HTML5 Programming for ASP.NET Developers

Bipin Joshi

Apress®

President and Publisher: Paul Manning
Lead Editor: Gwenan Spearing
Development Editor: Louise Corrigan
Technical Reviewer: Peter Vogel
Editorial Board: Steve Anglin, Ewan Buckingham, Gary Cornell, Louise Corrigan, Morgan Ertel, Jonathan Gennick, Jonathan Hassell, Robert Hutchinson, Michelle Lowman, James Markham, Matthew Moodie, Jeff Olson, Jeffrey Pepper, Douglas Pundick, Ben Renow-Clarke, Dominic Shakeshaft, Gwenan Spearing, Matt Wade, Tom Welsh
Coordinating Editor: Anamika Panchoo
Copy Editor: Tiffany Taylor
Compositor: Bytheway Publishing Services
Indexer: SPI Global
Artist: SPI Global
Cover Designer: Anna Ishchenko

Distributed to the book trade worldwide by Springer Science+Business Media New York, 233 Spring Street, 6th Floor, New York, NY 10013. Phone 1-800-SPRINGER, fax (201) 348-4505, e-mail orders-ny@springer-sbm.com, or visit www.springeronline.com.

For information on translations, please e-mail rights@apress.com, or visit www.apress.com.

Apress and friends of ED books may be purchased in bulk for academic, corporate, or promotional use. eBook versions and licenses are also available for most titles. For more information, reference our Special Bulk Sales–eBook Licensing web page at www.apress.com/bulk-sales.

Any source code or other supplementary materials referenced by the author in this text is available to readers at www.apress.com. For detailed information about how to locate your book's source code, go to www.apress.com/source-code.

At the holy feet of Lord Shiva.
    – Bipin Joshi

Contents at a Glance

Contents

About the Author

Bipin Joshi is an independent blogger and author who writes about apparently unrelated topics—yoga and technology. A former software consultant and trainer by profession, Bipin has been programming since 1995 and has worked with the .NET framework since its inception. He is a published author and has authored or co-authored more than a half dozen books and numerous articles on .NET technologies. Bipin was a Microsoft Most Valuable Professional (MVP) and a Microsoft Certified Trainer (MCT) during his tenure as a software consultant and trainer. He has also penned a few books on yoga. Having embraced yoga way of life, he enjoys the intoxicating presence of God and writes about yoga, life, and technology. He can be reached at www.bipinjoshi.com.

About the Technical Reviewer

Peter Vogel began working in information technology in 1984 and by 1994 was the head of the IT department for a multinational heavy-equipment manufacturer. He has received many awards throughout his career, including the President's Award for excellence at Imperial Oil, marking only the second time the award had been given to the IT department; and the Quality in IT award at Bayer AG. Peter branched out as an independent consultant in 1997, supplying both management insight and technical support to companies including Bayer AG, Exxon, Christie Digital, Volvo, the Canadian Imperial Bank of Commerce, Service Brands International, and Microsoft, among others. As an industry expert, Peter has presented at conferences in Canada, the US, the UK, Australia, and Europe and is frequently a keynote speaker at software conferences.

In addition to providing consulting services, Peter has had a parallel career as a technical writer. Currently, Peter is an editor for *Visual Studio Magazine*, where he also writes the "Practical .NET" column and the occasional feature article. He has written several articles for *MSDN Magazine*. Peter was the editor of the *Smart Access* newsletter, the founding editor of the *XML Developer* newsletter, and the editor of *Advisor* magazine. He currently edits Learning Tree's *Management Insights* newsletter. Peter has had four books published (his *Visual Basic Object and Component Handbook* was called "the definitive guide to 'thinking with objects'"). He recently self-published a book on creating effective user manuals (*rtfm*: the little book on how to write and actually get read*). He also wrote the "Contractor Skills" column for *Contract Professional* magazine.

Peter also teaches for Learning Tree International. In addition to teaching in Canada, the US, England, Sweden, and Hong Kong, Peter has written four courses for Learning Tree in both the management and technical curricula. He has also acted as a technical editor or subject matter expert for an equal number of courses, mostly in management curricula.

Peter has a BA from the University of Western Ontario, has an MBA from Wilfrid Laurier University, has been a Microsoft MVP, and was one of the first Microsoft Certified Solution Developers.

Peter lives in Goderich, Ontario, Canada—officially the "prettiest town in Canada."

Acknowledgments

Although name of an author alone appears on the book, many contribute to the process directly or indirectly. I must express my deep feeling of devotion toward Lord Shiva. Without His blessings and yogic teachings this would not have been possible.

Writing a book is about teamwork. Input from the technical reviewer, Peter Vogel, was very useful in rendering the book accurate. The whole team at Apress—Gwenan, Anamika, Louise, Tiffany, and others —were very helpful. Thank you, team, for playing your part wonderfully.

Introduction

Welcome to the exciting world of HTML5! If you're an ASP.NET developer looking to turbocharge your ASP.NET applications with HTML5 features, you've picked the right book. Compared to its successors, HTML5 offers a much richer and complex set of features. HTML5 isn't just about additional markup tags—it's about APIs that you can program using client-side script.

On one hand, HTML5 simplifies tasks that weren't possible previously; but at the same time, it calls for a detailed understanding of HTML5 features and ways to integrate those features into your applications. This is the reason you need a book that specifically talks about integrating HTML5 into your web development framework: ASP.NET. When ASP.NET was initially released, the core focus was on server-side programming. However, due to the popularity of Ajax, the client side became increasingly rich. Most professional web sites developed today tap the power of JavaScript and Ajax to provide a better user experience. Because many HTML5 features are programmable using JavaScript, the overall work done at the client side will continue to increase. ASP.NET, JavaScript, Ajax, and HTML5 may sound like independent pieces, but in reality they complement each other to form a complete picture of modern web application development. This book is intended to help you understand what this picture looks like and how to tap the full potential of HTML5 features in your ASP.NET web applications.

Who Is This Book For?

This book is for ASP.NET web developers who want to tap the power of HTML5 in their existing or new web applications. This book doesn't teach about ASP.NET features as such. I assume you're already comfortable working with ASP.NET and doing web application development in general.

All the code samples discussed in this book use C# as the server-side programming language. So, you should also know C#. For the client-side code, the book uses jQuery—a JavaScript-based library. Although no prior knowledge of jQuery is expected, I assume you're familiar with the basics of JavaScript.

The examples illustrated throughout the book use SQL Server and Entity Framework. Although you need not have a detailed understanding of these, you should be familiar with them.

Finally, the book uses Visual Studio as the development tool. You should know how to work with Visual Studio to perform basic tasks such as creating projects and debugging code.

Web Forms or MVC

ASP.NET offers two options for developing web applications: ASP.NET Web Forms and ASP.NET MVC. Using the HTML5 features discussed in this book is more or less the same whether you're developing Web Forms–based applications or MVC-based applications. So, this book presents the code samples as a mix of

Web Forms and MVC applications. Where there is difference in the usage of HTML5 features, both options are covered. All the MVC applications use ASPX views.

Software Required

In order to work through the examples discusses in this book, you need the following software:

- Visual Studio 2012

- SQL Server 2012

- Web browsers: Internet Explorer 9, Firefox, Chrome, Opera, and Safari

Although I used Visual Studio Professional 2012 to develop the book's examples, most of the examples can also be developed using Visual Studio Express 2012 for Web.

All the data-driven examples were developed using SQL Server 2012 Express Edition. I use the Northwind sample database in many examples, and I suggest that you install it at your end. You can download the Northwind database and its script from the MSDN downloads web site. Some examples (especially those needing Web Socket protocol support) require Windows 8 in order to run successfully.

HTML5 is an evolving specification. As of this writing, various browsers support HTML5 features to varying degrees. Throughout the book, I use different browsers (IE9, Firefox, Chrome, Opera, and Safari) to illustrate HTML5 features. When you're developing a web application that uses HTML5 features, it's recommended that you test the features in these browsers. So, you should install the latest versions of all these browsers on your development machine.

Structure of This Book

This book is organized in 13 chapters and 1 appendix. A quick overview follows:

- Chapter 1 gives you a brief overview of the HTML5 features discussed in the book. Some Visual Studio 2012 features that are important from an HTML5 point of view are also discussed.

- Many features of HTML5 can be programmed using JavaScript. Chapter 2 teaches you the basics of jQuery—a popular JavaScript library. You use jQuery throughout the book. If you're unfamiliar with jQuery, this chapter gets you up and running.

- Playing audio and video files is now easy because HTML5 provides native support for playing media files. Chapter 3 covers these two areas in detail.

- Chapter 4 covers the HTML5 canvas, a feature that allows you to draw inside a browser window using JavaScript objects intended for that purpose.

- If you develop data-driven web applications using ASP.NET, Chapter 5 is bound to catch your attention: it covers new HTML5 input types and enhancements to HTML forms.

- Chapter 6 discusses the history API and custom data attributes (data-*). The history API lets you add entries to the browser history programmatically, and custom data attributes allow you to define metadata for an element.

- HTML5 introduces a new type of client-side storage called web storage. Using web storage, you can store pieces of information as key-value pairs. Chapter 7 covers this useful topic.

- Although most web applications require a live network connection in order to function properly, some applications can be developed to work offline. Chapter 8 discusses what offline web applications are and how to develop one.

- Chapter 9 shows how you can use the file API to read file information and the content of files selected by the user. This chapter also teaches you to use HTML5 native drag-and-drop.

- Web workers let you develop web pages such that JavaScript processing can be run in the background. This way, the user interface is responsive to user interactions processing logic behind the scenes. Chapter 10 covers this important and useful feature.

- HTML5 has added new ways in which the client and server can communicate. They include the postMessage API, server-sent events, XMLHttpRequest (Level 2), and Web Sockets. All of them are the subject matter of Chapter 11.

- As mobile devices become more and more popular, web applications that customize themselves according to the user's current location are finding their way into handheld gadgets. Chapter 12 discusses geolocation—the feature that lets you develop location-aware web applications.

- Chapter 13 covers some of the important enhancements to Cascading Style Sheets version 3 (CSS3). Using these features, you can add fancy frills to your HTML elements, such as web fonts, shadows, transparency, gradients, and borders with rounded corners.

Appendix A lists some learning resources for HTML5.

Downloading the Source Code

The complete source code for the book is available for download at the book's companion web site. Visit www.apress.com, and go to this book's information page. You can then download the source code from the Source Code/Download section.

Contacting the Author

You can reach me via my web sites www.bipinjoshi.com and www.bipinjoshi.net. You can also follow me on popular social-networking web sites such as Facebook and Twitter (see the "Subscribe" section on my web sites for the links).

CHAPTER 1

■ ■ ■

Overview of HTML5 and ASP.NET 4.5

Until recently, ASP.NET developers didn't need to bother much about the version number of HTML—and now suddenly everybody is talking about HTML5! That's the kind of impact the evolved HTML standards will have on the web pages we develop now and in the future. Of course, the old functionality provided by traditional HTML (such as HTML 4.01) isn't going away. The previous version is an integral part of HTML5, but the new improvements offered by HTML5 are appealing to any ASP.NET developer.

This chapter gives you a quick overview of HTML5 features. It also explains how HTML5 and ASP.NET fit into a web application. An overview of the ASP.NET web stack and step-by-step tour of project creation in Visual Studio give you a quick brush-up of your ASP.NET skills.

This chapter specifically covers:

- A brief history of HTML5

- HTML5 page layout

- New markup tags

- HTML5 programmable features

- Where and how HTML5 fits in an ASP.NET application

History of HTML5

To understand the magic behind the number 5, it would be worthwhile to peek into the history and inspiration behind the evolution of HTML standards over a decade. If you've been designing web pages since the early days of the Web, you'll recollect that back then, a web page was basically a collection of static HTML elements. Web pages lacked the interactivity, responsiveness, and complexity you see today. The old HTML was merely a set of markup tags that web developers and designers used to create web pages. It was also careless about the strictness of the markup.

After completing the majority of work on HTML 4, the World Wide Web Consortium (W3C) decided to develop a standard—XHTML—for HTML markup. The XHTML specifications introduced strict rules for HTML markup such as requiring that start tags have corresponding end tags, tags be properly nested, and so on. These rules were introduced with good intentions and were appreciated by the developer community. However, it became apparent that nobody wanted to give up web pages developed using the old HTML that didn't meet the rules enforced by XHTML. Neither web-page developers nor browser companies stopped their support for traditional HTML markup in favor of the new XHTML standards. As a result, web pages became a mix of old HTML and XHTML. There were efforts to evolve XHTML further, but the browser and developer community simply refused to give up support for plain old HTML markup. The XHTML rules, although good from a theoretical point of view, weren't compelling enough to make the web community abandon support for traditional HTML.

In 2004, a group of people, mostly from browser manufacturing companies (such as Apple, Mozilla, and Opera), formed the Web Hypertext Application Technology Working Group (WHATWG). The newly formed group began looking at HTML from a different perspective. Instead of talking in terms of rules, standards, and strictness, they brainstormed about features that, if added to HTML, would add value for web designers and developers. Traditional HTML (official version 4.01) coupled with these additional features became HTML5. This initiative got support from the community, developed momentum, and was taken over by W3C for standardization in 2007. In January 2008, W3C published a working draft of HTML5. In addition, XHTML5 (a set of standards for HTML5 documents) was introduced; it's essentially an update to XHTML and is being defined alongside the HTML5 specifications.

The past showed that it's impossible to abandon HTML and replace it with something else. So, HTML is considered a current standard: although it's called HTML5 to refer to its new capabilities, from the browser and specifications point of view it's just HTML. The next section makes this clear when you learn the basic layout of an HTML5 page.

■ **Note** Although XHTML could never replace HTML, it had a positive impact on web developers and designers. Due to XHTML's strict rules, web page developers and designers became more conscious of improving the structure of their web pages. The web-design tools also improved by highlighting markup-level errors caused by improper nesting and missing end tags.

HTML5 Page Structure

Now that you know the brief history of HTML5, let's see a simple HTML5 web page in action. Open any text editor, such as Windows Notepad, TextPad, or Visual Studio's default text editor, and key in the markup shown in Listing 1-1.

Listing 1-1. A Simple HTML5 Page

```
<!DOCTYPE html>
<html>
  <head>
      <title>Welcome to HTML5</title>
  </head>
  <body>
      <h1>Hello HTML5!</h1>
  </body>
</html>
```

Save the file as Hello.htm, and double-click it to open in your default browser. Figure 1-1 shows a sample run of Hello.htm in Internet Explorer 9 (IE9).

Figure 1-1. A sample run of `Hello.htm`

Although constructing this web page isn't rocket science, it throws light on some interesting things. First, look at the `<!DOCTYPE>` declaration in Listing 1-1: it tells you that this document is an HTML document. Notice that there is no mention of the HTML version in the `DOCTYPE`. That means even if new features are added to HTML in the future (and they undoubtedly will be) the document is still an HTML document and not an HTML4 or HTML5 document. Compare this simple `DOCTYPE` declaration with the following pre-HTML5 declaration:

```
<!DOCTYPE html PUBLIC "-//W3C//DTD XHTML 1.0 Transitional//EN" "http://www.w3.org/TR/xhtml1/DTD/
xhtml1-transitional.dtd">
```

The complex `DOCTYPE` declaration is reduced to a simple form in HTML5.

Listing 1-1 includes properly nested markup tags such as `<head>`, `<title>`, and `<h1>`. However, HTML5 and web browsers forgive most nesting errors, just like old HTML. Of course, as a good practice you should follow the guidelines of well-formed and -structured markup.

In the preceding example, you used a text editor to create `Hello.htm`. As an ASP.NET developer, you probably use Visual Studio or Visual Studio Express for Web to develop your web pages. Luckily, these tools understand and support HTML5 markup. Figure 1-2 shows the Options dialog in Visual Studio, where you can configure the relevant settings.

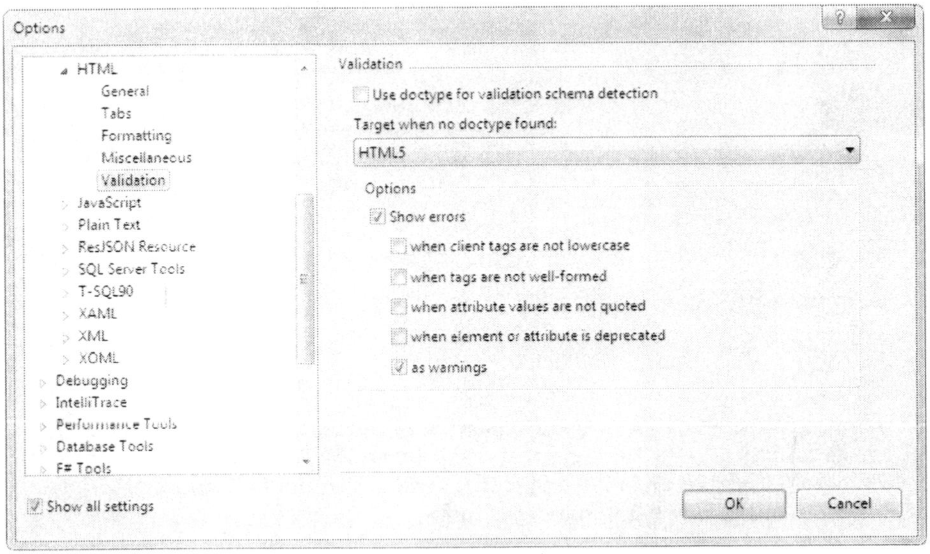

Figure 1-2. Options dialog in Visual Studio

When you configure Visual Studio to use HTML5 (Visual Studio 2012 uses HTML5 by default), all the HTML pages and Web Forms you create use the HTML5 style of DOCTYPE declaration. The markup in Listing 1-2 shows the default web form markup created in an ASP.NET web site.

Listing 1-2. Default Markup for a Web Form

```
<%@ Page Language="C#" %>

<!DOCTYPE html>
<script runat="server">
</script>

<html xmlns="http://www.w3.org/1999/xhtml">
<head runat="server">
    <title></title>
</head>
<body>
    <form id="form1" runat="server">
    <div>
    </div>
    </form>
</body>
</html>
```

You can also see HTML5-specific markup tags in Visual Studio IntelliSense (Figure 1-3).

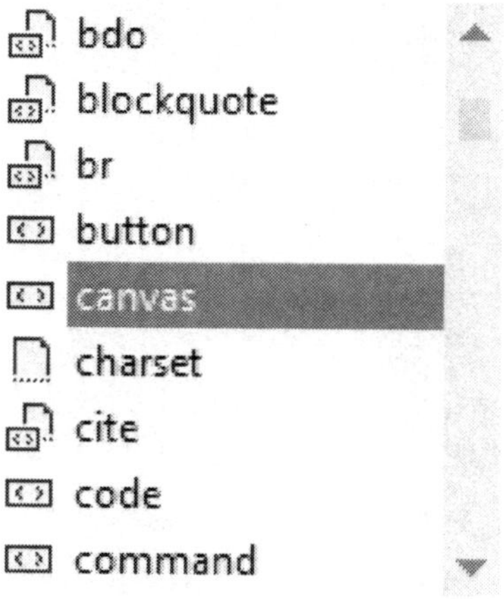

Figure 1-3. HTML5-specific tags in Visual Studio IntelliSense

Although HTML5 and web browsers forgive most markup errors, as a good developer you should ensure that your HTML5 page markup follows the recommended usage rules. To assist with this task, you can use the W3C Markup Validation Service: an online utility that validates your HTML and XHTML documents. Figure 1-4 shows this utility with Hello.htm as the input.

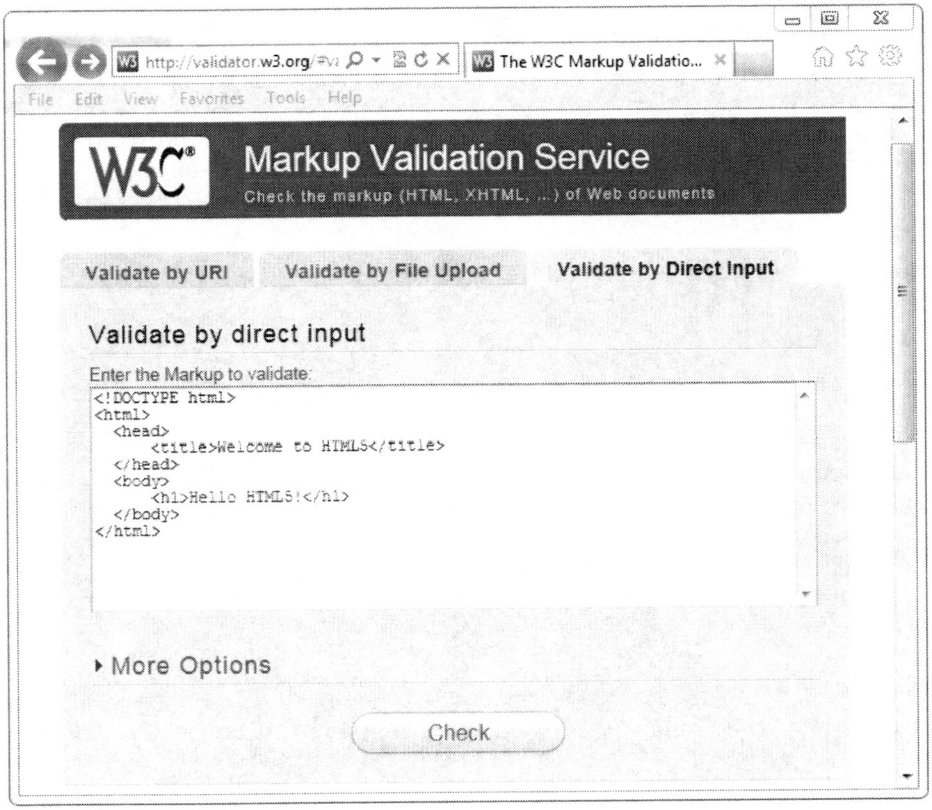

Figure 1-4. Validating an HTML5 document

Note that this tool may not correctly validate ASP.NET server-side markup. For example, the `runat="server"` attribute may be flagged as an error. If you're using Visual Studio, your job is simpler because validation errors are automatically highlighted as you key in your markup (see Figure 1-5).

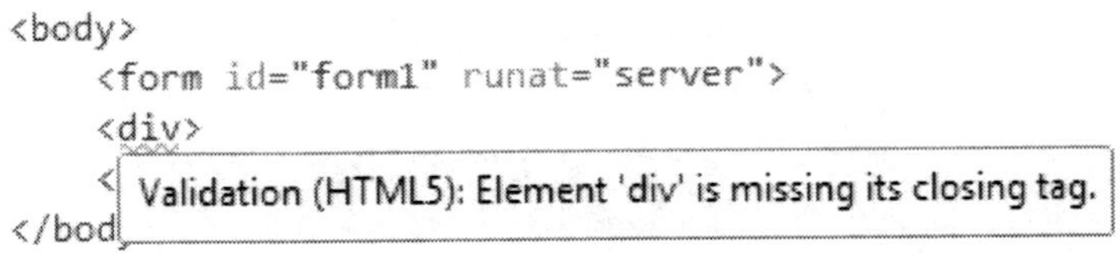

```
<body>
    <form id="form1" runat="server">
    <div>
    <
    Validation (HTML5): Element 'div' is missing its closing tag.
</bod
```

Figure 1-5. HTML5 document validation in Visual Studio

■ **Note** You might wonder why HTML pages created in Visual Studio have `xmlns` set to `http://www.w3.org/1999/xhtml`. This namespace indicates that an HTML5 document is using validation rules from the XHTML5 specifications; Visual Studio editor flags validation errors accordingly.

A Quick Look at HTML5-specific Tags

Before you move ahead to the programmable features of HTML5, it would be helpful to glance over a few newly added elements. Table 1-1 presents a list of elements that not only allow you to design more structured web pages but also provide functionality that has never before been part of HTML markup. Note, however, that any detailed discussion of the elements related to the well-structuredness of web pages (the first couple of rows in Table 1-1) is beyond the scope of this book.

■ **Note** You can fine a neat and handy HTML5 tag reference at `http://w3schools.com/html5/default.asp`.

You come across some of the elements mentioned in Table 1-1 in the chapters to follow. They're explained as and when required.

Table 1-1. Newly Added HTML5 Elements

Elements	Description
`<article>`, `<header>`, `<hgroup>`, `<footer>`, `<section>`, `<summary>`, `<aside>`, `<nav>`	These elements allow you to design a page in a more structured manner (such as an article or blog post). Previously, developers used a combination of `<div>`, `<span>`, and `<p>` to design HTML pages. Although that approach is perfectly acceptable, even under HTML5, the new layout elements can come in handy to mark specific areas of pages such as headers, footers, summaries, and sidebars. The new elements are more readable and meaningful in a given context, and you can design your CSS styles specifically for them. These elements also make it possible for third-party tools and utilities to parse the HTML document and automate page processing.
`<figure>`, `<figcaption>`	Using images in a web page is a common task for which you use `<img>`. The `<figure>` and `<figcaption>` tags are used to mark figures that serve as illustrations in an article or document.
`<input>`	The `<input>` tag itself isn't a new addition to HTML5. However, it now has many new values for its type attribute: Email, URL, Telephone, Color, and so on.
`<audio>`, `<video>`	Showing audio and video files used to be tricky and often required dependency on a plug-in (Flash or Silverlight, for example). The new `<audio>` and `<video>` elements provide a native way for browsers to identify (and play) media files.
`<canvas>`	The `<canvas>` element is a region where you can draw shapes, text, and images using JavaScript code.

HTML5 Features of Interest

Enhanced markup is just a small part of the HTML5 story. HTML5 is more than markup; it includes a set of features that you can program using client-side script.

Over time, web applications have moved beyond static markup. Almost all modern web applications use technologies such as JavaScript, jQuery, Ajax, validations, data access, and more. To cope with the changing nature of web applications, HTML5 has taken steps in the right direction by offering native support for features that are commonly needed by web developers. Rather than rely on a third party to provide support or develop such a feature from scratch, it's easy to consume the native support provided by HTML5. For example, ASP.NET developers used validation controls or custom validation libraries to validate user input. But HTML5 natively supports many of the commonly needed validations. Thus HTML5 is an umbrella that covers markup tag, markup standards, programmable APIs, and new JavaScript objects.

The subsequent chapters of this book dissect the HTML5 APIs and associated JavaScript objects one by one. This section's overview of these programmable features gives you an idea of what's coming.

Audio and Video

Playing audio and video files used to be tricky and often involved dependency on third-party plug-ins such as Flash and Silverlight. HTML5 introduces <audio> and <video> elements so a web page can play media files with ease. This native support means that playing media files requires no special plug-ins, applets, or ActiveX controls. HTML5 also provides audio and video APIs to control various aspects of the audio and videos being played. This programmability gives you better control over the media files and how to play them.

Canvas

One of the reasons for the popularity of the Web is the GUI offered to end users: images, animations, fonts, and other interactive effects make a web site appealing from an end user's perspective. However, web developers often encounter limitations when drawing graphics in the browser. Developers commonly use Flash or Silverlight plug-ins to generate graphics on the server side and then send them to the client browser as pictures.

HTML5 does a great job in client-side graphic rendering by offering the <canvas> element. You do your actual drawing using the canvas API. Some of the areas in which the canvas API can be useful include charting, gaming, and online drawing tools.

History API

Before the advent of HTML5, web developers had little control over session history and its manipulation. The HTML5 history API provides a means to perform tasks such as moving forward and backward in the session history, adding new entries to the history, and synchronizing page content when the user navigates within the history. The history API is a standardized way to manipulate the browser history via JavaScript and is especially useful in Ajax-driven applications that have no one-to-one mapping between the page URL and the content being displayed at a given point in time.

Web Storage

As an ASP.NET developer, you may have used cookies to store small pieces of data on the client side. One limitation of using cookies is the amount of data that can be saved. For example, many browsers limit each cookie to 4,096 bytes.

HTML5 web storage allows you to store more data on the client side using JavaScript code. Web storage comes in two flavors: local storage and session storage. Local storage is persisted on the client machine across browser sessions, whereas session storage is persisted only for the current session. These storages are exposed as two new JavaScript objects: localStorage and sessionStorage.

Offline Web Applications

Normally, web applications require a live connection with the server in order to function. This always-connected behavior can create problems when the server goes offline for some reason or the network connection is lost temporarily. The HTML5 application caching feature addresses these scenarios with the help of the offline application caching API. Offline applications use a cache manifest file that stores a list of files that are to be cached locally. A typical cache manifest includes a list of web pages, images, style sheets, and script files. This way, these files are accessible even if the network connection is unavailable temporarily. Your application can also use the offline application cache API to deal with updated versions of pages.

File API

Traditionally, client-side code never had access to the local file system. But HTML5 allows you to read and find information about local files. Such a feature lets you perform custom processing before a file or its data is sent to the server. HTML5 drag-and-drop features and the file API can be used hand in hand to drag files from the local machine onto a web page and then take further action (say, upload the file to the server or show a thumbnail of an image file).

Web Workers

The web workers API brings multithreading to browser-based applications. Web workers essentially allow you to load and execute JavaScript code in a separate thread without affecting the responsiveness of the user interface. This means the end user can continue to work with the user interface while web workers run some processing in the background. When the processing is complete, the user is notified or the page is updated with the processing results.

Web Sockets

If you've ever programmed a desktop chat application, then you're probably aware of socket programming. Sockets are essentially programmable interfaces that plug into each other over a network. Once they're plugged in, the two systems can communicate with each other: client to server and server to client.

On the other hand, web pages are based on a request-response model. When a web server sends a response to the client, it doesn't hold a constant connection with the client. So, if the server wants to notify the client about something interesting, it doesn't have any way to do so. A popular way around this is to periodically ping back to the server using Ajax requests. But this pull technique is still one-way communication and isn't always efficient due to the possibility of too many requests.

Web sockets, on the other hand, provide a two-way communication channel that lets the server send data to the client browser. They offer socket programming capabilities for web applications.

Geolocation

Geolocation has the potential to become a popular feature of HTML5 because it brings location awareness to web applications. Using geolocation, you can develop applications that are dependent on the user's location (assuming the device on which the page is running can report position). For example, a web site may offer discounted rates or special offers to people living in a specific locality. In addition, geolocation can be of great use on mobile devices such as mobile phones and tablets.

CSS3

Strictly speaking, CSS3 isn't a direct feature of HTML5 but is evolving along with HTML5. It's worthwhile for any HTML5 and ASP.NET developer to know CSS3. ASP.NET developers rely heavily on CSS for the sake of look and feel and formatting Web Forms, views, and pages, and CSS3 introduces cool new features that are bound to grab developers' attention. Features such as boxes, shadows, web fonts, transforms, transitions, and media queries are particularly worth noting because they let developers accomplish things that weren't easy before.

HTML5 and Browser Support

Even though HTML5 is not yet an official standard, you can start using many of its features in your ASP.NET web applications. All the leading browsers—Mozilla Firefox, Google Chrome, Opera Software's Opera, Apple Safari, and Microsoft IE—support HTML5 in varying degrees. These days, most browsers release updated versions frequently, and HTML5 support improves in each new version. IE is lagging slightly behind as far as the frequency of new releases is concerned, but IE9 does support several HTML5 features.

As a good programming practice, you should always test your Web Forms, views, and plain HTML pages in the browser you're targeting. There are two ways to check whether the target browser supports a specific HTML5 feature:

- Statically at development time

- Dynamically at runtime

Checking for HTML5 Support Statically

With this approach, you manually ensure that the features used in your web pages are supported by your target browser. You can get help from any of the online utilities that tell you whether a specific browser version supports certain HTML5 features. Consider, for example, http://html5test.com, which provides a nice way to detect browser support for HTML5. Figure 1-6 shows the home page of the HTML5 test site displaying the HTML5 support score for the browser being used to view the site.

Figure 1-6. http://html5test.com browser score

As you can see in Figure 1-6, IE9 on Windows 7 scores 138 points out of 500. You can also check how other browsers score. Figure 1-7 shows a feature comparison between Firefox 11, Chrome 18, and Opera 12.

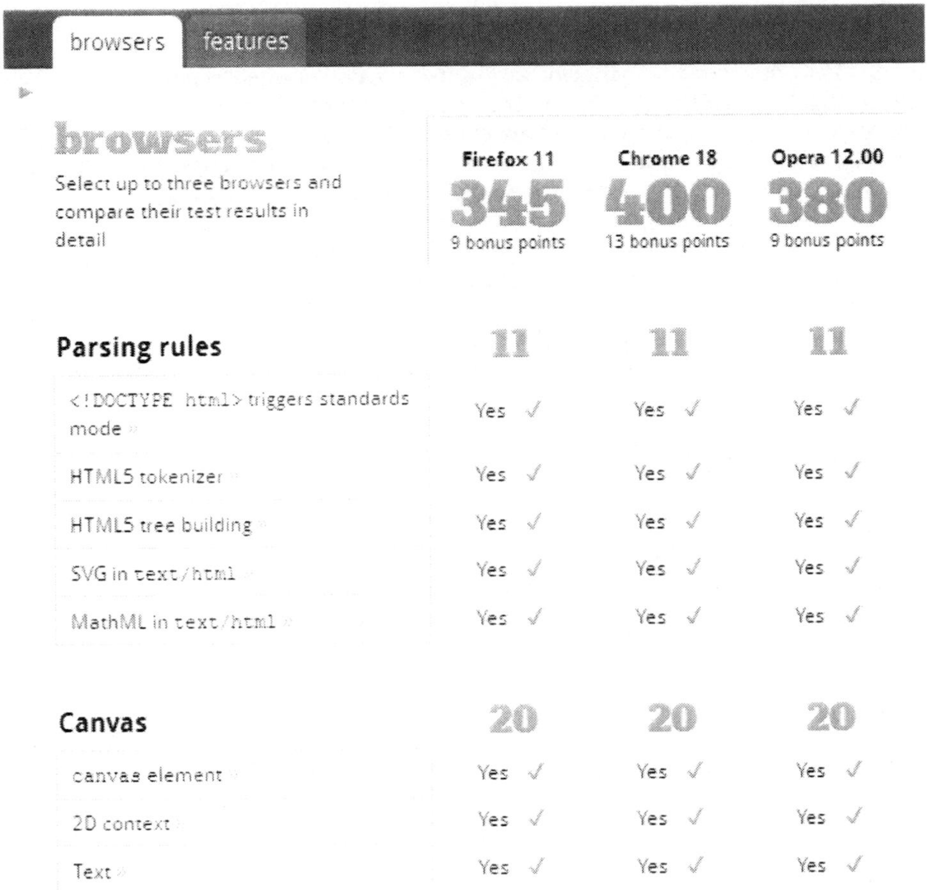

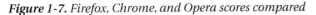

browsers	features

browsers

Select up to three browsers and compare their test results in detail

	Firefox 11	Chrome 18	Opera 12.00
	345	**400**	**380**
	9 bonus points	13 bonus points	9 bonus points
Parsing rules	**11**	**11**	**11**
`<!DOCTYPE html>` triggers standards mode	Yes ✓	Yes ✓	Yes ✓
HTML5 tokenizer	Yes ✓	Yes ✓	Yes ✓
HTML5 tree building	Yes ✓	Yes ✓	Yes ✓
SVG in `text/html`	Yes ✓	Yes ✓	Yes ✓
MathML in `text/html`	Yes ✓	Yes ✓	Yes ✓
Canvas	**20**	**20**	**20**
canvas element	Yes ✓	Yes ✓	Yes ✓
2D context	Yes ✓	Yes ✓	Yes ✓
Text	Yes ✓	Yes ✓	Yes ✓

Figure 1-7. Firefox, Chrome, and Opera scores compared

IE9 scores poorly compared to other browsers. In addition, IE9 runs only on Windows 7, limiting its audience further. As of this writing, Internet Explorer 10 is still in the development stage, but other browsers are quite aggressive in releasing the new versions or updates. In real-world situations, rather than targeting a single browser, you have no choice but to target multiple browsers and their varying support for HTML5 features.

Checking for HTML5 Support Dynamically

Checking for HTML5 feature support statically works well only if you know the target browser. For example, if you're developing an intranet web application that is supposed to be used only by the employees of a particular company, you may standardize on a specific browser and program HTML5 features accordingly. However, in today's modern age, users can access web sites from many browsers and devices—some of which only offer a specific browser choice—so relying on such browser standardization may not be the best approach. If your web application is in widespread use, then you can't guarantee which browser the end users are using. A fact of real-world web application development is that you need a robust and safe approach to detect browser support for HTML5 features at runtime. You need to plug in code that detects the browser and its HTML5 support at runtime; then, based on the result, your web page should either use those features or use some alternative.

You can manually add JavaScript code that performs various tests to detect whether a particular HTML5 feature is supported by the target browser, but testing and managing such code is too complex because there are so many things to check for. Luckily, utility libraries are available that make your life easy. One such popular utility library is Modernizr. Modernizr is an open source JavaScript library that helps you build HTML5- and CSS3-powered web sites. To use the Modernizr library, you first need to download the development version or production version from http://modernizr.com. Unless you wish to debug a script, the production version is recommended due to its compact size. You can also specify which feature tests you would like to include in the library. The downloaded Modernizr library can then be used in your web pages for feature detection.

To give you can idea of how Modernizr can be used, let's develop a simple web page— HelloModernizr.htm—and test for a few HTML5 features. Listing 1-3 shows the complete HTML markup of HelloModernizr.htm.

Listing 1-3. Detecting Features Using Modernizr

```
<!DOCTYPE html>
<html>
  <head>
      <title>Welcome to HTML5</title>
      <script type="text/javascript" src="jquery-1.7.2.min.js"></script>
      <script type="text/javascript" src="modernizr-2.5.3.js"></script>
      <script type="text/javascript">
          $(document).ready(function () {
              if (Modernizr.audio) {
                  $("#Message").append("Your browser supports the HTML5 audio tag. <br/>");
              }
              if (Modernizr.video) {
                  $("#Message").append("Your browser supports the HTML5 video tag. <br/>");
              }
              if (Modernizr.canvas) {
                  $("#Message").append("Your browser supports the HTML5 canvas tag. <br/>");
              }
              if (Modernizr.draganddrop) {
                  $("#Message").append("Your browser supports HTML5 drag-anddrop. <br/>");
              }
          });
      </script>
  </head>
  <body>
      <h1>Hello HTML5!</h1>
      <div id="Message"></div>
  </body>
</html>
```

As you can see, HelloModernizr.htm includes two JavaScript libraries in the head section. The first <script> tag refers to a jQuery library, and the other refers to Modernizr. The <script> block that follows tests for four HTML5 features: audio, video, canvas, and drag-and-drop. The feature-detection code runs when the page is loaded in the browser. Notice the use of the Modernizr object, which has various properties representing HTML5 features. If a particular feature is supported by the browser, this sample page appends a message to a `<div>` element with the ID `Message`.

▓ **Note** The jQuery code used in `HelloModernizr.htm` is fairly easy to understand. The `ready()` function runs when a web page is fully loaded in a browser. To select an HTML element with a specific ID, you use # syntax. The `append()` method called on the `<div>` appends the supplied text/markup to the element. You learn about jQuery in more detail in Chapter 2.

Figure 1-8 shows a sample run of `HelloModernizr.htm` in Firefox.

Figure 1-8. Sample run of `HelloModernizr.htm` *in Firefox*

Notice how support for the `<audio>`, `<video>`, and `<canvas>` tags and drag-and-drop is confirmed to be available on the browser.

HTML5 and ASP.NET

You've learned the history of HTML5 and its features. You also created a couple of simple HTML5 pages and used the Modernizr library to detect browser support for HTML5 features. Now, let's see how HTML5 fits into the overall ASP.NET stack. Figure 1-9 shows the ASP.NET technology stack.

Web Forms	MVC	Web API	ASMX
Web Sites		Services	
ASP.NET Core Features & Services			
.NET Framework			

Figure 1-9. ASP.NET stack

As you can see, ASP.NET is part of the overall .NET Framework and relies heavily on .NET Framework base class libraries. On the top of the .NET Framework, ASP.NET provides features and services that are specific to web applications. These features and services include authentication, authorization, membership, role management, and profile management, all of which can be consumed in ASP.NET web sites and services. The two prominent ways of building ASP.NET web sites are Web Forms and MVC applications. To develop services, you can use ASMX web services (available since version 1.0 of ASP.NET) or other better options such as Windows Communication Foundation (WCF) services and the Web API.

Figure 1-9 shows that Web Forms and MVC views are going to use of HTML5. At first glance, you may think the use of HTML5 is restricted to the display part of an ASP.NET application. Although the user interface is where you use HTML5 heavily, the integration goes deeper. Figure 1-10 shows the integration between HTML5 and ASP.NET.

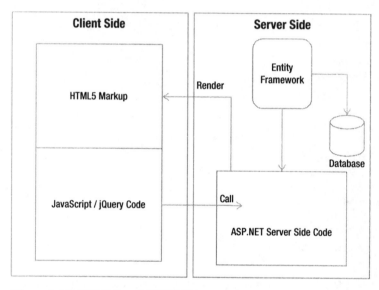

Figure 1-10. HTML5 and ASP.NET interaction

The ASP.NET server-side infrastructure sends HTML5 markup to the browser when a request is received. The ASP.NET server-side infrastructure consists of code in a web form code file or MVC controller. Most real-world web applications use data residing in a data store such as SQL Server. To access this business data, you can use a combination of ADO.NET and Plain Old CLR Objects (POCOs) or Entity Framework.

When the ASP.NET server-side infrastructure sends HTML5 markup to the client browser, the browser renders the user interface and allows the end user to work with the page. Many HTML5 features mentioned earlier expose programmable APIs that can be consumed using JavaScript code. The JavaScript code can, in turn, talk with the server to retrieve data or configuration needed for processing. For example, suppose you let the end user plot a simple bar graph in the browser using the HTML5 canvas API. After the graph is finished, you may want the user to save its data and related information to a database. This requires transfer of data from the client browser to the server. To facilitate this data transfer, you can use jQuery and send an Ajax request to a piece of server-side code. The server-side code then saves the data into a database.

Some features of HTML5 may not need any server-side interaction once the page is rendered. For example, you can display an HTML <form> that uses the new <input> types such as Email and URL. Doing so doesn't require any talk-back with the server.

Now that you know where HTML5 fits in with ASP.NET, it's worthwhile to know some features of Visual Studio HTML editor that can make your life easy.

Features of the Visual Studio HTML Editor

The Visual Studio HTML editor offers many features that simplify web page design. As an ASP.NET developer, you're probably familiar with many features of the HTML editor, so this section doesn't discuss each and every one; instead, it examines some interesting aspects.

■ **Note** You can refer to the MSDN documentation for all the available features of the Visual Studio HTML editor. Searching for *visual studio html editor* in the MSDN library should get you started.

HTML Formatting

While you're designing an HTML page, formatting various markup tags makes navigating and locating a specific element easy. The Visual Studio HTML editor does a good job of formatting the markup tags for you. If you need to tweak the default formatting behavior, you can do so via the Tools > Options dialog; see Figure 1-11.

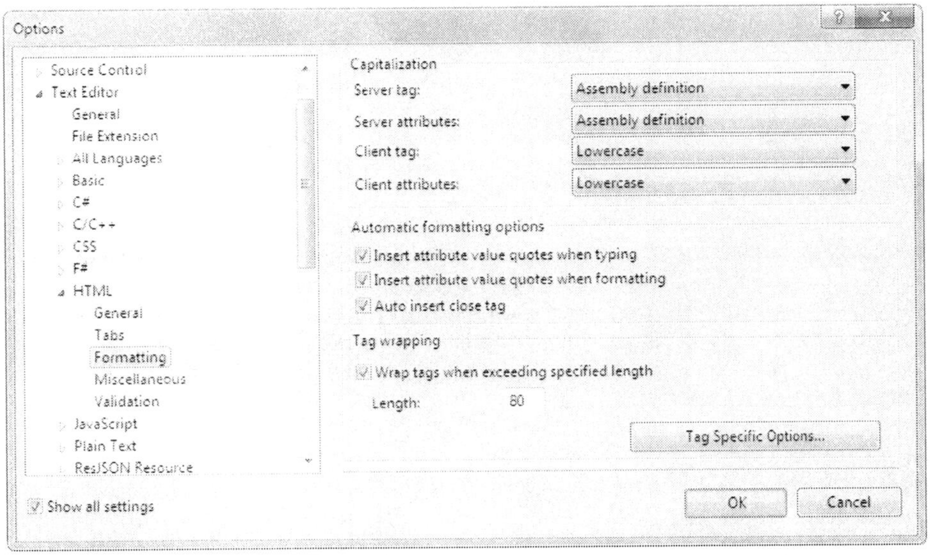

Figure 1-11. Changing HTML formatting options

Using formatting options you can, for example, configure whether closing tags should be automatically added, attribute values should be enclosed in double quotes, and so on. Clicking the Tag Specific Options button opens a dialog in which you can configure individual markup tags and their settings (Figure 1-12).

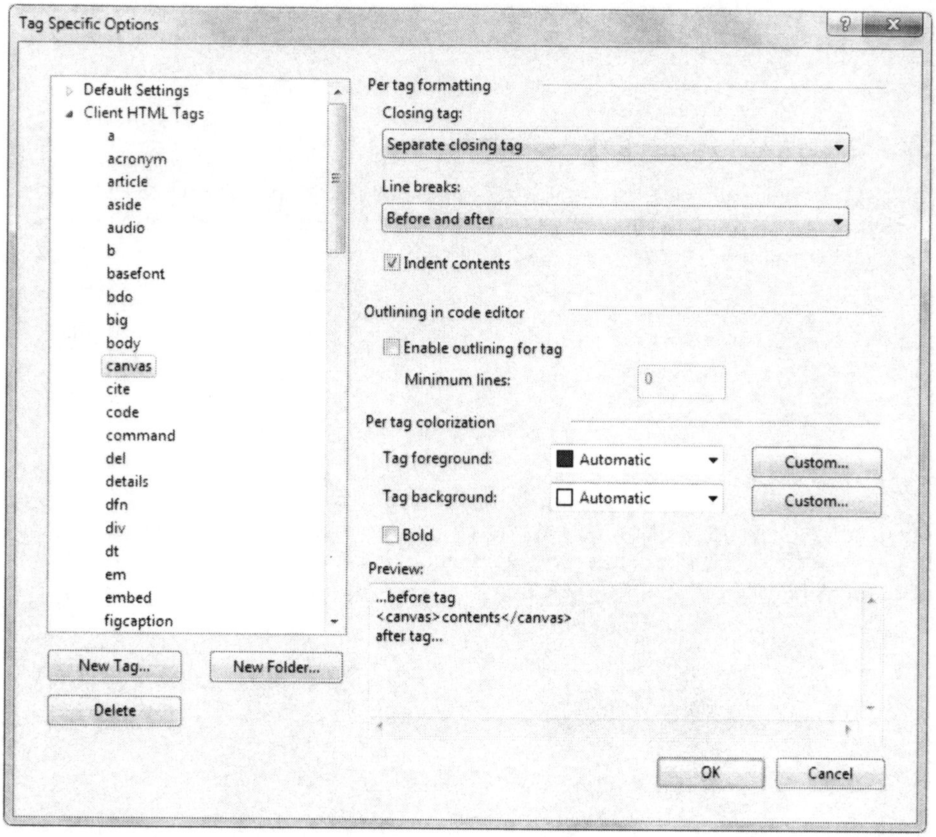

Figure 1-12. Configuring formatting options for individual tags

Tag-specific options include outlining specifications (whether you can collapse and expand a tag, and the minimum lines needed to enable this behavior), the tag's foreground and background colors in the HTML editor, line breaks, and so on. For most tags, the defaults set by Visual Studio work fine. However, in some case you may want to alter the default values. For example, while working with web sites that use <audio> and <video> tags heavily, you may want to consider changing the default tag foreground and background colors to make them easier to locate.

IntelliSense and Validations for HTML5 Tags

One feature of the Visual Studio HTML editor that is popular among developers is IntelliSense. Although IntelliSense is commonly used, a few things are worth noting because they aren't obvious at first glance.

The IntelliSense list doesn't show all possible HTML tags. Which tags are displayed for you to select from is governed by the HTML validation scheme you're using. You can configure the validation options from the Options dialog, as shown in Figure 1-13.

By default, the Visual Studio 2012 HTML editor uses HTML5 and also shows errors when any of the conditions listed under Show Errors are found.

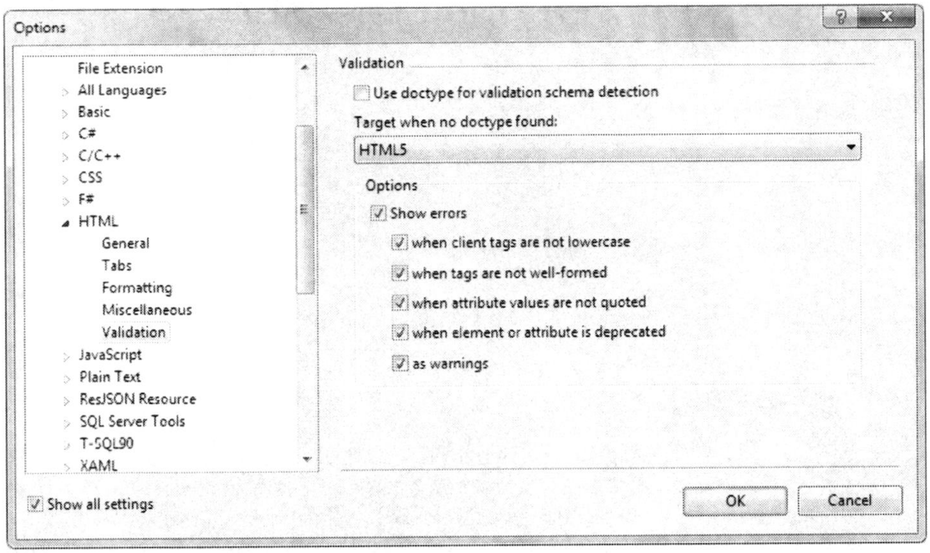

Figure 1-13. Configuring validation options

After you save the configuration, if you try to enter invalid HTML markup in a web page, the editor shows it as a validation error. Figure 1-14 shows the error message that appears when attribute values aren't enclosed in quotes.

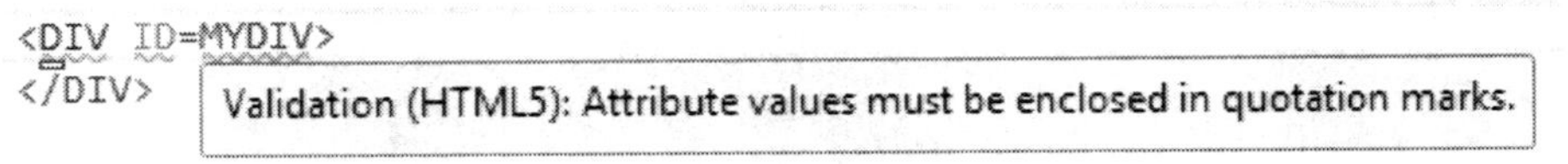

```
<DIV ID=MYDIV>
</DIV>     Validation (HTML5): Attribute values must be enclosed in quotation marks.
```

Figure 1-14. Validation error shown by the HTML editor

Also note that if you set the Validation option to something other than HTML5 (say, HTML 4.01), HTML5-specific tags (such as `<canvas>`, `<audio>`, and `<video>`) won't appear in IntelliSense.

HTML5 Snippets

Another time-saving feature of the Visual Studio HTML editor is HTML5 snippets. HTML5 snippets add a commonly used fragment of HTML5 markup to the web page you're editing. You can then customize the fragment as needed. Figure 1-15 shows the HTML5 audio snippet in the IntelliSense window.

Figure 1-15. HTML5 snippet in IntelliSense

17

After you select an HTML5 snippet in IntelliSense, press the Tab key twice to fully expand the snippet and add it at the current cursor location (Figure 1-16).

```
<audio controls="controls">
    <source src="file.mp3" />
    <source src="file.ogg" />
</audio>
```

Figure 1-16. HTML5 audio snipped expanded after pressing the Tab key twice

Once the snippet is added in the editor, you can modify it to suit your needs.

Automatically Renaming End Tags

Sometimes you may accidently misspell HTML tags while keying them in a web page. For example, let's say that instead of <audio>, you enter <aidio>. By default, when you close a start tag, Visual Studio automatically adds a corresponding end tag: the markup becomes <aidio></aidio>. To correct the error, you don't have to modify both the start and end tags—correcting the start tag automatically fixes the end tag too.

JavaScript IntelliSense

Visual Studio offers IntelliSense not just for HTML5 markup tags but also for JavaScript code. Earlier, this chapter looked at the jQuery and Modernizr libraries. Visual Studio provides IntelliSense for the objects, methods, and properties of these libraries too. Figure 1-17 shows the properties of a Modernizr object listed in the IntelliSense window.

Figure 1-17. JavaScript IntelliSense

Note that to display Modernizr members as shown in Figure 1-17, you must refer to the Modernizr library in the page using <script> tag.

Testing a Web Page in a Specific browserTesting

To ensure that your web page renders correctly in different browsers, you may need to run it in the individual browsers. A feature of Visual Studio that comes handy in such situations is shown in Figure 1-18.

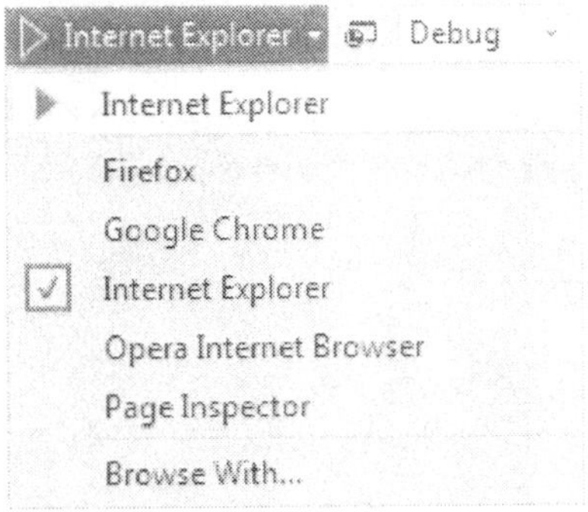

Figure 1-18. Running a web page in different browsers

The Run command on the standard toolbar shows a drop-down with all the browsers installed on a machine. You can select any browser from the list, and Visual Studio will launch your web application in the selected browser.

There is another way to browse HTML files in multiple browsers at once. If you right-click any HTML file in Solution Explorer and select the Browse With menu option, a dialog opens as shown in Figure 1-19.

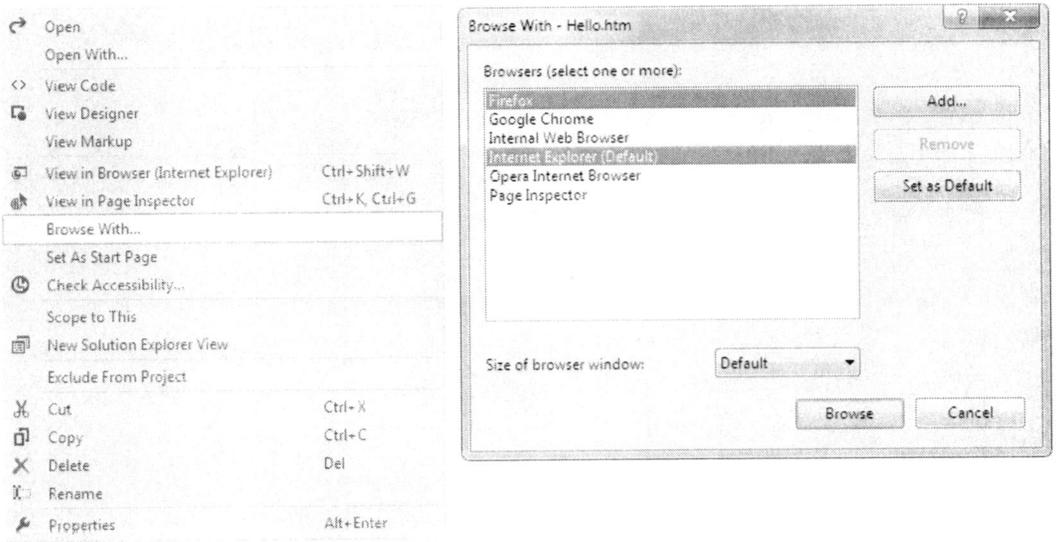

Figure 1-19. Selecting multiple browsers to view an HTML page

When you click Browse, the web page is launched in all the selected browsers.

Sample Web Applications

Now that you have a basic understanding of what HTML5 has to offer you as an ASP.NET developer, let's conclude this chapter by developing two simple ASP.NET web applications that use HTML5 features. The first web application uses ASP.NET Web Forms, and the second uses ASP.NET MVC.

■ **Note**   At this stage, you don't need to worry too much about jQuery syntax and HTML5 feature utilization in these web applications. The examples are meant to give you a quick and simplified understanding of what has been discussed so far. Later chapters present thorough coverage of these topics.

A Simple ASP.NET Web Forms–based Web Application Using HTML5

In this section, you develop an ASP.NET Web Forms–based application that plays audio and video files using HTML5 <audio> and <video> tags. The audio and video files to be played are retrieved at runtime using jQuery code.

Creating the ASP.NET Web Forms Project

To begin developing the application, create a new ASP.NET web application in Visual Studio using C# as the coding language. Figure 1-20 shows the New Project dialog in Visual Studio.

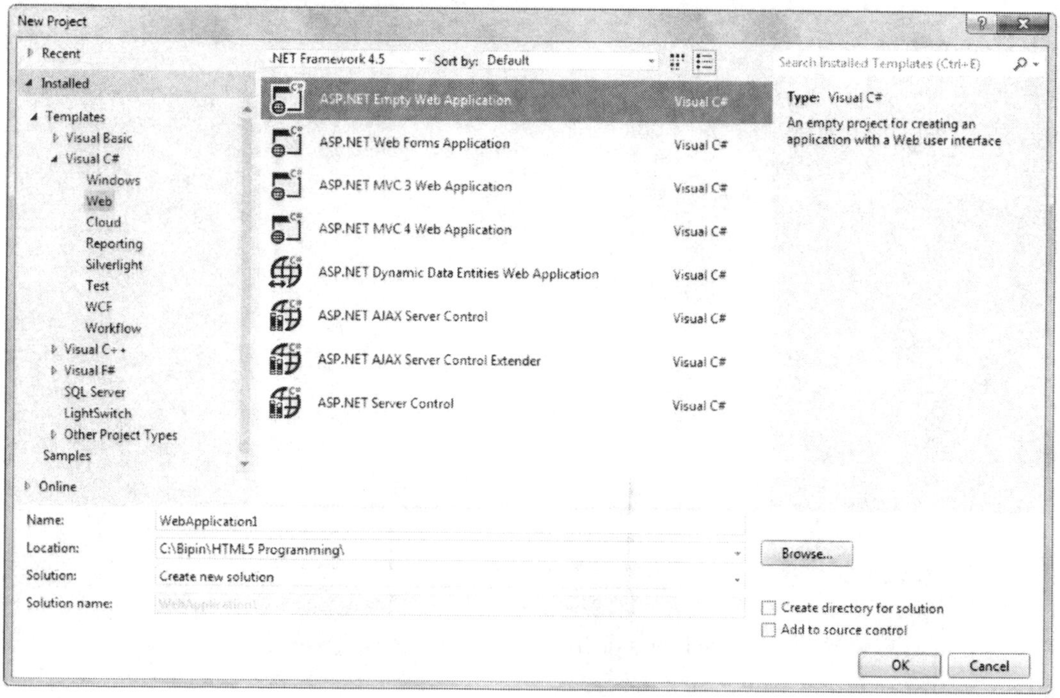

Figure 1-20. Creating a new Web Forms project in Visual Studio

Add three folders to the application: Images, Media, and Scripts. These folders store images, media files (audio/video), and script files, respectively. Place a few MP3 audio files and MP4 video files in the Media folder. Also copy jQuery and Modernizr library files into the Scripts folder. Figure 1-21 shows the Solution Explorer after setting up these folders.

■ **Note** If you haven't downloaded the latest versions of the jQuery and Modernizr JavaScript libraries yet, you can do so by visiting the respective web sites (http://jquery.com and http://modernizr.com). Keep a copy of these files handy, because you use them in the examples throughout this book. You can also access them from the Microsoft Content Delivery Network (CDN); that way, you don't need to maintain a local copy of the files. Visit http://www.asp.net/Ajaxlibrary/cdn.ashx for more details.

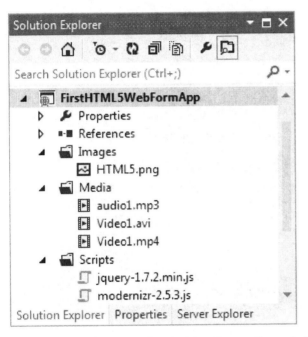

Figure 1-21. Solution Explorer with script, audio, and video files

Adding a Master Page and a Content Page

After you create the project, add a master page to the web application using the Add New Item dialog (Figure 1-22).

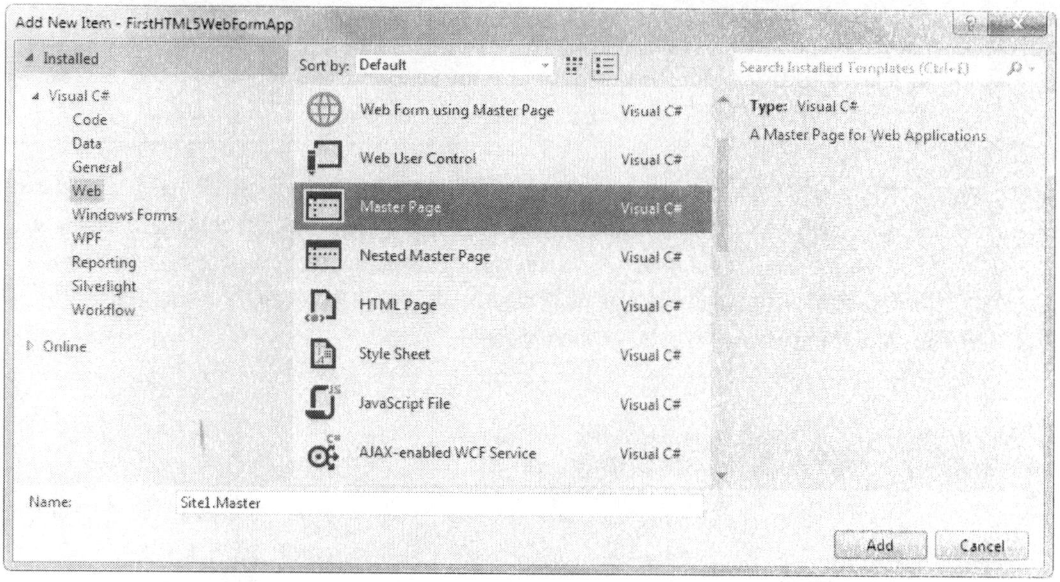

Figure 1-22. Adding a master page

Name the master page `MasterPage.master`, and add the markup shown in Listing 1-4.

Listing 1-4. Markup from `MasterPage.master`

```
<%@ Master Language="C#" AutoEventWireup="true" CodeBehind="MasterPage.master.cs"
                    Inherits="Example_03.MasterPage" %>
<!DOCTYPE html>
<html xmlns="http://www.w3.org/1999/xhtml">
<head runat="server">
  <title>Welcome to my HTML5 web site!</title>
  <link rel="stylesheet" type="text/css" href="StyleSheet.css" />
  <script type="text/javascript" src="Scripts/jquery-1.7.2.min.js"></script>
  <script type="text/javascript" src="Scripts/modernizr-2.5.3.js"></script>
</head>
<body>
  <aside class="sidebar">
    <figure>
      <img src="images/html5.png" alt="HTML5" />
      <br />
      <figcaption>HTML5 rocks!</figcaption>
    </figure>
  </aside>
  <section id="content" class="content">
    <article>
      <form id="form1" runat="server">
      <asp:ContentPlaceHolder ID="ContentPlaceHolder1" runat="server">
      </asp:ContentPlaceHolder>
      </form>
```

```
  </article>
 </section>
</body>
</html>
```

Notice that the markup shown in Listing 1-4 uses several HTML5-specific tags mentioned earlier in Table 1-1. Also notice that the jQuery and Modernizr script files are referenced in the master page so that not every content page has to refer to them again. As you enter the markup, notice how Visual Studio IntelliSense shows HTML5-specific tags, making your job easy.

Now add a new web form with a master page using Add New Item dialog, and select MasterPage.master as its master page (Figure 1-23).

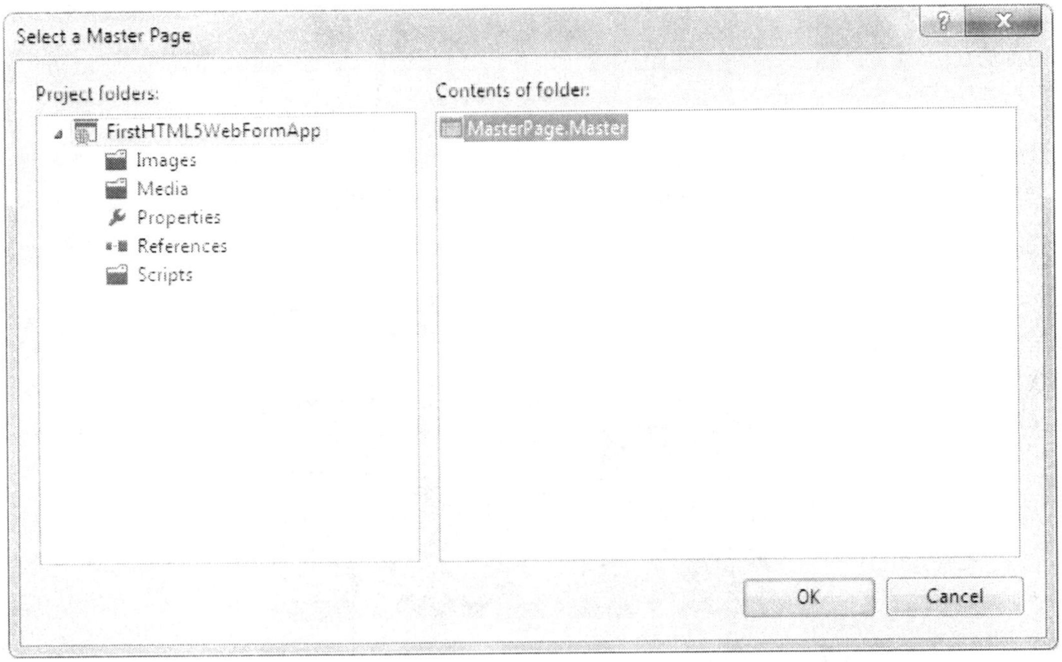

Figure 1-23. Adding a web form with master page

Next, add the markup shown in Listing 1-5 to Default.aspx.

Listing 1-5. Markup for Default.aspx

```
<%@ Page Title="" Language="C#" AutoEventWireup="true" MasterPageFile="~/MasterPage.Master"
CodeBehind="Default.aspx.cs" Inherits="Example_03.Default" %>

<asp:Content ID="Content1" ContentPlaceHolderID="ContentPlaceHolder1"
                      runat="server">
  <header>
    <h1>Play random Audio and Video files!</h1>
  </header>
  <div>
    <input type="button" id="playmusic" value="Play Random Audio File" />
```

```
        <br />
        <br />
        <audio id="audio" src="media/audio1.mp3" controls></audio>
        <br />
        <input type="button" id="playvideo" value="Play Random Video File" />
        <br />
        <br />
        <video id="video" src="media/video1.mp4" controls></video>
    </div>
</asp:Content>
```

The markup shown in Listing 1-5 renders two buttons, one <audio> tag, and one <video> tag. The <audio> and <video> tags have their src attribute set to default media files, but later you'll change src programmatically. The two buttons call server-side code that returns a random media file to be played. The returned media file is then assigned to the src attribute of the <audio> or <video> tag so as to set the media files dynamically. Figure 1-24 shows Default.aspx at runtime in IE9.

Figure 1-24. Default.aspx in IE9

Adding Web Methods

Currently, clicking the Play Random Audio File and Play Random Video File buttons doesn't do anything. You need to write server-side and client-side code to make them functional. Go into the code-behind file of Default.aspx, and add two web methods called GetAudio() and GetVideo() as shown in Listing 1-6.

Listing 1-6. Web Methods to Be Called from the Client Side

```
[WebMethod]
public static string GetAudio()
{
    //write logic to return random audio file
    return "audio1.mp3";
}
```

```
[WebMethod]
public static string GetVideo()
{
    //write logic to return random video file
    return "video1.mp4";
}
```

Notice that both methods are static and are decorated with the [WebMethod] attribute. This attribute is required so the methods become web callable and can be called from client-side code. GetAudio() and GetVideo() don't return a random file from a set of files, but you could add that logic inside the methods; currently they return predefined audio and video file names.

Writing jQuery Code to Call Web Methods

To call the GetAudio() and GetVideo() web methods from the client-side code, you need to add some jQuery code in the Default.aspx file. Listing 1-7 shows that code.

Listing 1-7. jQuery Code for the Call GetAudio() and GetVideo() Web Methods

```
<script type="text/javascript">
  $(document).ready(function () {
    if (!Modernizr.audio) {
      alert('Your browser does not support the HTML5 audio tag.');
      return false;
    }
    if (!Modernizr.video) {
      alert('Your browser does not support the HTML5 video tag.');
      return false;
    }

    $("#playaudio").click(function () {
      $.ajax({
        type: "POST",
        url: 'default.aspx/GetAudio',
        contentType: "application/json; charset=utf-8",
        dataType: "json",
        success: function (results) {
          $("#audio").src = results.d;
          $("#audio").trigger("play");
        },
        error: function (err) {
          alert(err.status + " - " + err.statusText);
        }
      })
    });

    $("#playvideo").click(function () {
      $.ajax({
        type: "POST",
        url: 'default.aspx/GetVideo',
        contentType: "application/json; charset=utf-8",
```

```
            dataType: "json",
            success: function (results) {
              $("#video").src = results.d;
              $("#video").trigger("play");
            },
            error: function (err) {
              alert(err.status + " - " + err.statusText);
            }
          })
        });
    });
</script>
```

The <script> block shown in Listing 1-7 consists of four parts:

- ready() function for the HTML document
- HTML5 audio and video feature detection using Modernizr
- Click event handler for the playaudio button
- Click event handler for the playvideo button

The ready() function is executed when the HTML DOM tree is fully loaded in the browser. It first checks whether the browser supports HTML5 audio and video features using Modernizr's audio and video properties (see the code marked in bold). If the browser doesn't support audio or video, an error message is displayed to the user.

The click event handler for the playaudio button is wired next. It calls GetAudio() using jQuery $.ajax() (see the bold code inside the event handler). When GetAudio() returns an audio file, the src property of the <audio> element is set to the returned file name, and its play() method is triggered to play the audio file. Notice how the return value of GetAudio() is accessed using results.d syntax. If there is an error while calling GetAudio(), an error message is displayed.

> ■ **Note** $.ajax() is one of several techniques you can use to call server-side code from HTML pages. You learn more about $.ajax() and other Ajax techniques offered by jQuery in Chapter 2.

The click event handler for the playvideo button is very similar to that for the playaudio button. The only difference is that it calls GetVideo() and plays a video file in the <video> element.

Run Default.aspx in IE9, and try clicking both buttons. See if audio and video files are played properly.

> ■ **Note** The web application also uses a CSS file that takes care of the web form's look and feel. You can get the complete source code for the project, including the CSS file, from the Chapter 1 code download.

A Simple ASP.NET MVC-Based Web Site Using HTML5

In this section, you develop an ASP.NET MVC application that displays an HTML5 canvas. You can draw a string on the canvas and then send the string to the server to be saved in a data store.

Creating an ASP.NET MVC Project

Begin by creating an ASP.NET MVC project in Visual Studio (Figure 1-25).

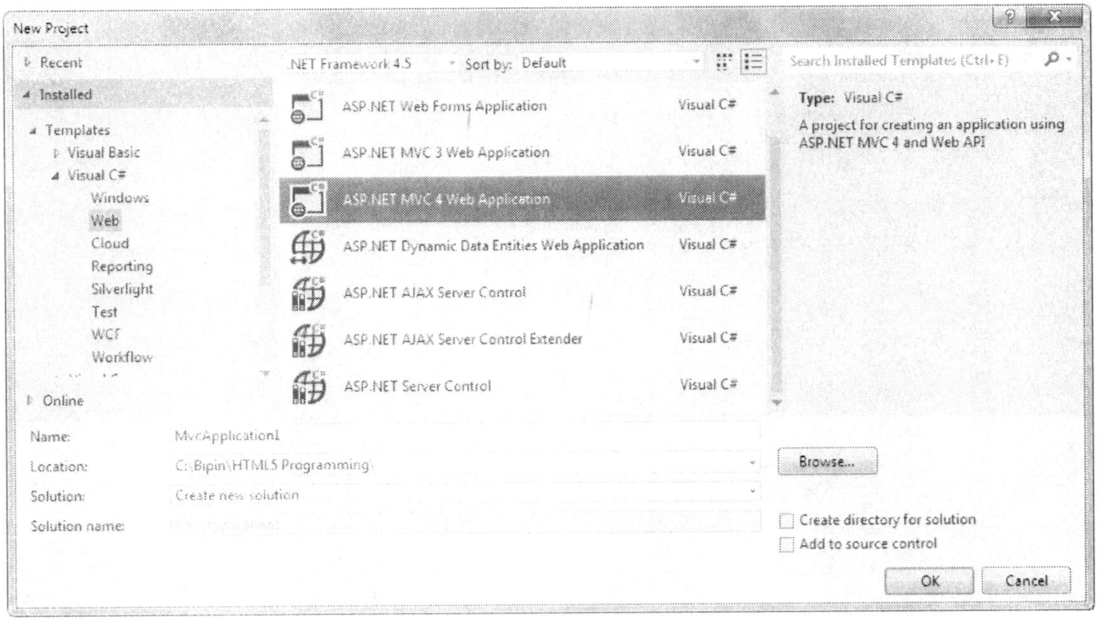

Figure 1-25. *Creating a new ASP.NET MVC project*

Make sure you select the Empty project template with ASPX as the view engine (Figure 1-26).

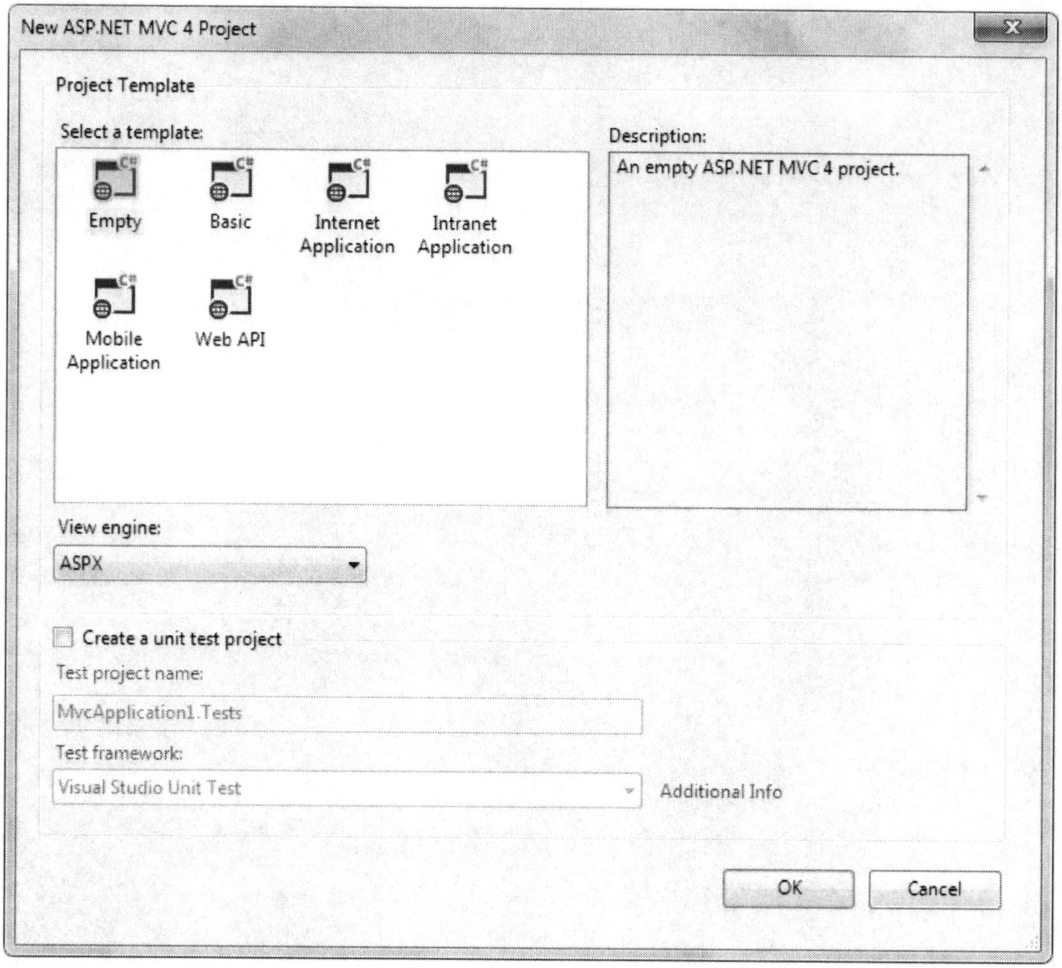

Figure 1-26. Select the ASPX view engine.

■ **Note** Although the web application you're building in this section isn't dependent on a specific version of MVC, the screenshots shown here assume that you've selected the MVC4 project template.

Unlike the ASP.NET Web Forms project you created earlier, the MVC project already contains a Scripts folder with jQuery and Modernizr libraries added to it. Of course, if you're keen to use the latest (or some specific) versions of these libraries, you can add them to the Scripts folder as before. Figure 1-27 shows the folder structure and script files for a newly created MVC project.

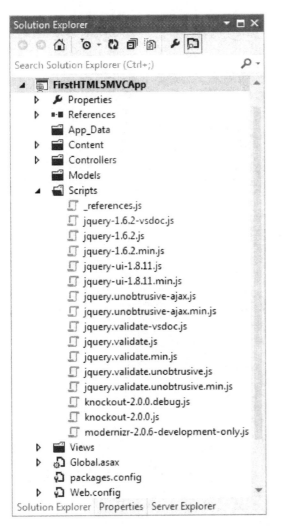

Figure 1-27. *Folder structure and script files from an ASP.NET MVC project*

Adding a Controller and Action Methods

Right-click the Controllers folder, select Add Controller from the menu, and add a new controller named HomeController (Figure 1-28).

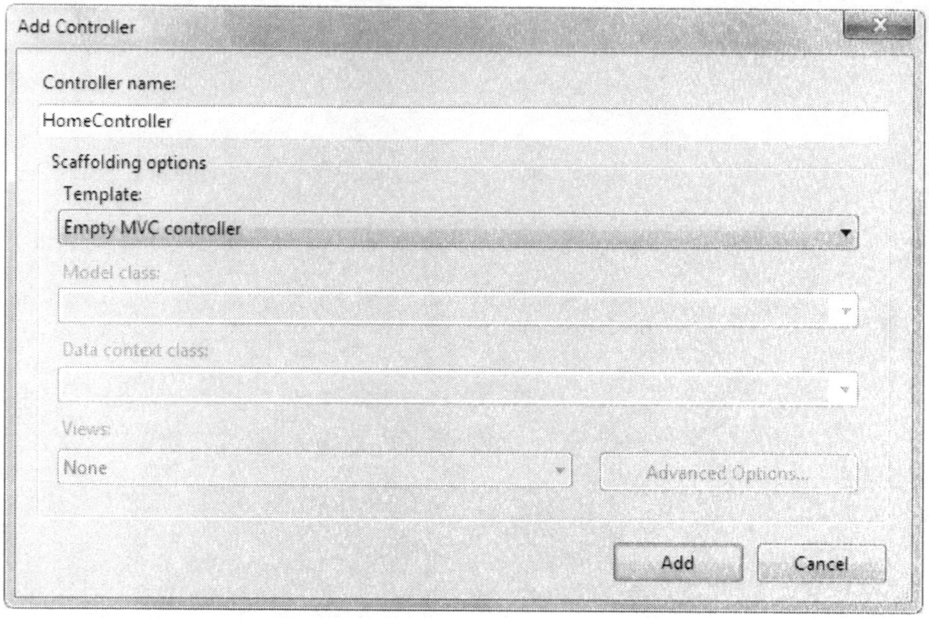

Figure 1-28. Adding HomeController

Add two action methods named Index() and SaveCanvas() to the HomeController class, as shown in Listing 1-8.

Listing 1-8. Action Methods of HomeController

```
public ActionResult Index()
{
    return View();
}

public JsonResult SaveCanvas(string data)
{
    //add code to store canvas data in some database
    Session["canvas_data"] = data;
    return Json("Canvas data stored successfully!");
}
```

The Index() action method simply returns the Index view, which you create in a moment. The SaveCanvas() method is called from the client-side jQuery code. The return type of SaveCanvas() is a JsonResult object, which represents a JavaScript Object Notation (JSON) representation of .NET data types.

■ **Note**   JSON is a lightweight data-interchange format. It's a text-based format and is based on a subset of the JavaScript programming language. Due to its text-based nature, it's easy to generate, read, write, and parse.

To keep the things simple, SaveCanvas() doesn't perform any database operations, but you could add them if you wish to persist the data in a database . The code stores the data in a session variable named canvas_data. A success message is returned to the caller by wrapping it in JSON format using the Json() method.

Adding a View

Next, right-click the Index() action method and select Add View from the shortcut menu. Add a new ASPX view named Index (Figure 1-29).

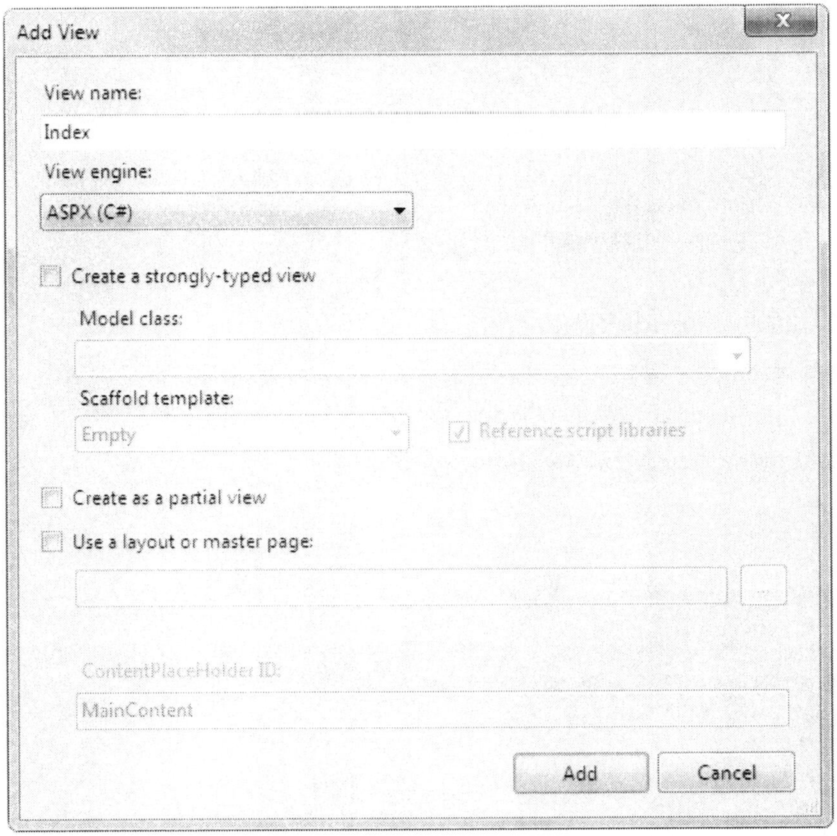

Figure 1-29. Adding an Index view

Add the markup shown in Listing 1-9 to the Index view located in the Views/Home folder.

Listing 1-9. Markup for the Index View

```
<%@ Page Language="C#" Inherits="System.Web.Mvc.ViewPage<dynamic>" %>

<!DOCTYPE html>
<html>
<head runat="server">
```

```
  <meta name="viewport" content="width=device-width" />
  <title>Index</title>
  <script type="text/javascript" src="../../Scripts/jquery-1.6.2.min.js"></script>
  <script type="text/javascript" src="../../Scripts/modernizr-2.0.6-development-only.js"></
script>
</head>
<body>
  <span>Enter Text : </span>
  <input type="text" id="Text1" value="<%= Session["canvas_data"] %>"  />
  <input type="button" id="Button1" value="Draw" />
  <input type="button" id="Button2" value="Save" />
  <br />
  <br />
  <canvas id="myCanvas" width="500" height="200"></canvas>
</body>
</html>
```

There are a couple of things to notice about this markup. First, it uses the HTML5 <canvas> tag and defines a canvas 500 pixels wide and 200 pixels high. Second, it uses the session variable canvas_data to populate the TextBox so the TextBox contains the value of canvas_data.

Writing jQuery Code to Call Action Methods

Now you need to wire event handlers for the Draw and Save buttons. You do that using jQuery code, as shown in Listing 1-10.

Listing 1-10. jQuery Code to Draw on the Canvas and Save the Session Data

```
<script type="text/javascript">
  $(document).ready(function () {
    if (!Modernizr.canvas) {
      alert('Your browser does not support the HTML5 canvas tag.');
    }
    $("#Button1").click(function () {
      var canvas = document.getElementById('myCanvas');
      var context = canvas.getContext("2d");
      context.fillStyle = 'silver';
      context.fillRect(0, 0, 500, 200);
      context.fillStyle = 'Black';
      context.lineWidth = 10;
      context.font = '20pt Arial';
      var x = canvas.width / 2;
      var y = canvas.height / 2;
      context.textAlign = "center";
      context.fillText($("#Text1").val(), x, y);
    });

    $("#Button2").click(function () {
      var data = '{ "data" : "' + $("#Text1").val() + '"}';
      $.ajax({
        type: "POST",
```

```
      url: '/home/SaveCanvas',
      data: data,
      contentType: "application/json; charset=utf-8",
      dataType: "json",
      success: function (result) {
        alert(result);
      },
      error: function (err) {
        alert(err.status + " - " + err.statusText);
      }
    })
  });
 });
</script>
```

This jQuery code first checks whether the browser supports the HTML5 canvas using the Modernizr library. It then wires click event handlers for Button1 (Draw) and Button2 (Save). Notice the bold code. The first fragment essentially gets hold of the Canvas object and its drawing context. Several properties of the drawing context are then set, such as fillStyle and font. The fillRect() method draws the canvas background. The fillText() method draws the supplied text at a specified x and y location. The string to be drawn is taken from the TextBox, and the text alignment is set to center.

The click event handler for Button2 uses $.ajax() and sends a POST request to the SaveCanvas() action method. The message returned from SaveCanvas() is then shown to the user.

Figure 1-30 shows a sample run of the Index view.

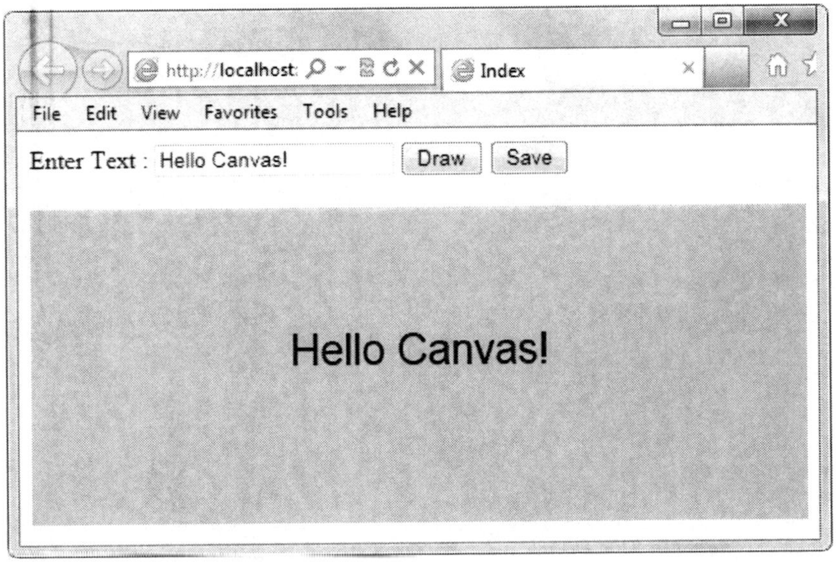

Figure 1-30. Sample run of the Index view

Summary

HTML5 is more than a set of markup elements. It offers many programmable features that are often required in modern web applications. These features include native support for playing audio and video

33

files, canvas, web storage, a history API, a file API, web sockets, web workers, offline applications, and geolocation.

This chapter gave you an overview of HTML5 and its features. You also learned how ASP.NET and HTML5 fit together. You used the Modernizr library to detect HTML5 feature support at runtime. Finally, you developed two simple web applications that illustrate how HTML5 and ASP.NET can go hand in hand. These applications also demonstrated how jQuery can make Ajax requests to the server and invoke server-side code without posting the entire page to the server.

Although HTML5 features can be programmed using plain JavaScript, in many real-world cases you use JavaScript-based libraries such as jQuery for client-side scripting. Chapter 2 delves into the details of jQuery and makes you familiar with many of its programming constructs.

CHAPTER 2

■ ■ ■

Overview of jQuery

To take advantage of many HTML5 features, you need to use client-side scripting techniques. Although you can use JavaScript to accomplish this task, using jQuery is easier and more beneficial. If you're developing a modern web application, chances are you're already using jQuery for your client-side scripting needs. So, sticking with jQuery for programming HTML5 features will make your code more readable, consistent, and manageable. In addition, jQuery offers many benefits over plain JavaScript (selectors and Ajax calls, for example, as discussed in this chapter) that you can use in your client-side code. Some HTML5 features require you to send data from the client to the server. This data transfer can be done effectively through Ajax requests to the server, and jQuery offers rich support for making Ajax requests. All the benefits mentioned here make jQuery an ideal choice for programming HTML5 features.

This chapter gives you an introduction to various jQuery features and constructs. However, the chapter doesn't attempt to discuss every minuscule feature of jQuery. It focuses on features that are frequently needed when programming HTML5 and that are used in the remainder of this book. Specifically, you learn the following:

- Event handling in jQuery
- jQuery selectors
- Manipulating the DOM using jQuery
- Ajax techniques in jQuery

■ Note   This chapter covers the basics of jQuery and how to use jQuery in ASP.NET applications. If you're already familiar with jQuery, feel free to skip this chapter.

What Is jQuery?

The official jQuery web site (http://jquery.com) defines jQuery as follows:

> *jQuery is a fast and concise JavaScript Library that simplifies HTML document traversing, event handling, animating, and Ajax interactions for rapid web development. jQuery is designed to change the way that you write JavaScript.*

Let's try to understand this definition of jQuery in a bit more detail.

jQuery Is a JavaScript Library

As an ASP.NET developer, you must have used JavaScript in one way or the other while developing ASP.NET web sites. Without a doubt, plain JavaScript helps you code rich, interactive, more responsive web pages; but you often need to write too much code. For example, if you wish to write a client script that shows a fancy pop-up menu complete with animation effects using plain JavaScript, it's a time-consuming task.

To simplify your client-side scripting and make you more productive, several JavaScript libraries are available, and jQuery is one of them. There are others, such as MooTools, Prototype, and Dojo. The fact that Microsoft uses jQuery extensively in ASP.NET projects clearly indicates jQuery's popularity and Microsoft's intention to support it in ASP.NET. As you would expect, jQuery is cross-browser and supports all leading browsers including Internet Explorer, Firefox, Chrome, Opera, and Safari.

jQuery Is Fast and Concise

jQuery is highly optimized library. Moreover, it's compact. The production version of jQuery 1.7.2 is just 32KB, and the development version is 247KB. This compactness means less data to be downloaded on the client side without compromising stunning UI effects.

jQuery Simplifies Traversing HTML Documents, Event Handling, Animation, and Ajax Interactions

jQuery simplifies HTML DOM navigation and manipulation considerably. It offers many ways to transverse DOM trees and parent-child elements. Most JavaScript functionality goes in client-side event handlers. jQuery is handy when it comes to event handling because it's easy to wire event handlers and process the events. jQuery also allows you to make Ajax calls to ASP.NET web services, web methods, Windows Communication Foundation (WCF) services, and MVC controller actions.

jQuery Is Designed to Change the Way You Write JavaScript

jQuery dramatically changes the way you write JavaScript code. If you've never used jQuery before, initially you may find its syntax a bit odd; but once you get hang of it, you'll probably never look at any other library (or at least the traditional way of writing JavaScript). For example, a common JavaScript file contains several functions, and you call them individually whenever required. With jQuery, the chain of operations makes your code compact. jQuery lets you chain methods together so the output from one method is automatically processed by the next method in the chain. This makes it easier to invoke multiple methods on the same output.

Downloading and Referring to jQuery

Before you use any of jQuery's features and constructs, you need to refer to it in your Web Forms or MVC views. You can refer to the jQuery library in two ways:

- Refer to a local copy of the jQuery library.
- Refer to the jQuery library from Microsoft's Ajax Content Delivery Network (CDN).

To refer to a local copy of the jQuery library, you should first download it from jQuery official web site (http://jquery.com) to your local machine. If you create a new ASP.NET MVC project, the jQuery library is automatically placed in the Scripts folder (Figure 2-1). Of course, if you wish to use the latest version of the jQuery library, you need to download it separately.

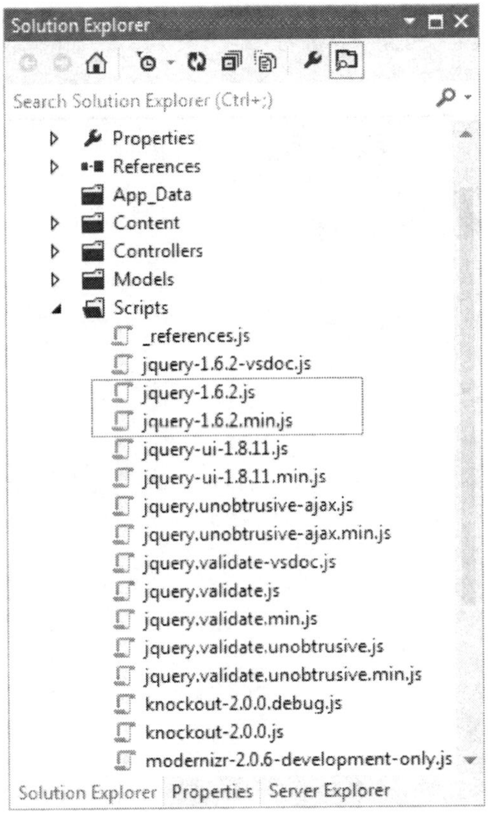

Figure 2-1. jQuery library from ASP.NET MVC projects

To refer to the jQuery library from Microsoft's Ajax CDN, you don't need to maintain a local copy of the jQuery library—you can refer to it directly. You can find a list of files available on the Microsoft Ajax CDN at www.asp.net/ajaxlibrary/cdn.ashx. Figure 2-2 shows a list of files you can use from Microsoft Ajax CDN.

The URLs for minified and non-minified versions of jQuery 1.7.2 are as follows:

```
http://ajax.aspnetcdn.com/ajax/jQuery/jquery-1.7.2.min.js
http://ajax.aspnetcdn.com/ajax/jQuery/jquery-1.7.2.js
```

The minified version is a compressed version obtained by applying several script-minification techniques such as removal of whitespaces and comments from the code. The minified version is ideal for production use because of its compact size. You can use non-minified version during the development phase when script debugging might be needed.

■ **Note** A CDN is a network of servers situated at key locations across the globe. This network maintains cached copies of files that are to be delivered to the client. When a client tries to access any file that is being maintained by the CDN, the server nearest to the requesting client fulfills the request. This technique is known as *edge caching* because the servers toward the edge supply the content. In addition to Microsoft Ajax CDN, you can also use the Google Libraries API for referring to the jQuery library.

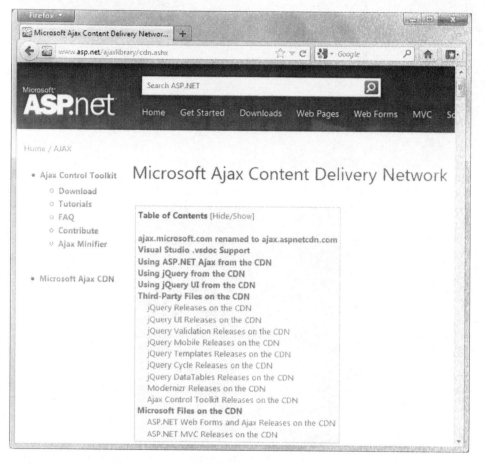

Figure 2-2. Files available on the Microsoft Ajax CDN

Whether you keep a local copy of the jQuery library or refer to it from the Microsoft Ajax CDN, you need to add a <script> reference to it as shown in Listing 2-1.

Listing 2-1. Referring to the jQuery Library

```
<!-- Referring to a local copy of the jQuery library -->

<script type="text/javascript" src="Scripts/jquery-1.7.2.min.js"></script>

<!-- Referring to the jQuery library from the Microsoft Ajax CDN -->

<script type="text/javascript"
          src="http://ajax.aspnetcdn.com/ajax/jQuery/jquery-1.7.2.js">
</script>
```

In Listing 2-1, the first <script> tag refers to the jQuery library from a local folder named Scripts. Make sure you change this path to match your project folder structure. If you use the Microsoft Ajax CDN to refer to the jQuery library, your development machine must have Internet connectivity. You can, of course, use a local copy of the jQuery library during development and switch to the Microsoft Ajax CDN once the application goes into production.

Now that you know how to refer to the jQuery library in your ASP.NET web applications, let's examine the core features of jQuery in the sections to come.

Event Handling

Handling events raised by HTML page elements such as buttons, lists, and images is one of the most frequently programmed operations in client-side scripts. jQuery offers an easy and cross-browser event-handling mechanism that allows you to wire event handlers on the fly and also provides rich information about the event being handled.

Table 2-1 lists many of the commonly used client-side events in web applications.

Table 2-1. Commonly Used Client-Side Events in Web Applications

Event	Description
blur	Occurs when focus leaves an element
change	Occurs when the value of <input>, <textarea>, and or <select> changes.
click	Occurs when the user clicks an element.
dblclick	Occurs when the user double-clicks an element.
focus	Occurs when an element receives focus.
hover	Allows you to trap mouse entry and exit from an element.
keydown	Occurs when a keyboard key is pressed but is yet to be released.
keypress	Occurs when any of the input key is pressed. Normally used when you're only interested in data entered and not in the state of the Shift or Ctrl key.
keyup	Occurs when a keyboard key is released.
mousedown	Occurs when a mouse button is pressed but not yet released.
mouseup	Occurs when a pressed mouse button is released.
select	Occurs when text is selected from <input> or <textarea>.
submit	Occurs when a form is being submitted. Valid only on <form> elements.

To handle the events in Table 2-1, jQuery offers a set of corresponding functions. These functions serve a dual purpose:

- They let you specify an event-handler function that should be executed when the event is raised.

- They let you trigger the event programmatically.

For example, to wire an event-handler function named OnClick to the click event of a button whose ID is Button1, you write

```
$("#Button1").click(OnClick);
```

On the other hand, if you wish to programmatically trigger the click event of Button1, you write:

```
$("#Button1").click();
```

This dual purpose will be clearer when you use it in the example developed in this section.

One nice feature of jQuery event handling is that the event object is passed to the event handler in a standard way and contains the same set of properties across all browsers. The event object passed to an event handler contains several pieces of information, as listed in Table 2-2.

Table 2-2. Properties of Event Object Passed to an Event Handler

Property	Description
altKey	Returns true/false depending on whether the Alt key is pressed
ctrlKey	Returns true/false depending on whether the Ctrl key is pressed
data	User-specific data passed to the event handler. This is optional.
pageX	X coordinate of the mouse within the document.
pageY	Y coordinate of the mouse within the document.
shiftKey	Returns true/false depending on whether the Shift key is pressed.
target	A reference to the DOM element that triggered the event.
type	Type of event, such as click or keydown.
which	The key code of the keyboard key that was pressed.

The event object also provides a handy method preventDefault() that cancels the default action on an event.

To understand how events can be handled using jQuery, let's develop an ASP.NET Web Forms application as shown in Figure 2-3.

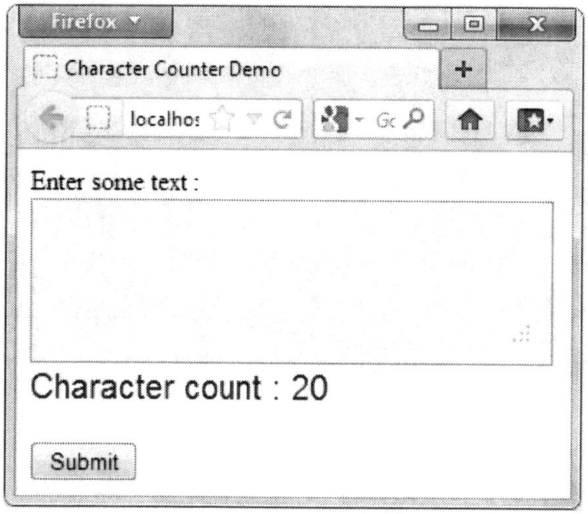

Figure 2-3. Character counter using jQuery event handling

The web form shown in Figure 2-3 has a <textarea> to enter free-form text data. However, you can set a maximum number of characters that can be entered. At runtime, as the user starts typing, a character counter displays the number of characters that can still be entered. If the length of the entered text exceeds a predefined value, you can either prohibit further entry or display a negative character count with colored highlighting. When the user clicks the Submit button, they're asked to confirm whether they want to submit the form; accordingly, either the form is submitted to the server or the action is cancelled.

Listing 2-2 shows the HTML markup of the web form.

Listing 2-2. HTML Markup of the Character Counter Form

```
<form id="form1" runat="server">
<span>Enter some text :</span>
<br />
<textarea id="textarea" rows="3" cols="50" class="TextArea"></textarea>
<br />
<span class="NormalCounter">Character counter : </span>
<span id="counter" class="NormalCounter"></span>
<br /><br />
<asp:Button ID="submit" runat="server" Text="Submit" OnClick="submit_Click" />
<br />
<asp:Label ID="lblMessage" runat="server" Text=""></asp:Label>
</form>
```

The Submit button and the associated message label are server controls. As usual, the CSS classes used in the markup reside in a style-sheet file. Next, you need to write jQuery code that wires several event handlers and makes the character counter functional. Listing 2-3 shows the ready() function that wires event handlers for keyup, blur, and click events. The keyup and blur event handlers ensure that the number of characters entered in the textarea are less than or equal to the maximum length. They also update the character count in the corresponding <span> element.

Listing 2-3. Event Wiring of the Character Counter

```
$(document).ready(function () {
  var eventData = {
    MaxLength: 20,
    Type: 'Remaining',
    AllowOverflow: true,
    CounterId: 'counter',
    NormalCss: 'NormalCounter',
    WarningCss:'WarningCounter'
  };
  $("#textarea").keyup(eventData, OnKeyUp);
  $("#textarea").blur(eventData,OnBlur);
  $("#textarea").keyup();

  $("#submit").click(function (event) {
    if (!confirm("Do you wish to submit the form?")) {
      event.preventDefault();
    }
  });
})
```

The ready() function is automatically called by jQuery when the entire HTML DOM tree is loaded in the browser. You can pass your own function to the ready() function that wires event handlers for various elements such as textarea and <button>. The code declares a variable (eventData) that stores configuration settings you need to pass to the event handlers. Once the event handlers are wired, the eventData object is automatically passed to the event handlers every time the event is raised. Notice that eventData is a JSON object and takes the form of key-value pairs. A key and its value are separated by a colon (:) and multiple key-value pairs are delimited by comma (,). Table 2-3 explains the purpose of each of the settings of the eventData object.

Table 2-3. Configuration Settings Passed via the eventData Object

Option	Description
AllowOverflow	This setting governs the behavior of the <textarea> if the length of the text exceeds the MaxLength value. If you set AllowOverflow to true, you can enter text even if the length exceeds MaxLength; otherwise you can't enter any further text after MaxLength is reached.
CounterId	CounterId indicates the ID of an HTML element (typically a <span> or <div>) that is displaying the character counter.
MaxLength	This setting indicates the maximum number of characters that can be entered in the <textarea>.
NormalCss	NormalCss is a CSS class that is applied to the counter element when the length of the text entered is less than MaxLength.
Type	You can display the character counter in two ways: show the total number of characters entered so far, or show the number of characters that can still be entered. If you pass Total, the former setting is used; if you pass Remaining, the latter setting is used.
WarningCss	When the length of the text entered in the <textarea> exceeds MaxLength, the character counter is displayed with a CSS class indicated by WarningCss.

The code then selects the <textarea> element. Notice the jQuery way of selecting an element based on its ID: you need to pass the ID of an element prefixed with the # character. The keyup and blur events of <textarea> are wired to the OnKeyUp and OnBlur event-handler functions, respectively. You write these event-handler functions shortly. Notice that the code also passes the eventData object while wiring the event handlers. Then the code programmatically triggers the keyup event of the <textarea> by calling the keyup() function. This causes the counter <span> element to display the initial character count.

The event handler for the click event of the Submit button is wired using a different syntax. Instead of creating a separate function and then attaching it as an event handler, the code creates an anonymous event handler (also known as *inline function*) function. The event-handler function takes a parameter (event) that is automatically passed when the click event is raised. The click event handler of the Submit button asks the user whether to submit the form. If the user decides to cancel the form submission, the click event is cancelled using the preventDefault() method of the event object.

The event-handler function OnKeyUp() is shown in Listing 2-4.

Listing 2-4. Handling the keyup Event

```
function OnKeyUp(event) {
  var id = "#" + event.target.id;
  var counterid = "#" + event.data.CounterId;
  var text = $(id).val();
  if (text.length > event.data.MaxLength) {
    if (!event.data.AllowOverflow) {
      $(id).text(text.substring(0, event.data.MaxLength));
    }
  }
  var diff = 0;
  if (event.data.Type == 'Remaining') {
...
  }
  else {
...  }
  $(counterid).text(diff);
}
```

Notice how event.target.id is used to retrieve the ID of <textarea> and event.data.CounterId is used to retrieve the ID of <span>. These IDs are stored in two variables (id and counterid) for later use. The val() method returns the text entered in the <textarea> and is stored in another local variable (text). Depending on the type of counter (Remaining or Total), the code checks the length of the text data entered in the <textarea> against the MaxLength value. If Type is Remaining, the check is performed as follows:

```
diff = event.data.MaxLength - $(id).val().length;
if (diff < 0) {
  $(counterid).removeClass(event.data.NormalCss);
  $(counterid).addClass(event.data.WarningCss);
}
else {
  $(counterid).removeClass(event.data.WarningCss);
  $(counterid).addClass(event.data.NormalCss);
}
```

If the difference between the length of the text and MaxLength is less than 0, it indicates that the text has exceeded its maximum allowed length. In that case, you should display the counter with the WarningCss class. To do this, you first remove the NormalCss class using the removeClass() method and then apply the WarningCss class using the addClass() method. If the difference is greater than 0, you should apply the NormalCss class by removing the WarningCss class.

If the counter Type is Total, the CSS classes are applied as shown here:

```
diff = $(id).val().length;
if (diff > event.data.MaxLength) {
  $(counterid).removeClass(event.data.NormalCss);
  $(counterid).addClass(event.data.WarningCss);
}
else {
  $(counterid).removeClass(event.data.WarningCss);
  $(counterid).addClass(event.data.NormalCss);
}
```

If the length of the text entered is more than the MaxLength value, the NormalCss class is removed using the removeCss() method and the WarningCss class is applied using addClass(). Otherwise, WarningCss is removed and NormalCss is applied.

Finally, after the code performs the length checking based on the Type setting, the counter value is assigned to the <span> element using the text() method.

If the AllowOverflow setting is false, further text entered by the user is trimmed to the value of MaxLength using the substring() JavaScript function. The trimmed text is assigned to the <textarea> using the text() method.

The OnBlur() event-handler function is shown in Listing 2-5.

Listing 2-5. *Handling the blur Event*

```
function OnBlur(event) {
  var id = "#" + event.target.id;
  $(id).keyup();
}
```

The OnBlur() event-handler function simply triggers the keyup event programmatically. This way, even if the user enters text in the <textarea> using a copy-paste technique (Ctrl+V or a shortcut menu), the counter still reflects the correct value when the user exits the <textarea>.

Figure 2-4 shows a sample run of the web form with text exceeding the MaxLength value. You can also test the Submit button's functionality. Observe that if you click Cancel, the form isn't posted back to the server.

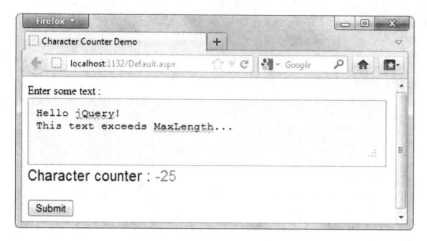

Figure 2-4. *Character counter showing a warning*

In the character counter you just developed, you used #id syntax to select a DOM element matching a specific ID. By doing so, you uses one of jQuery's many selectors. The next section introduces some other important selectors in jQuery.

Event Wiring Using the bind() Method

In the preceding example, you wired event handlers of the standard events click and change using the jQuery functions click() and change(), respectively. As of this writing, jQuery doesn't include event functions for HTML5-specific events. For example, the video element you learn about in Chapter 3 has play and pause events, but jQuery doesn't have built-in functions to wire event handlers for these events. Luckily, jQuery provides a generic way to wire events to their handlers: the bind() method. You can use it as follows:

```
$("#Button1").bind("click",OnClick);
```

This line of code wires the click event of Button1 to an event-handler function named OnClick. The bind() method takes two parameters. The first parameter indicates the event you wish to handle, and the second parameter specifies the event-handler function.

jQuery Selectors

While working with client-side scripts, you often need to perform certain tasks only on specific elements. For example, you may want to read the value of a text box whose ID is TextBox1 or display all the rows of a table that contain a negative value in red. jQuery selectors let you match HTML elements against certain criteria and select them for further processing. Thus jQuery selectors return a collection with zero or more elements matching a selection criterion.

jQuery selectors can be grouped into the following categories:

- *Basic selector:* Selects elements based on basic criteria such as ID, CSS class, and HTML tag name.

- *Basic filter:* Filters an element set based on conditions such as first occurrence, last occurrence, and odd or even elements.

- *Attribute selector:* Selects elements by matching their attribute values.

- *Child filter:* Filters an element set based on conditions such as first-child, last-child, *n*th-child, and only-child.

- *Content filter:* Filters elements based on their content.

- *Form selector:* Selects form elements based on their type (button, check box, and so on) and state (selected or checked).

- *Hierarchy selector:* Selects elements from a hierarchy (children, descendents, siblings, and adjacent).

- *Visibility filter:* Selects elements based on their visibility status (visible or hidden).

The selectors that are needed frequently and that are used in this book's examples are discussed in the following sections.

■ **Note** Some of the examples discussed in the following sections use the Northwind database, a sample database developed by Microsoft for SQL Server. So, you may consider installing it in your local SQL Server or SQL Server Express instance. You can download the T-SQL script of the Northwind database from the MSDN download center.

Selecting Elements Based on ID, Tag Name, and CSS Class

Selecting HTML elements based on their ID, tag names, or CSS class is a common requirement in client-side scripting. From the previous sections, you already know how to select HTML elements by specifying their ID. Listing 2-6 shows these three types of selections.

Listing 2-6. Using ID, Tag Name, and CSS Class to Match Elements

```
$(document).ready(function () {
  $("#myDiv").html("<h1>Hello jQuery !</h1>");
  $("div").css("background-color", "#ded8d8");
  $(".MyClass").text("We have the same CSS class!");
})
```

The first line in the ready function selects a DOM element whose ID is myDiv. It then sets the HTML content of the selected element to some markup using the jQuery html() method. The second line selects all the <div> elements from the page and sets their background color to #ded8d8 using the css() method. Finally, the third line of code selects all the elements that have a CSS class named MyClass applied to them and sets their HTML content to a string.

Figure 2-5 shows a sample run of the page.

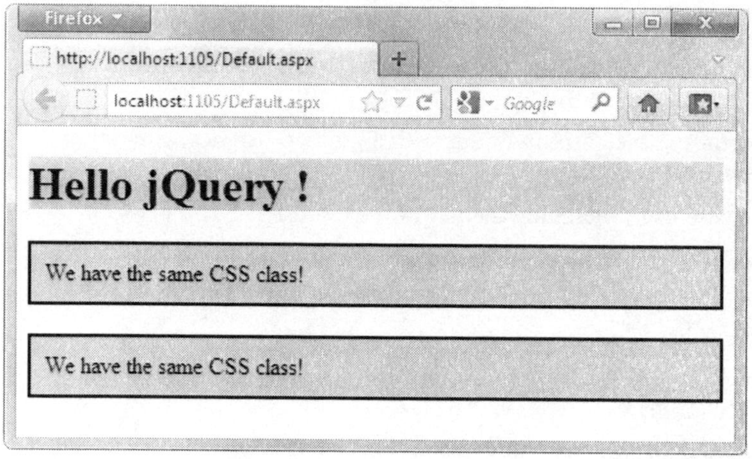

Figure 2-5. Selecting HTML elements based on ID, tag name, and CSS class

Notice how all the <div> elements have the same background color because the color was applied to the background-color attribute for all HTML elements with tag name div. Similarly, both <div> elements with the CSS class MyClass have the same text content.

Now, let's develop a more meaningful example based on this knowledge. Figure 2-6 shows a GridView server control populated with data from the Employees table of the Northwind database.

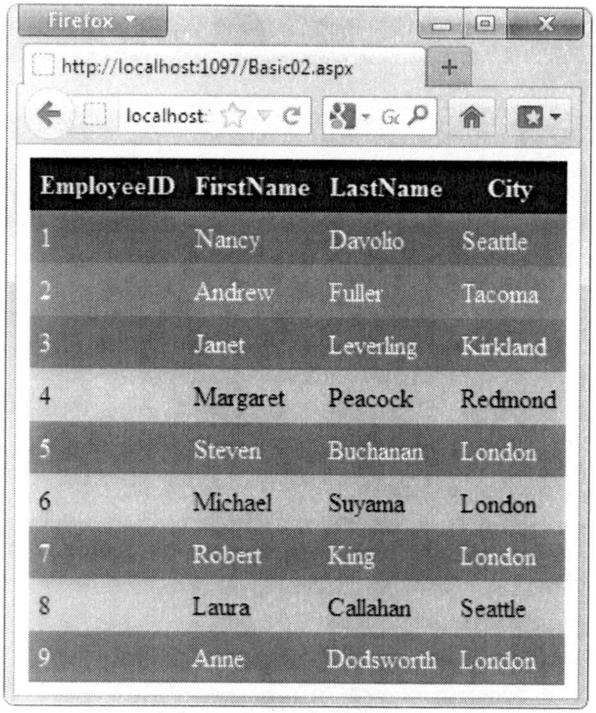

Figure 2-6. GridView with alternate rows displayed with different styles

The GridView control renders itself as an HTML table in the browser. The GridView shown in Figure 2-6 has alternate rows displayed with different CSS styles. Also, the header row is displayed with another CSS style. Further, the rows show a highlighted marker when the mouse pointer hovers over them. Clicking any row displays the EmployeeID of that row in an alert box. All this is done through jQuery. The <script> block from the web form reveals the jQuery code shown in Listing 2-7.

Listing 2-7. Marking Odd and Even Rows with Different Styles

```
$(document).ready(function () {
  $("#GridView1 th").parent().addClass("HeaderRow");
  $("#GridView1 tr:not(.HeaderRow):odd").addClass("Row");
  $("#GridView1 tr:not(.HeaderRow):even").addClass("AlternateRow");
  $("#GridView1 tr:not(.HeaderRow)").hover(function () {
    $(this).addClass('HoverRow');
  }, function () {
    $(this).removeClass('HoverRow');
  }).click(function () {
    if ($(this).hasClass("HeaderRow")) {
      alert("This is header row. Can't get EmployeeID!");
    }
    else {
      alert("You selected Employee ID :" + $("td:first", this).text());
    }
  });
});
```

The code shown in Listing 2-7 uses a combination of selectors discussed earlier in this section and a few additional filters. First, the code sets a CSS class for the header row of the table. Notice how the <th> elements from a specific GridView (with ID GridView1) are selected. This way, even if there are multiple tables on the same web form, the styling is applied only to GridView1. The parent() method returns a parent element of <th> (<tr> in this case), and the HeaderRow CSS class is applied to that table row using the addClass() method.

The next two lines of code select all the odd and even rows from the table excluding the header row. This is done using the :not(), :odd, and :even selectors. The :not() selector ensures that the header row isn't selected for applying odd and even styling. The :odd and :even selectors return odd and even elements, respectively. Once selected, the CSS classes Row and AlternateRow are applied to them, respectively.

Next, a mouse-hover effect is added to the table rows using the hover() method. The first parameter to the hover() method is a function that is called when the mouse pointer enters a table row, and the second parameter is a function that is called when the mouse pointer leaves that table row. In the callback functions, the keyword this represents the current table row. The hover() method functions essentially add and remove the HoverRow CSS class to the table row under consideration.

■ **Note** In any jQuery event handler, the keyword this refers to the DOM element to which the event handler is attached.

Notice the use of the jQuery chaining feature while wiring the click event handler. Instead of again selecting the rows and then wiring their click event handler, you can wire event handlers for the hover and click events at the same time.

The click event handler displays the EmployeeID from the row being clicked. The td:first selector returns the first <td> element in the current row. The text() method, when called without any parameter, returns the text content from that table column (EmployeeID in this case). If the header row is clicked, an error message is displayed. Notice how the hasClass() method is used to determine whether a row has a specific CSS class applied to it.

Selecting Elements Based on Their Attribute Value

Attribute selectors let you match attributes of HTML elements with certain criteria. It isn't limited to equal-to matching; several other options are also available, as outlined in Table 2-4. Using an attribute selector takes the following general form:

<element_name>[<attribute_name> <operator> <value_to_match>]

Table 2-4. Attribute Selectors

Attribute Selector	Operator	Description
Attribute equals	=	Selects elements whose specific attribute value exactly equals a specific string value.
Attribute not equal	!=	Selects elements whose specific attribute value doesn't match a specific string value *or* whose specified attribute is missing.
Attribute starts with	^=	Selects elements whose specified attribute value begins with a specific value.
Attribute ends with	$=	Selects elements whose specified attribute value ends with a certain string value.
Attribute contains	*=	Selects elements whose specified attribute value contains a specific string.
Attribute contains prefix	|=	Selects elements whose specified attribute value matches exactly the specified value or that starts with the specified value followed by a hyphen (-).
Has attribute selector		Selects an element if a specified attribute is present.

Let's consider some examples that show how the attribute selectors are used.

Suppose you have a web page with a bunch of hyperlinks, and you wish to select hyperlinks whose href attribute is exactly equal to http://www.microsoft.com. The following attribute selector does the trick. The alert box displays the total number of elements selected:

alert($("a[href = 'http://www.microsoft.com']").length);

Suppose you have a few hyperlinks: http://microsoft.com, http://msdn.microsoft.com, and http://www.asp.net. You need to select only those hyperlinks that contain the word *Microsoft*. The following attribute contains selector selects the first two hyperlinks but not the third one:

alert($("a[href *= 'microsoft.com']").length);

Let's say a product catalog page displays many images. Some of them are product images, and others are web site theme images (logo, menus, and so on). Also assume that the product images are stored in a folder named product. To select all the product images for processing, you can use this *attribute starts with* selector to return image elements whose src attribute begins with *product*:

alert($("img[src ^= 'product']").length);

Suppose you're building a photo album web application that displays photos in various formats including .png, .jpg, and .gif. Based on the image format, you may allow certain special effects to be added. In such cases, you may want to select images with a particular file extension. The following *attribute ends with* selector does that by selecting all the images whose src attribute ends with .gif:

```
alert($("img[src $= '.gif']").length);
```

Suppose a multilingual web site needs to render its content in different languages. The lang attribute is used to mark the language of a section of the page. If you wish to select all the <div> elements having their lang attribute set to some value, you can use this *has attribute* selector:

```
alert($("div[lang]").length);
```

Now, let's develop a more realistic example that uses attribute selectors, as shown in Figure 2-7.

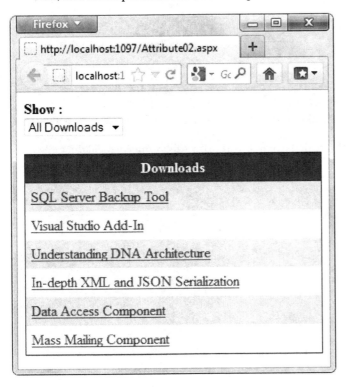

Figure 2-7. *Filtering download links using attribute selectors*

In Figure 2-7, the web form consists of a GridView control that displays links to files that can be downloaded. The download categories are listed in a DropDownList at the top. When the user selects a particular category, only downloads belonging to the selected category are displayed. The rest are kept hidden. The download links have a specific pattern:

- All download links for products contain the Products folder in the URL: for example, products/Product1Setup.exe.

- All download links for white papers are of the form paper-*xxxx*, where *xxxx* is the title of the paper: for example, Paper-Topic1.pdf.

- All download links for software components are of the form *xxxx*-comp.zip: for example, Component1-comp.zip.

This hiding and showing of download links happens on the client side using jQuery attribute selectors. Listing 2-8 shows the skeleton of this code.

Listing 2-8. Hiding or Showing Download Links Using Attribute Selectors

```
$(document).ready(function () {
  $("#DropDownList1").change(function () {
    switch ($("#DropDownList1").val()) {
      case "A":
      case "P":
      case "WP":
      case "C":
    }
  })
})
```

The ready function wires an event handler for the change event of DropDownList1. As you might guess, the change event is raised when the selection in the DropDownList changes. The change event handler consists of a JavaScript switch statement that checks for the selected value. Let's discuss what goes in each case section.

If the selected value is "A", meaning All Downloads, then the display CSS property of all the table rows is set to block. This ensures that all types of downloads (products, components, and white papers) are shown in the grid:

case "A":

```
  $("#GridView1 tr a").parent().css("display", "block");
  break;
```

If the selected value is "P" (Products), then the *attribute contains* selector (*=) is used to match all the anchor elements whose href attribute contains the string "products/". Once matched, the table rows containing the matched hyperlink elements are shown, and other rows are kept hidden:

case "P":

```
  $("#GridView1 tr a[href *= 'products/']").parent().css("display", "block");
  $("#GridView1 tr a[href |= 'Paper']").parent().css("display", "none");
  $("#GridView1 tr a[href $= '-comp.zip']").parent().css("display", "none");
  break;
```

If the selected value is "WP" (White Papers), the code uses the *attribute contains prefix* selector (|=) to select hyperlinks prefixed with the text "paper". Notice that the URLs for white papers begin with "Paper-", but the selector specifies only "Paper"; this is because while matching the elements, the *attribute contains prefix* selector automatically assumes a hyphen (-). Once selected, the table rows containing those hyperlinks are shown, and the other rows are kept hidden:

case "WP":

```
  $("#GridView1 tr a[href *= 'products/']").parent().css("display", "none");
  $("#GridView1 tr a[href |= 'Paper']").parent().css("display", "block");
  $("#GridView1 tr a[href $= '-comp.zip']").parent().css("display", "none");
  break;
```

Finally, if the selected value is "C" (Components), the code selects links related to components using the *attribute ends with* selector ($=) and displays and hides table rows accordingly:

```
case "C":
  $("#GridView1 tr a[href *= 'products/']").parent().css("display", "none");
  $("#GridView1 tr a[href |= 'Paper']").parent().css("display", "none");
  $("#GridView1 tr a[href $= '-comp.zip']").parent().css("display", "block");
  break;
```

Selecting Form Elements

Form selectors let you select HTML <form> elements based on their type (text box, check box, radio button, and so on) or their status (selected, checked, or disabled). Table 2-5 lists the various form selectors available.

Table 2-5. Form Selectors

Selector	Elements Selected
:button	<input> elements of type button, and <button> elements
:checkbox	<input> elements of type checkbox
:checked	Check boxes and radio buttons that are checked
:disabled	Elements that are disabled
:enabled	Elements that are enabled
:file	<input> elements of type file
:image	<input> elements of type image
:input	Elements of type <input>, <textarea>, <select>, and <button>
:password	<input> elements of type password
:radio	<input> elements of type radio
:reset	<input> elements of type reset
:selected	Options of a <select> element that are selected
:submit	<input> elements of type submit
:text	<input> elements of type text

Listing 2-9 shows some of the selectors mentioned in Table 2-5.

Listing 2-9. Basic Usage Syntax of Form Selectors

```
$(document).ready(function () {
  $("#form1 :text").attr("disabled", "disabled");
  $("#form1 :checkbox").attr("checked", "checked");
  $("#Button1").click(function () {
    alert($("#form1 input[type='checkbox']:checked").length + " checkboxes are checked.");
    alert($("#Select1 option:selected").length + " options are selected.");
  });
});
```

The first form selector in Listing 2-9 selects all text boxes and disables them by adding the disabled attribute. The jQuery attr() function is used to set attribute values of an element. The first parameter of attr() is the name of the attribute, and the second parameter is its value. In this case, the disabled attribute is set to a value of disabled so as to disable the text boxes.

The second form selector selects all check boxes and programmatically checks them by adding the checked attribute.

The click event handler of Button1 selects all the check box elements that are checked. A jQuery selector may return zero or more elements. The total number of elements selected can be obtained using the length property. In this case, an alert box displays the total number of check boxes that are checked.

Finally, the last alert box displays the count of all the selected options from a <select> element.

The web form shown in Figure 2-8 demonstrates a more realistic use of form selectors. The web form shows a GridView with records from the Employees table of the Northwind database. Each row of the GridView has a check box and a radio button to select that row. The check-box column also has a check box in the header to toggle selection of all the check boxes. The list box at the top displays cities; if you select one or more cities in the list box, only the employee records belonging to the selected cities are enabled. Other records' check boxes and radio buttons are disabled. Clicking the Clear Selection button clears any selection made in the list box and enables all the employee rows. The jQuery code responsible for this functionality consists of four event-handler functions: the change event handler of the check boxes, the change event handler of the radio buttons, the change event handler of the list box, and the click event handler of the button. These event handlers are wired in the ready() function and are discussed next.

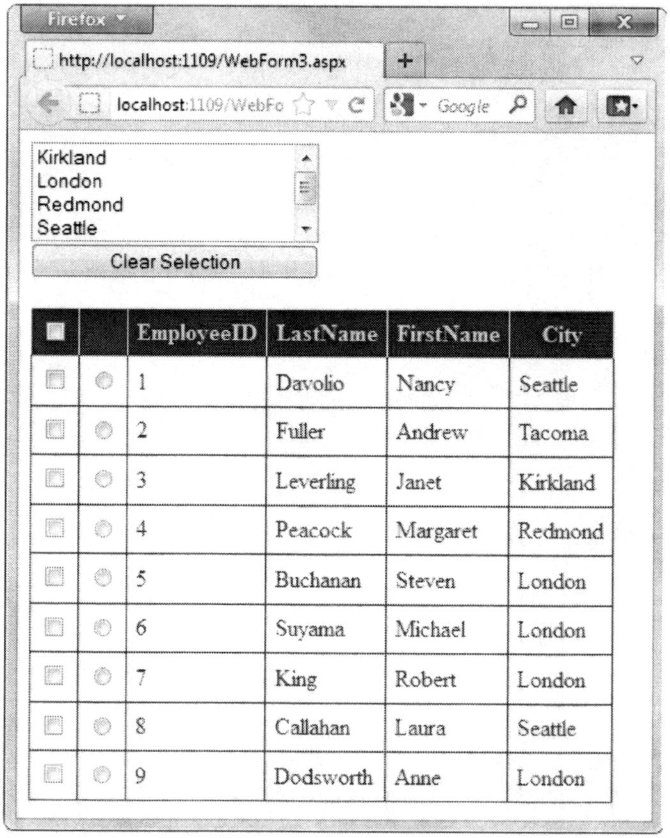

Figure 2-8. A GridView showing check boxes and radio buttons to select employee rows

Listing 2-10 shows the change event handler of the check boxes.

Listing 2-10. Change Event Handler of the Check Boxes

```
$("#GridView1 :checkbox[id$='chkHeader']").change(function () {
  if ($("#GridView1 :checked[id $='chkHeader']").is(":checked")) {
    $("#GridView1 :checkbox[id *='chkItem']").attr("checked", "checked");
  }
  else {
    $("#GridView1 :checkbox[id *='chkItem']").removeAttr("checked");
  }
})
```

The code shown in Listing 2-10 wires the change event handler for the check box in the header row. It does so using the *ends with* attribute selector because at runtime, the GridView generates unique IDs for the check boxes. While generating these unique IDs, the design-time ID set by the developer is appended at the end of a unique string value. For example, the header check box has its ID property set to chkHeader, and at runtime its client-side ID becomes GridView1$ctl01$chkHeader. The change event handler of the header check box selects all the check boxes from the GridView rows and toggles their state depending on the header check box state. The check box state is toggled by adding or removing the checked attribute using the jQuery attr() method.

The change event handler of all the radio buttons is wired as shown in Listing 2-11.

Listing 2-11. Change Event Handler of the Radio Buttons

```
$("#GridView1 :radio[id *='radItem']").change(function () {
  var newId = this.id;
  $("#GridView1 :radio[id *='radItem']").each(function (index) {
    if (this.id != newId) {
      $(this).removeAttr("checked");
    }
  })
})
```

By default, radio buttons placed in a GridView aren't mutually exclusive, and you can select more than one radio button. This happens because the GridView generates a different name for each of the radio button rather than treating them as a group. To tackle this problem, the change event handler of the radio buttons iterates through the radio buttons and unchecks all of them other than the one being selected. To iterate through the radio buttons, the code uses the jQuery each() method. The each() method takes a function that is executed on each element from the matched set. The callback function receives a zero-based index of the current element from the matched set. To uncheck a radio button, its checked attribute is removed using the removeAttr() method.

The change event handler of the list box displaying the cities is shown in Listing 2-12.

Listing 2-12. Change Event Handler of the List Box

```
$("#ListBox1").change(function () {
  $("#GridView1 :input").attr("disabled", "disabled");
  $("#ListBox1 option:selected").each(function () {
    $("#GridView1 tr:contains('" + this.value + "')").each(function () {
      $(":input", this).removeAttr("disabled");
    })
  })
})
```

This event handler disables all input elements including check boxes and radio buttons. It then selects the options selected in the list box and iterates through them one by one using the each() method. The code in the each() block checks whether the current row contains a selected city. This checking is done using the :contains() selector. This selector accepts a string and returns only those rows that contain the specified string value. If a city is found in a row, the disabled attribute of the corresponding check box and radio button is removed using the removeAttr() method.

The click event handler of the Clear Selection button is shown in Listing 2-13.

Listing 2-13. Click Event Handler of the Clear Selection Button

```
$("#Button1").click(function (event) {
  $("#ListBox1 option").each(function () {
    $(this).removeAttr("selected");
  })
  $("#GridView1 :input").removeAttr("disabled");
  event.preventDefault();
})
```

The button's click event handler iterates through all the list-box options using the each() method and unselects them one by one by removing the selected attribute. All the <input> elements are enabled by removing the disabled attribute, because no city is now selected in the list box.

Modifying the DOM Using jQuery

By now, you know how to alter existing elements and their attributes. jQuery also lets you insert, append, remove, and replace elements from the HTML DOM so you can modify the document structure. For example, suppose you're calling a remote service from client-side jQuery code and, based on what the service returns, you need to generate HTML markup on the fly. Such tasks can be accomplished using jQuery methods that let you manipulate the HTML DOM. Table 2-6 lists some of the most commonly used DOM-manipulation methods.

Table 2-6. jQuery Methods for Modifying the HTML DOM

Method	Description
after()	Inserts content after a specific element
append()	Appends content as specified by the parameter to the end of the matched elements.
appendTo()	Appends the matched elements to the end of a target element.
attr()	Gets or sets an attribute value
before()	Inserts content before a specific element
clone()	Makes a deep copy of an element and its contents
empty()	Removes all the child nodes of a specific element
html()	Returns the HTML markup of an element
insertAfter()	Inserts content after a specific element
insertBefore()	Inserts content before a specific element
prepend()	Inserts content as specified by the parameter at the beginning of the matched elements
prependTo()	Inserts the matched elements at the beginning of a target element
remove()	Removes a specific element and all its child elements

`removeAttr()`	Removes an attribute from an element
`replaceWith()`	Replaces target element with specific content
`text()`	Returns the text content of an element including all child elements
`val()`	Returns the value from a form element
`wrap()`	Wraps every element of a matched set in a given element

You're already familiar with some of these methods, such as `val()`, `attr()`, `removeAttr()`, `text()`, and `html()`. Listing 2-14 shows the use of other methods from Table 2-6.

Listing 2-14. Using DOM-Manipulation Methods

```
$("#container").append("<div>Hello</div>");
$("<div>Hello</div>").appendTo("#container");
$("span").replaceWith("<div class='class1'>Hello Universe!</div>");
$("<div class='class2'>Hello World!</div>").replaceAll("div.class1");
```

The first line of code from Listing 2-14 adds `<div>Hello</div>` at the end of the container element. So, if the container is a `<span>` element, then after calling the `append()` method, the effective markup is

```
<span id='container'><div>Hello</div></span>
```

▨ **Note** Most browsers let you view the HTML source of the web page being displayed. However, this HTML source doesn't include any HTML markup dynamically added at runtime using the jQuery methods listed in Table 2-6.

The second line of code uses the `appendTo()` method. This method is similar to the `append()` method with one difference: `append()` is invoked on the target element and accepts markup to be appended. The `appendTo()` method accepts a target element as a parameter and appends the specified markup at the end of the target.

The example of the `replaceWith()` method replaces all the `<span>` elements with `<div class='class1'>` elements. For example, if the original markup is `<span>Hello World!</span>`, then after calling the `replaceWith()` method, the new markup is `<div class='class1'>Hello Universe!</div>`.

Finally, the `replaceAll()` method replaces all the `<div>` elements with the CSS class `class1` with `<div>Hello World!</div>`.

jQuery Ajax Techniques

Many of the HTML5 features discussed in later chapters require you to pass data between the client browser and the server. Such a data transfer can be accomplished in two ways:

- Submitting an entire form to the server
- Making an Ajax request to the server

The first technique involves submitting the entire form to the server using `GET` or `POST` requests. Although this is a classic technique and easy to implement (using a Submit button or the `submit()` JavaScript method), it suffers from a drawback: the entire page needs to be refreshed, which affects the responsiveness and overall performance of the web application. No wonder many modern web applications tend to use the second way of sending data to the server.

The second technique involves making an Ajax request to the server. The advantage of using Ajax is that you don't need to send all the form data to the server. Instead, you can send only the pieces of data that are required for processing at a given point of time. The result of the processing returned by an Ajax request can be used to dynamically update the web page. Thus Ajax improves the responsiveness and overall performance of a web application.

Note that although Ajax implies using XML as a data format, JSON is more commonly used than XML due to its compactness. Most of the examples in this book that require data transfers between client and server use Ajax and JSON.

jQuery offers many ways to make Ajax requests to the server. They're listed in Table 2-7.

Table 2-7. jQuery Ajax Methods

Technique	Request Method	Description
`$.ajax()`	GET / POST / other HTTP verbs also supported	Generic function that can be used to make Ajax calls to the server. All the techniques listed below internally use `$.ajax()`to perform their operations.
`$("...").load()`	GET / POST	Fetches HTML markup or text from the server dynamically and then sets it to the contents of a selected DOM element.
`$.get()`	GET	Makes generic GET requests to the server. For example, using the `$.get()` method you can make a request to an MVC action method and fetch data from the database.
`$.post()`	POST	Makes generic POST requests to the server. For example, using the `$.post()` method you can submit a form to an MVC action method for further processing.
`$.getJSON()`	GET	Makes a GET requests to the server and fetches data in JSON format.
`$.getScript()`	GET	Loads remote script files dynamically so you can execute them further in the code.

Using jQuery Ajax techniques, you can invoke the following types of ASP.NET server-side code:

- Web services (`.asmx`)
- Web methods
- WCF services (`.svc`)
- ASP.NET MVC controller action methods
- Web API
- Generic HTTP handlers (`.ashx`)

Although jQuery Ajax techniques let you call ASMX web services, whenever possible you should avoid using them because newer techniques are available.

■ **Note** Technically speaking, you can make Ajax request to any server-side resource not listed here. However, in most common cases it's best to encapsulate the code to be called from the client side in one of the mechanisms discussed.

Detailed discussion of all the jQuery Ajax techniques listed in Table 2-7 is beyond the scope of this book. The examples that follow illustrate the use of the $.ajax() function because it's the mother of all the other techniques.

The examples in this section show how you can use $.ajax() in Web Forms as well as MVC applications. Both of the applications you develop display a simple web page, as shown in Figure 2-9.

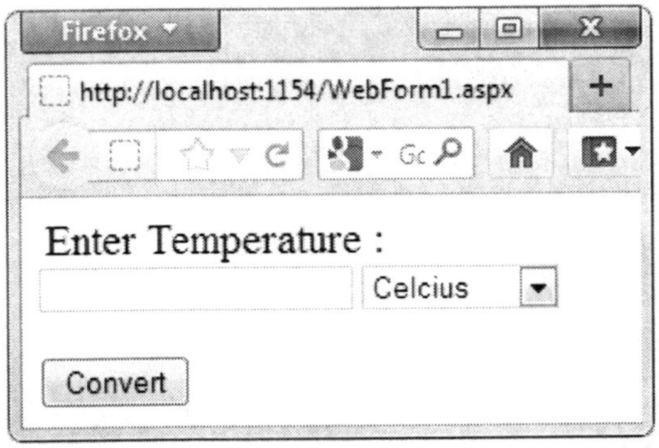

Figure 2-9. *Web page to convert a temperature between Celsius and Fahrenheit*

The web page allows you to enter a temperature value in Celsius or Fahrenheit and converts it to the other scale. The temperature conversion happens in a WCF service for the Web Forms application and in a controller action method for the MVC application.

Using the jQuery $.ajax() Method in a Web Forms Application

The WCF service that converts temperature values between Celsius and Fahrenheit is shown in Listing 2-15.

Listing 2-15. *WCF Service for Converting Temperature Values*

```
namespace AjaxWebForm
{
    [DataContract]
    public class TemperatureData
    {
        [DataMember]
        public decimal Value { get; set; }
        [DataMember]
        public string Unit { get; set; }
    }

    [ServiceContract]
    public interface IService
    {
        [OperationContract]
        [WebInvoke(Method = "POST",
          RequestFormat = WebMessageFormat.Json,
          ResponseFormat = WebMessageFormat.Json)]
```

```
        TemperatureData Convert(TemperatureData t);
    }

    public class Service : IService
    {
        public TemperatureData Convert(TemperatureData t)
        {
            if (t.Unit == "C")
            {
                t.Value = (t.Value * 1.8m) + 32;
                t.Unit = "F";
            }
            else
            {
                t.Value = (t.Value - 32) / 1.8m;
                t.Unit = "C";
            }
            return t;
        }
    }
}
```

The TemperatureData class represents the data contract of the WCF service and contains two data member properties: Value and Unit. The IService interface represents a service contract for the service and defines a single method Convert(). The Convert() method accepts a TemperatureData object and returns a TemperatureData object after converting the temperature value to the other scale.

Notice that Convert() is decorated with an [WebInvoke] attribute. Due to this attribute, Convert() becomes callable from the client-side jQuery code. The RequestFormat and ResponseFormat properties of the [WebInvoke] attribute specify JSON as the communication format during request and response, respectively. The Method property specifies that Convert() can be invoked by HTTP POST requests. The Service class implements Convert(). The Convert() method checks the Unit of the incoming TemperatureData object and, depending on the Unit, converts the Value to the other scale.

The Service class's Convert() method can be called using jQuery's $.ajax() function as shown in Listing 2-16.

Listing 2-16. Using $.ajax() to Call the WCF Service Convert() Method

```
$(document).ready(function () {
  $("#Button1").click(function () {
    url = "Service.svc/Convert";
    data = '{"Value":"' + $("#Text1").val() + '","Unit":"' + $("#Select1").val() + '"}';
    $.ajax({
      type: "POST",
      url: url,
      data: data,
      contentType: "application/json; charset=utf-8",
      dataType: "json",
      success: OnSuccess,
      error: OnError
    })
  });
});
```

```
function OnSuccess(results) {
  alert("Converted Temperature : " + results.Value + " " + results.Unit);
}

function OnError(err) {
  alert(err.status + " - " + err.statusText);
}
```

The Convert button's `click` event handler contains the jQuery code for invoking the `Convert()` method. The `$.ajax()` function has many configurable settings. Some common ones are used in Listing 2-14. The `url` setting allows you to specify the remote resource URL. For a WCF service, the URL takes the form `<path_to_svc_file>/<method_name>`.

The `type` option lets you specify the HTTP request type to be used while making the request. The `Convert()` method is configured with the `[WebInvoke]` attribute to use a `POST` method, and hence `type` is `POST`. The `data` setting indicates the data to be sent to the server (if any) while making the call. Notice how data is captured in JSON format. A JSON object takes the form of key-value pairs: a key and its value are separated by a colon (`:`), and multiple key-value pairs are delimited by a comma (`,`).

The `dataType` setting governs the data type of the response (XML, JSON, and so on). Recollect that the `[WebMethod]` attribute specified `ResponseFormat` as JSON, so `dataType` here must be set to JSON to correctly process the data coming from the server.

If `Convert()` returns successfully, the function specified by the success option (`OnSuccess`) is called. If there is any error while calling the WCF service, a function specified by the error option (`OnError`) is called. The `OnSuccess()` function is where you process the data returned from the WCF service. `OnSuccess()` receives the return value of `Convert()` (the `TemperatureData` object) as a parameter. You can access its `Value` and `Unit` properties and display an alert box to the user.

In the `OnError()` function, you typically flag the error to the user or take some corrective action. `OnError()` receives an error object; you can display its `status` and `statusText` properties to the user.

Figure 2-10 shows a sample run of the Web Forms application.

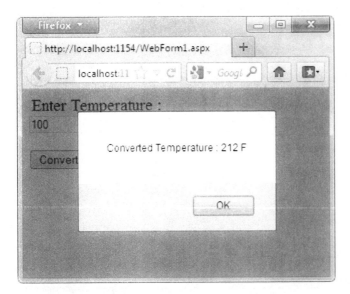

Figure 2-10. Sample run of Web Forms application that converts temperatures

Using the jQuery $.ajax() Method in an MVC Application

Working with MVC applications and calling server-side code from jQuery is simple. You don't need to create a separate service (of course, you can if you so wish). Instead, you can encapsulate the code in a controller action method. For example, Listing 2-17 shows the Convert() action method that encapsulates the temperature-conversion logic.

Listing 2-17. Convert() Action Method in an MVC Controller

```
public JsonResult Convert(TemperatureData t)
{
    if (t.Unit == "C")
    {
        t.Value = (t.Value * 1.8m) + 32;
        t.Unit = "F";
    }
    else
    {
        t.Value = (t.Value - 32) / 1.8m;
        t.Unit = "C";
    }
    return Json(t);
}
```

As you can see, the Convert() action method accepts a parameter of type TemperatureData and returns a JsonResult. The JsonResult class wraps a return value in JSON format. Notice how the JsonResult object is returned using ASP.NET MVC's Json() method; this method accepts data to be returned and converts it into JSON format.

You can call the Convert() action method from the client side by writing the jQuery code shown in Listing 2-18.

Listing 2-18. Calling a Controller Action Method Through $.ajax() ()

```
$(document).ready(function () {
  $("#Button1").click(function () {
    url = "/Home/Convert";
    data = '{ Value: "' + $("#Text1").val() + '", Unit: "' + $("#Select1").val() + '" }';
    $.ajax({
      type: "POST",
      url: url,
      data:data,
      contentType: "application/json; charset=utf-8",
      dataType: "json",
      success: OnSuccess,
      error: OnError
    })
  });
});

function OnSuccess(results) {
  alert("Converted Temperature : " + results.Value + " " + results.Unit);
}
```

```
function OnError(err) {
  alert(err.status + " - " + err.statusText);
}
```

This code is similar to Listing 2-16, with a minute difference: the URL where the POST request is sent is of the form <controller_name>/<action_method_name>. If you run the MVC application, you should get the same results as in the case of the Web Forms application.

Summary

HTML5 features can be programmed with plain JavaScript, but using a library such as jQuery provides greater richness of functionality and ease of use. jQuery is a popular JavaScript library that makes your client-side scripting a breeze. Using the power of jQuery selectors, you can select HTML DOM elements based on complex conditions. You can also manipulate the HTML DOM on the fly. jQuery comes to the rescue when you need to pass data between client and server. And jQuery Ajax techniques let you make requests to the server without submitting the entire page.

This chapter gave you an overview of core jQuery features such as event handling, selectors, DOM manipulation, and Ajax techniques. You use these features (and a few more) throughout the remainder of the book. With these skills under your belt, it's time to explore the HTML5 audio and video APIs in the next chapter.

CHAPTER 3

▓ ▓ ▓

Working with Audio and Video

Web sites built more than a decade ago were mainly collections of static HTML pages. Then came JavaScript, and web pages became more interactive and animated. However, media-rich web sites were still in their infancy. Over the years the situation has changed to a great extent. Web sites supporting audio and video aren't at all uncommon. Video-sharing web sites such as YouTube have become immensely popular. To add to this media madness, social networking web sites such as Facebook and Google+ let you share videos with just a click of your mouse. The bottom line is that media-rich web sites will become more and more common in the years to come.

For pre-HTML5 web applications, developers need to rely on third-party plug-ins to display audio and video files. That is because HTML 4.01 doesn't have native support for playing media files. *Native support* means the HTML markup and the browser can display media files without needing any external plug-in or application. HTML5 is set to change the picture: it offers native support for playing audio and video files. Not only that, it exposes audio and video APIs that allow you to control how media files are played in the browser. This chapter covers all you need to know to use HTML5's audio and video features. Specifically, you learn about the following:

- Using the <audio> element

- Using the <video> element

- Media formats supported by leading browsers

- Providing a fallback mechanism in cases where the browser doesn't support HTML5

- Creating a custom video player using audio and video API and jQuery

Embedding Media Files Using the <object> Tag

Before discussing the HTML5-specific ways you can play audio and video files, let's glance at the techniques that are commonly in use today. Although HTML5 provides native support for embedding audio and video files in a web page, not all browsers support HTML5. To ensure that your web page works as expected in such browsers, you can use the techniques discussed in this section as a fallback mechanism.

The HTML <object> tag is a general-purpose tag that lets you embed objects in your web page: media files, ActiveX controls, Java applets, or even PDF files. However, more commonly it's used to display audio and video files. The <object> tag needs a third-party plug-in to load and play media files; you can use Adobe Flash, Apple QuickTime, and Microsoft Silverlight based plug-ins. If the target machine doesn't have the required plug-in installed, the media file will refuse to play.

The following sections illustrate how to use the <object> tag to play audio and video files.

Embedding Audio Files

To embed an audio file into a web page, you can use an <object> tag as shown in Listing 3-1.

Listing 3-1. Using the <object> Tag to Play Audio Files

```
<body>
<h2>Play Audio File</h2>
<object data="Media/Song.mp3" />
</body>
```

The data attribute of the <object> tag points to an MP3 audio file residing in the Media folder.

Embedding Flash Video Files

Adobe Flash is one of the most popular ways of embedding video files in web pages. Due to its popularity, all the leading browsers support the Flash plug-in. You can use the <object> tag to embed Flash videos in a web page; Listing 3-2 shows how.

Listing 3-2. Embedding a Flash Video Using the <object> Tag

```
<object id="flash1" data="Media/Video1.swf" type="application/x-shockwave-flash"
height="200" width="200">
  <param name="movie" value="Media/Video1.swf">
</object>
```

The <object> tag this time plays a Flash video file Video1.swf. The type attribute specifies the MIME type for Flash videos (application/x-shockwave-flash).

Embedding Silverlight Video Files

Microsoft's solution to displaying media files in a web page is Silverlight. Silverlight is seen as a competitor to Flash, but because it's a relatively recent invention, it lags behind Flash in terms of popularity and widespread use. However, Silverlight is a flexible and powerful platform that can be programmed using .NET tools such as Visual Studio and Visual C#. You can also encode existing media files into a Silverlight-specific format using Expression Web. Listing 3-3 shows how to embed and play a video using Silverlight.

Listing 3-3. Embedding Silverlight Media Files

```
<object data="data:application/x-silverlight-2"
type="application/x-silverlight-2" width="300" height="300">
  <param name="source" value="silverlightvideos/CleanTemplate.xap"/>
  <param name="background" value="white" />
  <param name="minRuntimeVersion" value="4.0.50401.0" />
  <param name="autoUpgrade" value="true" />
  <param name="enableHtmlAccess" value="true" />
  <param name="enableGPUAcceleration" value="true" />
  <param name="initparams" value='playerSettings =
```

```
<Playlist>
  <DisplayTimeCode>false</DisplayTimeCode>
  <EnableCachedComposition>true</EnableCachedComposition>
  <EnableCaptions>true</EnableCaptions>
  <EnableOffline>true</EnableOffline>
  <EnablePopOut>true</EnablePopOut>
  <StartMuted>false</StartMuted>
  <StartWithPlaylistShowing>false</StartWithPlaylistShowing>
  <StretchNonSquarePixels>NoStretch</StretchNonSquarePixels>
  <Items>
    <PlaylistItem>
      <AudioCodec>WmaProfessional</AudioCodec>
      <Description></Description>
      <FileSize>1349539</FileSize>
      <FrameRate>25</FrameRate>
      <Height>360</Height>
      <IsAdaptiveStreaming>false</IsAdaptiveStreaming>
      <MediaSource>silverlightvideos/Video2.wmv</MediaSource>
      <ThumbSource></ThumbSource>
      <VideoCodec>VC1</VideoCodec>
      <Width>640</Width>
    </PlaylistItem>
  </Items>
</Playlist>'/>
<a href="http://go2.microsoft.com/fwlink/?LinkID=124807" style="text-decoration: none;">
<img src="http://go2.microsoft.com/fwlink/?LinkId=108181"
alt="Get Microsoft Silverlight" style="border-style: none;"/>
</a>
</object>
```

Notice how the `<object>` tag now includes many pieces of information. The `<param>` and `<Playlist>` elements supply a great deal of data such as the path of the Silverlight compressed output file (`.xap`) and the configuration of the video being played.

HTML5 Audio and Video Tags

In the previous sections, you learned how pre-HTML5 web applications play audio and video files using `<object>` tag. Now let's turn our attention to HTML5 and see how HTML5 natively supports audio and video playback.

HTML5 audio and video support comes in the form of the `<audio>` and `<video>` markup elements, respectively. Each of these tags has a set of attributes you can use to configure how files are played. Additionally, these elements expose properties, methods, and events that you can program using JavaScript or jQuery. The following sections discuss the `<audio>` and `<video>` elements in detail.

Playing Audio

The HTML5 `<audio>` tag allows you to embed and play audio files in a web page. In its basic form, the `<audio>` tag looks like Listing 3-4.

Listing 3-4. Simple Use of the <audio> Tag

```
<body>
  <audio src="Audio1.mp3" controls="controls"></audio>
</body>
```

The src attribute points to an audio file (Audio1.mp3), and the controls attribute indicates that the audio playback controls such as Play, Pause, and Volume should be displayed. Figure 3-1 shows how an <audio> tag is rendered in IE9, Firefox, Chrome, and Opera.

■ Note   Not all the browsers support all the audio and video formats. You learn how to deal with the different levels of support in various browsers later in this chapter.

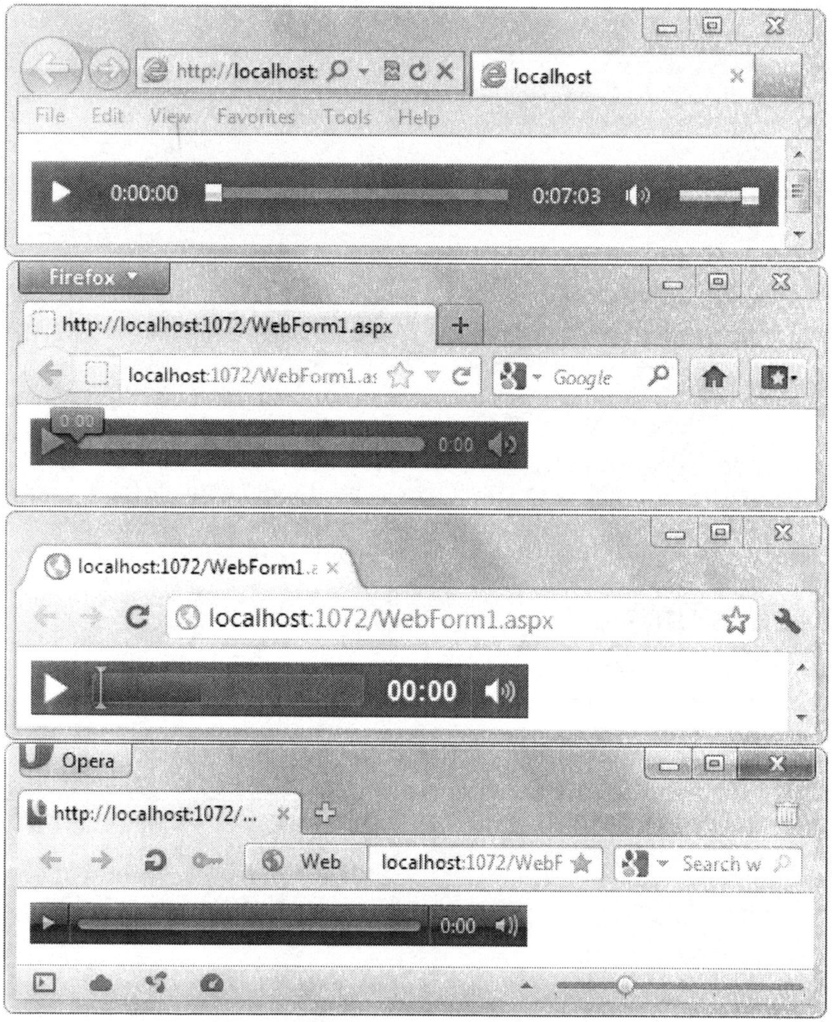

Figure 3-1. <audio> element in different browsers

```
Play
Mute

Save Audio As...
Copy Audio URL

Play Speed                    ▶
```

Figure 3-2. Shortcut menu for the audio player in IE9

All the browsers also reveal a shortcut menu if you right-click the audio player (see Figure 3-2). You can use the shortcut menu to control audio playback.

The <audio> tag also provides some useful attributes that let you fine-tune how audio files are played. By default, when you run a page using <audio>, the audio file isn't played until you click the Play button. If you wish to play the file automatically, you can add the autoplay attribute as follows:

```
<audio src="Audio1.mp3" controls="controls" autoplay="autoplay"></audio>
```

The autoplay attribute is handy for playing a background sound as users read the content of your web page.

By default, an audio file isn't replayed when it completes. To play the same file over and over again, you can set the loop attribute:

```
<audio src="Audio1.mp3" controls="controls" loop="loop"></audio>
```

The loop attribute is useful in scenarios when users tend to be on a page a long time and you wish to play background audio without interruption.

There is also a preload attribute that governs how an audio file is loaded by the browser. This attribute has three possible values: auto, metadata, and none. The auto value indicates that the entire audio file should be loaded as soon as the web page loads in the browser. metadata indicates that only metadata information such as the length of the audio file should be loaded. Finally, none indicates that the file shouldn't be loaded at all. In this case, the file is loaded only when it's played in the browser. The default value for the preload attribute varies from browser to browser. If the preload attribute is omitted, the result varies from one browser to another. The following markup shows how to use the preload attribute:

```
<audio src="Audio1.mp3" controls="controls" preload="auto" ></audio>
```

Using the preload attribute, you can control how much media data is downloaded on the client side. For example, if you're displaying a long list of audio files on a single page, setting preload to auto might download too much data. Setting preload to metadata can be more efficient in such cases. Note that preload is ignored if the autoplay attribute is present.

Playing Video

The HTML5 <video> element lets you play video files. It supports the same set of attributes as the <audio> tag and provides a few more. The basic use of <video> is shown here:

```
<video src="Video1.mp4" controls="controls"></video>
```

The src attribute points to a video file, and the controls attribute displays the playback controls. Figure 3-3 shows a video file being played in IE9.

Figure 3-3. `<video>` *element in IE9*

In addition to the autoplay, loop, and preload attributes, you can also use the muted and poster attributes with the `<video>` element. The muted attribute indicates whether the audio output of the video file being played should be muted. You can use this attribute when you want the user to view the video without background sound, like this:

```
<video src="Video1.mp4" controls="controls" muted="mute d"></video>
```

The poster attribute points to an image file that is displayed while the video is being downloaded or until the user clicks the Play button. You can use poster to display additional information about the video. Here's an example:

```
<video src="Video1.mp4" controls="controls" poster="poster.jpg" preload="none"></video>
```

Figure 3-4 shows the poster attribute in action.

Figure 3-4. Using the poster *attribute*

In addition to the attributes discussed so far, you can use the height and width attributes to control the dimensions of the video player.

■ **Note** HTML5 <audio> and <video> elements don't hide the location of the media file from the end user. Just like an image, you can easily save a media file that's being played by looking at the web page's HTML source and grabbing the file URL or by right-clicking the video player and choosing the Save As menu option.

Supported Audio and Video Formats

In the preceding sections, you worked with the <audio> and <video> tags to display audio and video files. These tags are simple to use, but there is a gray area that you need to be aware of as a web developer: audio and video *formats*. Although HTML5 provides native support for audio and video playback, this support isn't uniform across all browsers. Different browsers don't agree on the audio and video file formats that can be played. For example, IE9 and Chrome play MP4 files just fine; but if you try to play them in Firefox, you get the error "Video format or MIME type is not supported" (see Figure 3-5).

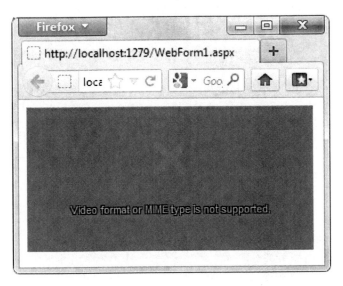

Figure 3-5. Firefox is unable to play MP4 files.

■ **Note** You may wonder why not all browsers support all of the popular media formats. There are various reasons for this lack of support including licensing issues, patenting issues, open standards, and so on. Detailed discussion of these issues is beyond the scope of this book.

Before examining browsers and their supported formats, it's worthwhile to look at some of the widely used media formats on the Web because all the leading browsers support one or more of these formats. Table 3-1 lists the file formats supported by the leading browsers.

Table 3-1. Common Audio and Video File Formats for HTML5

Format	File Extension	MIME Type	Description
MP3	.mp3	audio/mp3	MP3 is possibly the most popular and widely used format for audio files. The MP3 format was originally designed by the Moving Picture Experts Group (MPEG) as part of its specifications. The main reasons some browsers don't support this format are licensing and patent issues.
MP4	.mp4	video/mp4	Just like MP3, MP4 is a popular web format for videos. The MP4 standard is a part of MPEG-4. It's widely used by H.264 codecs; saying that a browser supports MP4 video actually refers to H.264.
Ogg Vorbis	.ogg	audio/ogg	Ogg Vorbis is a free and open format for audio files.
Ogg Theora	.ogv	video/ogg	Ogg Theora is a format for videos and, just like Ogg Vorbis, is a free and open standard.
WAV	.wav	audio/wav	WAV or Waveform is a format for audio files. It was designed for PCs by Microsoft and IBM. WAV is an uncompressed file format and hence file sizes tend to be larger.
WebM	.webm	video/webm	WebM is a royalty-free and open video format intended for use with HTML5. Its development is sponsored by Google.

Notice the MIME Type column in Table 3-1. You must ensure that your web server has the correct mapping of file extensions and MIME types. If this mapping doesn't exist, the web server may not serve the media files, and consequently the web page may not play the audio/video. For example, while using the development web server that ships with Visual Studio, you may need to add the markup shown in Listing 3-5 to the web.config file so that all the file extensions mentioned in Table 3-1 work as expected.

Listing 3-5. Adding MIME Type Mappings in web.config

```
<system.webServer>
  <staticContent>
      <mimeMap fileExtension=".mp4" mimeType="video/mp4" />
      <mimeMap fileExtension=".ogg" mimeType="audio/ogg" />
      <mimeMap fileExtension=".oga" mimeType="audio/ogg" />
      <mimeMap fileExtension=".ogv" mimeType="video/ogg" />
      <mimeMap fileExtension=".webm" mimeType="video/webm" />
  </staticContent>
</system.webServer>
```

As you can see the `<staticContent>` subsection of `<system.webServer>` contains several `<mimeMap>` elements. Each `<mimeMap>` element maps a file extension with its MIME type.

If you're using a stand-alone installation of Internet Information Services (IIS) rather than the Visual Studio development web server, you can also configure MIME types in the IIS Manager. Figure 3-6 shows the relevant IIS Manager dialog in Windows 7.

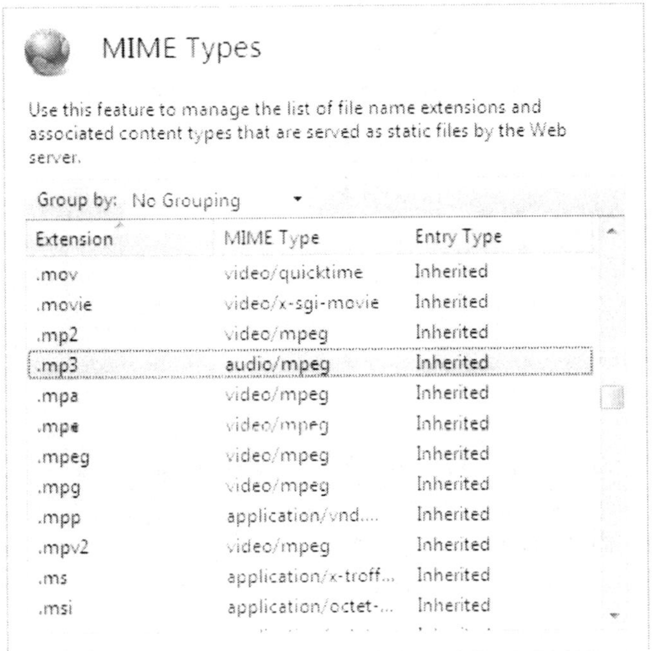

MIME Types

Use this feature to manage the list of file name extensions and associated content types that are served as static files by the Web server.

Group by: No Grouping ▾

Extension	MIME Type	Entry Type
.mov	video/quicktime	Inherited
.movie	video/x-sgi-movie	Inherited
.mp2	video/mpeg	Inherited
.mp3	audio/mpeg	Inherited
.mpa	video/mpeg	Inherited
.mpe	video/mpeg	Inherited
.mpeg	video/mpeg	Inherited
.mpg	video/mpeg	Inherited
.mpp	application/vnd....	Inherited
.mpv2	video/mpeg	Inherited
.ms	application/x-troff...	Inherited
.msi	application/octet-...	Inherited

Figure 3-6. MIME mappings in IIS

■ **Note** Multipurpose Internet Mail Extension (MIME) is a specification for the format of non-text e-mail attachments. Although it was originally designed to work with e-mailing systems, it's now used extensively on the Web to indicate the content type of web resources.

Now that you have some idea about various media formats, let's see how different browsers support them. Table 3-2 shows the leading browsers' support of the media types from Table 3-1.

Table 3-2. Media Supported by Leading Browsers

Media Type	IE9	Firefox	Chrome	Opera	Safari
MP3	Yes	No	Yes	No	Yes
MP4	Yes	No	Yes	No	Yes
Ogg Theora	No	Yes	Yes	Yes	No
Ogg Vorbis	No	Yes	Yes	Yes	No
WAV	No	Yes	Yes	Yes	Yes
WebM	No	Yes	Yes	Yes	No

───

■ **Note**   It's best to test the media support mentioned in Table 3-2 in the latest versions of these browsers. The specification is evolving, and all the browser companies are actively working to improve and standardize their support for media formats.

───

Implementing a Fallback Mechanism

From the discussion in the preceding section, you may have realized that relying on browsers to support media files of a specific MIME type isn't practical when you're building Internet web applications. Additionally, when your target browser is unknown, you can't guarantee that it supports HTML5 <audio> and <video> tags. Some form of fallback mechanism is necessary to provide alternatives to the user if the target browser doesn't support HTML5 audio and video playback.

You need to provide fallback schemes for two scenarios:

- The target browser supports HTML5 <audio> and <video> tags but doesn't support a particular MIME type.

- The target browser doesn't support HTML5 <audio> and <video> tags.

To handle these scenarios, you can use the following fallback mechanisms, respectively:

- Create media files in multiple file formats (MIME types).

- Use Flash or Silverlight as an alternate playback mode.

The following sections detail how to implement these techniques.

Supporting Multiple Media Formats

The <audio> and <video> elements allow you to specify multiple media sources. Until now, you've used the src attribute of these tags to specify a media file, but <audio> and <video> can also use nested <source> elements to specify multiple source files. At runtime, depending on the supported media type, a browser picks up an appropriate version of the file. Listing 3-6 shows a <video> element that lists three sources.

Listing 3-6. Using the <source> Element

```
<video controls>
  <source src="media/video1.mp4" type="video/mp4" />
  <source src="media/video1.ogv" type="video/ogg" />
  <source src="media/video1.webm" type="video/webm" />
</video
```

As shown in Listing 3-6, each <source> element sets src and type attributes. The src attribute points to a video file, and the type attribute indicates the file's MIME type.

The downside of using <source> is that you need to maintain multiple file formats for each audio or video file under consideration. This may require additional media-converter software, which increases the overall cost of the project.

▨ **Note**   When you play an audio or video file with multiple `<source>` elements, it isn't apparent which of the file formats the browser is using. A quick and easy way to find out is to right-click the `<audio>` or `<video>` element in the browser and select Save As from the shortcut menu. The Save As dialog displays the source file name of the `<source>` element that is being played.

Flash or Silverlight Fallback

The fallback mechanism using the `<source>` element works well if you're sure the target browser supports HTML5. However, it's possible that the target browser doesn't understand HTML5 `<audio>` and `<video>` elements. In such cases, you can use a Flash- or Silverlight-based fallback system. Listing 3-7 shows how an example using Flash.

Listing 3-7. *Using a Flash-Based Fallback System*

```
<video controls>
  <source src="media/video1.mp4" type="video/mp4" />
  <source src="media/video1.ogv" type="video/ogg" />
  <source src="media/video1.webm" type="video/webm" />
  <object id="flash1" data="Media/Video1.swf" type="application/x-shockwave-flash">
    <param name="movie" value="Media/Video1.swf">
  </object>
</video>
```

The `<video>` element now has an `<object>` tag nested inside it. This way, if a browser doesn't understand the `<video>` tag, it skips to the `<object>` tag and plays the Flash video file.

If you decide to provide a Silverlight fallback, you need to embed Silverlight media using the `<object>` tag. Listing 3-8 shows how this can be done.

Listing 3-8. *Using a Sliverlight-Based Fallback System*

```
<video controls>
  <source src="media/video1.mp4" type="video/mp4" />
  <source src="media/video1.ogv" type="video/ogg" />
  <source src="media/video1.webm" type="video/webm" />
  <object data="data:application/x-silverlight-2"
type="application/x-silverlight-2" width="300" height="300">
    <param name="source" value="silverlightvideos/CleanTemplate.xap"/>
    ...
  </object>
</video>
```

In Listing 3-8, the Silverlight media is embedded using the `<object>` tag inside the `<video>` element. If a browser encounters the `<video>` tag but doesn't support it, the browser skips to the `<object>` tag and plays the Silverlight video.

If you don't want to provide Flash, Silverlight, or another fallback, then instead of an `<object>` tag you can simply include some HTML markup that informs the end user what went wrong.

■ **Note** To test the Flash or Silverlight fallback scheme, you need a browser version that doesn't support HTML5 `<audio>` and `<video>` elements.

Programming with the Audio and Video APIs

So far, you've been using static `<audio>` and `<video>` elements to play audio and video files. HTML5 also provides a programmatic way to play and control media files using JavaScript. To give you a glimpse of what you can configure, Table 3-3 shows a list of the properties, methods, and events of the `<audio>` and `<video>` DOM elements that you have at your disposal. Note that Table 3-3 lists only the commonly used members of `<audio>` and `<video>`.

■ **Note** You can browse all the available members of the `<audio>` and `<video>` elements at www.w3schools. com. This web site also provides a good reference for the other HTML5 tags, properties, methods, and events.

Table 3-3. Properties, Methods, and Events of the `<audio>` and `<video>` DOM Elements

Member	Property / Method / Event	Description
canPlayType()	Method	The canPlayType() method returns true/false depending on whether a particular MIME type can be played by the `<audio>` or `<video>` element.
currentTime	Property	The currentTime property indicates the current time instance of a media file in seconds.
duration	Property	The duration attribute returns duration of the media file being played in milliseconds. This property returns correct value only if the metadata of the file is available at the time of reading the property.
ended	Event	The ended event is raised when the media file is played completely.
pause	Event	The pause event is raised when a media file is paused.
pause()	Method	The pause() method pauses a media file being played.
play	Event	The play event is raised when a media file is played.
play()	Method	The play() method plays a media file specified by the src property.
playbackRate	Property	The playbackRate property governs the speed at which a media file is played. Default is 1 which means normal speed. Value of 2 means twice the normal speed and so on.
playing	Event	The playing event is raised when the media file is ready to play.
src	Property	The src property indicates a URL of the media file to be played.
timeupdate	Event	The timeupdate event is raised when the current playback position is changed.
volume	Property	The volume property indicates the volume level of the audio/video player. Possible values are between 0 and 1, 1 being maximum volume and 0 being mute.
volumechange	Event	The volumechange event is raised when the volume of a media file being played is changed.

■ **Note** It's always a good practice to check whether the browser supports `<audio>` and `<video>` tags before you attempt to play the media files. As discussed in Chapter 1, you can use Modernizr library for that purpose. A sample check looks like this:

```
$(document).ready(function () {
  if (!Modernizr.audio) {
    alert("This browser doesn't support HTML5 audio!");
  }
  if (!Modernizr.video) {
    alert("This browser doesn't support HTML5 video!");
  }
});
```

Creating a Custom Video Player Using the Video API

To see the properties, methods, and events of the `<video>` element in action, let's build a custom video player in an ASP.NET MVC application. The video player looks like the one shown in Figure 3-7.

Figure 3-7. A custom video player

75

The custom video player shown in Figure 3-7 provides a drop-down list of video files that can be played. This list resides in a SQL Server database and is fetched using jQuery $.ajax() method. You can play, pause, or stop a video using the Play and Stop buttons. (A single button is used to play as well as pause a video.) The playback speed and volume can be set using the respective range input controls. Once a video starts playing, the overall percentage of progress (%) is shown along with the video's total duration. The player also includes a poster that tells the user to select a video file from the drop-down list.

HTML5 Markup

The HTML5 markup for the custom video player resides in an MVC view (Index.aspx) and is shown in Listing 3-9. For the sake of clarity, Listing 3-9 shows only the markup required for the video player rather than the complete view.

Listing 3-9. HTML Markup for the Custom Video Player

```
<div class="PlayList">
  Select Video To Play : <br />
  <select id="ddlPlayList" class="DropDownList">
  </select>
</div>
<div>
  <video id="videoPlayer" controls class="Video" poster="/content/media/poster.jpg" ></video>
</div>
<div class="Progress">
  <span id="spanDuration" class="Duration"></span><br />
  <span>Progress :</span>
  <span id="spanProgress"></span>
</div>
<div>
  <input type="button" id="btnPlayPause" value="Play" class="Button" />
  <input type="button" id="btnStop" value="Stop"  class="Button"/>
</div>
<br />
<div class="Speed">
  <span>Playback Speed (1-5) :</span>
  <input type="range" id="rngPlaybackRate" value="1" step="1" min="1" max="5" class="Range"/>
</div>
<div class="Volume">
  <span>Volume (0-1) :</span>
  <input type="range" id="rngVolume" value="1" step="0.1" min="0" max="1" class="Range"/>
</div>
```

This HTML5 markup consists of six <div> elements. The first <div> contains a <select> element that displays a list of videos that can be played.

The second <div> element contains an HTML5 <video>tag. The id attribute of the <video> element is set to videoPlayer, and its poster attribute points to the poster.jpg file. The image indicated by the poster property is displayed initially when no file is yet being played in the videoPlayer. Notice that the src attribute of the <video> tag isn't set because the actual video URL is selected from the drop-down list. Even though the markup sets the controls attribute, you can skip it if you wish because you control the play and pause operations programmatically.

The third <div> element shows the total duration of the video and a progress indicator specifying the percentage of the video already played.

The fourth <div> element holds two buttons: Play/Pause and Stop. btnPlayPause toggles between Play and Pause modes.

The fifth and sixth <div> elements display a range selector for video playback rate and volume. Notice that both <input> elements representing the range selectors have their type attribute set to range. (You learn about several new <input> types available in HTML5 in Chapter 5.) The min and max attributes of these range selectors indicate the minimum value and maximum value that can be selected. The step attribute indicates a step by which a range can be incremented or decremented.

The CSS classes used by the Index.aspx view reside in the application's Site.css file. For the sake of reducing clutter, the CSS classes aren't shown here.

SQL Server Database and Entity Framework Data Model

The application stores a list of videos that can be played in a SQL Server Express database (VideoDb.mdf). VideoDb consists of a single table (Videos) that stores the titles and URLs of video files. Figure 3-8 shows the schema of the Videos table in Server Explorer.

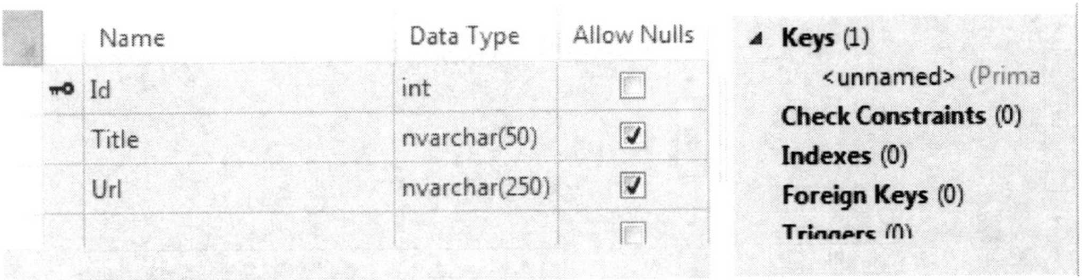

Figure 3-8. Schema of the Videos table

To represent the Videos table at the code level and get data out of this table, you use an Entity Framework data model. The data model resides in the Models folder and looks like Figure 3-9.

Figure 3-9. Entity Framework data model class for the Videos table

The `Video` data model class has three properties—`Id`, `Title`, and `Url`—that correspond to the corresponding columns in the `Videos` table.

Fetching the Video Playlist

To display a list of videos in the drop-down list, you need to fetch the data from the `Videos` table using jQuery's `$.ajax()` method. The controller class (`VideoPlayerController`) contains an action method—`GetPlayList()`—that returns a list of `Video` objects. The `GetPlayList()` method and the associated jQuery code that calls it are shown in Listing 3-10 and Listing 3-11, respectively.

Listing 3-10. GetPlayList() Action Method

```
public JsonResult GetPlayList()
{
    VideoDbEntities db=new VideoDbEntities();
    var data = from items in db.Videos
               select items;
    return Json(data.ToArray());
}
```

Listing 3-11. Calling the GetPlayList() Method Using $.ajax

```
$.ajax({
    type: "POST",
    url: '/VideoPlayer/GetPlayList',
    dataType: 'json',
    contentType: "application/json; charset=utf-8",
    success: OnSuccess,
    error: OnError
});

function OnSuccess(playListItems) {
  for (var i = 0; i < playListItems.length; i++) {
    $("#ddlPlayList").append("<option value='" + playListItems[i].Url + "'>" +
    playListItems[i].Title +
    "</option>");
  }
}

function OnError(err) {
  alert(err.status + " - " + err.statusText);
}
```

Notice that the `GetPlayList()` method selects all the records from the `Videos` table and returns an array of `Video` objects as `JsonResult`. The jQuery `$.ajax()` method then makes a `POST` request to the `GetPlayList()` action. The success function `OnSuccess()` receives a JSON array of `Video` objects. The `OnSuccess()` function then iterates through this JSON array and, with each iteration, appends an `<option>` element to the drop-down list using the `append()` method. The URL of a video file is assigned to the `value` attribute of an `<option>` element, and its title is displayed in the drop-down list.

The `OnError()` function displays information about any errors encountered while invoking the `GetPlayList()` method.

Playing, Pausing, and Stopping a Video

You need to handle various client-side events in order to make the video player functional. These events fall into two categories:

- Events of supporting elements such as the Play/Pause and Stop buttons, the volume control, and the drop-down list

- Events of the <video> element

The events in the first category can be handled using the jQuery event-handling syntax you learned about in Chapter 2. Listing 3-12 shows various event handlers in this category.

Listing 3-12. Handling Events of Supporting Elements

```
videoPlayer = $("#videoPlayer").get(0);

$("#ddlPlayList").change(function () {
  var extension = $(this).val();
  extension=extension.substr(extension.lastIndexOf('.') + 1);
  var mime = "";
  switch (extension) {
    case 'mp4':
      mime = "video/mp4";
      break;
    case 'ogv':
      mime = "video/ogg";
      break;
    case 'webm':
      mime = "video/webm";
      break;
  }
  if (videoPlayer.canPlayType(mime)) {
    $("#btnPlayPause").val("Play");
    videoPlayer.src = $(this).val();
    $("#btnPlayPause").click();
  }
  else {
    alert("Cannot play this video format!");
  }
});

$("#btnPlayPause").click(function () {
  if ($(this).val() == "Play") {
    videoPlayer.playbackRate = $("#rngPlaybackRate").val();
    videoPlayer.play();
  }
  else {
    videoPlayer.pause();
  }
});
```

```
$("#btnStop").click(function () {
  videoPlayer.pause();
  videoPlayer.currentTime = 0;
});

$("#rngVolume").change(function () {
  videoPlayer.volume = $(this).val();
});
```

The code in Listing 3-12 stores a reference to the <video> DOM element in a global variable, videoPlayer. Notice the use of the get() method, which returns a DOM element at a specified index. Any jQuery selector returns a collection of zero or more elements matching the selection criteria. You can retrieve an element from this collection using get() by specifying its zero-based index. In this case, the <video> element is selected using its ID. Naturally, the collection has only one element, and hence index is specified as 0.

The drop-down list's change event handler takes care of playing a video when the selection in the drop-down list changes. First it checks whether the <video> element can play the selected video file using the canPlayType() method. The canPlayType() method accepts the MIME type of a media file and returns true if that media type can be played. If the <video> element is capable of playing the selected video file, its src property is set to the URL of the selected video file, and the Play/Pause button's click event is triggered programmatically.

The Play/Pause button's click event handler checks its own value. Inside the handler, the keyword this refers to the DOM element being clicked (that is, the Play/Pause button) and the val() method returns the current value of the button. If the value is Play, the playbackRate property is set to a value selected in the speed range selector, and the <video> element's play() method is called. This way, the video is played at a chosen playback speed. If the value is Pause, the <video> element's pause() method is called so that video playback is paused.

The Stop button's click event handler sets the currentTime property to 0 to indicate the beginning of the media file and calls the pause() method.

The Volume range selector's change event handler changes the volume of the video playback by setting the volume property of the <video> element.

Displaying Duration and Progress

To display the total length of the selected video file and its playback progress, you need to handle the timeupdate and loadmetadata events of the <video> element. These events need to be wired a bit differently than before. Events such as click and change are standard HTML DOM events and are natively included in the jQuery library. However, that's not the case with video events. Because the <video> element is a new addition in HTML5, the jQuery library doesn't have native support for its events. Therefore you need to wire the event handlers as shown in Listing 3-13.

Listing 3-13. Wiring Events Using the jQuery bind() Method

```
$(videoPlayer).bind("loadedmetadata", OnLoadedMetadata);
$(videoPlayer).bind("timeupdate", OnTimeUpdate);
$(videoPlayer).bind("play", OnPlay);
$(videoPlayer).bind("pause", OnPause);
```

As you can see, jQuery's bind() method essentially binds an event with its handler. The first parameter of the bind() method is the event to be handled, and the second parameter is the event-handler function.

You could use anonymous functions here, but for the sake of clarity Listing 3-13 uses stand-alone JavaScript functions.

■ **Note** As of this writing, jQuery doesn't include event functions for HTML5-specific events such as play and pause. That is why this example uses the bind() method. Refer to Chapter 2 for details of using the bind() method for event wiring.

You might be wondering why Listing 3-13 handles play and pause events. It does so because you can also play and pause videos in the video player using the shortcut menu. If a user decides to use the shortcut menu instead of the Play/Pause button to play or pause a video, the functionality of the Play/Pause button becomes out of sync. The play and pause events are raised when the video is played or paused using either means (button or shortcut menu). By handling these events, you ensure that the Play/Pause button always reflects the correct state of the player.

The event-handler functions OnLoadedMetadata, OnTimeUpdate, OnPlay, and OnPause are shown in Listing 3-14.

Listing 3-14. Event-Handler Functions Used in the bind() Method

```
function OnLoadedMetadata() {
  $("#spanDuration").html("Duration : " + videoPlayer.duration.toFixed(1) + " seconds.");
}

function OnTimeUpdate() {
  var percentage = Math.floor((videoPlayer.currentTime / videoPlayer.duration * 100));
  $("#spanProgress").html(percentage + " % ");
}


function OnPlay() {
  $("#btnPlayPause").val("Pause");
}

function OnPause() {
  $("#btnPlayPause").val("Play");
}
```

The loadmetadata event is raised when the metadata of the video file being played is loaded. In order to display a video's duration, the video's metadata must be available; hence the loadmetadata event is used to display the duration in a <span> element. The duration property returns the duration in seconds; for the sake of proper display, it's converted to a fixed decimal number using the JavaScript toFixed() method.

The timeupdate event is raised every time the current playback position of the video changes. The OnTimeUpdate() function calculates a percentage of video played so far with the help of the <video> element's currentTime and duration properties. The progress thus calculated is displayed in a <span> element.

The OnPlay() event handler sets the Play/Pause button's text to Pause when the video starts playing. On the same lines, the OnPause() event handler sets the Play/Pause button's text to Play when the video is paused.

That's it! Your custom video player is ready. You can test the player by adding a few entries in the Videos table and then running those files by selecting from the drop-down list.

Summary

Prior to HTML5, embedding audio and video files in a web page required third-party plug-ins such as Flash and Silverlight. Developers used <object> tags to embed Flash or Silverlight media in web pages. HTML5 provides native support for playing audio and video files using <audio> and <video> elements, respectively. As of this writing, there is yet to be standardization on the audio and video formats supported by the various browsers, but we can hope that in the future all browsers will agree on a common set of media formats.

Because not all browsers support HTML5, you may need to implement a fallback scheme so that if a browser doesn't understand HTML5 <audio> and <video> elements, the Flash or Silverlight player takes over. Using <audio> and <video> tags coupled with jQuery, you can develop database-driven media catalogs or playlists.

The <audio> and <video> elements allow you play existing media files. The HTML5 <canvas>, the subject of the next chapter, lets you draw shapes, text, and images in a browser, thus opening a plethora of possibilities for building graphic-rich web applications.

■ ■ ■

CHAPTER 4

Drawing with the Canvas

One of the reasons for the popularity of the Web is the graphical user interface offered to end users. Images, animations, fonts, and other interactive effects make a web site appealing from an end user's perspective. However, one limitation that web site developers may have encountered when developing pre-HTML5 web applications was drawing graphics in the browser using client-side capabilities. ASP.NET developers have been using the System.Drawing namespace to generate graphics on the fly on the server and then send them to the client, but there is no native support for drawing graphics in the browser window.

HTML5 does a great job at client-side graphic rendering by offering the *canvas*. As the name suggests, a canvas is a rectangular area of a web page in which you can perform drawing operations with the help of the canvas API and JavaScript/jQuery. In this chapter, you learn about the HTML5 canvas in detail. Specifically, you look into the following:

- Drawing lines, curves, paths, shapes, and text on the canvas

- Applying special effects such as shadows, gradients, pattern fills, and transparency to drawing objects

- Saving the canvas state on the server for later use

The chapter concludes by building a sample application that incorporates what you've learned.

The <canvas> Element

As mentioned previously, an HTML5 canvas is a rectangular space on a web page where you carry out drawing operations. An HTML5 canvas is represented by the <canvas> tag. As of this writing, the latest versions of all the leading browsers (IE, Firefox, Chrome, Opera, and Safari) support the <canvas> element, although the support varies in terms of the canvas features offered.

You can place a canvas on a web page using the markup from Listing 4-1.

Listing 4-1. Basic <canvas> Element

```
<head runat="server">
    <script type="text/javascript" src="Script/jquery-1.7.2.min.js"></script>
    <script type="text/javascript" src="Script/modernizr-2.5.3.js"></script>
    <script type="text/javascript">
      $(document).ready(function () {
```

```
            if (!Modernizr.canvas) {
                alert("This browser doesn't support HTML5 Canvas!");
            }
        });
    </script>
    <style>
        canvas {
            border: 2px solid #808080;
        }
    </style>
</head>
<body>
    <form id="form1" runat="server">
        <canvas id="MyCanvas" height="200" width="200"></canvas>
    </form>
</body>
```

The markup in Listing 4-1 declares an HTML5 canvas using a <canvas> element. Although they're optional, the width and height of the canvas are also set to mark the dimensions of the canvas. If you don't specify dimensions for a canvas, the browser creates a canvas with the default width and height. For example, if dimensions aren't specified, Firefox and Google create a canvas with a width of 300 pixels and a height of 150 pixels. The <head> section also contains jQuery code that checks for canvas support using Modernizr. The <style> section adds a border to the canvas so its boundaries can be seen on the web page. Figure 4-1 shows how the canvas looks.

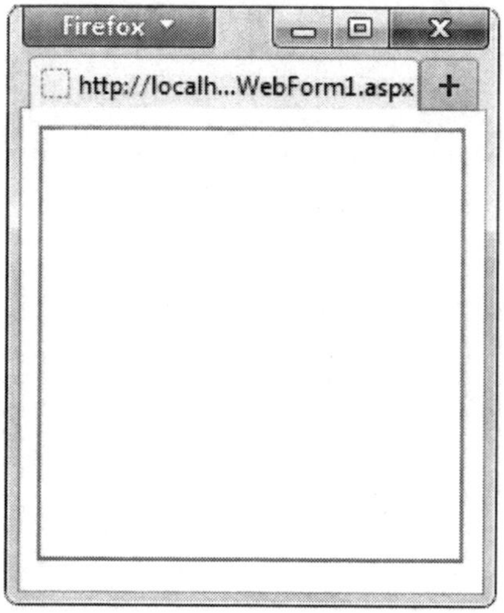

Figure 4-1. Basic canvas rendered in a browser

Drawing on the Canvas

In order to draw anything on the canvas, you need to get its drawing context. A *drawing context* is an object that provides methods and properties for drawing graphics on the canvas. Any changes to the context properties are applied to subsequent drawing operations. Additionally, you can perform different drawing operations using different context objects.

To get a reference to the drawing context in your code, you use the getContext() method of the <canvas> DOM element. Listing 4-2 shows how.

Listing 4-2. Getting a Drawing Context

```
$(document).ready(function () {
  var canvas = $("#MyCanvas").get(0);
  var context = canvas.getContext("2d");
});
```

As you did in the previous chapter, here you use the jQuery get(0) method to get a reference to the <canvas> element with ID MyCanvas. As mentioned in Chapter 2, jQuery selectors return a collection of matching elements. You can retrieve an element from this collection using the get() method by specifying its zero-based index. In this case, the <canvas> element is selected using its ID. Naturally, the collection has only one element, and hence index is specified as 0. You then call the getContext() method of the canvas object to retrieve its drawing context. The getContext() method takes a parameter indicating the type of context. A value of 2d indicates two-dimensional drawing content (the only mode currently available).

Once you get the drawing context object, you're ready to draw on the canvas. While performing drawing operations on the canvas, you need to specify the coordinates where graphics are to be drawn, and hence you should be aware of the canvas coordinate system. The unit for specifying canvas coordinates is the pixel. The top-left corner of the canvas has coordinates (0,0). Figure 4-2 explains canvas coordinates with an example.

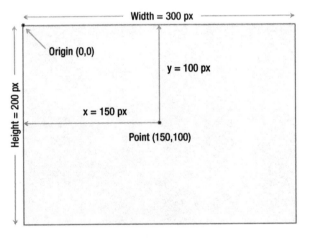

Figure 4-2. HTML5 canvas coordinate system

The figure shows a canvas 300 pixels wide and 200 pixels high. The origin of the canvas is at (0,0). Another point at (150,100) is also shown.

Drawing Lines

Drawing a line is possibly the simplest operation you can perform on a canvas. To draw a line, you need to perform these operations:

- Shift the current drawing position to a required start point.

- Specify the end-point coordinates of the line.

- Draw the line.

Listing 4-3 shows all three operations.

Listing 4-3. Drawing a Line

```
context.moveTo(10, 100);
context.lineTo(190, 100);
context.stroke();
```

This code assumes that the context variable holds a reference to a drawing context. To draw a line with start coordinates of (10,100) and end coordinates of (190,100), you use three methods of the drawing context: moveTo(), lineTo(), and stroke().

The moveTo() method moves the current drawing coordinates to specified x and y points (10 and 100 in this case). The lineTo() method specifies the end coordinates of the line (190,100 in this case). The line isn't drawn immediately after you call the lineTo() method. You inform the drawing context that the drawing operation is to be performed using the stroke() method. The code from Listing 4-3 results in the line shown in Figure 4-3.

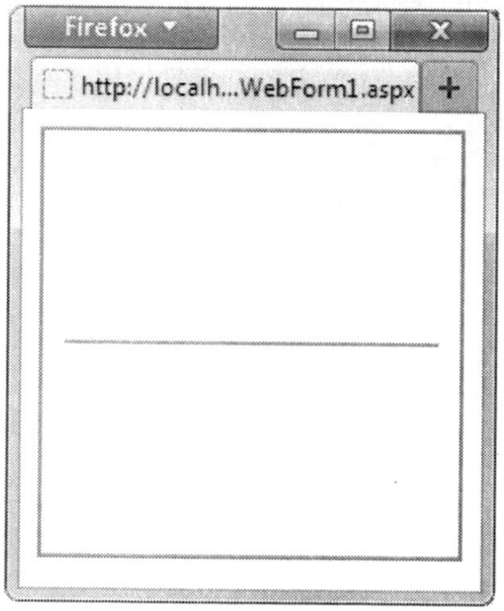

Figure 4-3. Drawing a line

The line drawn in this case assumes a default width. You can, however, change the width of the line being drawn as explained in the next section.

Changing the Line Width and Cap

In the preceding example, you used the default values for the line width and line cap while drawing a line. You can change these defaults using the lineWidth and lineCap properties.

The lineWidth property specifies the width of a line in pixels. All lines drawn after you set lineWidth assume the newly specified width while rendering.

The line *cap* refers to how the end of a line is drawn. The lineCap property has three possible values: butt, round, and square. The default is butt. Figure 4-4 shows the difference between the three line endings.

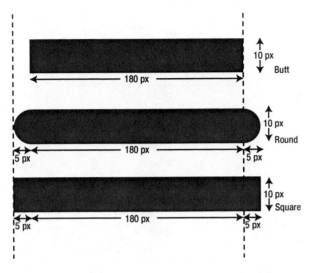

Figure 4-4. *Differences between* butt, round, *and* square

As you can see in Figure 4-4, a lineCap value of butt ends exactly at the end coordinates specified in the lineTo() method. On the other hand, lineCap values of round and square extend the line by an amount equal to the width of the line, because additional pixels equal to half of the line width are used for the cap. For example, consider a line with width of 10 pixels, a start point (10,100), and an end point (190,100). The length of the line including the start and end points is 180 pixels. If you specify a lineCap mode of butt, the resulting line has a length of exactly 180 pixels. However, with a lineCap mode of round or square, the length of the line is 190 pixels (180 pixels + an additional 5 pixels at the start + an additional 5 pixels at the end for a line).

Listing 4-4 shows how to use the lineWidth and lineCap properties, and Figure 4-5 shows the resulting lines.

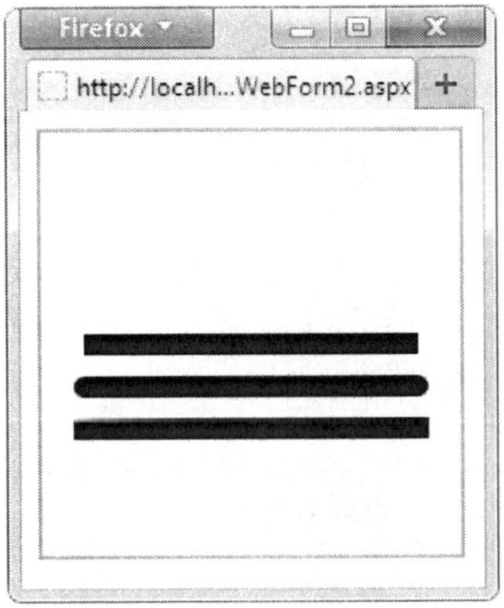

Figure 4-5. *Different* lineCap *settings in action*

Listing 4-4. Setting the `lineWidth` and `lineCap` Properties

```
context.lineWidth = 10;

context.beginPath();
context.moveTo(20, 100);
context.lineTo(180, 100);
context.lineCap = "butt";
context.stroke();

context.beginPath();
context.moveTo(20, 120);
context.lineTo(180, 120);
context.lineCap = "round";
context.stroke();

context.beginPath();
context.moveTo(20, 140);
context.lineTo(180, 140);
context.lineCap = "square";
context.stroke();
```

In this listing, the width of the lines to be drawn is set to 10 pixels using the `lineWidth` property. Then the code draws three lines by setting `lineCap` to `butt`, `round`, and `square`, respectively.

Notice the use of the `beginPath()` method, which begins a new drawing path. (Paths are covered in a later section.) Here, suffice to say that a path is a series of drawing operations. If you don't call `beginPath()`, all lines are redrawn with the last `lineCap` setting you specified (`square` in this example).

Notice how the last two lines in Figure 4-5 add extra pixels to the overall length, whereas the first line is precisely drawn as per the start and end coordinates.

Drawing Curves

You can draw three types of curves on the canvas: arcs, quadratic curves, and Bezier curves. These three types of curves are drawn using the `arc()`, `arcTo()`, `quadraticCurveTo()`, and `bezierCurveTo()` methods. Drawing an arc is necessary in order to draw circles and rounded rectangles. You can probably do all the drawing you need with `arc()` and `arcTo()`, but if you need something more complicated, you can investigate quadratic and Bezier curves. The following sections discuss `arc()` and `arcTo()`.

A Quick Introduction to Radians

While working with arcs, you frequently come across angles specified in radians. The radian is the standard unit of angular measurement and describes the ratio between the length of an arc of a circle and its radius. One radian is defined as the angle subtended when the length of the arc of a circle is equal to the radius of that circle. A radian is therefore equal to (Length of the arc / Radius of the arc).

The circumference of a circle is given by the formula $2\pi r$, where r is the radius of the circle. A full circle means 360° or $2\pi r/r$—that is, 2π and 1 radian = $(180/\pi)°$. To convert radians to degrees, you need to multiply a radian value by $180/\pi$. Along the same lines, to convert degrees to radians, you multiply a degree value by $\pi/180$.

■ **Note**   This discussion is limited to the bare minimum understanding required to use the `arc()` and `arcTo()` methods. Explaining the mathematical treatment involved in drawing these curves is beyond the scope of this book.

Drawing an Arc Using the arc() Method

To draw an arc on a canvas, you use the drawing context's `arc()` method. The general syntax of `arc()` is as follows:

```
context.arc(x, y, radius, start_angle, end_angle, direction)
```

The first two parameters of the `arc()` method indicate the coordinates of the center of the arc. The radius parameter indicates the arc's radius. The start and end angles are the angles in radians for the start point and end point of the arc, respectively. Finally, the `direction` parameter indicates whether the arc should be drawn in a clockwise or counterclockwise direction. To better understand these parameters, look at Figure 4-6.

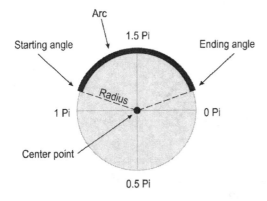

Figure 4-6. Pictorial representation of the arc() method's parameters

Listing 4-5 shows a code fragment that draws an arc using the `arc()` method.

Listing 4-5. Using the arc() Method

```
var canvas = $("#MyCanvas").get(0);
var context = canvas.getContext("2d");
var x = canvas.width / 2;
var y = canvas.height / 2;
var radius = 100;
var start_angle = 0.5 * Math.PI;
var end_angle = 1.75 * Math.PI;
context.arc(x, y, 75, start_angle, end_angle, false);
context.lineWidth = 20;
context.stroke();
```

This code calculates the center of the canvas and uses those coordinates as the x and y coordinates of the arc. Notice how the start and end angles are calculated in radians using the Math.PI constant. The direction parameter is set to false, indicating that the arc should be drawn in the clockwise direction. Figure 4-7 shows how the code from Listing 4-5 renders in the browser.

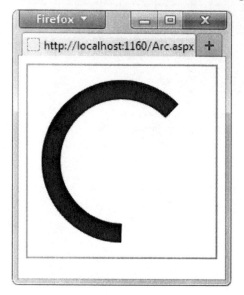

Figure 4-7. The arc() method in action

There is also a different way to draw an arc: using the arcTo() method. This method takes the following form:

```
context.arcTo(x1, y1, x2, y2, radius)
```

In this method signature, x1, y1, x2, and y2 are the control points, and radius is the radius of the arc. Determining the control points is bit complex; Figure 4-8 illustrates.

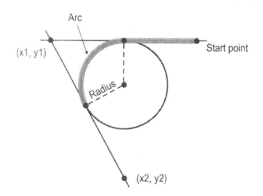

Figure 4-8. Coordinates used in the arcTo() method

■ **Note** Without going into too much detail, *control points* are special points attached to a curve that are used to alter the curve's shape and angle. Stretching a control point changes the shape of a curve, whereas rotating a control point changes the curve's angle.

The arcTo() method comes in handy for drawing rounded rectangles. Listing 4-6 shows how.

Listing 4-6. *Using the arcTo() Method*

```
var canvas = $("#MyCanvas").get(0);
var context = canvas.getContext("2d");
var x = 25;
var y = 50;
var width = 150;
var height = 100;
var radius = 20;
context.lineWidth = 10;
// top and top right corner
context.moveTo(x + radius, y);
context.arcTo(x + width, y, x + width, y + radius, radius);
// right side and bottom right corner
context.arcTo(x + width, y + height, x + width - radius, y + height, radius);
// bottom and bottom left corner
context.arcTo(x, y + height, x, y + height - radius, radius);
// left and top left corner
context.arcTo(x, y, x + radius, y, radius);
context.stroke();
```

This code calls the arcTo() method four times. The first call draws the top edge and upper-right corner of the rectangle. The second call draws the right edge and lower-right corner. The third call draws the bottom edge and lower-left corner. Finally, the fourth call draws the left edge and upper-left corner. Figure 4-9 shows how the rounded rectangle looks at runtime.

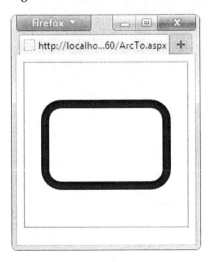

Figure 4-9. *Drawing a rounded rectangle using the arcTo() method*

The `arc()` and `arcTo()` methods discussed in this section are very useful for drawing circles, sectors, and rounded rectangles.

Drawing Paths

In the preceding sections, you learned to draw lines and curves. You can combine lines and curves to draw a path or a shape. Simply put, a *path* is a sequence of drawing operations that result in a shape. A path can be open or closed. A closed path can also be filled with some color or pattern.

To draw a path, you first call the `beginPath()` method and then draw lines or curves as before. To flag the end of the path, you call `stroke()` (to draw the outline of a shape) or `fill()` (to draw a filled shape).

Listing 4-7 draws a smiley using the `moveTo()` and `arc()` methods.

Listing 4-7. Drawing a Smiley

```
var canvas = $("#MyCanvas").get(0);
var context = canvas.getContext("2d");
context.beginPath();
//face
context.arc(100, 100, 80, 0, Math.PI * 2, false);
//smile
context.moveTo(160, 100);
context.arc(100, 100, 60, 0, Math.PI, false);
//left eye
context.moveTo(75, 70);
context.arc(65, 70, 10, 0, Math.PI * 2, true);
//right eye
context.moveTo(135, 70);
context.arc(125, 70, 10, 0, Math.PI * 2, true);
context.stroke();

context.lineWidth = 5;
context.stroke();
```

In all, there are four calls to the `arc()` method: they draw the outline of the face, the smile, the left eye, and the right eye, respectively. To actually draw the path, the code calls the `stroke()` method—`stroke()` draws the outline of the path. Figure 4-10 shows what the smiley looks like in the browser.

You can also draw closed paths that are filled by a color. For example, Listing 4-8 draws a triangle that is filled with blue color.

Listing 4-8. Drawing a Filled Shape

```
context.beginPath();
context.moveTo(50,20);
context.lineTo(50,100);
context.lineTo(150, 100);
context.closePath();
context.lineWidth = 10;
context.strokeStyle = 'red';
context.fillStyle = 'blue';
context.stroke();
context.fill();
```

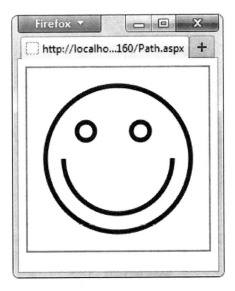

Figure 4-10. Drawing a smiley

Notice the use of two methods not used so far: closePath() and fill(). The closePath() method closes a path by joining the start point of the first drawing operation and the end point of the last drawing operation. Thus to draw a triangle, you need to draw only two lines using lineTo(); calling closePath()draws the third side of the triangle. Until now, you used the stroke() method to draw an outline of a shape. The fill() method fills the shape with a color. Of course, you can use stroke() as well as fill() with a single shape. The strokeStyle and fillStyle properties can be used to specify a color with which the outlining or filling operation should be performed. Figure 4-11 shows how a filled triangle is rendered as a result of running the code from Listing 4-8.

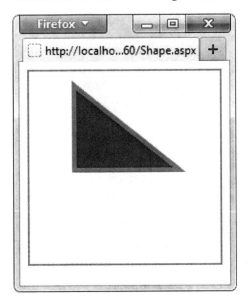

Figure 4-11. Drawing a filled triangle

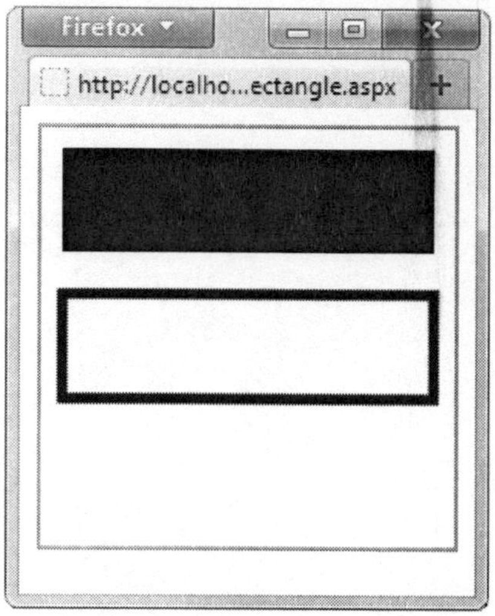

Figure 4-12. *Rectangles drawn on a canvas*

Just like a triangle, a rectangle can also be drawn using the path-drawing techniques discussed earlier. However, drawing a rectangle is such a commonly needed operation that there are readymade methods— strokeRect() and fillRect()—that simplify your job. These methods accept the coordinates of the upper-left corner of a rectangle and its width and height. The strokeRect() method draws an outline of the rectangle, whereas fillRect() draws a filled rectangle. Listing 4-9 show how these methods are used, and Figure 4-12 shows the resulting rectangles.

Listing 4-9. Drawing a Rectangle

```
var canvas = $("#MyCanvas").get(0);
var context = canvas.getContext("2d");
context.lineWidth = 5;
context.fillRect(10,10,180,50);
context.strokeRect(10,80,180,50);
```

▪ **Note** There is also a method—rect()—that you can use to draw rectangles. However, if you use rect(), you also need to call stroke() or fill() to actually draw the rectangle. The strokeRect() and fillRect() methods perform these two steps in one go.

Drawing Text

So far, you've learned to draw lines, curves, and shapes on the canvas. Often you need to incorporate text as a part of the drawing itself, and sooner or later you'll want to draw text on the canvas. As you might expect, the drawing context provides rich support for drawing text using the strokeText() and fillText() methods. Additionally, you can specify the font, font size, alignment, and baseline for drawing the text.

Listing 4-10 show how to draw text with the help of these properties and methods.

Listing 4-10. Drawing Text on the Canvas

```
var canvas = $("#MyCanvas").get(0);
var context = canvas.getContext("2d");
var x = canvas.width / 2;
var y = canvas.height / 2;
context.font = "30px Arial";
context.textBaseline = "middle";
context.textAlign = "center";
context.lineWidth = 1;
context.strokeStyle = "red";
context.fillStyle = "blue";
context.strokeText("Hello Canvas!",x,y-50);
context.fillText("Hello Canvas!",x,y+50);
```

This code sets the font for the text to be drawn using the font property. Note that the font size and attributes such as bold and italics must be mentioned before the font family in order for the text to be drawn correctly.

The textBaseLine property governs the baseline for the text. Some of the common values for textBaseLine property are top, bottom, and middle. These values affect the vertical positioning of the text with respect to the y coordinate. For example, setting the textBaseLine property to middle means the text is drawn with its vertical midpoint corresponding to the y coordinate. The textAlign property controls the text alignment on the canvas. Common values for textAlign are left, right, and center. The textAlign property controls the alignment of the text with respect to the x position of the text. For example, if the x coordinate is set to 100px and textAlign is set to center, then the center of the text is placed at 100px.

You can use the strokeStyle property to specify the text outline color. The strokeText() method draws the text on the canvas with the specified strokeStyle.

The fillStyle property governs how the text is filled, and the fillText() method draws the text with the specified fillStyle.

Figure 4-13 shows how the code from Listing 4-10 renders the specified text.

Figure 4-13. The strokeText() and fillText() methods in action

---

■ **Note**   There is no built-in way to wrap a long line of text into multiple lines of text. You have to write your own code to segment the text according to your needs.

Drawing Images

Drawing on the HTML5 canvas is not limited to lines, curves, shapes, and text. You can also draw existing image files on a canvas. This is particularly helpful when you wish to integrate an image that is more complicated than a simple shape. Consider, for example, if you want to display a company logo on a canvas. Re-creating the logo from scratch may not be the best option. Additionally, the logo may be too complex to be drawn using the available canvas API. It would be much easy to load an existing logo image and then render it on the canvas. Luckily, the drawing context offers the drawImage() method, which allows you to draw images on a canvas.

Listing 4-11 shows the simplest form of using drawImage().

Listing 4-11. Using the drawImage() Method in Its Simplest Form

```
var canvas = $("#MyCanvas").get(0);
var context = canvas.getContext("2d");
var img = new Image();
$(img).load(function () {
  context.drawImage(img, 10, 20);
});
img.src = "images/html5.png";
```

This code creates an image on the fly using JavaScript code. Notice that the jQuery code also wires an event handler for the load event of the image object. The load event is raised when an image is fully loaded. Unless an image is fully loaded, you can't draw it on a canvas. Therefore, you call the drawImage() method inside the load event handler. drawImage() accepts the image object to be drawn and x and y coordinates where the image is to be drawn. The code then sets the image's src property to an existing image file (images/html5.png). If you run the code in Listing 4-11, you see an image drawn on the canvas as shown in Figure 4-14.

At times you may need to resize an image while drawing it on the canvas. For example, the original image size may be larger than the canvas size, and you may wish to fit the image as per the canvas dimensions. To accomplish this, you can use a variation of the drawImage() method that accepts the width and height to which the image must be resized. Listing 4-12 shows how this is done.

Listing 4-12. Drawing an Image with a Specific Width and Height

```
var canvas = $("#MyCanvas").get(0);
var context = canvas.getContext("2d");
var img = new Image();
$(img).load(function () {
  context.drawImage(img,0,0, canvas.width,canvas.height);
});
img.src = "images/html5.png";
```

As you can see, in addition to x and y coordinates, the drawImage() method also specifies the image's width and height. In Listing 4-12, the image width and height are set equal to the canvas width and height.

Figure 4-14. drawImage() method in action

Of course, it's possible that the resized imaged may be distorted if the width and height proportions aren't maintained.

Yet another possibility while drawing images on a canvas is to draw just a portion of the source image instead of the entire image. To accomplish this image cropping, you use another variation of the drawImage() method that takes the coordinates and dimensions of the image slice along with other parameters discussed previously. Listing 4-13 make clear how to use this variation.

Listing 4-13. Drawing Just Part of an Image

```
var canvas = $("#MyCanvas").get(0);
var context = canvas.getContext("2d");
var img = new Image();
$(img).load(function () {
  context.drawImage(img, 0,0,200,40,0, 0, canvas.width/2 , canvas.height/2);
});
img.src = "images/html5.png";
```

The drawImage() method now takes four more parameters than the previous signature. The two parameters after the image parameter indicate the x and y coordinates (0,0) of the source image at which cropping should begin. The next two parameters indicate the width (200px) and height (40px) of the region from the source image that needs to be drawn on the canvas. The last four parameters have the same significance as in the previous example. Figure 4-15 shows how part of the image is drawn on the canvas.

Figure 4-15. Image cropping using the `drawImage()` *method*

As you can see, the HTML5 logo has been cropped such that only the text *HTML* is drawn on the canvas. Just like the previous variation of the drawImage() method, here too there can be distortion of the resultant image if the width and height proportions are not maintained.

Adding Special Effects

The canvas methods you've learned about so far allow you to render plain graphics. However, you can also add fancy and eye-catching effects to the graphics such as shadows, transparency, gradient fills, and pattern fills. In this section, you learn how.

To add special effects, you set certain properties of the drawing context and then call `stroke()` or `fill()`. Let's see how this is done with some examples.

Shadows

A common effect used while drawing graphics on a canvas is a shadow. You can add shadows to lines, curves, shapes, and text using four core properties of the drawing context object: `shadowColor`, `shadowBlur`, `shadowOffsetX`, and `shadowOffsetY`.

The `shadowColor` property indicates the color of the shadow. The `shadowBlur` property is a numeric property and configures the blurriness of the shadow. The lower the `shadowBlur` value, the sharper the shadow. For example, setting `shadowBlur` to 10 adds more blurriness to the shadow than a value of 5. The `shadowOffsetX` and `shadowOffsetY` properties allow you to control the positioning of the shadow. These x and y coordinates are relative to the target graphic object displaying the shadow. For example, if you set the `shadowOffsetX` and `shadowOffsetY` properties to 5 pixels, then the shadow is drawn 5 pixels to the right and 5 pixels down from the target graphic. You can also supply `shadowOffsetX` and `shadowOffsetY` properties as negative numbers to shift the shadow in the opposite direction (left and up).

Listing 4-14 adds shadows to a rectangle and text using the shadow properties discussed.

Listing 4-14. Using Shadow Properties to Configure Shadows

```
var canvas = $("#MyCanvas").get(0);
var context = canvas.getContext("2d");

context.shadowColor = "#808080";
context.shadowBlur = 5;
context.shadowOffsetX = 10;
context.shadowOffsetY = 10;
context.fillRect(20, 20, 150, 80);

context.shadowColor = "red";
context.shadowBlur = 15;
context.shadowOffsetX = -5;
context.shadowOffsetY = 5;
context.fillStyle = "blue";
context.textAlign = "center";
context.font = "bold 30px Arial";
context.fillText("Hello Canvas!",100,150);
```

This code draws a rectangle with a shadow color of #808080 and offsets of 10 pixels. The blur value is 5. The x offset value is -5, and shadowColor is red. Figure 4-16 show how the resulting rectangle and text look.

Figure 4-16. Adding shadows to a rectangle and text

The text drawn on the canvas has a negative x shadow offset value, and hence the shadow shifts to the left side. The y shadow offset is a positive value, and hence the shadow shifts toward the bottom.

Transparency

Until now, all the graphic objects drawn on a canvas have been totally opaque. You can, however, change the transparency of a graphic object using the strokeStyle and fillStyle properties. These properties let you set the color of a graphic such that in addition to RGB components, it also specifies a transparency level. This is accomplished using the rgba() function (instead of more commonly used rgb() function). Listing 4-15 shows how.

Listing 4-15. Setting the Transparency of a Drawing Object

```
var canvas = $("#MyCanvas").get(0);
var context = canvas.getContext("2d");

context.fillStyle = "black";
context.fillRect(20, 20, 150, 80);
context.fillStyle = "rgb(255, 0, 0)";
context.fillRect(40, 40, 150, 80);

context.fillStyle = "black";
context.fillRect(20, 150, 150, 80);
context.fillStyle = "rgba(255, 0, 0,0.5)";
context.fillRect(40, 170, 150, 80);
```

The first block of code draws two filled rectangles without any transparency. The second block of code draws two filled rectangles, with the second rectangle having a transparency of 50%. Notice how the rgba() function is used. The fourth parameter of rgba()—the alpha value—controls the transparency. The alpha value can be between 0 to 1, 0 being transparent and 1 being opaque. Figure 4-17 shows how both sets of rectangle are rendered.

Figure 4-17. Controlling the opacity of drawing objects

> **Note** In CSS, an RGB value can be obtained using the functional notation formats `rgb()` and `rgba()`. `rgb()` uses red, green, and blue components to form a color. `rgba()` uses an additional component—alpha—that controls the color's transparency.

Gradient Filling

A *gradient* specifies a range of colors that are used to fill a shape. The gradient effect applies color ranges continuously between the start and end positions, thus producing a smooth color transition. A gradient can be of two types: linear or radial.

A linear gradient is defined by two points and a color at each of those points. The colors along the line joining these two points vary based on a color stop.

A radial gradient is defined by two circles, each of which has a color. The gradient radiates out from the starting circle to the ending circle, and colors are calculated based on color stops.

To fill a shape with a linear or radial gradient, you first need to create a corresponding gradient object and then define the required color stops. Finally, you fill a shape with the fillStyle property set to the gradient object just created.

Listing 4-16 shows how you can fill a rectangle with a linear gradient.

Listing 4-16. Drawing a Linear Gradient

```
var canvas = $("#MyCanvas").get(0);
var context = canvas.getContext("2d");
var linearGradient = context.createLinearGradient(0, 100, 200, 100);
linearGradient.addColorStop(0, "blue");
linearGradient.addColorStop(0.5, "green");
linearGradient.addColorStop(1, "red");
context.fillStyle = linearGradient;
context.fillRect(0, 0, 200, 200);
```

This code creates a linear gradient object using the drawing context's `createLinearGradient()` method. The first two parameters of `createLinearGradient()` represent the x and y coordinates of the gradient's start point. Similarly, the last two parameters represent the x and y coordinates of the end point. The gradient is drawn from the start point to the end point.

The code adds three further color stops. The color-stop offset values range from 0 to 1 (from the start of the gradient to the end). The drawing context's fillStyle property is set to the linear gradient object, and then fillRect() is called. Figure 4-18 shows the resulting gradient-filled rectangle.

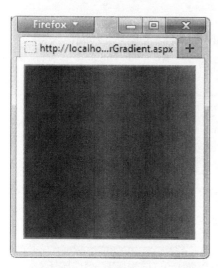

Figure 4-18. Linear gradient

Using the start and end points of the gradient, you can change how the linear gradient is drawn. For example, if you create a linear gradient object using start and end coordinates of (50, 10) and (200, 100), respectively, the resulting gradient is as shown in Figure 4-19.

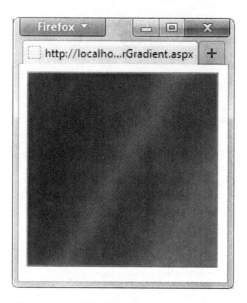

Figure 4-19. Changing the coordinates of the gradient line

The process of filling a shape with a radial gradient is similar to the preceding example, with a few differences. First, you use the `createRadialGradient()` method to create a radial gradient object. Second, instead of the start and end coordinates, you supply coordinates for the center of the start and end circles along with their respective radii. Listing 4-17 shows how this is done.

Listing 4-17. Drawing a Radial Gradient

```
var canvas = $("#MyCanvas").get(0);
var context = canvas.getContext("2d");
var radialGradient = context.createRadialGradient(100, 100, 5,100, 100,100);
radialGradient.addColorStop(0, "blue");
radialGradient.addColorStop(0.5, "green");
radialGradient.addColorStop(1, "red");
context.fillStyle = radialGradient;
context.fillRect(0, 0, 200, 200);
```

As you can see, the createRadialGradient() method takes six parameters. The first three represent the coordinates of the start circle (100,100) and its radius (5). The next three indicate the coordinates of the end circle (100,100) and its radius (100). Figure 4-20 shows the resulting rectangle.

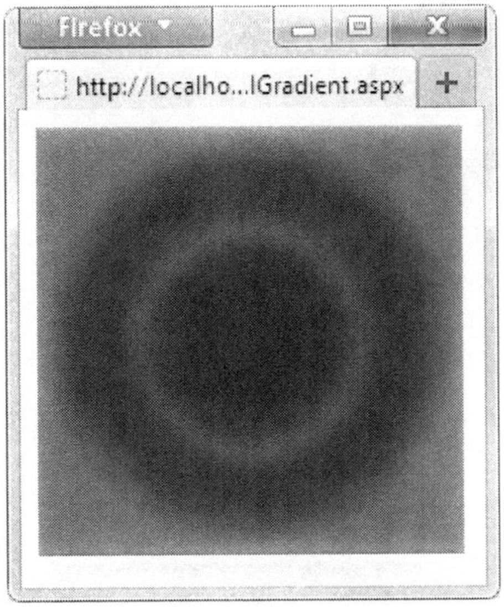

Figure 4-20. Radial gradient

The gradient starts out blue, then turns green, and then changes to red due to color stop values of 0, 0.5, and 1.

Pattern Filling

Pattern filling involves filling a shape with an image, typically repeated across x, y, or both axes. In order to use pattern filling, you use the drawing context's createPattern() method and then set the fillStyle property to the newly created pattern. Listing 4-18 shows how you create a pattern.

Listing 4-18. Creating and Filling a Pattern

```
var canvas = $("#MyCanvas").get(0);
var context = canvas.getContext("2d");
var img = new Image();
$(img).load(function () {
```

```
    var pattern = context.createPattern(img, "repeat");
    context.fillStyle = pattern;
    context.fillRect(0, 0, 200, 200);
});
img.src = "images/pattern.png";
```

This code creates a new instance of an Image object and sets its src property to an image that is to be used for pattern filling. The load event handler of the Image creates a pattern using the drawing context's createPattern() method. The first parameter of createPattern() is the image to be used, and the second parameter indicates a repeat direction. The possible values for the repeat direction are repeat-x (repeat horizontally), repeat-y (repeat vertically), and repeat (repeat in both the directions). The fillStyle property is then set to the newly created pattern object. Finally, a filled rectangle is drawn. Figure 4-21 shows how the rectangle is filled with a sample pattern.

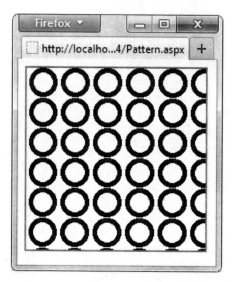

Figure 4-21. Filling a rectangle with a pattern

Saving the Canvas State

So far, you've been playing with the canvas by performing various drawing operations on it. Many times, you need to change the state of the canvas between drawing operations. For example, assume that you have a canvas with settings such as lineWidth and fillStyle set to some values. Now you wish to draw three rectangles on the canvas. However, lineWidth and fillStyle are different for all of them. In this case, you set the context properties for the first rectangle and then draw the rectangle. Doing so causes the original values to be overwritten. You repeat the same process to draw the other two rectangles. Now, if you wish to return the canvas to the original state it was in before you began drawing the three rectangles, you have to set those properties again because they were overwritten by the subsequent drawing operations. Saving the canvas state allows you to restore it at some later stage.

The term *state* can be bit misleading. Here, the *canvas state* means settings such as the strokeStyle, fillStyle, lineWidth, lineCap, shadowOffsetX, shadowOffsetY, shadowBlur, and shadowColor properties and a few other settings. You may want to save a snapshot of the canvas settings at a given point of time so you can revert back to those settings later in the current browser session. To perform these tasks, the drawing context object offers two methods: save() and restore(). As their names suggest, the save() method saves a canvas state, whereas the restore() method restores a previously saved state.

Using the save() and restore() Methods

Using save() and restore() is relatively straightforward. The save() method pushes a snapshot of the canvas state onto a stack, whereas the restore() method pops a saved snapshot of the canvas state. It's important to remember that *canvas state* doesn't refer to the actual drawing on the canvas. Listing 4-19 show how you use save() and restore().

Listing 4-19. Using the save() and restore() Methods

```
var canvas = $("#MyCanvas").get(0);
var context = canvas.getContext("2d");
//default state
context.lineWidth = 5;
context.fillStyle = 'blue';
context.fillRect(10, 120, 150, 50);
context.save();
//change state
context.lineWidth = 10;
context.fillStyle = 'red';
context.fillRect(20, 130, 150, 50);
//restore state
context.restore();
context.fillRect(30, 140, 150, 50);
```

As you can see, first canvas settings such as lineWidth and fillStyle are set and a rectangle is drawn. You save these settings using the save() method. Next, you change the canvas settings to new values, and a rectangle is drawn. Finally, before drawing a third rectangle, you restore the canvas settings using restore(). Figure 4-22 shows the effect of saving and restoring the canvas state.

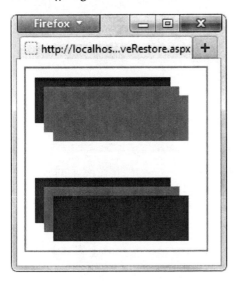

Figure 4-22. Effect of saving and restoring the canvas state

Notice that in Figure 4-22, the top three rectangles are drawn without using save() or restore(). The third rectangle assumes the canvas settings set for the second rectangle.

The rectangles at the bottom, however, use save() and restore(). After the code draws the first rectangle, the canvas state is saved using save(). Before the third rectangle is drawn, the canvas state is restored using restore(). That's why the third rectangle assumes the restored settings and not those with which the second rectangle was drawn.

Saving the Canvas Drawing

In the preceding sections you performed drawing operations during the active browser session. What if you close the browser window? What if you wish to persist a drawing for later use? That is where you need to deal with saving the canvas drawing. You may want to save the canvas drawing in a storage medium such as local storage (discussed in Chapter 7), a physical file system of the server, or a SQL server database residing on the server, so you can retrieve it later during the same or a different browser session.

To fulfill this requirement, the canvas (not the drawing context!) offers the toDataURL() method. However, this method alone won't persist data on the server. It returns a Base64 representation of the canvas drawing. It's your responsibility to send this Base64-encoded data to the server using a client-side technique such as the jQuery $.ajax() method.

In addition to the built-in techniques of saving the canvas drawing, you can implement custom techniques that mimic a save operation. For example, you can remember all the drawing steps performed by a user on the canvas. Instead of saving the canvas drawing, you can save these steps on the server and later replay the same steps to reproduce the canvas drawing. The saving mechanism you use depends on the kind of application you're building. The following sections you primarily focus on the built-in techniques for saving the canvas drawing.

Using the toDataURL() Method

The canvas's toDataURL() method returns a Base64-encoded representation of the drawing. It's up to you to decide what to do with this Base64 data. Some of the possibilities include the following:

- Display the canvas drawing in an HTML image object.

- Send the Base64-encoded string to the server, and save it in a database.

- Send the Base64-encoded string to the server, and save it as an image file on the server.

- Save the Base64-encoded string in web storage, and retrieve it later.

Your selection of a canvas-saving technique depends on the kind of application. In the following examples, you learn all the techniques except the last one; web storage is the subject of Chapter 7.

▓ **Note**   Base64 encoding is commonly used in scenarios where there is a need to convert binary data to text format for the sake of storing and transferring over wire. Base64 is commonly used to encode e-mail attachments and store binary data in XML documents.

Saving the Canvas Drawing in an <img> Object

At times you may want to allow users to save the canvas drawing as a physical image file. In such cases, saving a canvas drawing as an image can be useful. Once the image has been saved, users can right-click it and save the drawing in their local file system just like any other image loaded in the browser.

Saving a canvas as an image can also be used in situations where you wish to allow users to create multiple drawings without saving them explicitly and then load the previously created drawings again on the canvas. In such cases, you can save different drawings as images and then reload the drawings using the drawImage() method discussed earlier.

Saving a canvas drawing in an <img> object is straightforward. All you need to do is assign the src property of the DOM <img> element to the Base64-encoded data returned by the toDataURL() method. Listing 4-20 shows how this can be done.

Listing 4-20. *Saving a Canvas Drawing as an <img> Object*

```
var canvas = $("#MyCanvas").get(0);
var context = canvas.getContext("2d");
context.fillRect(20, 20, 160, 160);
var data = canvas.toDataURL();
$("#imgCanvas").attr("src", data);
```

As shown in this listing, a rectangle is drawn on the canvas, and then toDataURL() is called to retrieve the Base64-encoded representation of the canvas drawing. You load this Base64 data into an <img> element by setting its src attribute. A part of a sample Base64-encoded string is shown here:

```
data:image/png;base64,iVBORw0KGgoAAAANSUh...
```

As you can see, the string begins with a MIME type for the image. You can also specify the image type yourself using a variation of toDataURL():

```
var data = canvas.toDataURL("mage/png");
```

toDataURL() now takes the MIME type for the image. Typical values include image/png and image/jpg. The default image MIME type is image/png.

Saving the Canvas Drawing in SQL Server

Saving the canvas drawing in a SQL Server database calls for sending to the server the Base64-encoded data obtained as a result of calling toDataURL(). You can either use a hidden form field to accomplish this data transfer or, better yet, use the jQuery $.ajax() method. Listing 4-21 uses $.ajax() to send the Base64-encoded data to the server.

Listing 4-21. *Sending Base64 Canvas Data to the Server Using $.ajax()*

```
var canvas = $("#MyCanvas").get(0);
var context = canvas.getContext("2d");
context.fillRect(20, 20, 160, 160);

$('#btnSave').click(function () {
  var data = canvas.toDataURL();
  data = data.replace('data:image/png;base64,', '');
  $.ajax({
    type: 'POST',
```

```
      url: '/SaveInSQLServer.aspx/SaveToDb',
      data: '{ "data" : "' + data + '" }',
      contentType: 'application/json; charset=utf-8',
      dataType: 'json',
      success: function (msg) {
        alert('Image data saved to SQL Server database!');
      }
  });
});
```

As shown here, the click event handler of a button triggers the save operation. Inside the click event handler, toDataURL() is called and the Base64-encoded data is stored in a local variable. You need to send only the image data to the server; hence the beginning of the string ('data:image/png;base64,') is removed using the JavaScript replace() function. Of course, if you wish to render the images in image elements using the data URL technique discussed earlier, you need not remove the beginning of the string.

The $.ajax() method then makes a POST request to a web method named SaveToDb(). The Base64-encoded image data is passed to the server as a JSON object. The SaveToDb() web method is shown in Listing 4-22.

Listing 4-22. SaveToDb() Web Method

```
[WebMethod]
public static void SaveToDb(string data)
{
    ImageDbEntities db = new ImageDbEntities();
    Image img = new Image();
    img.ImageData = data;
    img.SaveDate = DateTime.Now;
    db.Images.AddObject(img);
    db.SaveChanges();
}
```

The SaveToDb() method receives the Base64-encoded image data as a parameter. Inside, it uses an Entity Framework data model class (Image) to save the data in a SQL Server table named Images. If you run this example and check the ImageDb database from the App_Data folder, you find that a record is added to the Images table every time you click the Save button.

Saving the Canvas Drawing as an Image File on the Server

At times, saving a canvas drawing as a physical disk file on the server is more convenient than storing the image in a database. For example, consider a case where you wish to send the canvas drawing as an e-mail attachment. In such a case, attaching a canvas drawing saved as a physical image file is more convenient and simplifies your task.

Saving a canvas drawing as a server-side image is similar to the previous technique. This time, however, you need to convert the Base64-encoded data back to its binary representation and then save it as a disk file. Converting Base64-encoded data to its binary form is necessary because you save it in a physical image file rather than a SQL Server database. The jQuery code remains almost identical to the previous example, but the web method needs some modifications. Listing 4-23 shows the $.ajax() call being made to a web method named SaveAsImageFile.

Listing 4-23. $.ajax() Method Calling the SaveAsImageFile Web Method

```
$('#btnSave').click(function () {
  var data = canvas.toDataURL();
  data = data.replace('data:image/png;base64,', '');
  alert(data);
  $.ajax({
    type: 'POST',
    url: '/SaveAsServerSideImg.aspx/SaveAsImageFile',
    data: '{ "data" : "' + data + '" }',
    contentType: 'application/json; charset=utf-8',
    dataType: 'json',
    success: function (msg) {
      alert('Image saved on the server!');
    }
  });
});
```

Once the Base64-encoded data is received in the web method, it's converted to binary form and saved as a physical file. Listing 4-24 shows the SaveAsImageFile() web method.

Listing 4-24. Saving the Canvas Drawing as a Physical Image File

```
[WebMethod]
public static void SaveAsImageFile(string data)
{
    Guid id = Guid.NewGuid();
    string path = HttpContext.Current.Server.MapPath("~/images/" + id.ToString() + ".png");
    byte[] binaryData = Convert.FromBase64String(data);
    FileStream file = new FileStream(path, FileMode.Create);
    BinaryWriter bw = new BinaryWriter(file);
    bw.Write(binaryData);
    bw.Close();
}
```

This code generates a random file name using a GUID and the Server.MapPath() method. The physical file has an extension of .png. To convert Base64-encoded data into binary form, you use the FromBase64String() method of the Convert class. This method accepts Base64-encoded data and returns a byte array. The byte array thus returned is written to a physical file using the FileStream and BinaryWriter classes.

Figure 4-23 shows a sample canvas drawing saved as an image file being viewed in Windows Photo Viewer.

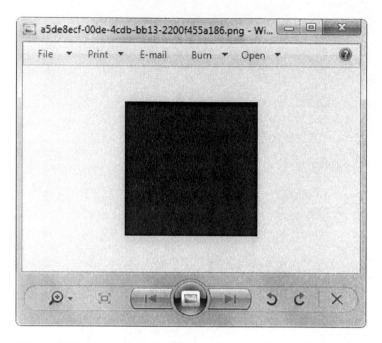

Figure 4-23. Canvas drawing after saving as a physical image file

As you can see in the title of the Photo Viewer, the file is saved with a GUID as the file name and .png as the file extension.

Creating Pie Charts Using Canvas Drawing Techniques

Now that you're familiar with the canvas API, it's time to develop a sample application that puts together what you've learned so far. In this section, you develop an ASP.NET MVC application that allows you to create pie charts using the HTML5 canvas.

Developers often resort to third-party charting components for their charting needs. However, at times you may find canvas-based charting useful. The <canvas> element is an integral part of HTML5, so you need not purchase a commercial component. Many third-party components are rich when it comes to server-side programming, but they often lack client-side programming support. You can use canvas-based charting when a chart is to be programmed using client-side code. Using canvas-based charting also lets you avoid dependency on third-party charting software. Of course, you can resort to a third-party charting component if your requirements call for it.

The example application's user interface is divided into two sections, as shown in Figure 4-24. The left side of Figure 4-24 shows how a final pie chart looks in the browser, and the right side shows the area where you can enter pie chart data such as sector names, values, and colors. You can also specify a title for the chart along with a gradient background. Clicking the Draw Chart button draws a pie chart on the canvas based on the data you enter. Clicking the Save Chart button does two things—it saves the pie chart as an image file on the server, and it also saves the pie chart sector information in a SQL Server database. This way, you can regenerate a pie chart based on the saved data and use the physical image file for other purposes such as sending as e-mail attachments, embedding in documents, or presentations.

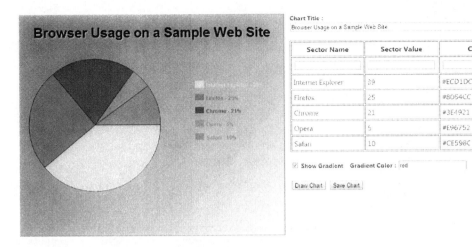

Figure 4-24. *Drawing pie charts using canvas API*

SQL Server Database

The application saves pie chart data such as sector names and their values in a SQL Server database (ChartDb). The ChartDb database consists of two tables: ChartMaster and ChartDetails. The actual data access happens through Entity Framework. The Entity Framework data model for the ChartMaster and ChartDetails tables physically resides in the Models folder of the web application and is shown in Figure 4-25.

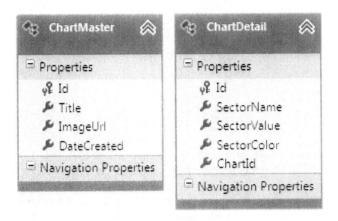

Figure 4-25. *Entity Framework data model for the ChartDb database tables*

As you can see, the `ChartMaster` table stores the pie chart title and the physical image file URL. The `ChartDetails` table stores sector information such as names, values, and colors. Although this application doesn't regenerate charts based on stored data, you could easily do so because the data is readily available in these tables.

MVC Controller

The ASP.NET MVC application has a single controller: `ChartController`. It contains code that saves a pie chart as an image. It also saves the pie chart data into the `ChartMaster` and `ChartDetails` tables. The action method of the `ChartController` class that does the job is shown in Listing 4-25.

Listing 4-25. Saving the Chart Image on the Server

```
[HttpPost]
public JsonResult SaveChart(string data, ChartMaster master, ChartDetail[] details)
{
    Guid id = Guid.NewGuid();
    string path = HttpContext.Server.MapPath("~/images/" + id.ToString() + ".png");
    byte[] binaryData = Convert.FromBase64String(data);
    FileStream file = new FileStream(path, FileMode.Create);
    BinaryWriter bw = new BinaryWriter(file);
    bw.Write(binaryData);
    bw.Close();

    ChartDbEntities db = new ChartDbEntities();
    master.Id = id;
    master.ImageUrl = "~/images/" + id.ToString() + ".png";
    db.ChartMasters.AddObject(master);
    foreach (ChartDetail detail in details)
    {
        detail.ChartId = master.Id;
        db.ChartDetails.AddObject(detail);
    }
    db.SaveChanges();
    return Json("Chart saved in the database!");
}
```

As you can see, the `SaveChart()` method accepts three parameters: canvas drawing data in Base64 format, a `ChartMaster` object, and an array of `ChartDetail` objects. These three parameters are sent from the client-side jQuery code.

The code in `SaveChart()` should look familiar because previous sections have discussed these canvas-saving techniques. Notice how a GUID serves dual purposes: acting as a chart ID and a physical file name. The `SaveChart()` method essentially does two things: it saves the pie chart as a physical `.png` file on the server and saves the chart data in the `ChartMaster` and `ChartDetails` tables. `SaveChart()` returns a success message as a `JsonResult` object after a chart is saved on the server.

MVC View

The HTML5 canvas markup, as well as jQuery code that invokes the controller actions, resides in a view: `Index.aspx`. The HTML markup of the index view is shown in Listing 4-26. For the sake of clarity, unwanted markup tags have been removed.

Listing 4-26. HTML Markup of Index.aspx

```
<div><strong>Chart Title :</strong></div>
<input type="text" id="txtTitle" size="87" class="textbox"/>
...
<table id="tblChartData" border="1" cellpadding="5">
  <tr class="HeaderRow">
    <th>Sector Name</th>
    <th>Sector Value</th>
    <th>Color</th>
    <th>Action</th>
  </tr>
  <tr>
    <td><input type="text" id="txtName"/></td>
    <td><input type="text" id="txtValue"/></td>
    <td><input type="text" id="txtColor"/></td>
    <td><input type="button" id="btnAdd"/></td>
  </tr>
</table>
<br />
<input type="checkbox" id="chkGradient" />
<span><strong>Show Gradient</strong></span>
...
<span><strong>Gradient Color : </strong></span><input type="text" id="txtGradient" />
...
<input id="btnDraw" type="button" value="Draw Chart" />
<input id="btnSave" type="button" value="Save Chart" />
...
<canvas id="MyCanvas" width="600" height="500"></canvas>
```

This HTML markup is straightforward and creates a canvas 600px wide and 500px high. The event handlers for the Add, Draw Chart, and Save Chart buttons are wired in jQuery code and are discussed next.

Adding Chart Data

Adding pie chart data involves capturing sector information such as the sector name, its value, and its color. Once captured, sector information is added to the HTML table (see Figure 4-24). The jQuery code responsible for adding sector information to the HTML table is shown in Listing 4-27.

Listing 4-27. Adding Chart Data to an HTML Table

```
$("#btnAdd").click(function () {
  var row = "<tr>";
  row += "<td>" + $("#txtName").val() + "</td>";
  row += "<td>" + $("#txtValue").val() + "</td>";
```

```
    row += "<td>" + $("#txtColor").val() + "</td>";
    row += "<td> </td>";
    row += "</tr>";
    $("#tblChartData").append(row);
    $("#txtName").val('');
    $("#txtValue").val('');
    $("#txtColor").val('');
    $("#txtName").focus();
});
```

As you can see, the jQuery code from the Add button's click event handler uses the val() method to retrieve values entered in the text boxes. The append() method is then used to dynamically add a new table row.

■ **Note**   You may find entering sector colors a bit tedious. The code download for this chapter includes a JavaScript function that automatically populates the color text box with a random hexadecimal color code upon receiving focus. For the sake of saving space, that function isn't discussed here.

Drawing a Pie Chart

The Draw Chart button's click event handler is responsible for drawing a pie chart on the canvas. The complete jQuery code for the click event handler is given in Listing 4-28.

Listing 4-28. Drawing a Pie Chart

```
var sectorNames = Array();
var sectorValues = Array();
var sectorColors = Array();

$("#btnDraw").click(function () {
  context.save();
  if ($("#chkGradient").is(":checked")) {
    var linearGradient = context.createLinearGradient(0, 0, canvas.width, canvas.height);
    linearGradient.addColorStop(0, $("#txtGradient").val());
    linearGradient.addColorStop(1, 'white');
    context.fillStyle = linearGradient;
    context.fillRect(0, 0, canvas.width, canvas.height);
    context.restore();
  }
  else {
    context.clearRect(0, 0, canvas.width, canvas.height);
  }
  context.save();

  $("table tr:gt(1)").each(function (i, v) {
    sectorNames[i] = $(this).children("td:eq(0)").text();
  })
  $("table tr:gt(1)").each(function (i, v) {
    sectorValues[i] = parseInt($(this).children("td:eq(1)").text());
```

```
})
$("table tr:gt(1)").each(function (i, v) {
  sectorColors[i] = $(this).children("td:eq(2)").text();
})

//draw title
context.textAlign = "center";
context.font = "bold 30px Arial";
context.shadowColor = "silver";
context.shadowOffsetX = 2;
context.shadowOffsetY = 2;
context.fillStyle = "black";
context.fillText($("#txtTitle").val(), 300,50 );
context.restore();

//draw sectors
var total = 0;
for (var i = 0; i < sectorValues.length; i++) {
  total += sectorValues[i];
}
var angle = 0;
for (var i = 0; i < sectorValues.length; i++) {
  context.fillStyle = sectorColors[i];
  context.beginPath();
  context.moveTo(170, 250);
  context.arc(170, 250, 150, angle, angle + (Math.PI * 2 *
  (sectorValues[i] / total)), false);
  context.lineTo(170, 250);
  context.fill();
  context.stroke();
  angle += Math.PI * 2 * (sectorValues[i] / total);
}

//draw legends
var offset = 150;
for (var i = 0; i < sectorColors.length; i++) {
  context.fillStyle = sectorColors[i];
  context.font = 'bold 12px Arial';
  context.save();
  context.shadowColor = "silver";
  context.shadowOffsetX = 2;
  context.shadowOffsetY = 2;
  context.fillRect(400, offset, 20, 15);
  context.restore();
  context.textBaseline = "middle";
  context.fillText(sectorNames[i] + ' - ' + sectorValues[i] + '%', 425, offset + 10);
  offset += 30;
}

});
```

The code in Listing 4-28 declares three global arrays—sectorNames, sectorValues, and sectorColors—for storing sector names, their values, and their colors, respectively.

Then the code determines whether a gradient is to be drawn by checking the state of the gradient check box. Accordingly, either a linear gradient is drawn or the canvas is cleared using the clearRect() method. Notice how the createLinearGradient() method is used and how the color stops are defined. The start color stop is picked up from the corresponding text box, but the end color stop is always white. Also notice the use of the canvas's save() and restore() methods for saving and restoring the canvas state. You restore the canvas settings to their initial values because you don't need a gradient for every drawing operation.

Next, you use the jQuery each() method to iterate through all the HTML table rows. The three sector arrays are populated by picking values from the respective table cells.

You then draw the title of the pie chart using fillText() method. Notice that the title has a shadow configured using the shadowOffsetX, shadowOffsetY, and shadowColor properties. For the same reason mentioned earlier, the canvas state is restored to the previous value.

Next, a for loop iterates through the sectorValues array and draws sectors of the pie chart using the arc() method. Notice how the angle is calculated based on the total of the sector values and the value of a sector being drawn.

Finally, the pie chart's legends are drawn. The associated for loop iterates through the sectorColors array, and for every sector a rectangle is drawn with the sector color. A label is also drawn in front of the rectangle.

Saving a Pie Chart

Once you draw a pie chart on the canvas, it can be saved to the database. The Save Chart button's click event handler contains jQuery code that calls the SaveChart() controller action method with the help of the $.ajax() method. Listing 4-29 shows how this is done.

Listing 4-29. Saving a Pie Chart on the Server

```
$('#btnSave').click(function () {
  var data = canvas.toDataURL();
  data = '"data": "' + data.replace('data:image/png;base64,', '') + '"';

  var master = '"master": {"Title" :"' + $("#txtTitle").val() + '"}';

  var details = '"details" : [';
  for (var i = 0; i < sectorNames.length; i++) {
    var sector = '{"SectorName" : "' + sectorNames[i] + '", "SectorValue":"' +
    sectorValues[i] + '", "SectorColor":"' + sectorColors[i] + '"}';
    details += sector
    if ((i+1) != sectorNames.length) {
      details += ",";
    }
  }
  details += ']';

  var finalData = '{' + data + ',' + master + ',' + details + '}';

  $.ajax({
    type: 'POST',
```

```
    url: '/Chart/SaveChart',
    data: finalData,
    contentType: 'application/json; charset=utf-8',
    dataType: 'json',
    success: function (result) {
      alert(result);
    }
  });
});
```

The code needs to pass a complex JSON object from the client side to the server because the SaveChart() method takes three parameters. Additionally, one of the parameters is an array of ChartDetail objects. The code from Listing 4-29 constructs a JSON object (finalData) by gathering various pieces of information (such as the chart title and sector details). The jQuery $.ajax() method then makes a POST request to the SaveChart() method and passes the JSON object along with the call. The success function displays the returned message from the server in an alert box.

Figure 4-26 shows a sample run of the application.

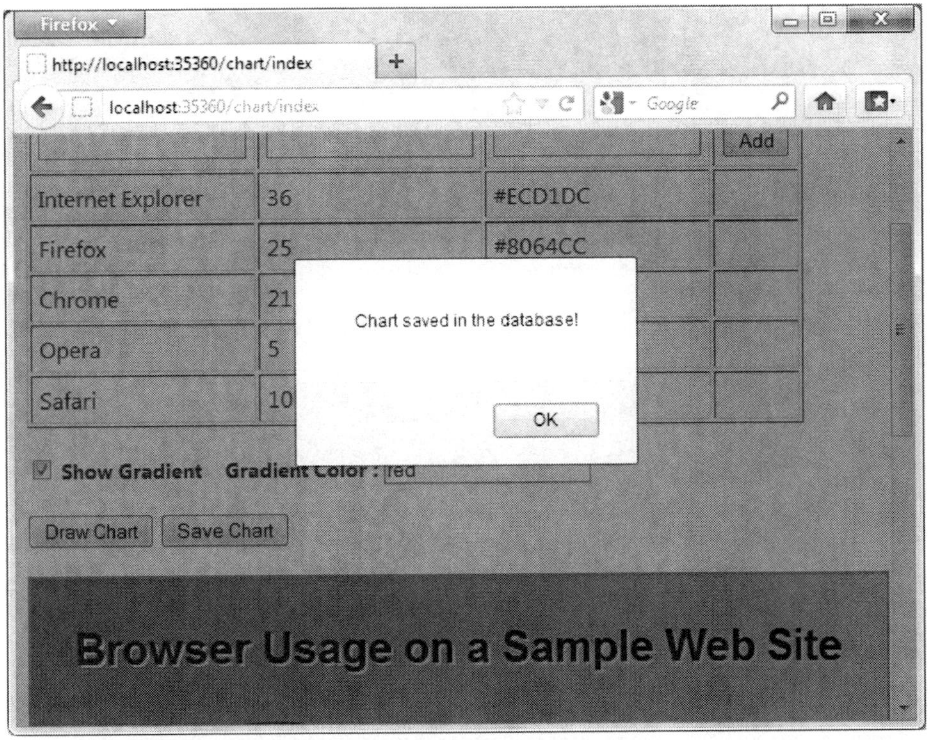

Figure 4-26. Successful run of the application

As you can see if you successfully save the chart on the server, a success message is displayed in an alert box. You can verify the save operation by checking for the existence of the data in the ChartMaster and ChartDetails tables.

Summary

The HTML5 canvas allows you to draw lines, curves, paths, shapes, images, and text using the canvas API. The drawing context object provides methods and properties to perform the drawing operations just mentioned. You can also add fancy frills to your drawing objects such as shadows, gradients, and transparency. The canvas also lets you save the canvas state programmatically. Using jQuery code, you can transfer the canvas drawing to the server as a Base64 string. In this chapter, you learned all this and also developed a simple yet functional charting application using the canvas API, jQuery, and ASP.NET MVC.

Chapters 3 and 4 discussed the audio, video, and graphics provisions of HTML5. One area that attracts any ASP.NET developer developing data-driven web applications is the forms enhancements such as new input types and validations. The next chapter dissects these enhancements and shows how you can use them in ASP.NET web forms as well as MVC applications.

CHAPTER 5

■ ■ ■

Working with Forms and Controls

One of the key areas where ASP.NET shines is developing data-driven web applications. Most ASP.NET web applications are more than collections of HTML pages. They involve a variety of database tasks ranging from simple listings of records to complex database operations. These tasks often include accepting user input, performing validation on the data entered by the user, processing the data on the server, and finally saving it in a data store.

A data-entry page typically presents a set of controls such as text boxes, check boxes, radio buttons, drop-down lists, and similar elements. These controls are housed in an HTML <form> element. Upon filling the form, the user can submit the form along with its data to the server for processing. Over the years, developing an HTML form has become more complex and demanding. For example, many forms call for complex data-format and business validations. They also need different types of controls for specific data types such date-time and numbers. Keeping these changing requirements and trends in mind, HTML5 offers a set of enhancements to the existing <form> features. It has also introduced new features that make overall form development easier. This chapter gives you a detailed introduction to these new and enhanced form features of HTML5. Specifically, you learn about the following:

- Using new HTML5 input types

- Improvements to the existing controls

- Using the newly added and enhanced features of HTML5 in ASP.NET Web Forms and MVC applications

- Validating user input using various techniques

Understanding HTML Forms in ASP.NET

Whenever you develop a data-driven ASP.NET or ASP.NET MVC application, the application's user interface is rendered with the help of Web Forms and views, respectively. Web Forms and views in turn use the HTML <form> element to house the data-entry region of the page. Before this chapter delves into the HTML5-specific features of the <form> element, it's worthwhile to briefly discuss how a <form> element appears in a typical ASP.NET Web Forms and ASP.NET MVC application.

The <form> Element in ASP.NET Web Forms

A typical ASP.NET web form consists of a <form> tag marked with the runat server. Additionally, it hosts one or more server controls such as text boxes, lists, and grids. Finally, it provides a mechanism to submit a form to the server for further processing. Listing 5-1 shows a simple web form that illustrates how these elements look in source view.

Listing 5-1. A Server-Side <form> Element in a Web Forms Application

```
<form id="form1" runat="server">
<asp:Label ID="Label1" runat="server" Text="Enter your Name : " ></asp:Label>
<br />
<asp:TextBox ID="TextBox1" runat="server"></asp:TextBox>
<br /><br />
<asp:Button ID="Button1" runat="server" Text="Submit" />
</form>
```

The <form> tag in Listing 5-1 has two attributes: id and runat. If you wish to process an HTML form on the server, it must be marked with runat. The runat attribute has only one possible value: server. In the <form> are a Label server control, a TextBox server control, and a Button server control. If you run this web form in a browser, you get the display shown in Figure 5-1.

Figure 5-1. A simple web form displayed in a browser

If you view the HTML source of the resulting page shown by the browser, it's as shown in Listing 5-2.

Listing 5-2. HTML Source of a Web Form

```
<form method="post" action="WebForm1.aspx" id="form1">
  <div class="aspNetHidden">
   <input type="hidden" name="__VIEWSTATE" id="__VIEWSTATE"
   value="kv16mNsClgHGNtkmN..." />
  </div>
  <div class="aspNetHidden">
   <input type="hidden" name="__EVENTVALIDATION" id="__EVENTVALIDATION"
    value="jIRq9NWtI2OO4IJRVRDv7..." />
  </div>
  <span id="Label1" >Enter your Name : </span>
  <br />
  <input name="TextBox1" type="text" id="TextBox1" />
```

```
<br /><br />
<input type="submit" name="Button1" value="Submit" id="Button1" />
</form>
```

As you can see, at runtime ASP.NET adds several pieces to the resulting HTML markup. Notice now the `<form>` tag has action and method attributes. Also notice that all the server controls are converted into their equivalent HTML markup. Finally, note the ViewState hidden form fields added at the top of the form. This bulky Base64-encoded ViewState (truncated in the listing for the sake of clarity) is one of the reservations ASP.NET developers have against Web Forms.

The following are a few things worth noting about the `<form>` tag used in a web form:

- Typically, a web form has only one `<form>` tag, although HTML doesn't impose any such restriction.

- A form method is always POST.

- A web form is posted to itself. That is, the action attribute of the `<form>` tag points to the same `.aspx` file.

- When you use master pages, the `<form>` tag is placed in the master page file (`.master`) rather than individual content pages (`.aspx`).

The `<form>` Element in ASP.NET MVC

The `<form>` element in the context of an ASP.NET MVC application is quite flexible. ASP.NET MVC applications have a couple of options when you place a `<form>` element in a view:

- An HTML `<form>` tag and HTML `<input>` tags can be placed directly in a view file.

- HTML helpers can be used to render `<form>` and `<input>` tags.

Listing 5-3 shows a form developed using plain HTML markup tags.

Listing 5-3. *A `<form>` in an MVC View Using Plain HTML Tags*

```
<form method="post" action="/Home/Index">
  <span id="Label1">Enter your Name : </span>
  <br />
  <input name="TextBox1" type="text" id="TextBox1"/>
  <br /><br />
  <input type="submit" name="Button1" value="Submit" id="Button1" />
</form>
```

This `<form>` uses plain HTML markup tags such as `<form>` and `<input>`. Notice that the action attribute of the `<form>` tag points to a controller action method (/Home/Index); you're free to point it to any controller class.

Listing 5-4 shows the same form developed using HTML helpers.

Listing 5-4. *A `<form>` Rendered Using HTML Helpers*

```
<% using(Html.BeginForm("IndexWithHelpers","Home","POST")) %>
<% { %>
<%= Html.Label("Enter your Name :") %>
<br />
<%= Html.TextBox("txtName") %>
```

```
<br /><br />
<input type="submit" value="Submit" />
<% } %>
```

As shown in Listing 5-4, the `<form>` tag is rendered using the `BeginForm()` method. The three parameters of the `BeginForm()` method represent the action method name, the controller name, and the form method, respectively. The `Label` and `TextBox` HTML helpers render a `<label>` and an `<input>` tag, respectively. The view's resulting markup closely matches Listing 5-3.

HTML5 Controls

An HTML5 form consists of a combination of text and controls. The text part of an HTML5 form usually consists of field labels, section headings, and explanatory text about the form. The HTML5 markup provides a plethora of controls. These controls can be broadly classified in the following categories:

- Data-input controls in which you type string data. Controls such as text boxes and `<textarea>` fall in this category.

- Option-selection controls that allow you to pick one or more options from a set of options. Controls such as check boxes, radio buttons, and drop-down lists belong to this category.

- Range-selector controls that let you pick a value between minimum and maximum values.

- Date- and time-picker controls that let you choose a date or a part of it (week, day, month, and so on).

- Color-picker control that allows you to pick color values.

- Button controls that render as Submit, Reset, Image, or push buttons.

- Miscellaneous controls that don't fit in any other category mentioned here.

HTML 4.01 provides many of the controls belonging to these categories. Most of the controls listed here are displayed using an `<input>` element. The `type` attribute of the `<input>` element is responsible for rendering a required type of control.

HTML5 adds many new input types; you learn about them in the following sections. Table 5-1 lists the available input types in HTML5 for your quick reference. Some controls that aren't `<input>` types but are used commonly in HTML forms are also listed.

Table 5-1. HTML5 `<input>` Types

Input Type / HTML Tag	New to HTML5?	Control Rendered	Additional Notes
text, password, `<textarea>`	No	Text box, password-entry field, free-form text area	The `<input>` element with type equal to text renders a single-line text box, whereas `<textarea>` renders a multiline text box.
checkbox, radio	No	Check box, radio button	More than one check box can be selected at a time, whereas only one radio button from a given group can be selected. You create a radio-button group by setting the `name` attribute to a common value.

email, url, tel	Yes	Text box that restricts the entered value to match the format of email, url, or tel (telephone number)	These controls validate data entered in them and display an error message if data doesn't meet the expected format. The type tel isn't implemented in all browsers.
date, datetime, datetime-local time, week, month	Yes	Date and/or time picker	Different browsers may display these controls in different fashions.
color	Yes	Color picker	Different browsers may display the color picker in different fashions.
number, range	Yes	Up-down control, range selector (slider)	You can specify minimum and maximum values as well as a step value.
file	Improved	Text box with a Browse button	This control is used to upload files from a client machine to the server.
hidden	No	Hidden form field (not displayed on the form)	This control isn't displayed on the web page but can be accessed programmatically. It's typically used to pass processed or hidden data between client and server.
submit, reset, button, image	No	Push button / image button for submitting, resetting the form, or triggering a custom action	These controls trigger an action. A Submit button submits a form to the server using a POST/GET request.
search	Yes	Search box	A search box can have special features that an ordinary text box doesn't have, such as the ability to clear the entered search criteria.
<select></select>	No	Drop-down list.	This control displays a list box or drop-down list. You can specify list items using <option> elements.

The next section discusses the new input types introduced by HTML5.

Using HTML5-Specific Input Types

Ensuring that data entered by a user meets the expected format is a common task in all data-driven web applications. Traditionally, developers used custom JavaScript code to perform checks such as these:

- Data entered is of correct format: for example, e-mail addresses, URLs, and telephone numbers.
- Data entered falls within certain range between minimum and maximum values: for example, age group and yearly income.
- Dates are entered in a common format, and values are valid dates.

Performing such validations through JavaScript is, no doubt, a good programming practice. However, a more logical approach is to enable the data-entry controls to accept data of the required format or range. This way, you need not write any JavaScript code to validate the user input. The new HTML5 input types attempt to do just that. Remember, though, that not all browsers support these new input types. Additionally, browser support for a particular input type may differ in terms of the control's user interface and validating capabilities.

As with other features of HTML5, it's recommended that you check browser support for the new input types using the Modernizr library. Listing 5-5 shows some sample jQuery code that checks whether the email input type is supported by the browser.

Listing 5-5. Checking Support for the New Input Types

```
$(document).ready(function () {
  if (!Modernizr.inputtypes.email) {
    alert("This browser doesn't support email input type of HTML5!");
  }
});
```

■ **Note** If a browser encounters an input type that it can't recognize, a normal text box is rendered. As of this writing, Chrome and Opera are leading as far as support of the new input types is concerned. Hence, all the input types discussed in the following sections are illustrated using either Chrome or Opera.

Note that individual browsers may perform the validations based on the input types bit differently. For example, Firefox highlights the <input> field containing an invalid value as soon as you leave the field. Chrome and Opera, on the other hand, don't give such instant visual feedback. All browsers, however, perform the validations when the form is submitted. At that time, the browser displays an error message (if any) for the first <input> field in error, and that input field gets the focus. Consider, for example, a form with three <input> fields, the first two of which contain invalid values. When such a form is submitted, the browser displays the validation error message for the first input field, and the first input field gets the focus. Only when a valid value is entered in the first input field is the validation error message for the second input field displayed. If there are any validation errors, the form isn't submitted.

The following sections discuss the new input types offered by HTML5. Remember that all the HTML 4.01 input types are available and can be used as before.

E-mail Addresses

E-mail addresses are commonly used on web sites for variety of reasons ranging from user registrations to contact forms. You can accept e-mail addresses using the email input type. Listing 5-6 shows how the email input type is used.

Listing 5-6. Using the email Input Type

```
<span>Enter your email address :</span>
<br />
<input id="email" type="email" />
<br />
<input type="submit" value="Submit"/>
```

As you can see, the type attribute is set to email. If you try to enter an invalid e-mail address, the browser displays an error message (see Figure 5-2).

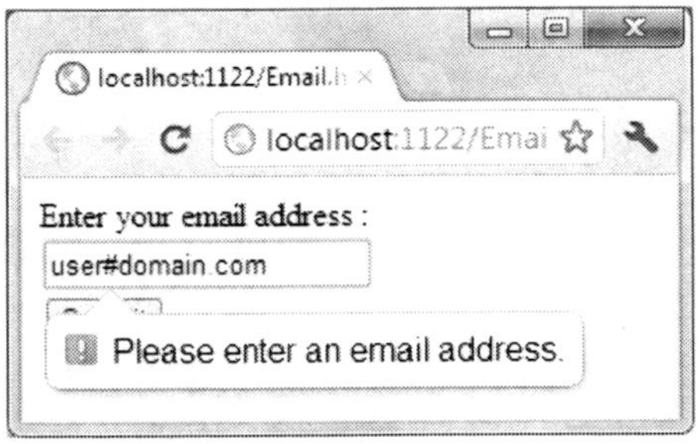

Figure 5-2. Chrome showing an error message when the user enters an invalid e-mail address

Notice that the error message is displayed only if the text box contains a value. If the text box is left empty, no validation is performed. This behavior is similar to ASP.NET validation controls.

URLs

Setting the input type to url ensures that the value entered matches a URL pattern. You use the url type as follows:

```
<input id="url" type="url" />
```

If you enter a valid Internet URL such as http://www.microsoft.com, the input field doesn't give any errors. Entering an invalid Internet URL, such as http://microsoft%com, causes the browser to display an error message. Note, however, that the current implementation of the url input type in most browsers doesn't perform strict checks on the URL format. For example, they allow whitespace to be part of the URL.

Numbers and Telephone Numbers

Numeric data is commonly accepted in web pages for things such as age, currency values, number of employees in an organization, and so on. You can use the number input type in such cases. Additionally, the number input type lets you specify an acceptable range for the number. For example, consider a web page that accepts an employee's current salary. Here is how to use the number input type:

```
<input id="salary" type="number" />
```

Figure 5-3 shows how Chrome displays the number input type as an up-down control.

Figure 5-3. The number input type shown in Chrome

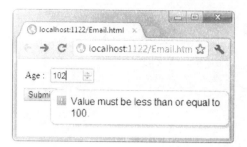

Figure 5-4. *The number input type with min and max attributes specified*

In addition to specifying the type attribute as number, you can also specify a minimum value, a maximum value, and a step value. The minimum and maximum values the control should accept are specified by the min and max attributes, respectively. The step attribute indicates a jump in the number when the number is incremented or decremented. The following markup shows how to use these three attributes to restrict a user's age to a range from 18 to 100:

```
<input type="number" min="18" max="100" step="2" />
```

Figure 5-4 shows the error message that's displayed if you try to exceed the maximum value.

By default, using the number input type allows you to enter only integers. If you wish to enter decimals, you need to specify an appropriate step value as follows:

```
<input type="number" min="10" max="50" step="0.5" />
```

■ **Note** The min, max, and step attributes work with these input types: number, range, date, datetime, datetime-local, month, time, and week.

To mark an input field as a telephone number, you use the tel type. But currently, browsers don't impose any special validations on the tel input type, and hence it acts more like a marker. You can use this information to perform custom JavaScript validations. Listing 5-7 shows how.

Listing 5-7. Custom Validation for the tel Input Type

```
$("#form1").submit(function (e) {
  var flag = false;
  $("input[type='tel']").each(function (i,v) {
    var pattern = /^(\([0-9]{3}\)|[0-9]{3}-)[0-9]{3}-[0-9]{4}$/;
    var value = $(this).val();
    if (!pattern.test(value)) {
      alert("Telephone no. is invalid!");
      flag = true;
    }
  });
  if (flag) {
    e.preventDefault();
  }
});
```

The code shown in Listing 5-7 shows a jQuery `submit()` function that handles the form's `submit` event. The `submit` event is raised when a form is submitted either using a Submit button or programmatically. The `submit` event handler function declares a flag variable that indicates whether the entered telephone number matches a certain pattern.

A jQuery attribute selector then selects all the input elements with the `type` attribute set to `tel`. The jQuery `each()` method checks each matched element against a regular expression, as indicated by the pattern variable. The regular expression's `test()` method returns `true` if a value specified in the parameter matches the pattern; otherwise it returns `false`. If the `test()` method returns `false`, an error message is displayed to the user using an alert box. Setting the flag variable to `true` indicates a validation error. The default action (form submission, in this case) is prevented using the `preventDefault()` method.

Range Selectors

At times, you need to select (rather than enter) values falling within a specific range. Recollect the custom video player you developed in Chapter 3: you provided the facility to change the player's volume. In such cases it isn't appropriate to expect the user to enter a volume level. Instead, it's better to let them select a volume level from a range. The following markup shows how you can use the `range` input type:

```
<input id="range1" type="range" min="1" max="5" step="1"  />
```

Attributes such as `min`, `max`, and `step` have the same significance as for the `number` input type (`min` and `max` control the control's minimum and maximum allowed values, and `step` controls the jump in the value). Figure 5-5 shows how the previous range selector is displayed in Chrome.

Figure 5-5. *Range selector in Chrome*

The resulting range selector has a minimum value of 1, a maximum value of 5, and a step of 1.

Dates and Times

Another commonly used data type in web applications is date and/or time. In ASP.NET Web Forms, the `Calendar` server control lets you pick dates. However, the biggest downside of `Calendar` is that it requires a post back when a date is selected. No wonder ASP.NET developers often used JavaScript-based pop-up date-time pickers in their web applications. It would be better if the browser itself could display a date-time picker, and that's where the `date` and `time` input types come into the picture. Using these input types, you can select a date, a time, or both. The user can also select a complete week or month rather than a specific day or time.

■ **Note**   As of this writing, Opera is the only browser that displays a pop-up date-time picker for the date and time input types. Chrome displays a pop-up date picker only when the input type is date; it renders a plain text box for other date and time types. Also, there is a difference in the display format for date. Opera, for example, displays dates in *yyyy-MM-dd* format, whereas Chrome displays them as per machine date format.

Listing 5-8 shows all the available date-time input types.

Listing 5-8. *Date and Time Input Types*

```
<input id="dt1" type="date" />
<input id="dt2" type="time" />
<input id="dt3" type="datetime" />
<input id="dt4" type="datetime-local" />
<input id="dt5" type="week" />
<input id="dt6" type="month" />
```

The six date-time input types allow you to accept date, time, date and time, local date and time, week, and month, respectively. The dates are displayed in *yyyy-MM-dd* format, whereas times are displayed in *hh:mm:ss* format. For weeks and months, the format is *yyyy-Www* and *yyyy-MM*, respectively. Figure 5-6 shows how Opera displays these date-time input types.

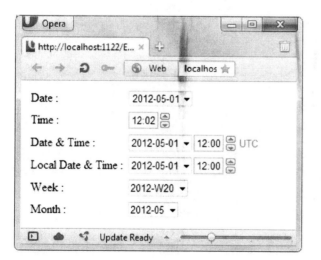

Figure 5-6. *Opera showing date-time input types*

If you click the down arrow of the date input type displayed in Figure 5-6, a pop-up date picker is displayed (see Figure 5-7).

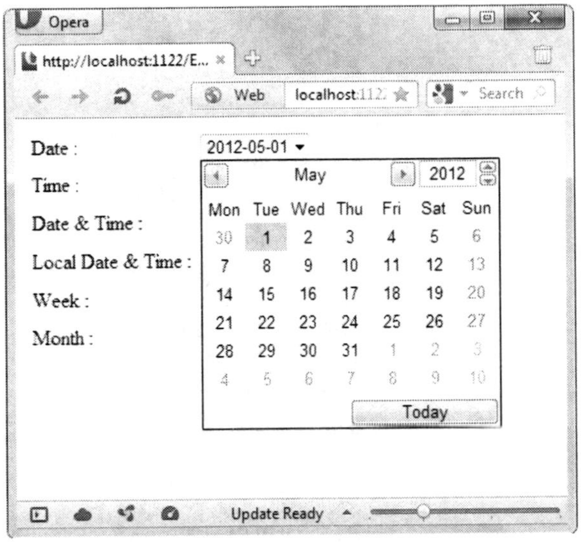

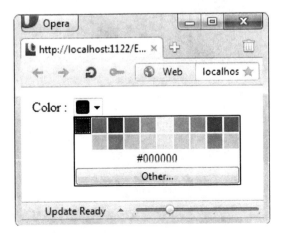

Figure 5-7. Opera showing a pop-up calendar

Note that you can also use the min and max attributes for dates to restrict the date selection to a particular date range.

Colors

An input type of color allows you to specify a color value. Recollect the pie chart canvas application you developed in Chapter 4. In that case, you specified sector colors in a plain text box. If your browser supports the color input type, it can prompt you with a color picker, making your job easy. Figure 5-8 shows how Opera displays a color input type.

Figure 5-8. Color picker in Opera

Using the `color` input type is just a matter of setting the type attribute of an `<input>` element to `color`, as shown here:

```
<input id="color1" type="color" />
```

Once the user selects a color, the value of the `<input>` field returns the corresponding hexadecimal color code. For example, selecting a white color returns `#ffffff`. By default, the color picker defaults to black (`#000000`).

Search

The `search` input type is intended to be used for search boxes. Currently, browsers don't provide anything special for the `search` input type except a few display changes. For example, Chrome displays a cross (X) as you start typing in the search box (see Figure 5-9). Clicking the X clears the search box.

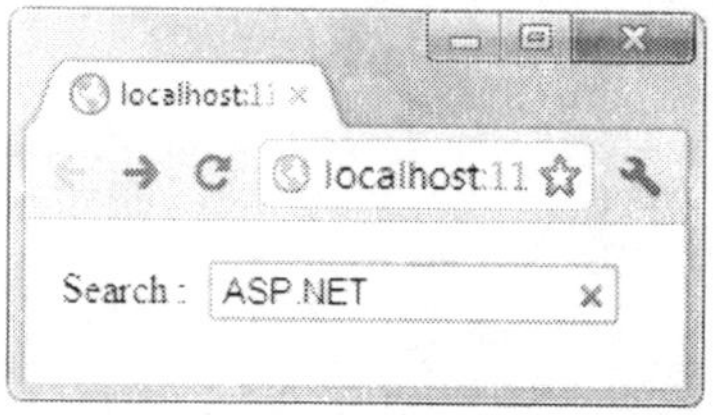

Figure 5-9. Search input type in Chrome

Now that you know what new input types are available and how to use them in a web page, it's time to see how you can use these input types in Web Forms and MVC views.

Using the New Input Types in Web Forms

In ASP.NET 4.5, you can set the `TextMode` property of a `TextBox` server control to the required input type. Prior to ASP.NET 4.5, the `TextMode` property took only two values: `SingleLine` and `MultiLine`. In ASP.NET 4.5, however, all the new input types are supported, as is evident in Figure 5-10.

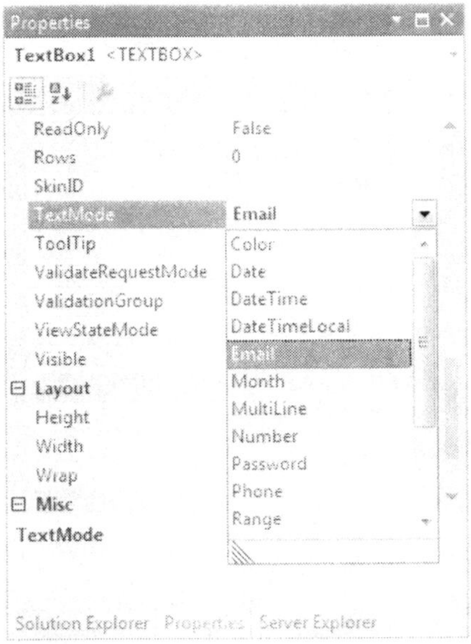

Figure 5-10. The TextMode *property supports the new input types.*

At runtime, the ASP.NET framework converts the TextMode setting to the appropriate input type attribute. Note that you can also set the type attribute directly in the <asp:TextBox> markup tag to get the same effect. However, the recommended way is to set the TextMode property. Of course, nothing prevents you from using a plain HTML5 <input> tag with the required setting for its type attribute. But if you wish to access the text box from the server-side code, then chances are you should use the TextBox server control.

If you wish to set attributes such as min, max, and step, you need add them directly to the <asp:TextBox> markup tag as shown here:

```
<asp:TextBox ID="TextBox1" runat="server" TextMode="Number"
min="18" max="100" step="2">
</asp:TextBox>
```

■ **Note**   If you're using Visual Studio 2010, you may need to install the latest Service Pack to be able to use the new input types.

Using the New Input Types in MVC Views

In MVC views, things are bit easier when it comes to using the new HTML5 input types. Because MVC views rely directly on the HTML markup rather than server controls, you can easily use <input> tags as discussed earlier. If you prefer to use HTML helpers instead of raw HTML markup, you can use the new input types as follows:

```
<%= Html.TextBox("txtNumber","18",new {type="number",min="18",max="100"}) %>
```

As you can see, the TextBox helper takes three parameters: the name of the resulting <input> element, its default value, and an object representing additional HTML attributes that need to be added to the element. In this example, you set the type, min, and max attributes.

131

If your views are strongly typed against some model, you can use TextBoxFor() instead of TextBox(), as follows:

```
<%= Html.TextBoxFor(m => m.Age, new {type="number",min="18",max="100"}) %>
```

In this line of code, the model is assumed to have a property named Age. The Age property is displayed in a text box that is of type number. The min and max attributes of the text box are set to 18 and 100, respectively.

Other Validation Attributes

In the preceding sections, you learned about HTML5 input types that let you validate the format of the data being entered. Beyond the input types, HTML5 adds several other attributes for controlling a few other aspects of the validation process. This section discusses these techniques.

Dealing with Required Fields

Many data-entry forms expect a value to be entered in one or more text boxes. To enforce this requirement, ASP.NET developers often use the RequiredFieldValidator control. HTML5 includes an easy alternative to indicate mandatory data-entry fields. Consider the following markup:

```
<input id="firstName" type="text" name="firstName" required="required"/>
```

Notice the required attribute at the end of the <input> element. This is the HTML5 way to indicate that a given field is mandatory. If you don't supply any value for the firstName text box, the browser shows an error message and refuses to submit the form even if you haven't written any validation script. Figure 5-11 shows how Chrome throws an error message.

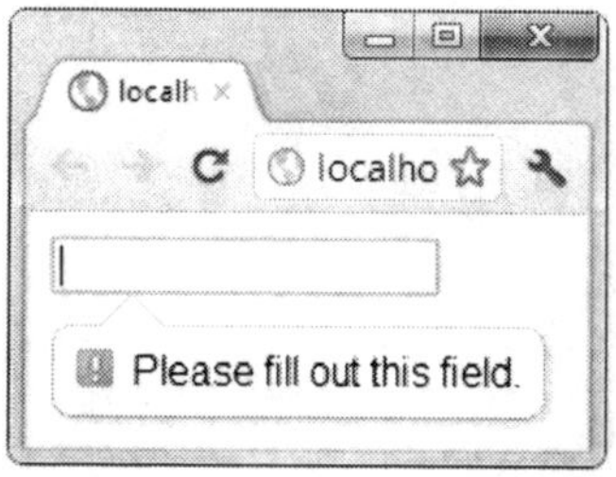

Figure 5-11. Using the required attribute

As you can see, trying to submit the form without entering a value in the text box generates an error prompting the user to fill out the field.

Pattern-Matching Using Regular Expressions

The new HTML5 input types allow you to validate a few commonly used data formats. However, at times you need to validate something more complex. A common way to validate such complex formats is regular expressions. HTML5 also relies on them for performing custom pattern-matching operations. Let's see how.

Suppose you wish to accept the user's first name. A name can contain only the letters *A* to *Z* in uppercase or lowercase. The HTML5 `<input>` element provides a `pattern` attribute that takes any valid regular expression and validates an inputted value against it. If the inputted value doesn't match the pattern specified by the regular expression, an error is shown. The following line of markup shows how to use the `pattern` attribute:

```
<input id="firstName" type="text" name="firstName" pattern="^\s*([a-zA-Z]+)\s*$"
required="required" />
```

The `pattern` attribute of this `<input>` tag is set to a regular expression that allows only alphabetic characters in the text box. If you try to enter a number as a first name, you get an error, as shown in Figure 5-12.

Figure 5-12. *Validating data using the* pattern *attribute*

Entering numeric data in the input field generates an error because the regular expression allows only alphabetic characters. The default error message leaves the user clueless about what exact format is expected or what went wrong; later, you learn to customize the error message displayed by the browser.

Turning HTML5 Validations On and Off

When you use the new input types and related validation techniques, your form is validated before it's submitted to the server. However, at times you may want to skip the form validation altogether. During the testing phase, you may want to test your server-side validations, and you may want to disable HTML5 validations temporarily. In certain cases, it might be all right to submit a form without performing any validations. For example, let's say you have a Cancel button or a Help button on a form. Because actions indicated by these buttons don't rely on the data, you can safely bypass the validations.

You can turn off the HTML5 validations at two distinct places:

- At the `<form>` tag level
- At the Submit button level

The former approach is good during the testing phase, and the latter approach is suitable for cases where a form needs to be submitted regardless of the control values.

To turn off the validations at the form level, HTML5 offers the `novalidate` attribute. At the Submit button level, the HTML5 `formnovalidate` attribute does the job. The following fragment of markup shows how to use both of these attributes:

```
<form id="form1" method="post" novalidate="novalidate"></form>
<input type="submit" formnovalidate="formnovalidate" />
```

The `<form>` element has the `novalidate` attribute set to `novalidate`. If you submit this form, no validations are performed on the input data based on input types or pattern.

The Submit button has the `formnovalidate` attribute set to `formnovalidate`. This has the same effect as the `novalidate` attribute.

Performing Custom Validations

In spite of the fact that HTML5 input types along with required and pattern attributes let you validate data, real-world web applications often still call for complex validations. In particular, validations that involve validating against data residing in a database are beyond the reach of the techniques discussed so far. Luckily, HTML5 also offers a technique you can use to perform such custom validations. It involves two steps:

1. Write a custom JavaScript function that performs the custom validation.

2. If the validation fails, call the `setCustomValidity()` method on the input field to inform the browser about the error.

Step 2 is your chance to supply a custom error message to the browser so the browser can pop it whenever validation fails. To understand how these steps work, look at Listing 5-9.

Listing 5-9. Custom Validation Function

```
$(document).ready(function () {
  $("#btnSubmit").click(OnSubmit);
});
function OnSubmit(evt) {
  $.ajax({
      url: '/home/ValidateCustomerID',
      type:'post',
      data: { id: $("#txtCustId").val() },
      dataType: 'json',
      async:false,
      success: function (result) {
        var textbox = $("#txtCustId").get(0);
        if (result == false) {
          textbox.setCustomValidity("Customer ID was not found in the database!");
        }
        else {
          textbox.setCustomValidity("");
        }
      }
    });
}
```

Listing 5-9 shows the `click` event handler of a Submit button. This event handler invokes a controller action named `ValidateCustomerID()` using `$.ajax()` and passes a customer ID entered in a text box (`txtCustId`). The `ValidateCustomerID()` action return `true` if the supplied customer ID is found in the `Customers` table of the `Northwind` database; otherwise it returns `false`. Notice the `success` function of the `$.ajax()` call: if a customer ID isn't found in the database, the `setCustomValidity()` method is called on the text box along with a custom error message. This error message is displayed to the user when the form is submitted. If a customer ID is found, setCustomValidity() method is called with an empty string indicating that there is no validation error. The ValidateCustomerID() action is shown in Listing 5-10.

Listing 5-10. ValidateCustomerID() Action Method

```
public JsonResult ValidateCustomerID(string id)
{
    NorthwindEntities db = new NorthwindEntities();
    var data = from item in db.Customers
               where item.CustomerID == id
               select item;
    if (data.Count() <= 0)
    {
        return Json(false);
    }
    else
    {
        return Json(true);
    }
}
```

The ValidateCustomerID() action uses the Entity Framework data model for the Northwind database to determine whether a CustomerID value exists in the database. Accordingly, a true or false flag is returned as JsonResult. Figure 5-13 shows a sample run of the view with an invalid customer ID.

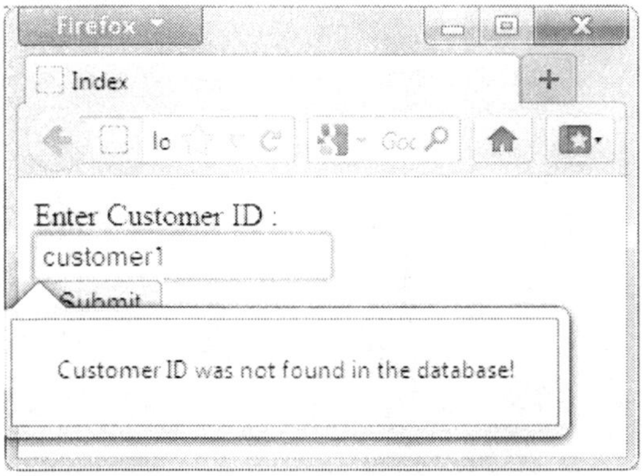

Figure 5-13. setCustomValidity() method in action

Notice an interesting thing about Listing 5-9: the $.ajax() call specifies an async option value of false. By default, $.ajax() makes an asynchronous request to the server. However, with this default behavior, the Submit button submits the form without waiting for ValidateCustomerID() to return. With the async option set to false, $.ajax() makes a synchronous request to the server rather than asynchronous, and the OnSubmit event handler waits for the ValidateCustomerID() method to complete.

HTML5 Input Types and ASP.NET Validation Techniques

Although the new HTML5 input types are great additions to the HTML markup, at times you need to mix HTML5 native validation techniques and ASP.NET validation techniques. ASP.NET Web Forms and

ASP.NET MVC provide good support for validation through server controls and HTML helpers, respectively. It's worthwhile to examine how these validation techniques fit in with HTML5. The following sections discuss various combinations in which HTML5 validation techniques can go hand in hand with ASP.NET built-in techniques.

HTML5 Input Types and Validation Controls

ASP.NET Web Forms provide validation controls for performing a common set of validation tasks. These validation controls emit client-side JavaScript that performs the job of validating the data. More important, you can use them along with the HTML5 input types. The validation controls as well as the HTML5 input types perform the validation when a form is submitted. If a text box has `TextMode` set to `Email` and also has a `RegularExpressionValidator` attached (see Listing 5-11), both schemes display an error message when a form is submitted.

Listing 5-11. Using TextMode and RegularExpressionValidator Together

```
<asp:TextBox ID="TextBox3" runat="server" TextMode="Email"></asp:TextBox>

<asp:RequiredFieldValidator ID="RequiredFieldValidator3" runat="server"
ControlToValidate="TextBox3" ErrorMessage="Please enter email address"
ForeColor="Red">*</asp:RequiredFieldValidator>

<asp:RegularExpressionValidator ID="RegularExpressionValidator1" runat="server"
ErrorMessage="Invalid email address" ForeColor="Red"
ValidationExpression="\w+([-+.']\w+)*@\w+([-.]\w+)*\.\w+([-.]\w+)*"
ControlToValidate="TextBox3">*</asp:RegularExpressionValidator>
```

Figure 5-14 shows how this works at runtime.

Figure 5-14. Validation controls and HTML5 input types used together

You might wonder why you would use validation controls and HTML5 input types together. Because HTML5 input types aren't supported on all browsers, you need to use validation controls as a fallback mechanism. So, in all you have the following options:

- Use only HTML5-specific input types and validation attributes. This approach works if the target browser supports the HTML5 input types; otherwise no validations are performed.

- Use a combination of HTML5 validation techniques and ASP.NET validation controls. This approach ensures that validations work in all browsers, but there may be some redundancy in the error messages as discussed earlier.

- Use a combination of HTML5 validation techniques and ASP.NET validation controls with client-side validation turned off. In this case, if the target browser supports HTML5, the HTML5 validation techniques execute; otherwise the form is posted back to the server, and validation controls validate the data. Of course, in the latter case, there is an overhead of the extra round trip to the server.

HTML5 Input Types and Server-Side Validations in an MVC Application

One way to combine HTML5's new validation techniques with ASP.NET MVC is to use HTML5 to provide client-side validation while using ASP.NET MVC to provide server-side validation in the controller. In this example, you validate first name, last name, and e-mail values using the MVC ValidationMessage and ValidationSummary HTML helpers. Listing 5-12 shows a view that renders a simple form with three fields: FirstName, LastName, and Email.

Listing 5-12. Validation Helpers and HTML5 Input Types in an MVC Application

```
<% using (Html.BeginForm()) { %>
<table cellpadding="3" cellspacing="0" class="style1">
    <tr>
        <td nowrap="nowrap" width="5%">
            <%= Html.Label("First Name :")%>
        </td>
        <td width="50%">
            <%= Html.TextBox("FirstName", "", new {required="required"})%>
            <%= Html.ValidationMessage("FirstName","*")%>
        </td>
    </tr>
    <tr>
        <td nowrap="nowrap" width="5%">
            <%= Html.Label("Last Name :")%>
        </td>
        <td width="50%">
            <%= Html.TextBox("LastName", "", new {required="required"})%>
            <%= Html.ValidationMessage("LastName","*")%>
        </td>
    </tr>
    <tr>
        <td nowrap="nowrap" width="5%">
```

```
                    <%= Html.Label("Email Address :")%>
            </td>
            <td width="50%">
                <%= Html.TextBox("Email", "", new {type="email"})%>
                <%= Html.ValidationMessage("Email","*")%>
            </td>
        </tr>
</table>
<input id="Submit1" type="submit" value="Submit" />
<%= Html.ValidationSummary() %>
<%}%>
```

As you can see, the Email text box has its type set to email. Also notice how the ValidationMessage and ValidationSummary MVC HTML helpers display validation errors. The HTML5 validations happen right in the browser. However, the MVC validations are performed in a controller, as shown in Listing 5-13.

Listing 5-13. Performing Validations in a Controller

```
[HttpPost]
public ActionResult Index(FormCollection form)
{
  if (form["FirstName"].Length < 3 || form["firstname"].Length > 50)
  {
      ModelState.AddModelError("FirstName",
        "Invalid First Name. Must be between 3 and 50 characters.");
  }
  if (form["LastName"].Length < 3 || form["LastName"].Length > 50)
  {
      ModelState.AddModelError("LastName",
        "Invalid Last Name. Must be between 3 and 50 characters.");
  }
  if (form["Email"].Length <= 0)
  {
      ModelState.AddModelError("Email", "Please enter Email Address.");
  }
  if(!Regex.IsMatch(form["Email"],@"\w+([-+.']\w+)*@\w+([-.]\w+)*\.\w+([-.]\w+)*"))
  {
      ModelState.AddModelError("Email", "Invalid Email Address.");
  }
  return View();
}
```

As you can see, the Index() action method performs validation on the form data and accordingly adds error messages in the ModelState. The validation helpers display these model errors in the browser (see Figure 5-15).

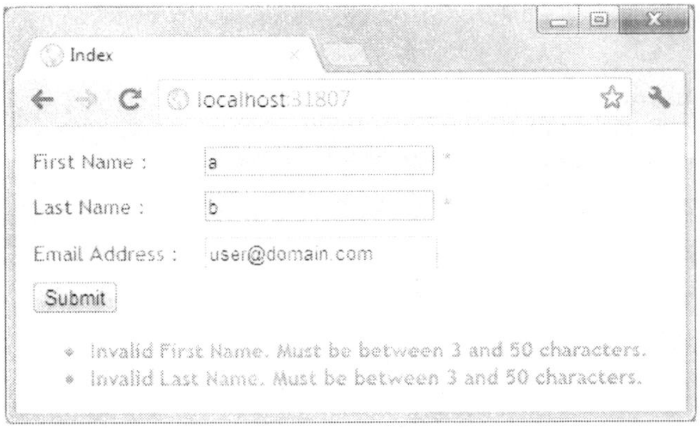

Figure 5-15. Validations in an MVC controller

When you have validation logic at the client side as well as the server side, the client-side validations are performed prior to submitting the form. In this example, the HTML5 validations are performed first, and only then is the form submitted. Once the control reaches the Index() action method. the server-side validations are performed.

HTML5 Input Types and Unobstructive Validation

Unobstructive validation is a technique implemented by ASP.NET that uses data-annotation attributes and jQuery. Under this scheme, a data model is decorated with data-annotation attributes that perform validations on the data model property values. At runtime, ASP.NET emits data-* attributes, a feature of HTML5. ASP.NET performs client-side validations with the help of these emitted data-* attributes and jQuery.

The data-* attributes are custom attributes and are just like any other built-in HTML attributes in terms of usage syntax. However, they differ from built-in HTML attributes in that they don't play any role in the visual rendering of the element. ASP.NET 4.5 Web Forms as well as MVC applications support unobstructive validation. I don't discuss the unobstructive validation scheme any further; suffice to say that you can use unobstructive validation along with HTML5 validation techniques if required.

■ **Note**   The data-* attributes are a feature of HTML5. You learn to use them in Chapter 6.

Customizing Validation Messages

So far, you've relied on the browser to display HTML5 validation messages. No doubt browsers supporting HTML5 validations do a good job of displaying validation messages neatly. However, you may want to customize them further. For example, you may want the error message font and color to match your web page theme, or you may want to give a strong highlight to any input control that violates the validation rules. HTML5 offers two ways to accomplish such customizations:

- Use CSS pseudo-classes to customize the appearance of an input field that violates a validation rule.

- Use JavaScript/jQuery code to customize the way validation messages for input fields are displayed.

The former technique is suitable in situations where you wish to customize the appearance of an input field and you aren't interested in changing the way validation messages are displayed. The latter approach gives you total control over how and where validation messages are displayed. It involves handling the input field's invalid event and writing custom logic to display validation messages.

Customizing the Appearance of an Input Field Using CSS Pseudo-Classes

Whenever there is a validation error, the browser pops up a callout that displays the validation error message (see Figure 5-2). Although browsers don't allow you to customize the appearance of the validation message callout, you can customize how an input field looks when a validation rule is broken. The trick is to write specific CSS pseudo-classes.

■ **Note** A CSS *pseudo-class* is a class that is applied to elements based on their state. For example, an anchor (<a>) tag has pseudo-classes link, visited, hover, and active, which represent the corresponding state of a hyperlink. The CSS pseudo-classes discussed in this section come from the CSS3 specification.

Table 5-2 lists the pseudo-classes you can use with HTML5 validations.

Table 5-2. Pseudo-Classes for Customizing Input Fields

Pseudo-Class	Description
valid	Applies to input elements that contain valid values.
invalid	Applies to input elements that contain invalid values.
in-range	Applies to input elements whose value is between the min and max values.
out-of-range	Applies to input elements whose value is outside the min and max limits.
required	Applies to input elements that are marked as required.
optional	Applies to input elements that aren't marked as required.

Listing 5-14 uses many of the CSS pseudo-classes mentioned in Table 5-2 to customize the appearance of input fields in the event of validation errors.

Listing 5-14. Sample Pseudo-Classes to Customize Input Fields

```
input:invalid {
  background-color: #ffd800;
  border: 2px solid #f00;
}
input:required {
  background-color: #ffd800;
  border: 2px solid #f00;
}
input:out-of-range {
```

```
  color: #fff;
  background-color: #242a59;
  border: 2px solid #f00;
}
```

Figure 5-16 shows a sample run of a web page with some invalid data.

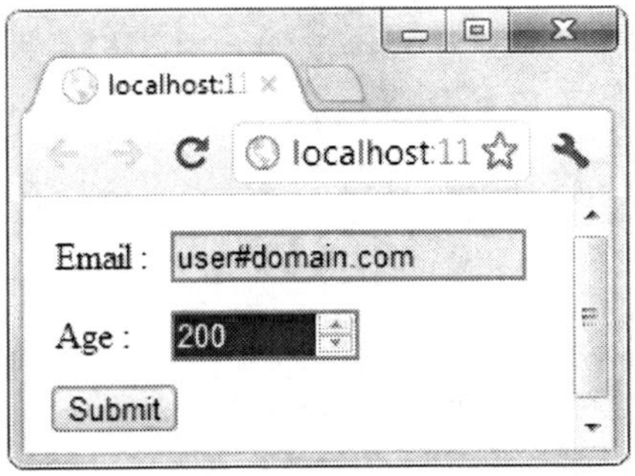

Figure 5-16. Validation pseudo-classes in action

Notice how the Email text box picks up the input:invalid class because the field's value doesn't meet the format of a valid e-mail address. Along the same lines, the Age text box picks up the input:out-of-range class when the age exceeds a maximum limit.

Customizing Validation Messages Through Code

After performing validations, the HTML DOM raises an invalid event for all input fields that violate validation rules. You can trap the invalid event and write custom code to suppress the default validation messages and display your own. In the invalid event handler, you can use the ValidityState object to find out more about the error. Listing 5-15 shows how this can be accomplished.

Listing 5-15. Handling the invalid Event

```
$(document).ready(function () {
  $("#txtEmail").bind("invalid", OnInvalid);
  $("#txtAge").bind("invalid", OnInvalid);
});

function OnInvalid(evt) {
  var input = evt.target;
  var validity = input.validity;

  if (validity.typeMismatch) {
    alert("Invalid email address");
  }
  if (validity.rangeOverflow) {
    alert("Age value too big");
  }
  if (validity.rangeUnderflow) {
```

```
      alert("Age value too small");
   }
   evt.preventDefault();
}
```

As you can see, the jQuery bind() method binds the invalid event handler for the two <input> fields. The OnInvalid() function gets the ValidityState object via the validity property of the input field. The ValidityState object provides several pieces of information about the current validity status of an input field. Table 5-3 lists the properties of the ValidityState object that can be used.

Table 5-3. ValidityState Properties

Property	Description
customError	Returns true if validation is performed via custom error techniques.
patternMismatch	Returns true if a control has a pattern attribute set and the control value doesn't match the pattern.
rangeOverflow	Returns true if an input type contains a value smaller than the max value.
rangeUnderflow	Returns true if an input type contains a value smaller than the min value.
stepMismatch	Returns true if an input type contains a value not in accordance with the step value.
tooLong	Returns true if data entered in a control exceeds its maxLength value.
typeMismatch	Returns true if a control contains data not that doesn't matching the required format (e.g. emaile-mail, URLs, number, and so on etc.)
valid	Returns true if a control contains valid value, or false otherwise.
valueMissing	Returns true if a control marked as "required" doesn't contain any input.

The code then displays an alert box with a customized validation message. The browser's default validation message is suppressed by calling the event object's preventDefault() method. If you don't prevent the default action using a preventDefault() call in addition to your alert box, the browser's validation error message callout is also displayed, which is unnecessary in most cases.

Figure 5-17 show a sample run of the code.

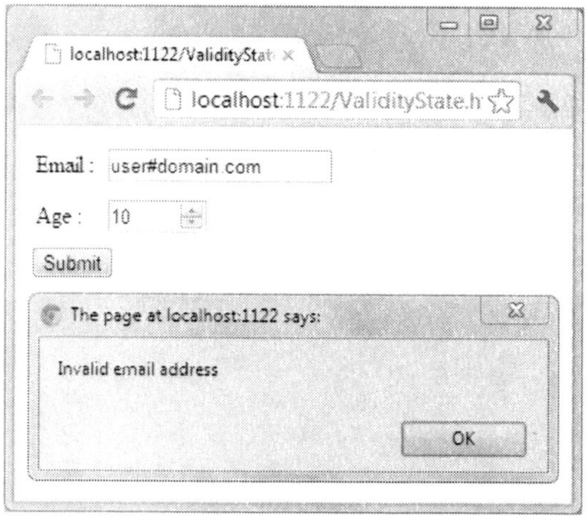

Figure 5-17. Customized validation message from the invalid event handler

As you can see, entering an invalid e-mail address and clicking the Submit button displays the validation error message in an alert box instead of the browser's default callout.

Other Improvements to the <input> Element

In the preceding sections, you learned about the new input types available in HTML5. HTML5 also enhances the <input> element with some features:

- Setting focus to a field when a form is loaded
- Displaying hint or help text using placeholders
- Spellchecking the entered text
- Turning browser autocomplete on or off
- Providing a drop-down list for an input field

These enhancements are discussed in the following sections.

Setting Autofocus

When a web page loads in the browser, it's a good idea to set the initial focus to a data-entry field that the user is supposed to fill out. You can indicate that an input field should receive focus using the autofocus attribute. The following markup shows how:

```
<input id="firstName" type="text" name="firstName" autofocus="autofocus"
  required="required"/>
```

This line of markup declares a text input field that has its autofocus attribute set to autofocus. When you open the web page in the browser, the firstName text box gets focus.

Displaying Help Text Using Placeholders

While filling out fields such as e-mail addresses, URLs, dates, and telephone numbers, it's a recommended practice to let the user know the format in which the data is to be entered. One way to do this is to simply place explanatory text in front of the data-entry field. The downside of this approach is that the label occupies extra screen space. HTML5 placeholders provide an elegant way to add hint or help text to an input control.

A placeholder is displayed as a watermark and is removed as soon as the user starts filling the field. You specify a placeholder using placeholder attribute of the <input> element. The following line of markup adds a placeholder that tells a user how to format a telephone number:

```
<input id="telephone" type="tel" placeholder="(123) 123-1234"/>
```

Figure 5-18 shows how this placeholder looks at runtime.

As you can see, the input field displays the placeholder as specified in the placeholder attribute. As soon as you start typing the telephone number, the placeholder text disappears. If the input field is emptied, the placeholder appears again.

Figure 5-18. Displaying a placeholder

Enabling Spell-Check

If your form accepts free-form text input from the user, you may want to enable spell-check on the content. Suppose, for example, that you're developing a blog engine that allows users to post and edit articles. It would be nice to enable spell-check for the content. This way, users can trap spelling errors easily. The `spellcheck` attribute does this job for you. Here is how you use it:

```
<textarea id="textarea1" rows="5" cols="50" spellcheck="true"></textarea>
```

The `spellcheck` attribute is a Boolean and can be set to `true` or `false`. If it's set to `true`, the `<textarea>` (or `<input>`) highlights spelling errors as shown in Figure 5-19.

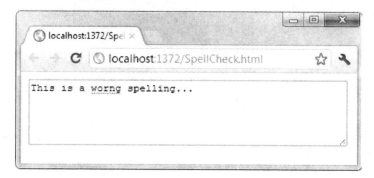

Figure 5-19. Enabling spell-check for a `<textarea>`

Notice how an incorrect spelling is highlighted with a red underline.

Turning Off Autocomplete

Most browsers try to help users fill data-entry forms with the help of the autocomplete feature. This feature lets users pick a value from a list instead of typing the entire value. At times, however, you may want to disable this feature for an input field. The `autocomplete` attribute allows you to do just that. The following markup shows how it's used:

```
<input id="firstName" type="text" autocomplete="off"/>
```

Of course, you can set `autocomplete` to on to explicitly turn on the feature. You can also turn autocomplete on or off for the entire form by adding the `autocomplete` attribute to the `<form>` tag instead of the individual `<input>` tag:

```
<form id="form1" autocomplete="off"></form>
```

If you set the autocomplete attribute of the <form> tag, autocomplete is disabled for all input fields belonging to that form.

Providing a Drop-Down List

At times, you want to let the user either enter a value manually or pick it from a list. For desktop applications, the combo box control is often used for such functionality. Suppose you're developing an order-entry page where customer details are provided. If an order is being placed by an existing customer, it's helpful to let the user choose existing details from a list rather than enter them again. You can provide such a list using a combination of the list attributes of the <input> and <datalist> element. Listing 5-16 shows how this can be accomplished.

Listing 5-16. Providing a Drop-Down List

```
<input id="country" type="text" list="pickuplist1" />
<datalist id="pickuplist1">
  <option label="India" value="India"></option>
  <option label="USA" value="USA"></option>
  <option label="UK" value="UK"></option>
</datalist>
```

As you can see, the <datalist> element essentially provides a list of key-value pairs. The value attribute governs what should be filled in the target text box when a selection is made. The label attribute acts as a description for the corresponding value. The <input> element's list attribute is set to the ID of the <datalist>. At runtime, a list is displayed as shown in Figure 5-20.

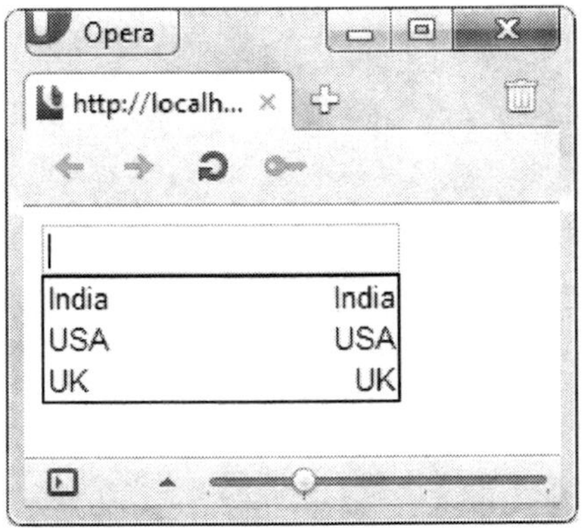

Figure 5-20. Drop-down list for an input field

The column at left in the drop-down list shows values as indicated in the value attribute, and the column on the right displays values specified by the label attribute.

Setting a Form's Action and Method

Normally, the <form> tag has action and method attributes to indicate the form action and HTTP method (GET/POST), respectively. In some cases, you may want to change these settings for individual Submit

145

buttons. You can do so using the `formaction` and `formmethod` attributes of the `<input>` element. Listing 5-17 shows how.

Listing 5-17. *Setting a Form's Action and Method Using the `<input>` Tag*

```
<form action="/Home/Index" method="get">
  <input id="btnSubmit" type="submit" value="Submit"
    formaction="/Home/Index2"
    formmethod="post" />
</form>
```

The `<form>` tag's `action` attribute is set to /Home/Index, and its `method` attribute is set to get. You override these defaults through the `<input>` tag by setting the `formaction` attribute to /Home/Index2 and the `formmethod` attribute to post. Other Submit buttons on the form (if any) use the action and method as specified at the form level.

Designing an Employee Data Form

Now it's time to put your knowledge of HTML5 form features to use and develop a complete form that deals with data from a SQL Server database. In this section, you develop an ASP.NET Web Forms application that inserts data into, updates data in, and deletes data from the Employees table of Northwind database. The main form of the application is shown in Figure 5-21.

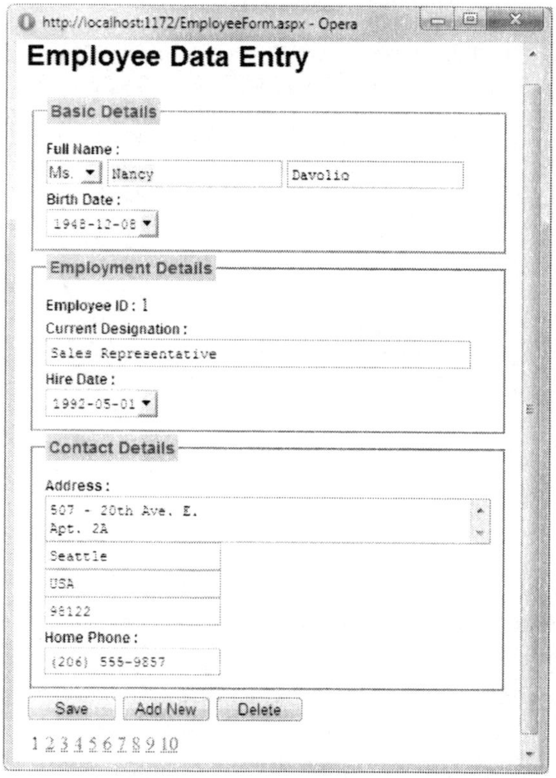

Figure 5-21. *Employee data form*

The form shown in Figure 5-21 doesn't update all the columns of the Employees table for the sake of simplicity. The Employee Data Entry form has the following validations and features:

- Columns FirstName, LastName, BirthDate, Title (Current Designation), HireDate, Address, City, Country, and PostalCode are mandatory fields, and they must be entered during data addition or modification.

- The legal age for employment is assumed to be 18, and hence there must be a difference of at least 18 years between BirthDate and HireDate.

- All the data-entry fields show a placeholder when empty.

- Current Designation can be entered manually or can be chosen from a list.

- PostalCode and HomePhone must match the pattern of US ZIP code and US telephone number, respectively.

Configuring the FormView Control

The form shown in Figure 5-21 is actually a FormView server control. Listing 5-18 shows the important properties of the FormView that need to be configured.

Listing 5-18. Properties of the FormView Control

```
<asp:FormView ID="FormView1" runat="server"
  AllowPaging="True"
  DefaultMode="Edit"
  DataKeyNames="EmployeeID"
  SelectMethod="GetEmployees"
  InsertMethod="InsertEmployee"
  UpdateMethod="UpdateEmployee"
  DeleteMethod="DeleteEmployee"
  ItemType="SampleAppWebForms.Model.Employee"
>
...
</asp:FormView>
```

By default, when the web form is shown in the browser, the FormView is in Edit mode so you can modify an employee record. You do so by setting the DefaultMode property to Edit.

Instead of relying on EntityDataSource control (or any other data source control), the FormView relies on custom methods to perform Create, Read, Update, and Delete (CRUD) operations. You can accomplish this by setting the four properties SelectMethod, InsertMethod, UpdateMethod, and DeleteMethod to appropriate methods. The GetEmployees(), InsertEmployee(), UpdateEmployee(), and DeleteEmployee() methods are written in the code-behind file of the web form and are discussed later.

The FormView templates are strongly typed to various properties of the Employee model. That is why the ItemType property is set to the fully qualified name of an Entity Framework data model class: Employee. The Employee model is discussed later along with the CRUD methods mentioned earlier.

Using HTML5 Input Types and Related Attributes

The FormView control uses EditItemTemplate and InsertItemTemplate to render the data-entry form's user interface in Edit and Insert mode, respectively. These templates are almost identical in terms of HTML and server control markup. Listing 5-19 shows `EditItemTemplate`. For the sake of readability, only the markup related to HTML5 validation techniques is shown.

Listing 5-19. *`EditItemTemplate` of the `FormView`*

```
<EditItemTemplate>
<fieldset>
  <legend>Basic Details</legend>
  <label for="FullName">Full Name :</label>
  <asp:DropDownList ... SelectedValue='<%# BindItem.TitleOfCourtesy %>'>
    ...
  </asp:DropDownList>
  <asp:TextBox ... required="required" Text="<%# BindItem.FirstName %>"
    PlaceHolder="First Name" autofocus="autofocus">...
  <asp:TextBox ... required="required" Text="<%# BindItem.LastName %>"
    PlaceHolder="Last Name">...
  <label for="txtBirthDate">Birth Date :</label>
  <asp:TextBox ... TextMode="Date" Text="<%# BindItem.BirthDate %>"
    required="required" PlaceHolder="Birth Date" >...
</fieldset>
<fieldset>
  <legend>Employment Details</legend>
  <label for="lblEmployeeID">Employee ID :</label>
  <asp:Label ... Text="<%# BindItem.EmployeeID %>">...
  <label for="txtDesig">Current Designation :</label>
  <asp:TextBox ... required="required" Text="<%# BindItem.Title %>"
    PlaceHolder="Designation" list="lstTitles">...
  <datalist id="lstTitles"></datalist>
  <label for="txtHireDate">Hire Date :</label>
  <asp:TextBox ... TextMode="Date" Text='<%# BindItem.HireDate %>'
    required="required" PlaceHolder="Hire Date">...
</fieldset>
<fieldset>
  <legend>Contact Details</legend>
  <label for="address">Address :</label>
  <asp:TextBox ... required="required" Text="<%# BindItem.Address %>"
    PlaceHolder="Street Address">...
  <asp:TextBox ... required="required" Text='<%# BindItem.City %>'
    PlaceHolder="City" >...
  <asp:TextBox ... required="required" Text='<%# BindItem.Country %>'
    PlaceHolder="Country" >...
  <asp:TextBox ... pattern="\d{5}(-\d{4})?" Text='<%# BindItem.PostalCode %>'
    required="required" PlaceHolder="Postal Code" >...
  <label for="txtPhone">Home Phone :</label><br />
  <asp:TextBox ... TextMode="Phone" Text='<%# BindItem.HomePhone %>'
    PlaceHolder="(123) 123-1234" >...
</fieldset>
<asp:Button ... Text="Save" CommandName="Update" />
<asp:Button ... ID="btnNew" Text="Add New"
  CommandName="New" formnovalidate="formnovalidate" />
```

```
<asp:Button ... ID="btnDelete" Text="Delete"
  CommandName="Delete" formnovalidate="formnovalidate" />
</EditItemTemplate>
```

Look carefully at the markup shown in Listing 5-19. In all, there are three <fieldset> elements that represent the three sections of the form: Basic Details, Employment Details, and Contact Details. A <fieldset> element is used to group related elements. To indicate the grouping visually, the <fieldset> element also draws a box enclosing the grouped elements. Because this is an Edit mode template, you want changes made to any field to propagate back to the database. Hence, all fields except EmployeeID are bound with the data model using a BindItem object. EmployeeID is the primary key, so it's read-only and hence uses an Item object.

If you look at the <asp:TextBox> elements, you find that many of them use HTML5 input types and related attributes. The BirthDate and HireDate text boxes have their TextMode property set to Date. Similarly, HomePhone has a TextMode value of Phone. The PostalCode text box's pattern attribute is set to a regular expression that matches US ZIP codes. Note that you could use the pattern attribute for the HomePhone text box too, but instead the application validates the phone number via jQuery code.

A <datalist> displays the existing values as soon as a text box gets focus. The <datalist> is linked to the text box using the list attribute. The actual <datalist> items are filled at runtime using jQuery.

The required attribute is set for all text boxes that must be filled. In addition, they all have their Placeholder attribute set to some help text. The three Button server controls—btnUpdate, btnNew, and btnDelete—invoke the appropriate actions. Notice that the CommandName property of these button controls is set to Update, New, and Delete, respectively. This way, the FormView control triggers the appropriate method. Also note that btnNew and btnDelete have their formnovalidate attribute set because there is no need to perform data validation when you click these buttons.

Taking Care of Date Formatting

The BirthDate and HireDate text boxes have TextMode set to Date. As you learned earlier, the default date format for the HTML5 date input type is *yyyy-MM-dd*. However, the Employees table stores dates in *MM/dd/yyyy* format. To take care of this mismatch in the date formats, you need to handle the DataBound event of the FormView and convert dates from *MM/dd/yyyy* format to *yyyy-MM-dd* format. Listing 5-20 shows how to do this conversion.

Listing 5-20. *Converting Date Formats*

```
protected void FormView1_DataBound(object sender, EventArgs e)
{
    if(FormView1.CurrentMode == FormViewMode.Edit)
    {
        DateTime dtBirthDate= ((Employee)FormView1.DataItem).
                                        BirthDate.GetValueOrDefault();
        DateTime dtHireDate = ((Employee)FormView1.DataItem).
                                        HireDate.GetValueOrDefault();
        TextBox txtBirthDate= (TextBox)FormView1.FindControl("txtBirthDate");
        TextBox txtHireDate = (TextBox)FormView1.FindControl("txtHireDate");
        txtBirthDate.Text = dtBirthDate.ToString("yyyy-MM-dd");
        txtHireDate.Text = dtHireDate.ToString("yyyy-MM-dd");
    }
}
```

This code checks whether the `CurrentMode` of the `FormView` is `Edit` and, if so, grabs the `BirthDate` and `HireDate` values being bound. The `DataItem` object represents an `Employee` being bound with the `FormView`. The text boxes showing `BirthDate` and `HireDate` are found using the `FindControl()` method. Finally, the date values are filled in the text boxes using *yyyy-MM-dd* format.

Writing the CRUD Methods

The web form code-behind contains four methods that perform CRUD operations on the database. These methods are shown in Listing 5-21.

Listing 5-21. Methods Performing CRUD Operations

```
public IQueryable<Employee> GetEmployees()
{
    NorthwindEntities db = new NorthwindEntities();
    var data = from item in db.Employees
               orderby item.EmployeeID
               select item;
    return data;
}

public void InsertEmployee(Employee e)
{
    NorthwindEntities db = new NorthwindEntities();
    db.Employees.AddObject(e);
    db.SaveChanges();
}

public void UpdateEmployee(Employee e)
{
    NorthwindEntities db = new NorthwindEntities();
    var data = from item in db.Employees
               where item.EmployeeID == e.EmployeeID
               select item;

    Employee obj = data.SingleOrDefault();
    obj.TitleOfCourtesy = e.TitleOfCourtesy;
    obj.FirstName = e.FirstName;
    obj.LastName = e.LastName;
    obj.BirthDate = e.BirthDate;

    obj.Title = e.Title;
    obj.HireDate = e.HireDate;

    obj.Address = e.Address;
    obj.City = e.City;
    obj.Country = e.Country;
    obj.HomePhone = e.HomePhone;

    db.SaveChanges();
}
```

```
public void DeleteEmployee(Employee e)
{
    NorthwindEntities db = new NorthwindEntities();
    var data = from item in db.Employees
                where item.EmployeeID == e.EmployeeID
                select item;
    Employee obj = data.SingleOrDefault();
    db.DeleteObject(obj);
    db.SaveChanges();
}
```

These CRUD methods are straightforward. The `GetEmployees()` method returns a collection of `Employee` objects to the caller. The `InsertEmployee()`, `UpdateEmployee()`, and `DeleteEmployee()` methods receive an `Employee` object as a parameter. This `Employee` object is then inserted into, updated in, or deleted from the database. The `Employee` model class contains all the columns of the `Employees` table, but you aren't using all of them. Hence, `UpdateEmployee()` assigns individual properties of the `Employee` object. The `Employee` model class is shown in Figure 5-22.

Figure 5-22. Employee data model class

The application doesn't use all the properties of the `Employee` class. The properties of interest are `EmployeeID`, `TitleOfCourtesy`, `FirstName`, `LastName`, `BirthDate`, `Title`, `HireDate`, `Address`, `City`, `Country`, and `HomePhone`.

jQuery Code

The web form also needs some jQuery code that does the following:

- Populates <datalist> items by fetching existing Titles (designations) from the Employees table

- Validates that an employee is at least 18 years old at the time of hiring

- Validates that telephone numbers match the US phone number format

To populate the <datalist> items, you need to make an Ajax call to the server and retrieve all existing Title values. You do so using the $.ajax() method, as shown in Listing 5-22.

Listing 5-22. Populating the <datalist> with Existing Title Values

```
$(document).ready(function () {
  $.ajax({
    url: 'employeeform.aspx/GetTitles',
    type: 'post',
    dataType: 'json',
    contentType: "application/json; charset=utf-8",
    success: function (results) {
      for (var i = 0; i < results.d.length; i++) {
        $("#lstTitles").append("<option label='" + results.d[i] +
                                      "' value='" + results.d[i] + "'></option>");
      }
    },
    error: function (err) { alert(err.status + " - " + err.statusText); }
  });
...
```

The $.ajax() method invokes a web method, GetTitles(), that resides in the EmployeeForm.aspx web form. GetTitles() returns a string array of existing titles. Once the titles are returned, they're added to the <datalist> using the jQuery append() method. The GetTitles() web method is shown in Listing 5-23.

Listing 5-23. GetTitles() Web Method

```
[WebMethod]
public static string[] GetTitles()
{
    NorthwindEntities db=new NorthwindEntities();
    var data = (from item in db.Employees
                select item.Title).Distinct();
    return data.ToArray();
}
```

GetTitles() selects distinct Title values from the Employees table and returns them to the caller as an array. Figure 5-23 shows how the <datalist> looks at runtime.

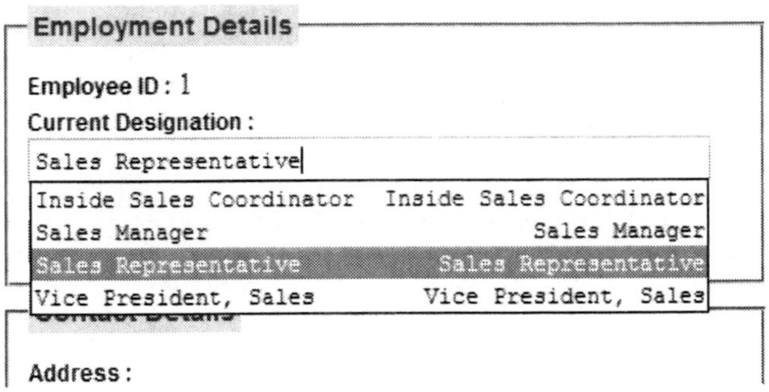

Figure 5-23. `<datalist>` populated using jQuery

In order to validate that an employee was at least 18 years old at the time of hiring, you need to find out the difference between BirthDate and HireDate. If this difference is greater than 18 years, the employee record can be added or updated. The HomePhone text box is of type tel (TextMode of Phone), and the telephone number entered should be a valid US telephone number. Both of these validations are performed when a record is added or updated. Listing 5-24 shows how this is done.

Listing 5-24. Validating the Age Requirement and Telephone Number Format

```
$("input[name$='btnUpdate']").click(function (e) {
  var birthDate = ToDate($("input[name$='txtBirthDate']").val());
  birthDate.setFullYear(birthDate.getFullYear() + 18);
  var hireDate = ToDate($("input[name$='txtHireDate']").val());
  var txtBirthDate = $("input[name$='txtBirthDate']").get(0);
  if ((hireDate.getTime() - birthDate.getTime()) < 0) {
    txtBirthDate.setCustomValidity("Invalid Birth Date or Hire Date!");
  }
  else {
    txtBirthDate.setCustomValidity("");
  }

  var pattern = /^\(?(\d{3})\)?[- ]?(\d{3})[- ]?(\d{4})$/;
  var value = $("input[name$='txtPhone']").val();
  var txtPhone = $("input[name$='txtPhone']").get(0);
  if (!pattern.test(value)) {
    txtPhone.setCustomValidity("Invalid Telephone Number!");
  }
  else {
    txtPhone.setCustomValidity("");
  }
});

function ToDate(input) {
  var parts = input.match(/(\d+)/g);
  return new Date(parts[0], parts[1] - 1, parts[2]);
}
```

A jQuery *attribute ends with* selector is used to select btnUpdate. This is necessary because the Update button is part of EditItemTemplate, and FormView assigns a unique name to the constituent controls (for example, FormView1$btnUpdate). The first block of code essentially calculates the difference between HireDate and BirthDate. If this difference is less than 0, it indicates that the age is less than 18. If so, a custom error message is added by calling the setCustomValidity() method on the BirthDate text box.

The second block of code validates the telephone number. It does so by matching the entered value against a regular expression. Notice the use of test(), which performs pattern matching. The test() method returns false if the value doesn't match the pattern. In that case, the setCustomValidity() method is called to set a custom validation message.

CSS Pseudo-Classes

Finally, you need to add a few pseudo-classes to highlight validation errors. These pseudo-classes are found in StyleSheet.css and are shown in Listing 5-25.

Listing 5-25. Pseudo-Classes for Validation Errors

```
input:invalid {
    background-color: #ffd800;
    border: 2px solid #f00;
}

input:required {
    background-color: #fff;
    border: 1px solid #ff6a00;
}
```

The invalid pseudo-class is applied to all invalid input fields, whereas the required pseudo-class is applied to all input fields for which the required attribute is set.

That's it! Figure 5-24 shows a sample run of the web form with a validation error.

Notice how the web form validates the Home Phone field upon form submission. Home Phone needs to be in the form (123) 123-1234. However, because the last part of the entered telephone number contains five digits rather than 4, the validation error is displayed.

Figure 5-24. Employee Data Entry form with a validation error

Designing a User Registration Form

In this section, you develop an ASP.NET MVC application that displays a User Registration page. Unlike the Employee Data Entry form you developed in the preceding section, the User Registration page performs validations on the client side as well as the server side. The client-side validations are performed using HTML5 features you learned about in this chapter, and the server-side validations use data annotation attributes. Further, the client-side validations are handled using the invalid event so that validation messages (client as well as server) are displayed in a consistent way. Figure 5-25 shows the User Registration page.

Figure 5-25. User Registration page

This page has the following validations and features:

- The Display Name, Email Address, Password, Confirm Password, and Legal Age fields must be completed.

- Duplicate display names and e-mail addresses aren't allowed.

- The e-mail address should be in the proper format.

- The Password and Confirm Password values must match.

- The blog URL must be in the proper format.

- Legal Age must be between 18 and 100.

- The Profile text area should have spell-check turned on.

- The Display Name, Email Address, Password, Blog/Website, and Profile fields have a minimum length and a maximum length.

All the features except the last are implemented through HTML5. The last set of validations is implemented on the server.

Entity Framework Data Model and Data Annotations

The example page stores user information in a SQL server table named Users. An Entity Framework data model is used to add user data in the Users table. Figure 5-26 shows the User model class.

Figure 5-26. User model class

To perform the server-side validations, you use data annotation attributes. Instead of decorating the User model class with the data annotations, it's a recommended practice to use a metadata class. A *metadata class* is a class that contains the data annotations for various properties of the main class. The metadata class is then associated with the main data model class. The advantage of using a metadata class is that it isolates validation-specific metadata in a separate class. This way, even if the User model class is regenerated for some reason, the data annotations won't be lost. The metadata class is shown in Listing 5-26.

Listing 5-26. UserMetadata Class

```
public class UserMetadata
{
    [Required]
    [StringLength(50,MinimumLength=3)]
    [DisplayName("Display Name")]
    public string DisplayName { get; set; }

    [Required]
    [StringLength(250, MinimumLength = 10)]
    [DisplayName("Email Address")]
    public string Email { get; set; }

    [Required]
```

```
        [StringLength(20, MinimumLength = 6)]
        public string Password { get; set; }

        [StringLength(50, MinimumLength = 10)]
        [DisplayName("Blog / Website")]
        public string BlogUrl { get; set; }

        [StringLength(500,ErrorMessage = "Bio size out of permissible limits.")]
        [DisplayName("Profile")]
        public string Bio { get; set; }

        [Required]
        [DisplayName("Legal Age")]
        public string Age { get; set; }

        [Required]
        [DisplayName("Yearly Income")]
        public string Income { get; set; }
}

[MetadataType(typeof(UserMetadata))]
public partial class User
{
}
```

As you can see, the UserMetadata class contains property definitions matching the User model class. The properties are then decorated with data annotation attributes such as [Required], [StringLength], and [DisplayName]. As you might have guessed, the [Required] attribute ensures that a property value is set. The [StringLength] attribute lets you specify minimum and maximum lengths for a string property. The [DisplayName] attribute is used to specify friendlier names for the properties. These names are used in the server-side error messages instead of the actual property names.

The UserMetadata class is a standalone class. To link it with the User model class, you need to create a User partial class and decorate it with [MetadataType] attribute.

■ **Note**   Data annotation attributes do a great job of implementing common validation criteria at the model level. ASP.NET validation mechanisms then use this information to provide the user with visual feedback about validation errors. A detailed discussion of data annotation attributes is beyond the scope of this book.

User Controller

The user registration application has a single controller (User) that contains two variations of Index() action methods. These action methods are shown in Listing 5-27.

Listing 5-27. Index Action Methods of the User Controller

```
public ActionResult Index()
{
    return View();
}
```

```
[HttpPost]
public ActionResult Index(User user)
{
    if (ModelState.IsValid)
    {
        UserDbEntities db = new UserDbEntities();
        db.Users.AddObject(user);
        db.SaveChanges();
        return View("Success");
    }
    else
    {
        return View("Index", user);
    }
}
```

The Index() action methods are straightforward. The second Index() action method accepts a User instance and adds it to the database. Notice the use of the ModelState.IsValid property, which returns true only if the data model (User object) meets all the validation criteria. If user registration is successful, the Success view is rendered. Otherwise Index view is displayed with validation errors.

The User controller also contains two action methods that are invoked from jQuery code. These methods check for duplicate display names and e-mail addresses and return true if a duplicate is found. Listing 5-28 shows these action methods.

Listing 5-28. Checking Duplicate Display Names and E-mail Addresses

```
[HttpPost]
public JsonResult IsDuplicateEmail(string email)
{
    UserDbEntities db = new UserDbEntities();
    var data = from item in db.Users
                where item.Email == email
                select item;
    bool flag=false;
    if (data.Count() > 0)
    {
        flag = true;
    }
    return Json(flag);
}

[HttpPost]
public JsonResult IsDuplicateDisplayName(string displayname)
{
    UscrDbEntitics db - new UserDbEntities();
    var data = from item in db.Users
                where item.DisplayName == displayname
                select item;
    bool flag = false;
    if (data.Count() > 0)
    {
```

```
        flag = true;
    }
    return Json(flag);
}
```

The IsDuplicateEmail() method accepts an e-mail address to be verified and returns true if it already exists in the database. Similarly, IsDuplicateDisplayName() accepts a display name and returns true if it already exists. Notice that both of these methods return true or false after wrapping the value as a JsonResult object.

Displaying the User Registration Form in an MVC View

The User Registration form is rendered using MVC HTML helpers. The Index view that displays the form is strongly typed with the User class. Listing 5-29 shows the form's markup. Note that to save space, table markup tags as well as jQuery code have been omitted and are indicated with ellipses.

Listing 5-29. Using HTML Helpers to Render the User Registration Form

```
<%@ Page Language="C#" Inherits="System.Web.Mvc.ViewPage
                                            <SampleAppMVC.Models.User>"  %>
...
  <% using (Html.BeginForm("Index","User","POST")) { %>
        <%= Html.LabelFor(model => model.DisplayName)%>
...
        <%= Html.TextBoxFor(model=>model.DisplayName,
                new {required="required"})%>
        <%= Html.ValidationMessageFor(model=>model.DisplayName,"*")%>
...
        <%= Html.LabelFor(model=>model.Email)%>
...
        <%= Html.TextBoxFor(model=>model.Email,
                new {required="required",type="email"})%>
        <%= Html.ValidationMessageFor(model=>model.Email,"*")%>
...
        <%= Html.LabelFor(model=>model.Password)%>
...
        <%= Html.PasswordFor(model=>model.Password,new {required="required"})%>
        <%= Html.ValidationMessageFor(model=>model.Password,"*")%>
...
        <%= Html.Label("Confirm password")%>
...
        <%= Html.Password("ConfirmPassword", "",new {required="required"})%>
        <%= Html.ValidationMessage("ConfirmPassword","*")%>
...
        <%= Html.LabelFor(model=>model.BlogUrl)%>
...
        <%= Html.TextBoxFor(model=>model.BlogUrl, new {type="url"})%>
        <%= Html.ValidationMessageFor(model=>model.BlogUrl,"*")%>
...
        <%= Html.LabelFor(model=>model.Age)%>
...
```

```
            <%= Html.TextBoxFor(model=>model.Age,
                    new {required="required",type="number",min="18",max="100"})%>
            <%= Html.ValidationMessageFor(model=>model.Age,"*")%>
...
        <%= Html.LabelFor(model=>model.Income)%>
...
            <%= Html.TextBoxFor(model=>model.Income,
                    new {type="range",min="2",max="20",step="4"})%>
            <%= Html.ValidationMessageFor(model=>model.Income,"*")%>
...
            <%= Html.LabelFor(model=>model.Bio)%>
...
            <%= Html.TextAreaFor(model=>model.Bio,
                    new {spellcheck="true",rows="3",cols="30"})%>
            <%= Html.ValidationMessageFor(model=>model.Bio,"*")%>
...
        <input id="btnSubmit" type="submit" value="Submit" />
...
        <%= Html.ValidationSummary() %>
        <div id="divErr" class="validation-summary-errors"></div>
...
<%}%>
```

Listing 5-29 uses many HTML helper methods such as LabelFor, TextBoxFor, ValidationMessageFor, and ValidationSummary. Notice how HTML5 input types and attributes are specified in the second parameter of the HTML helper methods. The validation conditions listed at the beginning of this section are implemented using HTML5 attributes. The server-side validation errors are displayed by the ValidationSummary() method. The <div> element below the validation summary is intended to display HTML5 validation messages.

Checking for Duplicate Display Names and E-mail Addresses

To ensure that the entered display name and e-mail address don't already exist in the database, you need to call the IsDuplicateDisplayName() and IsDuplicateEmail() methods from the jQuery code, discussed earlier. You call them using the jQuery $.ajax() method when the Submit button is clicked. Listing 5-30 shows how to check for duplicate display names.

Listing 5-30. *Checking for Duplicate Display Names*

```
if ($("#DisplayName").val() != "") {
  var data = '{ "displayname" : "' + $("#DisplayName").val() + '"}';
  $.ajax({
    url: '/User/IsDuplicateDisplayName',
    type: 'post',
    data: data,
    dataType: 'json',
    contentType: "application/json; charset=utf-8",
    async: false,
    success: function (result) {
      var displayname = $("#DisplayName").get(0);
      if (result == true) {
```

161

```
        $("#divErr").append("Duplicate Display Name!<br/>");
      }
    },
    error: function (err) { alert(err.status + " - " + err.statusText); }
  });
}
```

This code calls the IsDuplicateDisplayName() action method with the help of $.ajax(). Notice how the displayname parameter is passed as a JSON object. The success method receives a value of true if a display name already exists in the database. In that case, an error message is appended to divErr using the append() method.

Although it isn't discussed here, checking for duplicate e-mails works along similar lines.

Comparing the Password and Confirm Password Fields

Ensuring that the values entered in the Password and Confirm Password text boxes are the same is simple. Listing 5-31 shows how it's done.

Listing 5-31. Validating Password and Confirm Password

```
if ($("#Password").val() != $("#ConfirmPassword").val()) {
  $("#divErr").append("Password mismatch!<br/>");
}
```

The values entered in the text boxes are compared, and if there is any mismatch, an error message is added to the divErr element.

Handling the invalid Event and Displaying Validation Errors

To display other validation errors from input types (required field, min/max overflow, e-mail and URL patterns, and so on), you handle the invalid event on all the <input> elements. Listing 5-32 shows how this is done.

Listing 5-32. Handling the invalid Event

```
$(document).ready(function () {
  $("input").bind("invalid",OnInvalid);
  ...
})

function OnInvalid(evt) {
  var input = evt.target;
  var validity = input.validity;
  if (!validity.valid) {
    if (input.id == "DisplayName")
    { $("#divErr").append("Please enter Display Name!<br/>"); }
    if (input.id == "Email")
    { $("#divErr").append("Please enter Email Address!<br/>"); }
    if (input.id == "Password")
    { $("#divErr").append("Please enter Password!<br/>"); }
    if (input.id == "ConfirmPassword")
```

```
    { $("#divErr").append("Please enter Password Again!<br/>"); }
    if (input.id == "Age") {
      if (validity.valueMissing) {
        $("#divErr").append("Please specify age!<br/>");
      }
      if (validity.rangeUnderflow) {
        $("#divErr").append("Age must be between 18 and 100!<br/>");
      }
      if (validity.rangeOverflow) {
        $("#divErr").append("Age must be between 18 and 100!<br/>");
      }
    }
  }
  evt.preventDefault();
}
```

The code from Listing 5-32 binds the OnInvalid() function as an event handler of the invalid event. Look at the OnInvalid() function carefully. It uses the ValidityState object. First, the code checks whether a control contains a valid value using the valid property. If a control contains an invalid value, its id property is checked and an error message is appended in divErr. Notice the validation for Legal Age: it uses the valueMissing, rangeUnderflow, and rangeOverflow properties.

That completes the User Registration page. Figure 5-27 shows how the page responds to HTML5 validations.

Figure 5-27. HTML5 validations displayed by the invalid event handler

Figure 5-28 shows how validation errors are displayed for server-side errors.

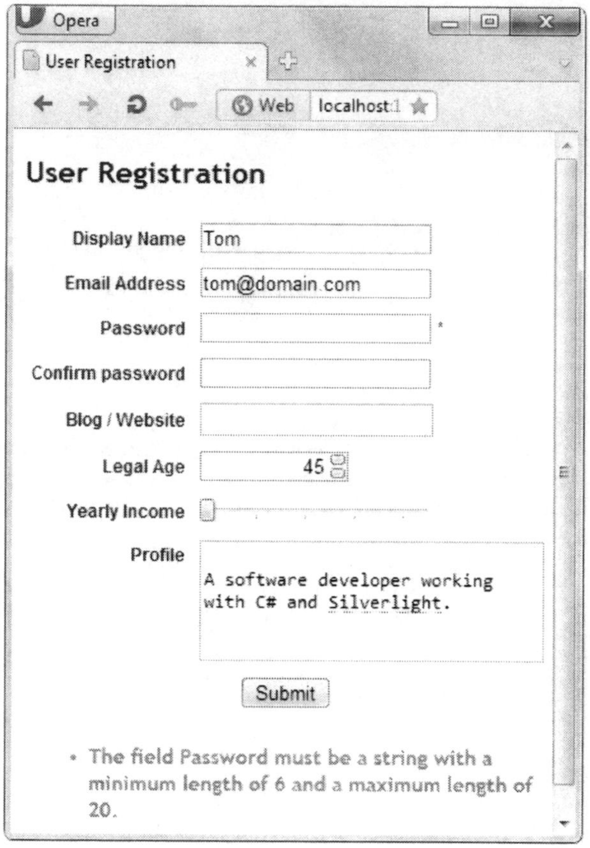

Figure 5-28. Server-side validations from data annotations and MVC

The error message shown in Figure 5-28 comes from the User data model class. Because this validation happens on the server, the Password field loses its value.

Summary

Most ASP.NET applications are data driven and involve forms in some way or another. HTML5 provides an array of features that enhance forms, the most noticeable being the new input types. Input types such as email, url, tel, and date allow you to enforce validations on the data being entered without needing any client-side script. Additionally, features such as required fields, pattern matching, autofocus, placeholders, and spell-check help you to develop rich forms with minimal markup and script.

Of course, you may still need to rely on server-side validation or custom validation as a fallback mechanism to deal with browsers that don't support HTML5. HTML5 also lets you customize validation messages and the way those messages are displayed.

HTML5 form features can be used by Web Forms as well as MVC applications. The TextMode property of the TextBox server control supports various HTML5 input types. MVC applications can use raw <input> tags or use HTML helpers to render HTML5 input types.

CHAPTER 6

■ ■ ■

Using History API and Custom Data Attributes

Whenever you navigate between various pages of your web application, the browser maintains a history of the pages you visited. You can navigate through the history using the browser's back and forward buttons. The same history is accessible to the JavaScript code through the History object. Although the History object isn't a new addition in HTML5, there are some enhancements to it that are worth knowing about. Especially in Ajax-driven applications, the new History API can prove to be very useful. An Ajax-driven application often changes the web page content without generating unique URLs for each different piece of content rendered in the page. This not only causes mismatches between the bookmarked URLs and the actual content but also makes content difficult for search engines to track. The History API provides a small object model as compared to other HTML5 APIs, but the functionality offered is often desirable when web applications need to synchronize the URL shown in the browser address bar and the page content.

After discussing the problems with traditional history management and how HTML5 addresses them, the chapter moves on to discuss another useful topic: custom data attributes, or data-* attributes. The standard HTML attributes are predefined by the HTML specifications and normally affect the behavior or appearance of an element in some way. The custom data attributes are developer-defined attributes that can be used to store metadata information about an element. This information can then be accessed using the client-side script.

The key topics discussed in this chapter include the following:

- The History object and HTML5 enhancements to it
- Scenarios when traditional history tracking can be problematic
- Using the HTML5 History API to add history entries
- Defining custom data attributes (data-*) on HTML elements
- Accessing custom data attributes using plain JavaScript and jQuery

The History Object

Whenever you navigate through pages of a web application, the browser tracks your visits in the form of the History object. You can access the History object via the history property of the DOM window object. In HTML 4.01 the History object has just one property and three methods, described in Table 6-1.

Table 6-1. Properties and Methods of the `History` *Object*

Property / Method	Description
`length`	Indicates the number of entries in the `History` object.
`back()`	Takes a user to the previous URL in the history.
`forward()`	Takes a user to the next URL in the history.
`go()`	Takes a user to a specified URL in the history. The `go()` method takes a single parameter that can be either a number or a URL string. If the parameter is a number, the user is taken to a URL at that specific position with respect to the current page. A negative number indicates movement backward through the history, and a positive number indicates movement forward through the history . For example, `window.history.go(-2)` takes the user two pages backward relative to the current page. If the parameter is a URL, the user is navigated to that URL.

Developers don't use the `History` object very often because users most commonly use the browser's back and forward buttons to navigate the history. However, if required for some reason, the properties and methods described in Table 6-1 are available to programmatically navigate to history entries.

To demonstrate the use of the `History` object, let's develop a simple Slide Show application in ASP.NET MVC. The Slide Show application displays images of some carpentry tools along with their descriptions, as shown in Figure 6-1.

Figure 6-1. User interface of the Slide Show application

As you can see in Figure 6-1, there are four buttons at the bottom of the page arranged in two rows. The top row of buttons (Previous and Next) cause the page to be submitted back to the server and then display either the previous slide or the next slide depending on the button clicked. The bottom row of buttons (< and >) use the History object to navigate backward or forward, respectively. The URL pattern used by the Slide Show application is like this:

```
http://localhost:1065/home/index/2
```

In this URL, home is the MVC controller name, index is the action method that handles the server-side logic of fetching a slide, and 2 is the ID of the slide being displayed. For different slides, the ID at the end of the URL is different.

■ **Note**   You may wonder why you're building a complete database-driven application just to illustrate couple of methods of the History object. You're starting with this project to demonstrate the use of History object in a non-Ajax application; then you move it to Ajax to see the problems that occur, and finally you see how the History object's new functionality can resolve that problem.

The Slide Show application stores its data in a SQL Server database named ImageDb. The ImageDb database contains a single table—Images—that stores image information such as title, description, and image URL. Figure 6-2 shows an Entity Framework data model for the Images table.

Figure 6-2. *Entity Framework data model for the Images table*

As shown in Figure 6-2, the Image data model class has four properties: Id, Title, Description, and ImageUrl. The Id column is the primary key for the Images table.

The main Controller class of the application (HomeController) contains just one action method—Index(). The skeleton of the Index() action method is shown in Listing 6-1. The code that retrieves the image information from the database is omitted for the sake of simplicity.

Listing 6-1. *Index( ) Action Method*

```
public ActionResult Index(int id=0)
{
    ImageDbEntities db = new ImageDbEntities();
    IQueryable<Image> data = null;
    ...
    ...
    return View(data.SingleOrDefault());
}
```

The Index() action method accepts an optional integer parameter that indicates an image ID. If this parameter is supplied, an image with that particular ID is displayed; otherwise the first image from the Images table is displayed.

The Previous and Next buttons submit the form to the server and display the previous or next slide. In order to navigate through the browser history, you need to handle the click event of the < and > buttons and call the back() and forward() methods of the History object, respectively. Listing 6-2 shows how this is done.

Listing 6-2. *Calling the back() and forward() Methods*

```
$(document).ready(function () {
  $("#btnBackward").click(function () {
    window.history.back();
  });
  $("#btnForward").click(function () {
    window.history.forward();
  });
});
```

As you can see, the click event handler of the btnBackward button calls the History object's back() method, whereas the click event handler of the btnForward button calls History object's forward() method.

To see how the back() and forward() methods work, run the application and navigate through the slides using the Previous and Next buttons. Then try clicking < and >. The browser address bar reflects the appropriate slide URL depending on the button clicked. You can also verify the behavior using the browser's back and forward navigation buttons.

Understanding the History-Tracking Problem

The History object discussed in the preceding section essentially tracks the URLs you visit through the browser address bar, hyperlinks, navigation menus, or code. For example, every time you click the Previous or Next button in the Slide Show application, the browser address bar reflects a different URL. This is possible because you submit the entire form to the server. In other words, for every slide, you have a unique URL. However, there can be situations where such a one-to-one mapping between the content of a page and its URL can't be maintained. Consider the following cases:

- You're developing a Web Forms based application, and the logic of displaying different slides is embedded in the server-side click event handlers of the Previous and Next buttons. You're using a single web form to display all the slides. An Image control on the page is updated with the new picture whenever the Previous or Next button is clicked. As a result, all the slides have the same URL. In such a case, there isn't a one-to-one match between slides and URLs.

- If you use Ajax techniques such as the jQuery $.Ajax() method or ASP.NET Ajax extensions, the complete page isn't submitted to the server. Instead, you make an Ajax call to the server and retrieve the next or previous slide. In this case, too, there isn't a unique URL for each slide.

In both cases, the browser history records a single URL for all the slides shown in a page. Because a single URL represents all the slides, the user can't bookmark a specific slide. A user may bookmark the page, thinking that a bookmark is being added for a specific slide; but if the bookmark is accessed, it always shows the first slide because the URL is common to all the slides. To understand this problem more clearly, let's convert the Slide Show application developed previously into an Ajax-driven application so that slides are loaded using the jQuery $.Ajax() method without refreshing the entire page.

The Ajax version of the Slide Show application consists of a controller named AjaxHomeController that contains the Index() action method, as shown in Listing 6-3.

Listing 6-3. Index() Action Method of AjaxHomeController

```
public ActionResult Index()
{
    ImageDbEntities db = new ImageDbEntities();
    IQueryable<Image> data = null;
    ...
    return View(data.SingleOrDefault());
}
```

This time, the Index() action method doesn't accept an image ID as a parameter because Index() is invoked only once when the index view is rendered initially. After that, various slides are fetched via Ajax calls. The Index() action method simply fetches the first image from the Images table and passes it to the index view.

Now the Previous and Next buttons don't submit the form to the server. Instead, clicking these buttons triggers Ajax calls to the server to fetch and display slides.

To display the previous or next slide, you need to handle the click event handlers of the Previous and Next buttons. These event handlers are shown in Listing 6-4.

Listing 6-4. Client-Side click Event Handlers of the Previous and Next Buttons

```
$("#prev").click(function () {
  $.Ajax({
    type: "POST",
    url: "/AjaxHome/GetImage",
    data:'{ id : "' + $("#id").val() + '", direction : "P"}',
    contentType: "application/json; charset=utf-8",
    dataType: "json",
    success: OnSuccess,
    error: OnError
  })
});

$("#next").click(function () {
  $.Ajax({
    type: "POST",
    url: "/AjaxHome/GetImage",
    data: '{ id : "' + $("#id").val() + '", direction : "N"}',
    contentType: "application/json; charset=utf-8",
    dataType: "json",
    success: OnSuccess,
    error: OnError
  })
});
```

These click event handlers of the Previous and Next buttons use the jQuery $.Ajax() method to invoke the GetImage() action method. The GetImage() method expects two parameters: the ID of the current image and a direction (N=Next or P=Previous). GetImage() then returns an Image object representing the previous or next image. The OnSuccess() function simply reads the Image object properties and displays a slide accordingly. Listing 6-5 shows the OnSuccess() function.

Listing 6-5. OnSuccess() Function

```
function OnSuccess(image) {
  $("#id").val(image.Id);
  $("#title").html(image.Title);
  $("#desc").html(image.Description);
  $("#img").attr("src",image.ImageUrl);
  $("#divMsg").html("History Length : " + history.length);
}
```

OnSuccess() receives an Image object returned from the GetImage() action method. Title, ImageUrl, and Description are then assigned to appropriate HTML elements. A <div> element also shows the number of entries in the History object to prove the point.

The skeleton of the GetImage() action method that is invoked using the $.Ajax() calls is shown in Listing 6-6.

Listing 6-6. GetImage() Action Method

```
public JsonResult GetImage(int id,string direction)
{
    ImageDbEntities db = new ImageDbEntities();
    IQueryable<Image> data = null;
    ...
    return Json(data.SingleOrDefault());
}
```

GetImage() accepts an ID of an image and a direction. It then finds the next or previous image in the specified direction. If no direction is specified, it fetches an image with the specified ID. The return type of GetImage() is JsonResult. The Json() method converts an Image object into its JSON equivalent and returns it to the caller.

Now, to understand the problem discussed at the beginning of this section, run the new Slide Show application and navigate through the slides using the Previous and Next buttons. Figure 6-3 shows slide 2 displayed in the browser, but the address bar still shows the base URL.

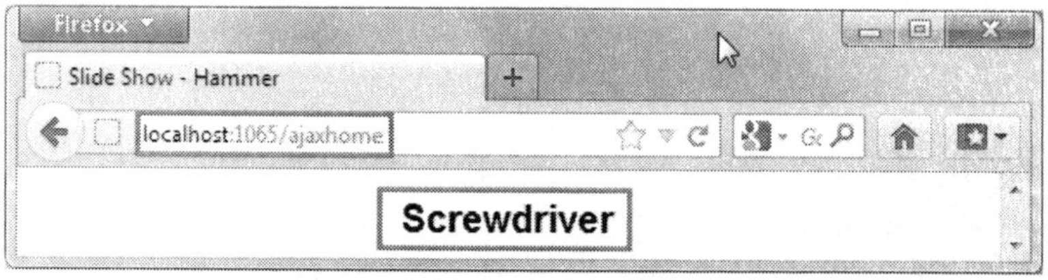

Figure 6-3. Changing the current slide doesn't change the URL in the address bar.

Because you're fetching slides using $.Ajax(), the browser address bar doesn't change the URL. Once you're finished, try clicking the < and > buttons. Even if you navigate through all the slides, you aren't taken forward or backward because the browser has just one entry in the History object: http://localhost:1065/Ajaxhome.

Effect on Browser Bookmarks

The history-tracking problem described in the preceding section also has an undue effect on bookmarks. Suppose a user is on slide 3, which displays information about a spanner. The user may want to re-read the same information later and so adds a bookmark to this page with the impression that slide 3 has been bookmarked. However, because there are no unique URLs for different slides, the browser adds a bookmark to the base URL (http://localhost:1065/Ajaxhome). The next time the user accesses this bookmark, the first slide is shown instead of the third because the server sends the first slide from the database for the URL.

Effect on Search Engine Listings

The Slide Show application also suffers from one drawback that no webmaster wants to have in their applications. Because there is just one URL for all the slides being displayed, search engines capture and list only this URL. If each slide was assigned its own unique URL (as in the non-Ajax version you developed earlier), then search engines could list all the slides in their databases. To allow users to search for and find unique information, you need a unique URL for each independent piece of information—in this case, each individual slide. The Ajax version of the Slide Show application in its current form violates this recommendation, affecting the application's search engine listings.

The Solution

Now that you understand the problems faced by Ajax-driven applications in terms of tracking history, bookmarks, and search engine listings, let's discuss the possible solutions. The basic cause of all the problem areas discussed earlier is that there are no unique URLs to identify independent pieces of content. To solve these issues, you need to create unique URLs for each such piece of information. As far as Ajax applications are concerned, there are two ways to generate such URLs:

* Using hash fragment in the URLs
* Using the new HTML5 History API

Using Hash Fragment in URLs

This technique involves generating URLs by adding a hash fragment at the end of the base URL. For example, consider the following URL:

```
http://localhost/slideshow.aspx#slideid=3
```

In this address, a slide ID is appended after the base URL using #. The browser ignores all information after # and doesn't send a separate request to the server. However, this is still a unique URL. You can append any number of key-value pairs in the # fragment, just like a query string; the only restriction is the size limit of the query string. Once you've created a hash-fragmented URL, you can navigate to it using standard navigation techniques (clicking a hyperlink or programmatically calling window.location.href, for example). You then need to write JavaScript code to read the hash fragment data and display the page content accordingly.

Although hash-fragmented URLs appear to solve the problem, they introduce problems of their own:

* Processing hash fragments often becomes too complex as the amount of data you want to pass increases. Some JavaScript libraries do the job for you, but over all the code tends to become tricky with hash-fragmented URLs.

- The URL becomes too complex and is rarely easy to remember. Although most web applications don't expect you to remember individual page URLs (they have navigation menus), in certain cases easy-to-remember URLs work great. Consider, for example, a social-networking application such as Facebook. Facebook offers shorter profile URLs that are much easier to remember than traditional profile URLs that have a complex ID in the query string.

- If you use hash-fragmented URLs, your processing logic may become tied to the hash-fragment parameters. If you add, remove, or change these parameters, you may also need to update your code due to the changes.

- In spite of the fact that hash-fragmented URLs are widely used in Ajax-driven web applications, search engines may treat them differently. For example, Google expects hash-fragmented URL data to begin with #! (a hash mark followed by an exclamation point). Once you do that, your application is considered *Ajax crawlable*.

■ **Note** ASP.NET Ajax extensions use the hash-fragment technique to generate URLs for multiple Ajax requests. The `ScriptManager` server control makes it easy for you to generate and handle hash-fragmented URLs through its `EnableHistory` property.

HTML5 History API

HTML5 comes to the rescue when it comes to creating different URLs for individual Ajax requests. Using the HTML5 History API, you can add entries to the browser history programmatically. These programmatically added URL entries need not exist physically on the server. When you navigate to an entry added via the History API, the browser raises an event to give you chance to synchronize the URL and the page content. By handling this event, you can fetch relevant content from the server and render it on the page. If you use the HTML5 History API, there is no need to use hash-fragmented URLs—you can avoid all the associated complexity. If a user bookmarks such a programmatically added URL and later navigates to it, the request is sent to the server as a fresh request, and you need to handle it on the server.

Understanding the History API

Earlier in this chapter, you learned about the `History` object (see Table 6-1). The HTML5 `History` API essentially adds two methods and one event to the traditional `History` object. These new methods and event are listed in Table 6-2.

Table 6-2. New Methods and Event of the `History` Object

Method / Event	Description
`pushState()`	Adds an entry to the browser session history with the given state, title, and URL.
`replaceState()`	Updates a current entry in the browser's session history with new details. You can use the `replaceState()` method if the data associated with a history entry changes.
`popstate`	A `popstate` event is raised by the `window` object when the current history entry changes. If the history entry was created by `pushState` or `replaceState`, the `popstate` event's `state` property contains a copy of the history `state` object.

To understand how you can use the new History API, you can modify the Ajax version of the Slide Show (MVC) application developed earlier. Recollect that the Slide Show application uses the jQuery $.Ajax() method to make Ajax requests to the server-side GetImage() action method and retrieve slides. Also recall that the browser address bar shows the same base application URL even if different slides are being shown to the user. Just for the sake of easy understanding, the Slide Show application's OnSuccess() function is given again in Listing 6-7.

Listing 6-7. OnSuccess() Function Without the HTML5 History API

```
function OnSuccess(image) {
  $("#id").val(image.Id);
  $("#title").html(image.Title);
  $("#desc").html(image.Description);
  $("#img").attr("src",image.ImageUrl);
  $("#divMsg").html("History Length : " + history.length);
}
```

■ **Note** For your convenience, the source code download contains three versions of the Slide Show MVC application. The controller names are HomeController, AjaxHomeController, and HTML5HomeController, respectively. While trying this example, you can modify AjaxHomeController and its index view instead of starting from scratch.

To use the HTML5 History API, you need to modify the OnSuccess() function as shown in Listing 6-8.

Listing 6-8. OnSuccess() Function Using the pushState() Method to Add a History Entry

```
function OnSuccess(image) {
  $("#id").val(image.Id);
  $("#title").html(image.Title);
  $("#desc").html(image.Description);
  $("#img").attr("src", image.ImageUrl);

  history.pushState(image, image.Title, "/HTML5Home/index/" + image.Id);
  $("#divMsg").html("History Length : " + history.length);
}
```

The OnSuccess() function receives a JSON object returned by the GetImage() action method that represents an image from the database. After assigning image details such as Title, Description, and ImageUrl, you add an entry to the History object using the pushState() method. The first parameter of pushState() is state information that you wish to access inside the popstate event handler. Here, the code passes the entire Image JSON object as the state information. The second parameter is a title that you're assigning to this history entry. This title is typically displayed in the browser's history menu or dialog. The third parameter is a URL that is to be associated with this history entry. The browser simply puts this URL in the address bar without navigating to it. Also, the browser doesn't check whether the URL really exists on the server. It's up to you to decide what that URL should be. The URL used by the Slide Show application is in the form /index/<image_id>. Later you modify the Index() action method to take care of the image ID passed.

173

Next, you need to handle the popstate event so that when you navigate to a history entry, you can generate the slide as per the history state information. This way, you can synchronize the current slide with the URL being shown in the address bar. Listing 6-9 shows how the popstate event is handled.

Listing 6-9. Handling the popstate Event

```
$(document).ready(function () {
  if (!Modernizr.history) {
    alert("This browser doesn't support the HTML5 History API!");
  }
  else {
    window.onpopstate = OnPopState;
  }
...
});

function OnPopState(evt) {
  $.Ajax({
    type: "POST",
    url: "/HTML5Home/GetImage",
    data: '{ id : "' + evt.state.Id + '", direction : "" }',
    contentType: "application/json; charset=utf-8",
    dataType: "json",
    success: function (image) {
      $("#id").val(image.Id);
      $("#title").html(image.Title);
      $("#desc").html(image.Description);
      $("#img").src = image.ImageUrl;
    },
    error: OnError
  })
}
```

Remember that the popstate event is raised for the window object, and hence you attach an event-handler function OnPopState to the window. Notice how support for the History API is detected. The OnPopState function makes an Ajax call to GetImage() using $.Ajax(). Recollect that while calling the pushState() method, you specified the Image JSON object as the history state. The same Image JSON object can be retrieved using the state property of the evt parameter. An ID of an image that is to be fetched is then passed to the GetImage() method. Upon successful completion of the Ajax call, Image details such as Title, Description, and ImageUrl are assigned to various <form> elements.

Finally, change the Index() action to take care of the optional image ID. Listing 6-10 shows the modified version of Index().

Listing 6-10. Index() Action Method, Which Now Takes Care of the Optional Image ID

```
public ActionResult Index(int id=0)
{
    ImageDbEntities db = new ImageDbEntities();
    IQueryable<Image> data = null;
    if (id == 0)
    {
        data = (from item in db.Images
```

```
                orderby item.Id ascending
                select item).Take(1);
    }
    else
    {
        data = from item in db.Images
                where item.Id == id
                select item;
    }
    return View(data.SingleOrDefault());
}
```

The Index() action method now checks whether an image ID is passed. If so, it returns an image with the specified ID; otherwise the first image from the database is returned.

Figure 6-4 shows a sample run of the modified Slide Show application. Notice how the browser address bar is showing a unique URL for every slide.

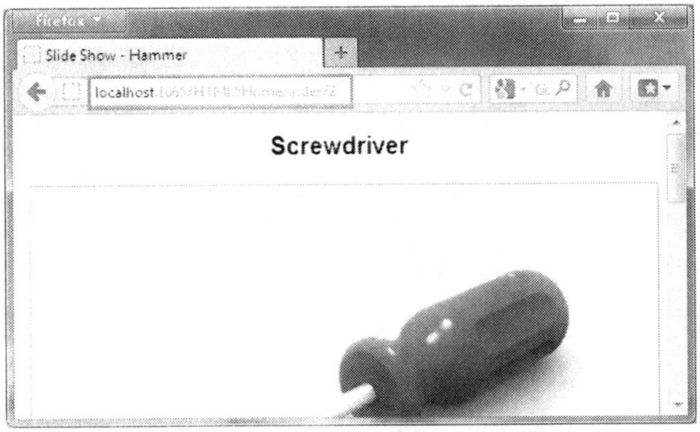

Figure 6-4. HTML5 pushState() method changing the URL in the address bar

The browser's history menu or dialog also lists the URLs added via the pushState() method, as shown in Figure 6-5.

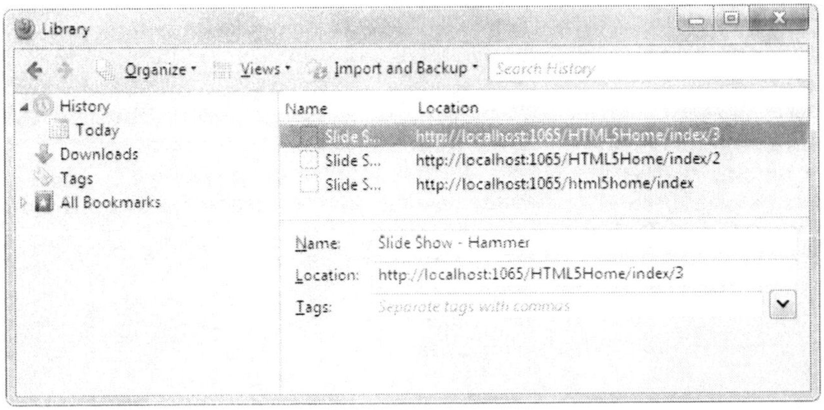

Figure 6-5. The browser's history dialog showing URLs added via the pushState() method

175

■ **Note**   Not all browsers use the `title` parameter of the `pushState()` method even if it's mentioned. For example, the history dialog shown in Figure 6-5 shows the title for all the URLs as "Slide Show – Hammer" even if their location is different. Future versions of browsers may use this parameter.

Browser Support

Almost all of the leading browsers except Internet Explorer 9 support the HTML5 History API. As with any other features of HTML5, it's always a good practice to check whether a browser supports the History API using Modernizr. The Slide Show application includes that check, as shown in Listing 6-11.

Listing 6-11. Checking Support for the History API Using Modernizr

```
if (!Modernizr.history) {
    alert("This browser doesn't support HTML5 History API!");
}
```

If a browser doesn't support the HTML5 History API, your application may still work, but it doesn't add any entries in the history; neither does it change the address bar. If you wish to provide some sort of fallback, you can resort to either of these two options:

- Use full-page refresh as you did in the first non-Ajax version of the Slide Show application.

- Use the hash-fragmented URL technique discussed earlier.

Custom Data Attributes

HTML markup elements use attributes to specify configuration information. For example, the `height` and `width` attributes of the `<canvas>` element govern the height and width of the canvas when displayed in the browser. Most of the attributes of HTML elements affect the user interface or visual display of the element under consideration.

While developing web applications, developers often find it necessary to emit metadata about an element to the client browser. Such metadata doesn't affect the display of the element directly. Nevertheless, the metadata holds pieces of information relating to that element.

Consider an example where an HTML form is to be validated using custom JavaScript code. When the JavaScript code validates the form fields, it's supposed to display validation errors if any of the fields hold invalid values. Often, the error message text is directly embedded in the JavaScript code. But what if the error message text is to be changed after the deployment? Embedding the error message text directly in the script calls for editing the script. This in turn amounts to changing the application's code-base. In such situations, it's helpful if the error message text is stored separately from the web pages (say, in a database table). At runtime, the error messages can be retrieved from the database and emitted to the client. These emitted messages form the metadata of the HTML elements. If any change is required in the error messages, you change the database entries, and the application begins using the new values from the next run.

Prior to HTML5, there wasn't a standard to deal with such metadata information. HTML5 introduces custom data attributes that can be used to define metadata about elements.

Overview of Custom Data Attributes

The HTML5 custom data attributes are special attributes that take the following form:

data-<name>="value"

Custom data attributes always begin with data- followed by a developer-defined name. For example, for the custom validation scenario discussed earlier, you can create a custom data attribute named data-errormessage.

The developer-defined name can contain a hyphen (-). For example, data-customer-id and data-customer-name are valid custom data attributes. Custom data attributes are also referred as data-* attributes due to the naming convention they follow. A data-* attribute can be assigned a value just like any other HTML attribute. ASP.NET uses data-* attributes extensively to provide unobstructive validation in web forms and MVC applications.

■ **Note** *Unobstructive validation* is a technique implemented by ASP.NET that uses data annotation attributes and jQuery. Under this scheme, a data model is decorated with data-annotation attributes that perform validations on the data-model property values. At runtime, ASP.NET emits data-* attributes based on these data-annotation attributes. The client-side validations are performed with the help of these data-* attributes and jQuery.

Unlike standard HTML attributes, data-* attributes don't affect the visual look and feel of the element. In fact, the browser doesn't use them automatically for any purpose. You need to programmatically access them and execute the intended logic on them. An HTML element can have any number of data-* attributes defined on it.

Although you can use data-* attributes for any custom requirement, you should avoid using them if the same purpose can be accomplished with a standard HTML attribute. For example, suppose you wish to display a tooltip for an element when the user hovers the mouse pointer on it. The tooltip changes based on programmatic conditions. In this case, it's better to use the HTML title attribute rather than create a new data-* attribute.

Listing 6-12 shows some sample HTML markup that uses custom data attributes.

Listing 6-12. Using Custom Data Attributes

```
<table border="1" cellpadding="3">
    <tr id='emp1' data-employeeid='1' data-title='Sales Representative'>
        <td>Nancy</td>
        <td>Davolio</td>
    </tr>
    <tr id='emp2' data-employeeid='2' data-title='Vice President, Sales'>
        <td>Andrew</td>
        <td>Fuller</td>
    </tr>
    ...
</table>
```

This listing shows an HTML table containing employee data. Each table row contains the name of the employee and additionally has two custom data attributes: data-employeeid and data-title. The data-employeeid attribute stores the employee's EmployeeID, and the data-title attribute stores the employee's job title.

Accessing Custom Data Attributes Using JavaScript

Now that you know what custom data attributes are, let's see how to access them in JavaScript code. Consider the JavaScript code shown in Listing 6-13, which illustrates how you can access the data-* attributes used in Listing 6-12 using JavaScript code.

Listing 6-13. Accessing data- Attributes in JavaScript Code*

```
var emp = document.getElementById('emp1');
alert('Employee ID : ' + emp.getAttribute('data-employeeid'));
alert('Title : ' + emp.getAttribute('data-title'));

emp.setAttribute('data-employeeid', '100');
emp.setAttribute('data-title', 'Senior Manager');
alert('New Employee ID : ' + emp.getAttribute('data-employeeid'));
alert('New Title : ' + emp.getAttribute('data-title'));
```

This code uses the DOM document's getElementById() method to grab a table row with ID of emp1. It then retrieves the values of the data-employeeid and data-title custom data attributes using the table DOM element's getAttribute() method. The values are displayed in an alert box. Further, the code changes the values of data-employeeid and data-title using the setAttribute() method. The changed values are also displayed in an alert box.

Although the technique of getting and setting data-* attributes from Listing 6-13 works as expected, HTML5 offers a technique exclusively designed for accessing data-* attributes. HTML5 data-* attributes are made available to your code through the dataset property of the underlying DOM element. Listing 6-14 shows how to use the dataset property to access data-* attributes.

Listing 6-14. Using the dataset Property to Access data- Attributes*

```
var emp = document.getElementById('emp1');
alert('Employee ID : ' + emp.dataset.employeeid);
alert('Title : ' + emp.dataset.title);
emp.dataset.employeeid = '200';
emp.dataset.title = 'Junior Manager';
alert('New Employee ID : ' + emp.dataset.employeeid);
alert('New Title : ' + emp.dataset.title);
```

To retrieve a data-* property value, you simply use the attribute name without data- against the dataset property. Similarly, to set a data-* attribute value, you use its name against the dataset property and assign a value to it.

If the custom data attribute contains a hyphen (-), you can access the attribute using camel casing. For example, to access the data-employee-birthdate attribute, you use the following code:

```
alert('Employee ID : ' + emp.dataset.employeeBirthdate);
```

As you can see, the attribute name contains employee-birthdate. But when you access it using the dataset property, it's referred to as employeeBirthdate.

Accessing Custom Data Attributes Using jQuery

The jQuery library also supports accessing custom data attributes by providing methods exclusively to work with data-* attributes. Listing 6-15 shows how you can use jQuery to retrieve and assign data-* attribute values.

Listing 6-15. Using jQuery to Access data-* Attributes

```
alert('Employee ID : ' + $("#emp1").data('employeeid'));
alert('Title : ' + $("#emp1").data('title'));

$("#emp1").data('employeeid', '100');
$("#emp1").data('title', 'Senior Manager');

alert('Employee ID : ' + $("#emp1").data('employeeid'));
alert('Title : ' + $("#emp1").data('title'));
```

The jQuery library provides a data() method to access custom data attributes. To retrieve a data-* attribute, you call data() on the underling DOM element and pass the attribute name without data-. For example, Listing 6-15 uses data('employeeid') to retrieve the value of the data-employeeid attribute. To assign a value to a data-* attribute, you call the data() method and supply the attribute name without data- and its new value. If the custom data attribute contains hyphen (-) in the name (data-employee-birthdate, for example) you can access it using the same camel-casing syntax, as shown here:

```
alert('Title : ' + $("#emp1").data('employeeBirthdate'));
```

If you call data() without any parameters, it returns an object of key-value pairs containing all the data-* attributes of that element and their values. Listing 6-16 shows how to use this variation of the data() method.

Listing 6-16. Using the data() Method to Obtain data-* Attributes as an Object

```
var obj = $("#emp1").data();
alert('Employee ID : ' + obj.employeeid);
alert('Title : ' + obj.title);
alert('Birth Date : ' + obj.employeeBirthdate);
```

As you can see, the data() method is called without any parameters. Doing so returns an object with key-value pairs. To read a particular data-* attribute value, you can use the data-* attribute name without data- against the object returned.

▪ **Note** You can also use the jQuery attr() method to get or set data-* attributes. However, it's better to use data() because it's designed specifically to deal with custom data attributes.

Using Custom Data Attributes to Emit Validation Messages

Now that you know how to use custom data attributes, let's develop a Web Forms application that illustrates how you can implement the validation scenario discussed at the beginning of this section with the help of data-* attributes. In this section, you develop a web form as shown in Figure 6-6.

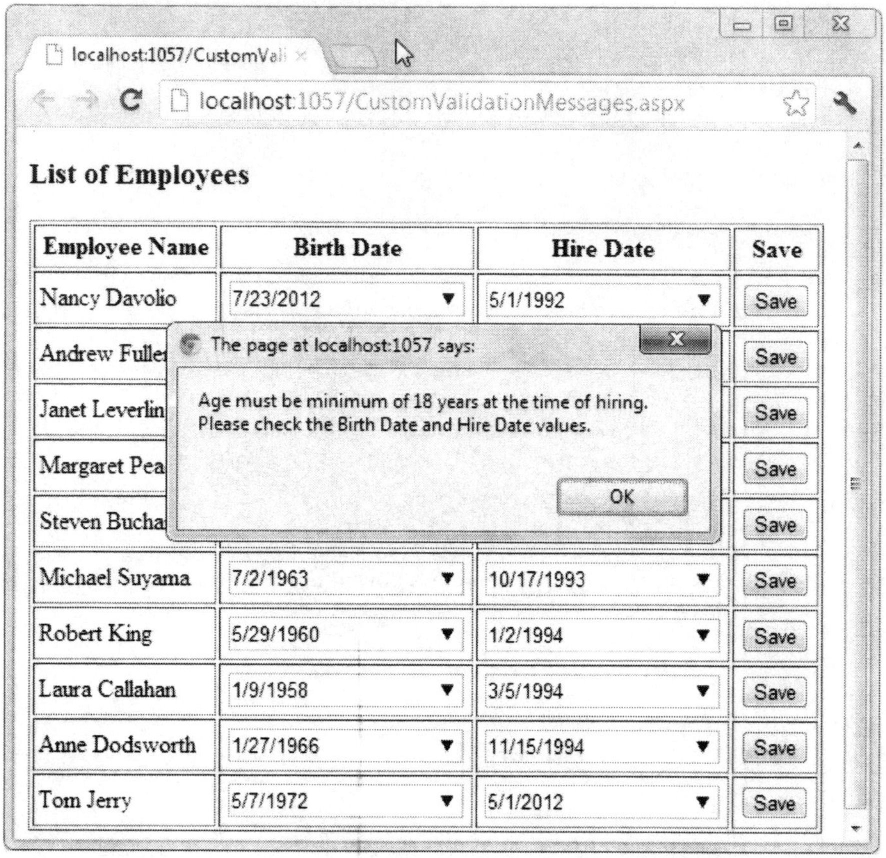

Figure 6-6. Employee list web form

The web form shows employee names from the `Employees` table of the `Northwind` database along with their `BirthDate` and `HireDate` values. The user can select the respective dates and click the Save button. Clicking Save triggers validation logic that checks whether the employee is at least 18 years old at the time of hiring. If not, an error message is displayed to the user in an alert box. The validation message isn't embedded anywhere in the code; rather, it's stored in a database table named `ErrorMessages`. The `ErrorMessages` table has a simple structure, as shown in its Entity Framework data model (Figure 6-7).

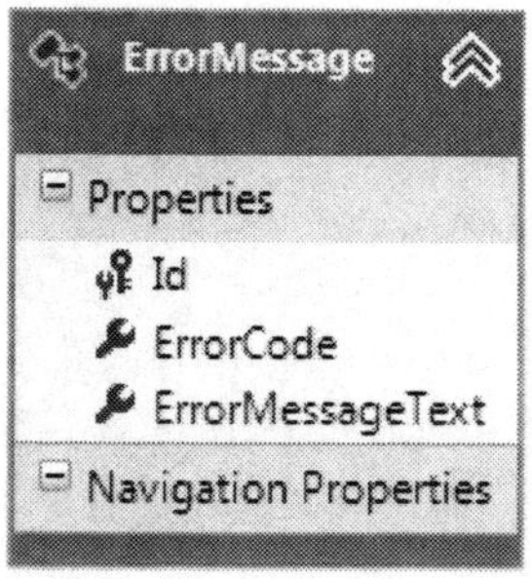

Figure 6-7. Data model for the `ErrorMessages` table

As you can see, the ErrorMessages table contains three columns: Id, ErrorCode, and ErrorMessageText. The ErrorCode column contains a short code for an error (such as INVALIDDATE), and the ErrorMessageText column holds the descriptive error message (for example, "The Hire Date must be later than Birth Date"). Listing 6-17 shows the markup for the ItemTemplate of the Repeater server control that renders the employee list.

Listing 6-17. Web Form Markup That Shows the Employee List

```
<ItemTemplate>
  <tr id='<%# Eval("EmployeeID","emp{0}") %>'
                   data-employeeid='<%# Eval("EmployeeID") %>'>
    <td><%# Eval("FirstName") %> <%# Eval("LastName") %></td>
    <td><asp:TextBox ID="txtBirthDate" runat="server" TextMode="Date"
           Text='<%# Eval("BirthDate") %>'
           data-error-invaliddate='<%# GetValidationMessage("INVALIDDATE") %>'>
         </asp:TextBox></td>
    <td><asp:TextBox ID="txtHireDate" runat="server" TextMode="Date"
            Text='<%# Eval("HireDate") %>'
            data-error-invaliddate='<%# GetValidationMessage("INVALIDDATE") %>'>
         </asp:TextBox></td>
    <td><input type="button" value="Save"/></td>
  </tr>
</ItemTemplate>
```

This markup consists of two TextBox server controls that display the BirthDate and HireDate column values, respectively. The TextMode property of these text boxes is set to Date so that a date-picker is displayed to select the dates. Each text box has a custom data attribute named data-error-invaliddate. The value of this attribute comes from the GetValidationMessage() function. GetValidationMessage() picks up the ErrorMessageText from the ErrorMessages table based on the ErrorCode passed:

```
public string GetValidationMessage(string errorCode)
{
    ValidationDbEntities db = new ValidationDbEntities();

    var data = from item in db.ErrorMessages
               where item.ErrorCode == errorCode
               select item.ErrorMessageText;
    return data.SingleOrDefault();
}
```

The jQuery code that performs the validation and displays the validation error, if any, resides in the Save button's click event handler. This code is shown in Listing 6-18.

Listing 6-18. Validating the Age of an Employee

```
$("input[value='Save']").click(function () {
  var birthDateTxtbox = $(this).closest('tr').children().eq(1).children().eq(0);
  var hireDateTxtbox = $(this).closest('tr').children().eq(2).children().eq(0);
  var birthDate = ToDate($(birthDateTxtbox).val());
  var hireDate = ToDate($(hireDateTxtbox).val());
  birthDate.setFullYear(birthDate.getFullYear() + 18);

  if ((hireDate.getTime() - birthDate.getTime()) < 0) {
```

```
    alert($(birthDateTxtbox).data('errorInvaliddate'));
    return;
}


//make $.Ajax() request to update the database
alert('Data saved!');
});
```

The Save button's click event handler begins by grabbing a reference to the BirthDate and HireDate input fields. The closest() method returns the row that holds the input fields and the Save button. The children() method returns all the child elements of the table row. The eq() method then returns a table cell at the specified index. Because the input fields are inside the table column, another call to the children() and eq() methods is necessary to grab the respective input fields.

The input fields hold the date value in yyyy-MM-dd format. These dates are converted into JavaScript date objects using a custom function ToDate(). The ToDate() function looks like this:

```
function ToDate(input) {
  var parts = input.match(/(\d+)/g);
  return new Date(parts[0], parts[1] - 1, parts[2]);
}
```

ToDate() should be familiar, because you used it in Chapter 5. It essentially parses the supplied input value and returns a JavaScript date object representing that value.

Next, the code checks the difference between the HireDate and BirthDate to determine if the employee is at least 18 years old at the time of hiring. If not, an error message as specified in the data-error-invaliddate custom data attribute is displayed to the user in an alert box. The jQuery data() method is used to retrieve the value of the data-error-invaliddate attribute.

Although the code doesn't actually save the changed data to the server, you can add that functionality if the age validation succeeds. In Listing 6-18, a success message is displayed after the age check is successful.

Summary

The HTML5 History API is a relatively small area of improvement, but it comes in handy in certain scenarios. In particular, modern web applications rely on Ajax techniques extensively to render page content without refreshing the entire page. At the same time, they need to take care of search engine optimization and the user experience. The new HTML5 History API allows you to add entries in the history programmatically. This way, you can also change the URL shown in the browser's address bar. When you navigate through the history, the History API gives you a chance to synchronize the page content with the URL being navigated to. The HTML5 History API not only provides a standard way of dealing with history entries but also takes away the complexity otherwise involved in the implementation.

Custom data attributes (data-*) allow you to embed metadata about an HTML element. They aren't processed by the browser and don't directly affect an element's behavior. You can use a DOM element's dataset property or the jQuery data() method to access data-* attributes.

Although the History API and custom data attributes let you deal with session history and metadata respectively, there is also a frequent need to store and retrieve session data. Traditionally, cookies have been used to store such data on the client side. The next chapter examines what is known as *web storage*—the ability to store and retrieve data locally on the client side.

CHAPTER 7

■ ■ ■

Storing Data in Web Storage

Most of the web sites developed today deal with data in one form or another. Naturally, this application data needs some sort of storage mechanism. As far as the server is concerned, there are sophisticated database engines such as SQL Server. However, storing data on the client side can be tricky. Traditionally, developers used cookies to persist data on the client side, but cookies suffer from their own limitations. To provide a streamlined data-storage mechanism at the client side, HTML5 provides web storage. This chapter examines what web storage is along with situations where it can be used. Specifically, you learn the following:

- What is web storage?
- Flavors of web storage
- Storing items in, retrieving them from, and removing them from web storage
- Storing non-string data in web storage
- Passing data from web storage to the server for further processing

Overview of Web Storage

The term *web storage* refers to HTML5's client-side data-storage mechanism. Web storage allows you to store data on the client side as key-value pairs. The W3C recommended a web storage size limit of 5MB per origin (see the section "Security Considerations for Web Storage" to learn more about origins). However, individual browsers may slightly deviate from this limit. For example, IE8 allows web storage of up to 10MB.

Although both web storage and cookies store data on the client side, they work differently. Cookies are passed between client and server with each and every request from a given web site. On the other hand, web storage is never passed to the server automatically. If you need to transmit data from web storage to the server-side code, you must resort to a programmatic approach such as jQuery calling server-side code or a hidden form field. Additionally, unlike cookies, you can't set an expiration time for web storage. You either need to write code to delete stale items or count on the user to delete the stale items using an option in the browser.

Web storage comes in two flavors: session storage and local storage. These two types are exposed as `sessionStorage` and `localStorage` attributes of the `window` object, respectively. As you might have guessed, session storage is persisted as long as the current browser (or its tab) instance is running. The moment you close the browser instance (or tab), the data is removed. If you load the web site again later, it can't access any of the previously stored data. Session storage is suitable for a single transaction. Local storage, unlike session storage, stores data across multiple instances of the browser and also beyond the current session.

In summary, web storage is good choice if

- You need to store data exceeding the size limits of cookie-based storage.

- You don't need to pass data to and from the server with every request.

- You don't need to set any specific expiration time for the data.

However, web storage may not be a good choice if

- You wish to store a huge amount of data.

- Your data can't be easily stored as key-value pairs (binary data or BLOBS, for example).

- Data to be stored is sensitive.

Session Storage and Local Storage Objects

As mentioned earlier, sessionStorage and localStorage objects store data as key-value pairs. Both of these objects have similar properties and methods. Table 7-1 lists them for your quick reference.

Table 7-1. Properties and Methods of sessionStorage *and* localStorage

Property / Method	Description
setItem()	Adds a key-value pair to a web storage object. If the key already exists, its value is changed.
getItem()	Retrieves the value of a specified key from a web storage object.
removeItem()	Removes a specified key and the value associated with it from a web storage object.
clear()	Removes all the key-value pairs from the web storage object.
key()	Takes a zero-based index and returns key name at that index.
length	Returns the total number of key-value pairs from the web storage object.
remainingSpace	Returns the amount of storage space (in bytes) still available for storing data. This property is currently supported only by IE.

Now that you have some idea about session storage and local storage, let's try these properties and methods in a Web Forms application.

▪ **Note** You can also test the sessionStorage and localStorage objects using plain HTML pages, but in that case you must host them in Internet Information Services (IIS). Unless your pages are part of a web site, the browser can't determine their originating domain and thus can't allocate storage space to them. You learn about these security restrictions later in this chapter.

Using the sessionStorage and localStorage Objects

In this section, you create the simple web form shown in Figure 7-1.

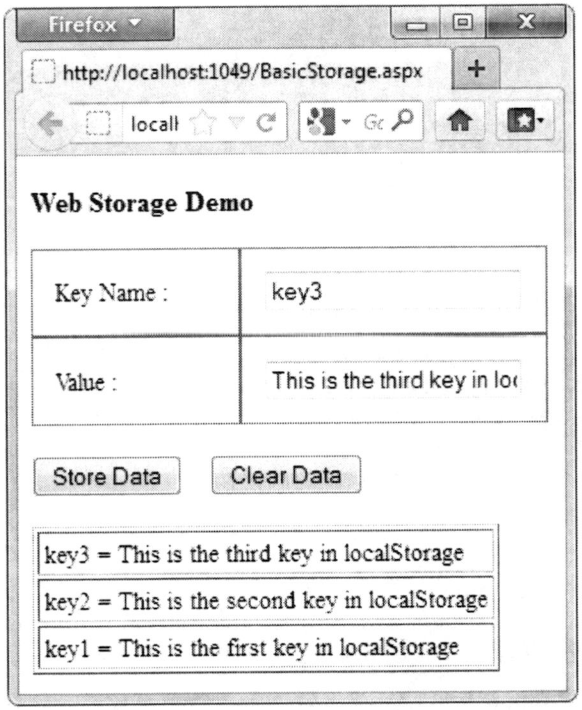

Figure 7-1. Simple web form using the localStorage *object*

The web form allows you to store key-value pairs in the localStorage object. It consists of two text boxes in which the user can enter a key and a value, respectively. Clicking the Store Data button stores a key and its value in the localStorage object. A list of all the keys and their values is shown in the bottom table. Clicking the Clear Data button removes all the entries from the localStorage. Listing 7-1 shows how the click event handlers of both buttons deal with the localStorage object.

Listing 7-1. Using the localStorage Object

```
var storage = window.localStorage;

$(document).ready(function () {
    if (!Modernizr.localstorage) {
      alert("This browser doesn't support HTML5 Local Storage!");
    }
    $("#store").click(OnStoreClick);
    $("#clear").click(OnClearClick);
});
```

```
function OnStoreClick(event) {
    var key = $("#keyName").val();
    var value = $("#keyValue").val();
    storage.setItem(key, value);
    $("#tblItems").empty();
    for (var i = 0; i < storage.length; i++)
    {
        $("#tblItems").append("<tr><td>" + storage.key(i) + " = " +
        storage.getItem(storage.key(i)) + "</td></tr>");
    }
}

function OnClearClick(event) {
    storage.clear();
    $("#tblItems").empty();
}
```

This code first stores a reference to the localStorage object in a variable: storage. This way, you don't always need to use window.localStorage syntax to call methods of the localStorage object. Additionally, if you decide to test sessionStorage instead of localStorage, you can just change this one line of code, and the rest of the code automatically uses sessionStorage object. Notice how support for localStorage is checked using Modernizr. If you wish to check support for sessionStorage, you can use the Modernizr.sessionstorage property instead.

The jQuery ready function wires the click events of the two buttons (Store Data and Clear Data) with event-handler functions: OnStoreClick() and OnClearClick().

The OnStoreClick() event-handler function stores a key-value pair in the storage object using the setItem() method of the localStorage object. It then iterates through all the keys. With every iteration, the code uses key() and getItem() to retrieve a key and its value. The key-value pair is then added to the tblItems table.

The OnClearClick() event-handler function simply removes all the items from the store using clear() method.

Storing Numbers, Dates, and Objects

Although the localStorage and sessionStorage objects allow you to store data, they suffer from a limitation as far as the data type of items being stored is concerned: all the data is stored as string. Even if you add values with numeric or date data types, they're still stored as plain strings. This is important because when you read the data back, you may need to convert it into an appropriate data type. In still more complex scenarios, you may want to store objects in web storage. Obviously, because web storage natively supports only string data to be stored, these types of conversions are your responsibility.

Consider the piece of code shown in Listing 7-2.

Listing 7-2. Storing Numbers in localStorage

```
$(document).ready(function () {
  var storage = window.localStorage;
  storage["number1"] = 10;
  storage["number2"] = 20;
  var sum1 = storage["number1"] + storage["number2"];
  var sum2 = Number(storage["number1"]) + Number(storage["number2"]);
```

```
    alert("Without conversion Sum = " + sum1 + "\r\n" +
          "With conversion Sum = " + sum2);
});
```

As you can see, two numbers are stored in `localStorage` with the keys `number1` and `number2`, respectively. Notice that this time, instead of using `setItem()` and `getItem()`, the code uses a familiar dictionary-access syntax to store the items. The `sum1` variable stores the sum of the values of these two keys without performing any conversion, whereas `sum2` stores their sum by first converting them to numbers using the `Number()` function. An alert box displays the values of `sum1` and `sum2`, as shown in Figure 7-2.

Figure 7-2. Adding numeric values after conversion

Figure 7-2 confirms that `localStorage` stores data in plain-text format and you need to convert it to an appropriate data format before using it in further processing.

Storing date values is similar to storing numbers in that you need to convert date strings into JavaScript `Date` objects. Listing 7-3 shows how this can be done.

Listing 7-3. Storing Dates in `localStorage`

```
$(document).ready(function () {
  var storage = window.localStorage;
  storage["date"] = new Date(2012,5,15);
  var date1 = storage["date"];
  try{
    alert("Without conversion Year = " + date1.getFullYear());
  }
  catch(e){
    alert("Data is not of date type!");
  }
  var date2 = new Date(storage["date"]));
  try {
    alert("With conversion Year = " + date2.getFullYear());
  }
  catch (e) {
```

```
            alert("Data is not of date type!");
        }
});
```

This code stores a date in `localStorage`. It then tries to access the year part of the date without performing any conversion. This results in an error, as indicated by the alert box. The second attempt parses the stored string into a `Date` object and then outputs its year. As you might have already guessed, the second attempt gives correct results.

In Listing 7-3, the date is stored in the `localStorage` object using the default JavaScript format (for example, Thu Mar 01 2012 00:00:00 GMT+0530 [India Standard Time]). In many cases, you may be using an input field as a date picker (you can do that in by setting the type attribute to date). The date picker returns dates in yyyy-MM-dd format. This format is also safe to store directly in `localStorage` because it can be easily parsed back into a JavaScript `Date` object later.

Storing objects sounds complex at first, but luckily most browsers support a handy way to convert objects into strings and vice versa. As far as JavaScript is concerned, objects are represented in JSON format; using the `JSON.stringify()` and `JSON.parse()` methods, you can easily convert a JSON object into a string and parse its string representation back into an object. Listing 7-4 shows how to do this conversion.

Listing 7-4. Converting JSON Objects

```
$(document).ready(function () {
  var storage = window.localStorage;
  var object1 = { "Name": "Tom", "Age": 50 };
  storage["object"] = JSON.stringify(object1);
  var object2 = JSON.parse(storage["object"]);
  alert(object2.Name + " (" + object2.Age + " years)");
});
```

This code defines a JSON object with two properties: `Name` and `Age`. While storing the JSON object into `localStorage`, the `JSON.stringify()` method converts the JSON object into its string representation. While retrieving the data from `localStorage`, the `JSON.parse()` method reconstructs the object. The alert box then correctly outputs the `Name` and `Age` properties (Figure 7-3).

Figure 7-3. Dealing with JSON objects

The JSON object used in this example contains the Name value Tom and the Age value 50. The resulting alert box displays these values to the user.

Session Storage and Local Storage Events

The sessionStorage and localStorage objects support a storage event that is raised whenever the underlying storage area changes. You should be aware of two things while dealing with this event. First, the storage event is raised on the window object. Second, for most browsers except IE, the storage event is fired on every browser instance (or tab) except the one that changed the storage object. In IE, the storage event is raised for all instances (or tabs) of the browser. So, if Example1.aspx is loaded in three tabs Tab1, Tab2, and Tab3, and Tab1 changes the web storage, Tab2 and Tab3 receive the storage event. In IE, Tab2 and Tab3 as well as Tab1 receive the storage event.

The storage event handler receives event information as a StorageEvent object. The properties of StorageEvent are shown in Table 7-2.

Table 7-2. Event Parameters of the storage Event

Parameter	Description
key	Represents the key of an item that is being added to the storage
oldValue	Old value of the key being changed (if an existing key is being changed)
newValue	New value being assigned to a key
url	URL of the page that is accessing the storage area
storageArea	Reference to the storage area: localStorage or sessionStorage

Just to check how the storage event works, modify the example shown in Figure 7-1 as shown in Listing 7-5.

Listing 7-5. Handling the storage Event

```
$(document).ready(function () {
    ...
    window.addEventListener('storage', OnStorage, false);
    ...
});

function OnStorage (event) {
    alert("Storage event fired for key : " + event.key + " in page " + event.url);
    alert("Old Value - New Value : " + event.oldValue + " - " + event.newValue);
}
```

Notice how the storage event handler is attached using the window object's addEventListener() method. The OnStorage() function uses various properties of the event parameter and displays them in a message box. To test the storage event, open the same web form in two Firefox tabs. Switch to the first tab, and add a key. You should see an alert box on the other tab as shown in Figure 7-4.

As you can see, adding a key to the first tab informs the user that the storage event has been raised for the second tab and the key name is key1.

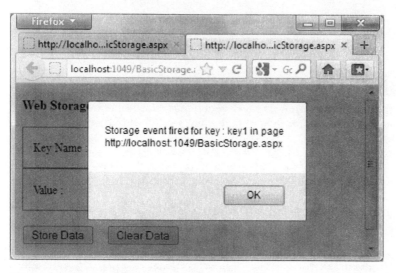

Figure 7-4. The storage *event is raised when a key is added.*

Clearing Web Storage Manually

If you add key-value pairs to localStorage and then close the browser without clearing the storage area, the data is preserved on the disk. As mentioned earlier, unlike cookies, you can't set a specific expiration date and time for local storage. One way to clear the localStorage data is to programmatically call the removeItem() method for each item or call the clear() method. Alternatively, you can manually delete the localStorage data using browser dialogs. For example, Figure 7-5 shows the Clear All History dialog in Firefox.

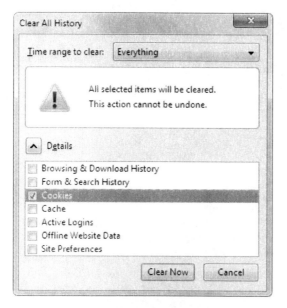

Figure 7-5. Clearing local storage manually

Make sure you select the Cookies check box and click the Clear Now button. In addition to cookies, this also deletes localStorage data.

Passing Data from Web Storage to the Server

Unlike cookies, web storage data isn't passed between the client and server with each request. If you wish to send web storage data to the server, you must devise a programmatic way to do so. Some options to accomplish this task are as follows:

- *Hidden form field:* In this approach, you first store data in localStorage or sessionStorage objects as usual. At the time of submitting the form, you transfer this web storage data into a hidden form field and then submit the form. The server-side code can then read this hidden field and process the data further.

- *Ajax calls:* Using this approach you make an Ajax call to the server and pass the web storage data to the server. The server-side code then processes the data further. In a Web Forms application, the Ajax call can be made to a web method, a web service, or a Windows Communication Foundation (WCF) service. In an ASP.NET MVC application, the Ajax call can be made to an action method.

In the example discussed in the next section, you use jQuery to call controller action methods.

An Example of Using Local Storage in a Survey Form

This section presents a more realistic example than the previous one that uses all the information about localStorage discussed so far. You develop a simple survey form that captures user feedback. As you may be aware, filling out a survey may not be a priority for end users while they're using your web site. They may begin completing the survey form and then navigate to some other part of the web site that interests them more. They may even close the browser and come back to your web site later. In such scenarios, it would be nice to persist the survey data locally as the user is entering it. Later, when the user comes back, you can reload the persisted data and save the user time. The survey application is developed using ASP.NET MVC, and its main view is shown in Figure 7-6.

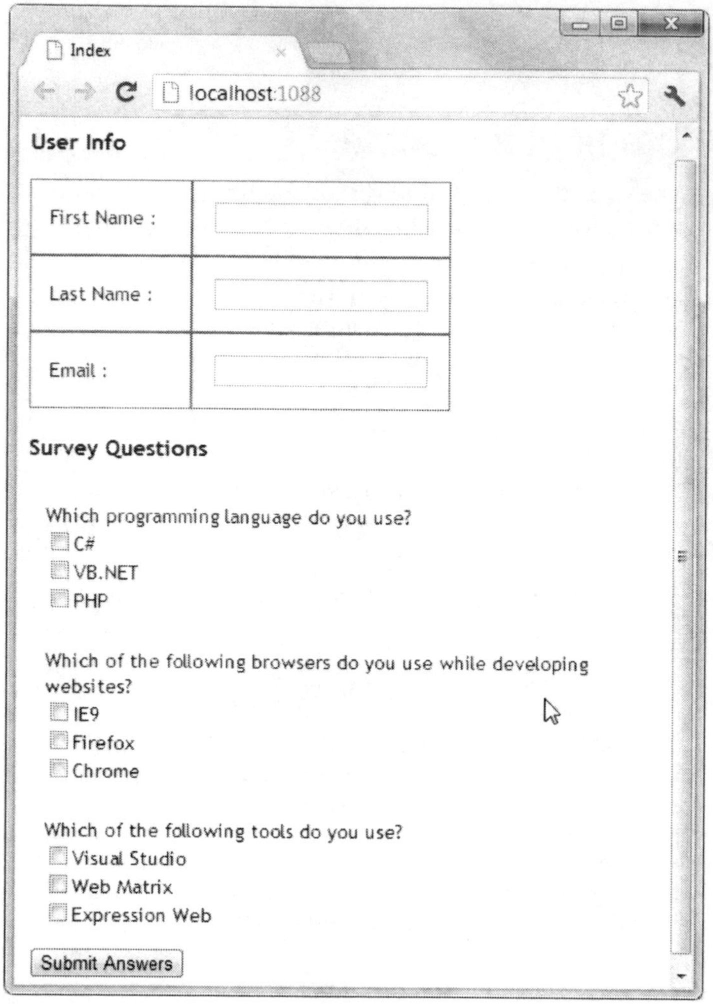

Figure 7-6. Survey form presented to users

As you can see, the survey form consists of two sections: User Info and Survey Questions. The User Info section captures user details such as First Name, Last Name, and Email. The Survey Questions section displays a list of survey questions and their answer choices. The survey questions as well as the choices are fetched from a SQL Server database (SurveyDb). As users start filling out the survey form, their input is stored in local storage. When they complete the survey and clicks the Submit Answers button, the user details and survey answers are sent to the server using jQuery $.ajax() method and stored in a database.

The SurveyDb database contains four tables: Questions, Choices, Results, and Users. Their purpose is listed in Table 7-3.

Table 7-3. Database Tables Used by the Survey Application

Table Name	Description
Questions	Contains the survey questions. Every question has a unique QuestionID.
Choices	Contains the answer choices for the survey questions. One question can have multiple choices. Every choice has a unique ChoiceID.
Results	Stores the survey answers as filled in by users.
Users	Contains user information such as FirstName, LastName, and Email.

The actual data access happens via an Entity Framework data model, shown in Figure 7-7.

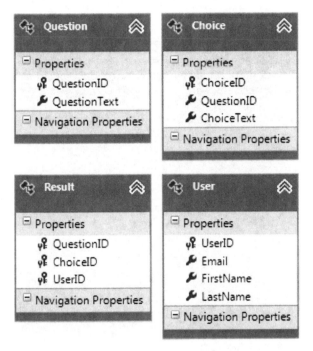

Figure 7-7. Entity Framework data model for SurveyDb *database tables*

To access the data residing in the SurveyDb database from the client side, you use jQuery code that calls certain action methods. In all three action methods of the controller (HomeController) are called from the jQuery code. They are GetQuestions(), GetChoices(), and SaveResults(). These action methods are discussed when they're used by the jQuery code.

When the view is loaded in the browser, a list of all the questions and their choices is displayed in the browser. This task is accomplished in the jQuery ready() method. ready() also wires event handlers for the buttons and the text boxes, as shown in Listing 7-6.

Listing 7-6. ready() Event Handler

```
var storage = window.localStorage;
$(document).ready(function () {
```

```
  if (!Modernizr.localstorage) {
    alert("This browser doesn't support HTML5 Local Storage!");
  }
  $("#submit").click(SubmitData);
  $("#firstName").change(function () { storage["FirstName"] = $(this).val(); });
  $("#lastName").change(function () { storage["LastName"] = $(this).val(); });
  $("#email").change(function () { storage["Email"] = $(this).val(); });
  $("#firstName").val(storage["FirstName"]);
  $("#lastName").val(storage["LastName"]);
  $("#email").val(storage["Email"]);
  GetQuestions();
})
```

A reference to the localStorage object is stored in a global variable—storage—for the sake of convenience. The click event of the Submit Answers button is wired to the SubmitData() function. The change event handlers of the firstName, lastName, and email text boxes are also wired. These change event handlers retrieve the text box value using the val() method and save it in localStorage. This way, as soon as users begin typing in these text boxes, their values are automatically saved in localStorage. If a user is revisiting the survey form and the firstName, lastName, and email values are already stored, then these pieces are retrieved from localStorage and filled in the text boxes.

The GetQuestions() function is then invoked to fetch survey questions. GetQuestions() is shown in Listing 7-7.

Listing 7-7. GetQuestions() Client-Side Function

```
function GetQuestions() {
  $.ajax({
    type: "POST",
    url: "/Home/GetQuestions",
    dataType: "json",
    contentType: "application/json; charset=utf-8",
    success: function (results) {
      for (var i = 0; i < results.length; i++) {
        $("#container").append("<div data-questions-questionid='" +
                               results[i].QuestionID + "'>" +
                               results[i].QuestionText + "</div>");
        $("div[data-questions-questionid]").addClass("paddedDiv");
      }
      GetChoices();
    },
    error: function (err) {
      alert(err.status + " - " + err.statusText);
    }
  })
}
```

The GetQuestions() function invokes the GetQuestions() action method using $.ajax(). The GetQuestions() action method returns an array of question items. The success handler function iterates through this array, and with each iteration, a <div> is dynamically added to the container. The GetQuestions() action method is shown in Listing 7-8.

Listing 7-8. GetQuestions() Action Method

```
public JsonResult GetQuestions()
{
    SurveyDbEntities db = new SurveyDbEntities();
    var data = from item in db.Questions
                   select item;
    return Json(data.ToArray());
}
```

The GetQuestions() action method selects all the question items from the Questions table and returns them as an array. Because the return value is to be accessed in jQuery code, it's converted into JSON format using the Json() method and then returned as a JsonResult.

Notice the use of data-* attributes in Listing 7-7. As discussed in Chapter 6, the data-* attributes are different than standard HTML attributes in that they're developer defined and don't directly affect the element in any way. All data-* attributes begin with prefix data- followed by a developer-defined attribute name. An element can have any number of data-* attributes, which you can access programmatically using jQuery code.

The dynamically generated <div> element defines one data-* attribute named data-questions-questionid. This attribute stores the QuestionID of a question from the Questions table. A sample dynamically generated <div> element looks like this:

```
<div data-questions-questionid='1'>Which programming language do you use?</div>
```

The success handler function then calls the GetChoices() function to populate choices for each of the questions. The GetChoices() function is shown in Listing 7-9.

Listing 7-9. GetChoices() Client-Side Function

```
function GetChoices() {
  $.ajax({
    type: "POST",
    url: "/Home/GetChoices",
    contentType: "application/json; charset=utf-8",
    dataType: "json",
    success: function(results){
      for (var i = 0; i < results.length; i++) {
        $("div[data-questions-questionid='" + results[i].QuestionID + "']").append(
          "<br /><input type='checkbox' data-choices-questionid='" +
          results[i].QuestionID +
          "' data-choices-choiceid='" + results[i].ChoiceID +
          "'/><span>" + results[i].ChoiceText + "</span>");
        if (storage[results[i].ChoiceID] != null) {
          var choiceId = results[i].ChoiceID;
          $("input[data-choices-choiceid='" +
              choiceId + "']").attr('checked', 'checked');
        }
      }
      $("input[data-choices-questionid]").change(function (event) {
        var key = $(event.target).attr("data-choices-choiceid");
        if ($(event.target).is(':checked') == true) {
          storage[key] = $(event.target).attr("data-choices-questionid");
        }
        else {
```

```
                    storage.removeItem(key);
          }
        });
      },
      error: function (err) {
        alert(err.status + " - " + err.statusText);
      }
    })
}
```

The GetChoices() function invokes the GetChoices() action method using the $.ajax() method. The GetChoices() action method returns an array of choice items. The success handler function iterates through all the choice items returned, and with each iteration, a choice is added to a question by dynamically generating a check box. You need to append all the choices belonging to a question inside that question's <div> element. Notice the jQuery selector that selects a <div> with data-questions-questionid attribute equal to the QuestionID. This way, the check boxes for choices are added to the <div> showing their question. Also notice how the code sets the data-choices-questionid and data-choices-choiceid attributes of the <input> element for later use. These two attributes represent the QuestionID and ChoiceID of a choice, respectively. A sample <div> with check boxes added looks like this:

```
<div data-questions-questionid='1'>Which programming language do you use?<br />
  <input type='checkbox' data-choices-questionid='1' data-choices-choiceid='1'/>
  <span>C#</span>
  <input type='checkbox' data-choices-questionid='1' data-choices-choiceid='2'/>
  <span>VB.NET</span>
  <input type='checkbox' data-choices-questionid='1' data-choices-choiceid='3'/>
  <span>PHP</span>
</div>
```

After you add the check boxes, you determine their checked status from localStorage, and accordingly they're checked or kept unchecked. If a user toggles the choice selection, you need to synchronize localStorage with the new selection. You do this in the change event handler of the dynamically added check boxes. The change event handler essentially determines whether a check box is checked (:checked selector), and an entry is added to or removed from the localStorage. When you add an item in localStorage, a ChoiceID acts as a key and its QuestionID acts as a value.

The GetChoices() action method used by the GetChoices() function discussed earlier is shown in Listing 7-10.

Listing 7-10. *GetChoices() Method*

```
public JsonResult GetChoices()
{
    SurveyDbEntities db = new SurveyDbEntities();
    var data = from item in db.Choices
               select item;
    return Json(data.ToArray());
}
```

The GetChoices() method is similar to the GetQuestions() method but returns all the choices from the Choices table.

When a user fills out the survey form and clicks the Submit Answers button, the SubmitData() function is called. This function in turn calls the SaveResults() action method using the jQuery $.ajax() method. The code in Listing 7-11 shows how this is done.

Listing 7-11. SubmitData() Client-Side Function

```
function SubmitData(event) {
  var data = '';
  for (var i = 0; i < storage.length; i++) {
    var key = storage.key(i);
    var value = storage[key];
    var pair = '"' + key + '":"' + value + '"';
    data = data + pair + ",";
  }
  if (data.charAt(data.length - 1) == ',') {
    data = data.substring(0, data.length - 1)
  }
  data = '{' + data + '}';
  $.ajax({
    type: "POST",
    url: "/Home/SaveResults",
    contentType: "application/json; charset=utf-8",
    data: data,
    dataType: "json",
    success: function(results){
      alert('Results saved!');
      window.localStorage.clear();
    },
    error: function (err) {
      alert(err.status + " - " + err.statusText);
    }
  })
}
```

The SubmitData() function forms a JSON representation of all the key-value pairs from localStorage by iterating through the keys. The function sends a JSON dictionary consisting of multiple question-choice pairs to the server all at once, not one question-choice at a time. The server-side code then needs to deserialize this JSON dictionary data into a .NET dictionary for further processing. To understand how SubmitData() sends the data to the server, you need to know what the JSON key-value pairs look like. Listing 7-12 shows some sample JSON data.

Listing 7-12. JSON Data Being Sent from the Client

```
{
    "FirstName":"Tom",
    "LastName":"Jerry",
    "Email":"tom@somedomain.com",
    "5":"2",
    "7":"3",
    "1":"1",
    "9":"3"
}
```

As you can see, there are several keys in the JSON data being sent to the server. These keys are described in Table 7-4.

Table 7-4. Keys Used in the JSON Dictionary

Key	Value
FirstName	A string value indicating the user's first name
LastName	A string value indicating the user's last name
Email	A string indicating the user's e-mail address
<choice_id>	<question_id> An integer indicating the QuestionID of the choice: for example, localStorage["3"] = 1 where 3 is a ChoiceID and 1 is a QuestionID

Note that localStorage is a key-value collection, and each key needs to be unique. Each choice in the Choices table has a unique ChoiceID. That is why you make ChoiceID the key and QuestionID the value. If you did it the other way around, you couldn't store multiple choices for a question—the latest ChoiceID would overwrite the previously stored ChoiceID because the QuestionID for both would be the same.

Once SaveResults() returns successfully, all the data from localStorage is removed using the clear() method. The SaveResults() action method that saves the survey results in the Results table is shown in Listing 7-13.

Listing 7-13. SaveResults() Action Method

```
public JsonResult SaveResults()
{
    string jsonData = string.Empty;
    using (StreamReader sr = new StreamReader(Request.InputStream))
    {
        jsonData = sr.ReadToEnd();
    }
    Dictionary<string, string> data =
    JsonConvert.DeserializeObject<Dictionary<string, string>>(jsonData);

    SurveyDbEntities db = new SurveyDbEntities();

    User usr = new User();
    usr.FirstName = data["FirstName"];
    usr.LastName = data["LastName"];
    usr.Email = data["Email"];
    db.Users.AddObject(usr);
    db.SaveChanges();

    string userEmail = data["Email"];
    int usrId = (from item in db.Users
                 where item.Email == userEmail
                 select item.UserID).SingleOrDefault();

    data.Remove("FirstName");
    data.Remove("LastName");
    data.Remove("Email");

    foreach (string str in data.Keys)
    {
        int choiceId = int.Parse(str);
```

```
        int questionId = int.Parse(data[str]);
        Result result = new Result();
        result.QuestionID = questionId;
        result.ChoiceID = choiceId;
        result.UserID = usrId;
        db.Results.AddObject(result);
    }
    db.SaveChanges();
    return Json("success");
}
```

The SaveResults() method is bit lengthy and requires careful observation. In order to convert JSON data passed from the client into a .NET dictionary, it uses the Json.NET library. Json.NET is a popular high-performance JSON framework for .NET that offers flexible ways to convert between JSON and .NET types. SaveResults() first reads the InputStream of the request into a string variable. It then uses the JsonConvert class of the Json.NET library to convert the JSON string into a .NET dictionary. Because localStorage stores all data as plain strings, the .NET dictionary uses string key and value data types (Dictionary<string,string>).

■ **Note**   Json.NET is a powerful open source framework and offer many other features. In this example, however, you need it only to convert a JSON dictionary to a .NET dictionary. Visit http://json.codeplex.com for more details about Json.NET.

SaveResults() then adds the user information to the Users table. The user's UserID is retrieved because it's also required while adding records to the Results table. The three keys—FirstName, LastName, and Email—are removed after a record is added in the Users table so that only ChoiceID keys are left. This way, you can simply run a for-each loop and add data to the Results table.

Figure 7-8 shows a sample successful run of the Survey application.

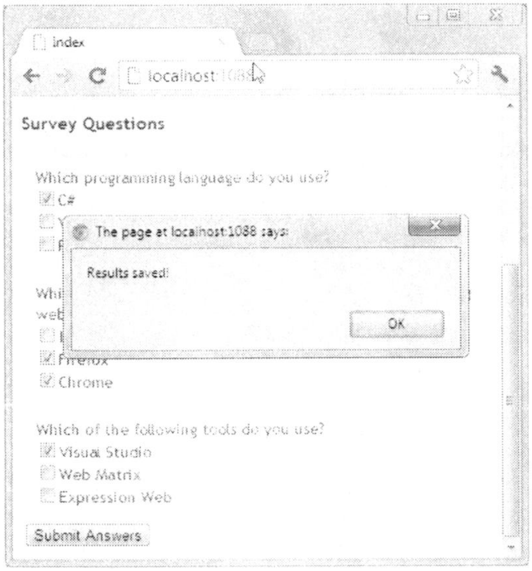

Figure 7-8. Sample run of the Survey application

You can test the application by making some selections and closing the browser window without saving the data. If you open the survey form again, it should show your earlier selections. You can then submit the answers and check whether they're saved in the SurveyDb database.

Passing Data as Hidden Form Field

In the Survey application that you just developed, data from the client side is passed to the server using the jQuery $.ajax() method. This works nicely because you don't submit the entire page to the server. However, in many cases you may want a full-page postback to the server.

Suppose you've developed the Survey application as a non-Ajax application. Further assume that the survey is split into three separate web pages like a wizard, such that each page displays a small subset of the total questions. In this case, data stored in localStorage needs to be sent to the server when the final wizard page is submitted. The application doesn't use Ajax, so how can you pass web storage data to the server? A simple way is to use a hidden form field. You can read key-value pairs from web storage, store them in a hidden field, and then submit the page to the server for further processing.

Assuming the Submit Answers button on the survey form causes a full-page postback, you can handle its click event and set a hidden form field using the client-side script shown in Listing 7-14.

Listing 7-14. Transferring localStorage Data into a Hidden Field

```
function OnPostback() {
  var data = '';
  for (var i = 0; i < storage.length; i++) {
    var key = storage.key(i);
    var value = storage[key];
    var pair = '"' + key + '":"' + value + '"';
    data = data + pair + ",";
  }
  if (data.charAt(data.length - 1) == ',') {
    data = data.substring(0, data.length - 1)
  }
  data = '{' + data + '}';
  $("#hiddenAnswers").val(data);
}
```

Listing 7-14 essentially generates the same JSON key-value pairs as in the previous case. This time, however, the JSON data is assigned to a hidden field with ID hiddenAnswers. On the server side, an action method handles the form postback. One such implementation is shown in Listing 7-15.

Listing 7-15. Handling the Postback on the Server

```
[HttpPost]
public ActionResult Index(FormCollection form)
{
    string jsonData = Request.Form["hiddenAnswers"];
    Dictionary<string, string> data =
    JsonConvert.DeserializeObject<Dictionary<string, string>>(jsonData);
    //save data here
    ...
    return Index();
}
```

As you can see, the `Index()` action method receives a `FormCollection`. The hidden field data is then retrieved and converted into a .NET dictionary using the `Json.NET` library as before. Once you have the . NET dictionary ready, you can easily store the survey results in the database just like the `SaveResults()` action method discussed earlier.

Security Considerations for Web Storage

When you're using web storage, it's important to be aware of some security aspects. Web storage isn't intended to store sensitive, secret data. So, you should never store sensitive information such as passwords, credit card numbers, Social Security numbers, and so on in web storage.

A browser allocates the same storage space to all the data that comes from the same origin. An *origin* means a combination of the scheme/host/port of the web site you're accessing. For example, `http://www.domain1.com` and `http://blog.domain1.com` are treated as two different origins by web storage. Along the same lines, `http://www.domain1.com` and `https://www.domain1.com` are also considered two different web sites. This, way malicious code can't trick web storage into storing dangerously huge amount of data. This same origin policy also prevents malicious scripts from using random subdomains to store unrestricted amounts of data.

As mentioned, web storage allocates storage spaces on a per-origin basis. However, someone could use DNS spoofing and pretend access was being attempted by an authentic domain. This way, the browser might grant malicious code access to that domain's storage area. To prevent such attacks, you can use Secure Socket Layer (SSL). Once SSL is in place, users can rest assured that the site they're visiting is from the authentic domain, and the browser will allocate the same storage space to all pages originating from that domain.

Summary

Web storage allows you to store data on the client machine. It doesn't suffer from the limitations of cookies and allows a reasonable amount of data to be stored on the client machine. The two objects `sessionStorage` and `localStorage` store key-value pairs of string data. `sessionStorage` can store data only for the current browser session, whereas `localStorage` can store data across browser sessions.

Web storage isn't transmitted to the server automatically with each request. You need to devise a programmatic approach such as Ajax calls or a hidden form fields to send web storage data to the server.

Web storage deals with data that is used in a live web application. The next chapter delves into another feature—offline applications—that lets you work with your web applications offline.

CHAPTER 8

■ ■ ■

Developing Offline Web Applications

Web applications are often looked on as wired applications that are connected to the network at all times. This "always on" nature of web applications is one of the reasons for their popularity and rapid growth. In today's Internet age, when network connectivity isn't a big deal, this characteristic of web applications doesn't pose a problem in most scenarios. However, sometimes you can't guarantee network connectivity. What should users of your application do then? Wouldn't it be nice if they could use your web application even in the absence of network connectivity? That is precisely what HTML5 offline web applications offer.

At first glance, you may find the concept of web applications functioning in a disconnected or stand-alone fashion slightly odd; but once you understand the scenarios in which they can help, you'll appreciate this feature of HTML5. This chapter explains the concept of offline web applications as applicable to HTML5. Specifically, you learn about the following:

- What offline web applications are, and when to use them

- The cache manifest file structure

- Creating and using a cache manifest in Web Forms and MVC applications

- Going online using Ajax techniques in situations where an offline application wants to talk with the server

- Using the applicationCache object and related events

When to Use Offline Applications

Offline applications are best suited in situations where there is little or no communication between client and server after the application files are downloaded at the client side. As the name suggests, offline applications are web applications that don't have live access to server-side resources such as databases and server-side code. Not all applications are good to go as offline applications. Therefore it's important to understand when to use offline applications and when to avoid them. While deciding whether your web application is a good candidate for going offline, you should consider these two basic questions:

- Does your application depend on live data?

- What impact will network downtime have on your web application and its users?

Suppose you're building a module for a sports portal that displays live cricket scores. Obviously your visitors will use this module to check the latest status of a cricket match. It doesn't make sense for such a module to go offline, because it relies on the latest data. The same can be said about web sites that provide stock quote information. Such web applications aren't good candidates to be implemented as offline applications.

Now, consider an online game. Assume that once downloaded, this game runs in a browser and needs no data from the server. The data used by the game is created and consumed on the client side. In such a case, the application doesn't depend on live data from the server and hence can be developed as an offline application.

Another important consideration is network downtime. Consider a web application that is used by sales executives. These sales executives are constantly travelling as part of their work and use the application on their laptops or mobile devices through wireless Internet connectivity. It's possible that they may not have Internet connectivity at all times; for example, they may travel to a remote location that is out of the coverage range of the wireless Internet service provider. Unavailability of network connectivity can hamper their work, so it makes sense to develop an offline application. On the other hand, network downtime may not make much difference to a web application used by operators for certain routine tasks, so there is no need to make it available as an offline application.

■ **Note** The term *offline application* doesn't necessarily indicate that all of a web site's pages work offline. A web site can have some pages that require network access to function and other pages that work offline. *Offline application* refers to the latter type of web pages.

HTTP Caching and Offline Applications

Before you delve into the details of offline applications, it's worthwhile to understand that they aren't same as traditional HTTP caching. Caching web resources such as web pages, images, style sheets, and JavaScript script files isn't a new invention. Browsers have been using these standard HTTP caching techniques for years. Whenever you access a web page, the browser downloads the page and its associated resources, such as images and style sheets, and stores them in a cache. This cache is maintained on the individual client machine. Browsers use this cache for the sake of efficiency and performance. Suppose, for example, that you're developing web pages that use the jQuery library. You refer to the jQuery library from the Microsoft Ajax Content Delivery Network (CDN) in all your web pages. If the browser already has the same version of the jQuery library in its cache, there is no need to download it again from the CDN. The same is true for images and style sheets.

Most of the time, the browser uses traditional HTTP caching behind the scenes. If you wish to check whether a browser has stored files in the local cache, you can test the behavior using the browser's offline mode. Almost all browsers provide an option to work offline. For example, Figure 8-1 shows Firefox's Work Offline menu option.

If you select this menu option, Firefox doesn't fetch pages from the server. Instead, it uses pages from the local cache if they already exist; otherwise it gives an error message.

The Work Offline menu option relies on the standard HTTP caching mentioned earlier. Usually you don't need to write any code on the server to enable this default behavior. If you wish to fine-tune or prohibit this behavior, you can do so using cache-control headers or IIS Manager.

At first glance, traditional HTTP caching may resemble the offline application caching introduced by HTML5. However, there are significant differences between them:

- Traditional HTTP caching doesn't need any code or configuration from your side unless you wish to alter the default browser behavior. On the other hand, HTML5 offline applications need certain explicit steps from your side.

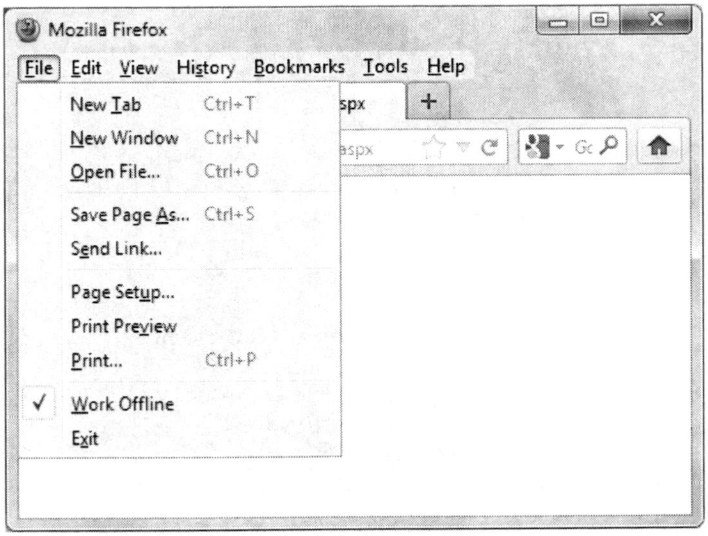

Figure 8-1. *Working offline in Firefox*

- Traditional HTTP caching can be fine-tuned using cache-control headers. HTML5 offline applications rely on a manifest file and always work in an offline fashion even if network connectivity is available.

- Traditional HTTP caching is an implicit mechanism, and no thought is given to how web pages should behave while the browser is in offline mode. HTML5 offline applications are explicitly developed with requirements such as data storage and network availability in mind.

Building an Offline Application

Offline applications essentially fetch server resources such as web pages, images, style sheets, and script files and store them in the browser's local cache. Once the files are on the local machine, there is no need for network connectivity. Of course, later you may need to go online to synchronize local and server-side data.

To develop an offline application, you need to follow these basic steps:

1. Create a cache manifest file.

2. Add references to the cache manifest file to all the web pages that are part of the offline application.

3. Configure the web server so that it recognizes the cache manifest file extension.

4. In JavaScript code, periodically check whether network connectivity with the server is available.

A *cache manifest* is a text file that lists all the file-based resources of an offline application. The resources listed in a cache manifest file include files that are to be cached, files that are to be fetched over a network rather than cached locally, and substitute files in case files can't be cached for some reason. An ASP.NET web application may contain many web pages out of which only a few are used as an offline application. So, there is no one-to-one mapping between the ASP.NET application and the offline application. One ASP.NET application may include multiple independent offline applications. Each such offline application needs its own cache manifest. There is no rigid requirement for the cache manifest's file extension, but .appcache and .manifest are commonly used.

Simply creating a cache manifest file isn't sufficient. All the web pages belonging to that offline application should refer the cache manifest. This way, whenever a browser downloads a web page, it knows that this page is part of an offline application. Additionally, the cache manifest tells the browser what resources the page requires (images, script files, and so on) so that the browser can ensure availability of those resources.

As mentioned, a cache manifest file can have any developer-defined extension. You need to inform IIS about the file extension you're using for your cache manifest file and associated MIME type. Without this information, IIS may not send the cache manifest to the browser, and the browser can't cache the required files.

Although offline applications behave like stand-alone applications, at some point in their lifetime they may need to interact with the web server. Suppose, for example, that you've developed a JavaScript-intensive game as an offline application. This means the end user doesn't need network connectivity while playing the game. However, at the end, the game may need to go online to store the user's score in an online account or profile. In this case, you need to check whether a network connection is available and, if so, perform the required data transfer. This step is, of course, optional and depends primarily on the nature of the application.

The following sections examine in detail the steps you follow to build an offline application. You develop a simple Web Forms–based offline application that uses the topics you've learn about. This offline application displays a JavaScript-driven digital clock on a web page (see Figure 8-2). There is also a provision to send the time shown on the clock to the server for further processing.

Figure 8-2. Clock offline application

Creating a Cache Manifest

As mentioned earlier, a cache manifest is a text file that lists files to be cached. In this example, you use .cachemanifest as the file extension and learn how to inform IIS about this extension.

The cache manifest file consists of a cache manifest declaration followed by one or more sections: CACHE, NETWORK, and FALLBACK. The cache manifest declaration looks like this:
CACHE MANIFEST

All cache manifest files must begin with this line. Other than the CACHE section, the other sections are optional and are discussed next.

■ **Note**   Cache manifest files are case sensitive. Be sure you key in the section names as well as file names exactly as shown in the example code.

The CACHE Section of the Cache Manifest

The CACHE section of a cache manifest lists all the files that are to be cached on the client side. The files may include web pages, images, style sheets, and JavaScript files. For example, the Clock application uses the files listed in Table 8-1.

Table 8-1. Files Used in the Clock Application

File Name	Description
Clock.aspx	The main web form where the clock is displayed
StyleSheet.css	The CSS file that includes styles being used in the Clock application
Scripts/jquery-1.7.2.min.js	A jQuery library that is necessary for the Clock application to work
Images/HTML5.png	An HTML5 logo that is displayed at the bottom of the Clock application

The files displayed in Table 8-1 are specified in the cache manifest as shown in Listing 8-1.

Listing 8-1. CACHE section of the Cache Manifest File

```
CACHE MANIFEST

CACHE:
Clock.aspx
Images/HTML5.png
StyleSheet.css
Scripts/jquery-1.7.2.min.js
```

Notice that the CACHE section name is followed by a colon (:) character. Files to be cached are listed one per line.

CACHE is an *implicit* section. That means if you don't explicitly specify CACHE, the files are assumed to belong to the CACHE section. So, Listing 8-1 and Listing 8-2 are equivalent.

Listing 8-2. Implicit CACHE Section

```
CACHE MANIFEST

Clock.aspx
Images/HTML5.png
StyleSheet.css
Scripts/jquery-1.7.2.min.js
```

The cache manifest file written so far conveys that the four files specified in the CACHE section are to be downloaded to the local cache.

■ **Note:**   The Clock application is an ASP.NET Web Forms application; if you developed it as an MVC application, then instead of Clock.aspx you would specify a controller action that renders the respective view (for example, Home/Index).

The NETWORK Section of the Cache Manifest

The CACHE section specifies what files the browser should cache for offline usage. The NETWORK section does exactly the opposite: it lists files that should not be cached. Suppose your application displays advertisements in addition to page content. They most likely come from an ad engine that keeps track of ad impressions and clicks. Obviously, such ads can't be stored offline. If your offline application uses such resources, they should be listed in the NETWORK section.

Listing 8-3 shows the Ads.js file listed in the NETWORK section.

Listing 8-3. NETWORK Section of the Cache Manifest File

```
CACHE MANIFEST

CACHE:
...

NETWORK:
Scripts/Ads.js
```

This way, Ads.js is never cached in an offline cache. Instead, it's always accessed over the network.

In a big application, there may be many candidates for the NETWORK section. At times you may not even know in advance that a resource needs to come over the network. In such cases, you can use the * wildcard character to inform the browser that all files not listed in the CACHE section should be accessed over a network. You use the * character like this:

```
NETWORK:
*
```

The NETWORK section is also useful when you're working with resources (images, scripts, and so on) that are hosted on a different server and referred to by your application. For example, you might be using images and script files hosted by a CDN rather than including them in your application. If you don't include these external resources in the NETWORK section (either explicitly or by using the * wildcard), then, strangely enough, your application won't load them when you're online.

The FALLBACK Section of the Cache Manifest

The FALLBACK section of the cache manifest file specifies alternate files in case a resource can't be cached or can't be accessed over a network. You can think of the FALLBACK section as an error-handling technique. If the original resource is unavailable, you substitute some other resource. You can use the FALLBACK section to provide substitute content or display an error message. For example, the Clock application uses the FALLBACK section to display a generic error message (see Listing 8-4).

Listing 8-4. *FALLBACK Section of the Cache Manifest File*

```
CACHE MANIFEST

CACHE:
...

NETWORK:
...

FALLBACK:
/ ErrorPage.aspx
```

Listing 8-4 uses ErrorPage.aspx as a generic error page for all resources (/) that can't be cached. Notice the use of the / character: it indicates that for any resource that can't be accessed, ErrorPage.aspx should be displayed. The / and the error page are separated by whitespace.

Before you proceed to the next section, make sure you save the cache manifest file as Clock.cachemanifest in the root folder of your web application.

Referring to the Cache Manifest in Web Forms and Views

Now that you've created the cache manifest for the Clock application, let's see how to refer it in web forms and views. Look at Listing 8-5.

Listing 8-5. *Referring to a Cache Manifest in* Clock.aspx

```
<%@ Page Language="C#" AutoEventWireup="true" CodeBehind="Clock.aspx.cs"
        Inherits="BasicOfflineApp.WebForm1" %>

<!DOCTYPE html>
<html xmlns="http://www.w3.org/1999/xhtml" manifest="Clock.cachemanifest">
<head runat="server">
    <link rel="stylesheet" type="text/css" href="StyleSheet.css" />
    <script type="text/javascript" src="Scripts/jquery-1.7.2.min.js"></script>
    <script type="text/javascript">
    ...
    </script>
</head>
<body>
    <script src="Scripts/Ads.js"></script>
    <form id="form1" runat="server">
        <div class="clock">
            <div id="date"></div>
```

209

```
            <div id="time">
              <span id="hours"></span><span id="colon1">:</span>
              <span id="min"></span><span id="colon2">:</span>
              <span id="sec"></span>
            </div>
        </div>
        <br />
        <center>
        <input id="Send" type="button" value="Send Time to Server" />
        <br /><br />
        <img src="Images/HTML5.png" width="125" height="125" />
        </center>
    </form>
</body>
</html>
```

Notice the markup shown in bold. The `<html>` tag contains a `manifest` attribute that points to the `Clock.cachemanifest` file. You need to add the `manifest` attribute in all the web forms (or MVC views) that are part of the offline application.

Also notice that the `<head>` section contains references to `StyleSheet.css` and the jQuery library. There is also a `<script>` block that contains the jQuery code responsible for displaying the clock (the code isn't shown in the listing for the sake of clarity). The `<body>` section uses `Ads.js` to display advertisements, followed by markup to display the clock. Recollect that the CACHE section of the `Clock.cachemanifest` file contains all these style sheet, script, and image files.

The remaining markup from the `<body>` section includes a few `<span>` elements that render hours, minutes, and seconds. The clock is displayed using the jQuery code shown in Listing 8-6.

Listing 8-6. jQuery Code that Displays the Clock

```
$(document).ready(function () {
  if (!Modernizr.applicationcache) {
    alert("This browser doesn't support HTML5 Offline Applications!");
  }
  var months = [ "January", "February", "March", "April", "May", "June",
                          "July", "August", "September", "October",
                          "November", "December" ];
  var days= ["Sunday","Monday","Tuesday","Wednesday","Thursday","Friday","Saturday"]
  var today = new Date();
  today.setDate(today.getDate());
  $('#date').html(days[today.getDay()] + " " + today.getDate() + ' ' +
                          months[today.getMonth()] + ' ' + today.getFullYear());

  setInterval(function () {
    var seconds = new Date().getSeconds();
    $("#sec").html(( seconds < 10 ? "0" : "" ) + seconds);
  },1000);

  setInterval( function() {
    var minutes = new Date().getMinutes();
    $("#min").html(( minutes < 10 ? "0" : "" ) + minutes);
  },1000);
```

```
  setInterval( function() {
    var hours = new Date().getHours();
    $("#hours").html(( hours < 10 ? "0" : "" ) + hours);
  }, 1000);
});
```

This code uses the `setInterval()` JavaScript function to update the time after every 1,000 milliseconds. The current date is also displayed at the top of the clock using the JavaScript `Date` object and its methods. Notice how browser support for offline applications is detected using the `Modernizr.applicationcache` property.

Configuring IIS to Recognize the Cache Manifest File

In order for an offline application to work as expected, the browser should be able to download the cache manifest file successfully from the web server. It's important that the web server (IIS) serve the cache manifest with the extension you use (`.cachemanifest` in this case). Earlier it was mentioned that `.manifest` and `.appcache` are commonly used file extensions for the cache manifest; be aware that `.manifest` is also used by .NET ClickOnce deployment, and IIS may already have an entry for it (see Figure 8-3).

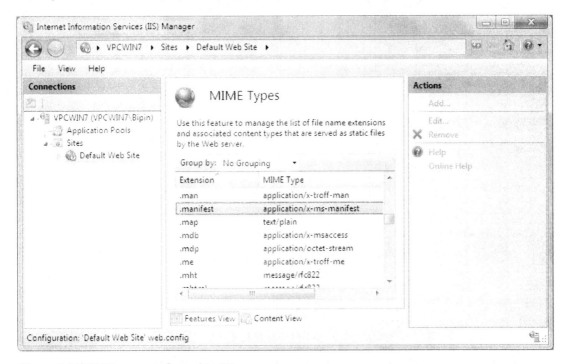

Figure 8-3. MIME types configured in IIS

Considering this, you may want to use another file extension (such as `.appcache` or `.cachemanifest`) to avoid confusion. Once you decide on a file extension, you need to add its MIME content type in IIS as `text/cache-manifest`. This way, IIS serves the cache manifest file correctly to the requesting browser.

There is also an alternative to using IIS Manager: your web application's `web.config`. You can configure the cache manifest file extension using the `mimeMap` element of `web.config`. Listing 8-7 shows how to map the `.cachemanifest` file extension to the MIME type `text/cache-manifest`.

Listing 8-7. Mapping the MIME Type Using web.config

```
<system.webServer>
  <staticContent>
      <mimeMap fileExtension=".cachemanifest" mimeType="text/cache-manifest" />
  </staticContent>
</system.webServer>
```

The fileExtension attribute of the <mimeMap> element specifies the file extension of the cache manifest file, and the mimeType attribute specifies the cache manifest's MIME type.

Testing an Offline Application

Now that you've completed all the steps required to create an offline application, let's test the Clock application using Chrome. Assuming that you have the project opened in Visual Studio, press Ctrl+F5 to run the application. Clock.aspx is loaded in the browser as shown in Figure 8-2 earlier. To ensure that the application is really being served from the browser cache, open the Visual Studio development web server (IIS Express) and stop the application (see Figure 8-4).

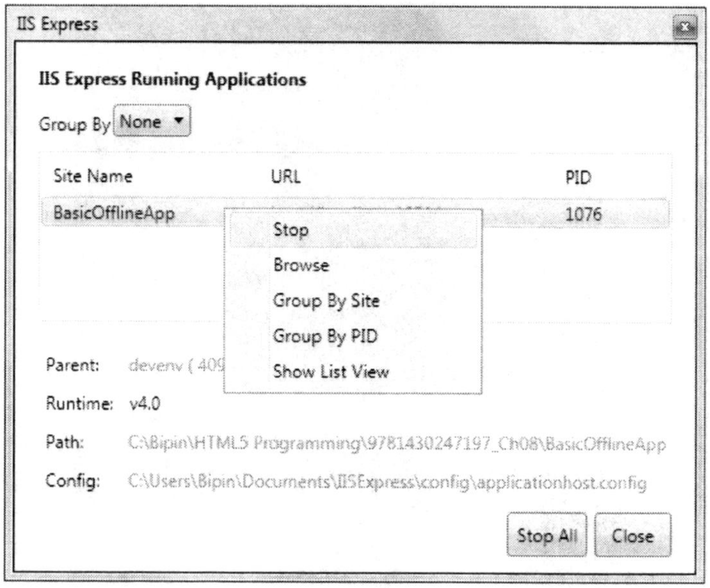

Figure 8-4. IIS Express list of applications

Now, refresh Clock.aspx. Ordinarily you would receive an error at this step because the web application is stopped; but because the browser has cached the application locally, Clock.aspx is refreshed from the cache.

Open another browser tab, type chrome://appcache-internals in the address bar, and press Enter. You should see a page similar to that shown in Figure 8-5.

Figure 8-5 shows how Chrome displays details of offline applications. You can see all the files listed in the cache manifest. You can also manually clear the cache by clicking Remove.

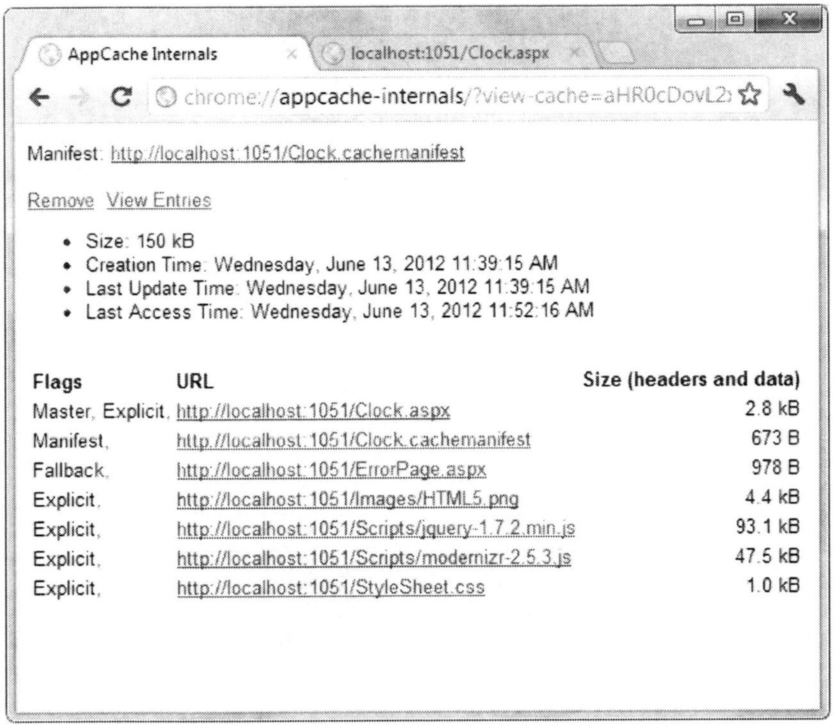

Figure 8-5. Chrome showing offline application details

▪ **Note** Different browsers have different ways to show details of offline applications. For example, Firefox shows these details in the Tools ➤ Options ➤ Advanced ➤ Network dialog. Additionally, Firefox informs you that a web application is requesting offline storage when the application is initially accessed.

Going Online Using Ajax

Although an offline application is disconnected from the server, during the lifetime of the application it may need to go online and communicate with the server. Suppose you wish to save the current time displayed in the Clock application in a database. You can do that only if a network connection is available. A sure way to tell if a network connection is available is to make a request to the server and see if the request is successful. The jQuery $.ajax() method can be used effectively for this purpose. Listing 8-8 shows how you can use $.ajax() to ping the server periodically.

Listing 8-8. Checking Whether a Network Connection Is Available Using $.ajax()

```
$(document).ready(function () {
  ...
  setTimeout(CheckOnline, 5000);
});
```

```
function CheckOnline() {
  $.ajax({
    type: "POST",
    url: 'Clock.aspx/IsOnline',
    contentType: "application/json; charset=utf-8",
    dataType: "json",
    success: function (result) {
      if (result.d == true) {
        $("#status").html("You are Online!");
        setTimeout(CheckOnline, 5000);
      }
    },
    error: function () {
      $("#status").html("You are Offline!");
      setTimeout(CheckOnline, 5000);
    }
  });
```

This code shows a function—CheckOnline()—that makes an $.ajax() request to a web method named IsOnline(). The IsOnline() web method returns a Boolean flag. If the $.ajax() method is able to invoke IsOnline() successfully, it indicates that a network connection is available. The success method then sets the content of a <div> to "You are Online!" If there is no network connectivity, the call to IsOnline() fails, and the error function is called. The error function sets the content of the <div> to "You are Offline!" You need to check for the online status periodically; hence the CheckOnline() function is called every 5,000 milliseconds using the setTimeout() function.

The IsOnline() web method used by the $.ajax() call is shown in Listing 8-9.

Listing 8-9. IsOnline() Web Method

```
[WebMethod]
public static bool IsOnline()
{
    return true;
}
```

The IsOnline() method returns true to indicate that a network connection to the server is available.

Updating an Offline Application

Once a cache manifest file is served to the browser, the browser begins using the application files from the cache. But you may need to change the web application after it has been cached. There are two possibilities in such cases:

- You can add files to or remove them from the web application and make changes to the cache manifest file.

- You can change one or more of the application files (their content or code) but not change the cache manifest file.

When you begin using an offline application, normally the browser checks with the server to see whether a cache manifest file is available that's newer than the one that has been cached. If so, the browser downloads the new cache manifest file and downloads the files as per that cache manifest. This browser behavior takes care of the first scenario listed because the timestamp of the modified cache manifest file is different than that of the previously downloaded cache manifest.

However, the second scenario is slightly tricky. In that case, you aren't changing the cache manifest file: you're changing the constituent files, and you expect the browser to use the new versions of those files. Unfortunately, the browser doesn't check the timestamp of each constituent file, and it keeps using the cached versions of the files. To rectify the problem, you need to change the timestamp of the cache manifest file residing on the server. There are different approaches to doing this:

- Whenever one or more constituent files change, run a utility that changes the timestamp of the cache manifest file (you can easily develop such a utility using System.IO classes).

- Open the cache manifest file and make a pseudo-change to it (say, add whitespace and remove it; or cut the entire contents of the file, save the file, paste in the contents, and save the file back to the disk) so it has a new timestamp.

- Maintain a version number in the cache manifest file, and change it whenever the constituent files change.

Of these options, the last is simplest to implement. The other options are more suitable if you're planning to build an automated way to update the cache manifest file.

Suppose the Clock.aspx file listed in Clock.cachemanifest changes due to a code-level revision, and you wish to use a version number as a way to change the cache manifest. You can do so as shown in Listing 8-10.

Listing 8-10. Cache Manifest with a Version Number

```
CACHE MANIFEST
# version 2.0

CACHE:
...

NETWORK:
...

FALLBACK:
...
```

Notice the bold code. The cache manifest file treats content following a # character as a comment. You specify a version number in the comment. Whenever you change any of the constituent files, you need to change the version number and save the modified cache manifest file. This way, the timestamp of the cache manifest is also changed, and the browser downloads the cache manifest and its constituent files again.

■ **Note** There can be some differences in the way cache manifest files are checked for a new version. If for some reason (HTTP caching, for example) the cache manifest file is cached on the client side, the browser won't check whether the file has been modified. If so, the user needs to manually remove the offline application files as mentioned earlier.

Offline Application Events

In the preceding sections, you created an offline application by creating a cache manifest. The browser did all the work of downloading and storing the application files in a local cache. When the browser is busy downloading and caching an application, it raises several applicationCache object events. applicationCache is an object whose properties, methods, and events can be handled using JavaScript code. Using applicationCache events, you can track various stages of an offline application's life cycle. Let's see what kind of events the applicationCache object fires:

1. Whenever you request a web page whose manifest attribute points to a cache manifest file, the checking event of the applicationCache object is raised. The checking event is raised regardless of whether the application is already cached.

2. If the browser has never cached this application before, it downloads the application's cache manifest as indicated in the manifest attribute and begins downloading files as listed in the cache manifest. At the same time, the downloading event of the applicationCache object is raised.

3. The cache manifest may contain many files, and the downloading operation may be lengthy. That is why periodically the applicationCache object raises a progress event notifying you about the progress of the download operation.

4. After all the files listed in the cache manifest are downloaded, the applicationCache object raises the cached event. This event is an indication that the entire application is now available offline.

5. If you're accessing an application that is already cached, the browser checks whether the application's cache manifest file has changed since the last download.

6. If the cache manifest file is unchanged, there is no need to update the offline cache, and the noupdate event of the applicationCache object is raised.

7. If the cache manifest has changed since the last download, the browser begins downloading the application files and raises the downloading and progress events of the applicationCache object as before.

8. When all the application files have been successfully downloaded, the updateready event of the applicationCache object is raised.

9. It's also possible that an application that was cached earlier is no longer an offline application—that is, its cache manifest has been removed from the server. In this case, the browser raises the obsolete event of the applicationCache object and removes the existing files from the cache. The application is now treated as a *connected* application and needs a live network connection with the server in order to function properly.

10. If there is an error in any of the previous steps, the error event of the applicationCache object is raised.

The applicationCache object events just discussed are listed in Table 8-2 for your convenience.

Table 8-2. Events of the applicationCache Object

Event	Description
checking	Raised when the browser detects a web page's manifest attribute.
downloading	Raised when the browser begins downloading files listed in an application's cache manifest file.
progress	Raised periodically during the download process.
cached	Raised when an application has been downloaded successfully and cached on the local machine.
updateready	Raised when the browser has successfully downloaded an updated version of a previously cached application.
noupdate	Raised when the browser detects that no update is required for an already cached application.
obsolete	Raised when the browser detects that the cache manifest of a previously cached application is no longer available on the server.
error	Raised when there is an error during any of the other events.

To understand how you can use these events, let's wire some of them into the Clock application (see Listing 8-11). The Clock application essentially uses these events to notify the end user about the associated operations.

Listing 8-11. Using applicationCache Object Events

```
$(document).ready(function () {
  ...
  $(applicationCache).bind("checking",NotifyUser);
  $(applicationCache).bind("downloading", NotifyUser);
  $(applicationCache).bind("progress", NotifyUser);
  $(applicationCache).bind("cached", NotifyUser);
  $(applicationCache).bind("updateready", NotifyUser);
  $(applicationCache).bind("noupdate", NotifyUser);
  $(applicationCache).bind("obsolete", NotifyUser);
  $(applicationCache).bind("error", NotifyUser);
});

function NotifyUser(evt) {
  alert(evt.type);
  if (evt.type == 'updateready') {
    if (confirm('An updated version of this application is available.' +
                     'Do you wish to use the new version now?'))
    {
      applicationCache.swapCache();
    }
  }
}
```

This code binds the applicationCache events listed in Table 8-1 to a common event handler function NotifyUser(). The NotifyUser() function displays the event type (checking, downloading, progress, and so on). Notice the if block: if the event type is updateready, it means an updated version of the application is available. In most cases, you want the user to use the updated version immediately. One way to

217

accomplish this is to call the `window.location.reload()` method. Alternatively, you can call the `applicationCache` object's `swapCache()` method. `swapCache()` replaces the older cache with the newly downloaded one and begins using the new cache without requiring any page refresh as in the case of `reload()`.

▦ **Note**   The `applicationCache` object also exposes a `status` property that returns a numeric status code depending on the state of the object (1 for Idle, 2 for Checking, and so on). However, in most cases, using `applicationCache` object events offers much more flexibility and control than using the `status` property.

ASP.NET MVC Example: the Survey Application Revisited

In the preceding sections, you worked with the Web Forms–based Clock application. To create an offline application using ASP.NET MVC, you follow the same steps. For the sake of completeness, let's convert the Survey application you developed in Chapter 7 into an offline application. The Survey application may not be the best candidate for offline use, but think of a slight variant of it.

Suppose a big software development company frequently recruits junior- and senior-level software developers. The company receives hundreds of job applications from interested candidates, and it's impossible to conduct personal one-to-one interviews with all the applicants. Hence the company wants to develop an online examination engine that presents a series of single-choice, multiple-choice, and descriptive questions to candidates. The candidates can take the online exam anywhere, at their convenience. This online test becomes a basis for filtering the candidates. Only successful candidates are then called for interview. In the case of an online examination engine, candidates may remain on a page for a long time because they're thinking about the correct answers. Such an application can be nicely developed as an offline application. By now you must have guessed that the Survey application, although not exactly an online exam engine, resembles this scenario.

Let's carry out the steps required to convert the Survey application into an offline application. The offline version of the Survey application is shown in Figure 8-6.

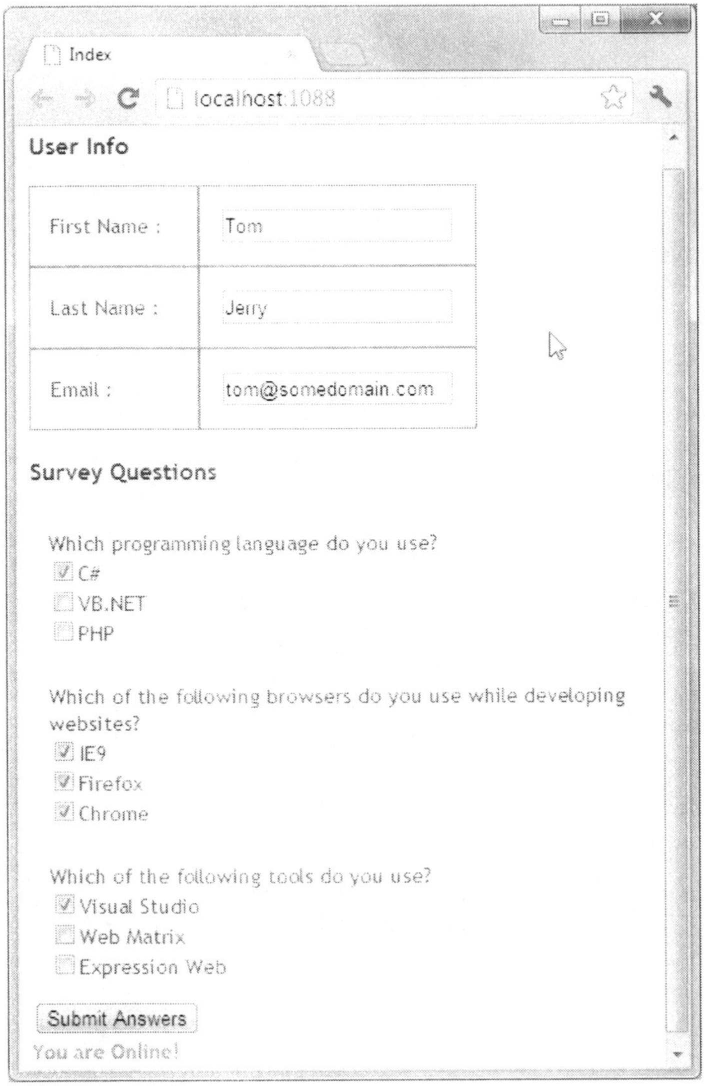

Figure 8-6. *Survey application converted to an offline application*

The modified Survey application is almost identical to the original in terms of look and feel, except for one change. Below the Submit Answers button, you now display the network status so the user knows whether survey data can be saved to the database.

Creating a Cache Manifest File

To begin converting the Survey application into an offline application, create a copy of the Survey application and open it in Visual Studio. Next, you need to create the cache manifest file for the application. So, create a text file named Survey.cachemanifest, and add the entries shown in Listing 8-12.

Listing 8-12. Survey.cachemanifest File

```
CACHE MANIFEST
# version 1.0

CACHE:
Home/Index
Content/Site.css
Scripts/jquery-1.6.2.js
Scripts/modernizr-2.0.6-development-only.js

FALLBACK:
/ Home/ErrorPage
```

Look at this listing carefully. The CACHE section lists four entries: one route URL, one CSS file, and two script files. The FALLBACK section specifies a generic error page: the ErrorPage view displays a generic error message to the user.

Next, open index view and specify the cache manifest file using the manifest attribute, like this:

```
<html manifest="/Survey.cachemanifest">...</html>
```

Getting the Questions and Choices

The overall functionality of the Survey application remains unchanged even when it's converted into an offline application. However, because the application relies on the questions and choices stored in the database, you need to cache them on the client side. Recollect that the GetQuestions() and GetChoices() functions call controller action methods to retrieve questions and choices, respectively. You should store this data into local storage so it's also available in offline mode.

■ **Note**   A real-world survey or online exam application has many questions and choices. Additionally, the questions may change frequently, and it would be impractical to cache all of them and their choices on the client side. A better approach is to fetch questions and choices in live mode every time and then inform users that they can go offline.

The modified versions of the GetQuestions() and GetChoices() functions are shown in Listing 8-13.

Listing 8-13. Storing data in local storage

```
function GetQuestions() {
 $.ajax({
    ...
     GetChoices();
   },
   error: function (err) {
     if (storage["container"] != null) {
       $("#container").html(storage["container"]);
     }
     else {
       alert(err.status + " - " + err.statusText);
     }
```

```
    }
  })
}

function GetChoices() {
  $.ajax({
      ...
        else {
          storage.removeItem(key);
        }
      });
      storage["container"]=$("#container").html();
    },
    error: function (err) {
      alert(err.status + " - " + err.statusText);
    }
  })
}
```

Notice the bold code. The GetQuestions() function fetches questions and then calls the GetChoices() function. Once GetChoices() completes successfully, the container <div> element is populated with questions and their choices. The code stores the entire dynamically generated HTML markup in local storage. This way, even if there is no network connectivity, the questions and choices are available to the code. Beginning the next time through, if GetQuestions() can't access the database due to network unavailability, the error function of the $.ajax() call (of GetQuestions()) retrieves the HTML markup stored in the local storage and populates the container <div> element.

Checking for a Network Connection

Finally, the Survey application needs to store the answers in a database. It makes an Ajax call to the server whenever the Submit Answers button is clicked. When the user clicks Submit Answers, the SubmitData() function is invoked; it calls the SaveResults() controller action method to save the survey data. This Ajax call succeeds only if there is network connectivity.

It would be beneficial to inform the user about the availability of a network connection and accordingly enable or disable the Submit Answers button. To do so, you need to periodically check whether a network connection is available. Listing 8-14 shows how this can be accomplished.

Listing 8-14. Enabling or Disabling the Submit Answers Button

```
$(document).ready(function () {
  ...
  setTimeout(CheckOnline, 5000);
})

function CheckOnline() {
  $.ajax({
    type: "POST",
    url: 'Home/IsOnline',
    contentType: "application/json; charset=utf-8",
    dataType: "json",
    success: function (result) {
```

```
      if (result == true) {
        $("#status").html("You are Online!");
        $("#submit").removeAttr('disabled');
        setTimeout(CheckOnline, 5000);
      }
    },
    error: function () {
      $("#status").html("You are Offline!");
      $("#submit").attr('disabled', 'disabled');
      setTimeout(CheckOnline, 5000);
    }
  });
}
```

This code should look familiar: you used a similar technique in the Clock application. Using the setTimeout() method, you call CheckOnline() every five seconds. CheckOnline() then calls the IsOnline() controller action method. If this call is successful, it indicates that a network connection is available; otherwise, the network is unavailable. Accordingly, the Submit Answers button is enabled or disabled by adding or removing the disabled attribute. IsOnline() is shown in Listing 8-15.

Listing 8-15. IsOnline() Action Methodpublic JsonResult IsOnline()

```
{
    return Json(true);
}
```

IsOnline() returns true in JSON format. You can now run the Survey application and test it by stopping the application in IIS Express, as explained earlier.

Summary

Most web applications need a live network connection to the web server in order to function properly. Such applications involve heavy interaction between client and server. Some web applications, however, can work without an active network connection to the web server. Such applications usually involve heavy client-side functionality. HTML5 allows you to develop such offline applications easily. Not every application is a good candidate, but if the need arises, you have native support for such offline applications.

At the heart of an offline application is a cache manifest file that lists all the files that are needed in offline mode. If required, an offline application can connect with the web server when a network connection is available and transfer data or execute server-side code. The applicationCache object introduced in HTML5 represents an offline application cache and helps you to track various application life cycle events by raising events.

HTML5 adds rich client-side capabilities to your web applications. Another such area is client-side file access. Traditionally, JavaScript couldn't access local files in any manner. The HTML5 File API provides a standardized way to deal with local files. The next chapter discusses this feature in detail.

■ ■ ■

CHAPTER 9

Dealing with Local Files Using the File API

It's a well-known fact that for the sake of security and privacy, browsers don't allow web applications to tamper with the local file system. Local files are used in a web application only when the user decides to upload them to the server using the HTML <input> element of type file. The title of this chapter may surprise you at first, because the term *File API* gives the impression of being a full-blown file-system manipulation object model like the System.IO namespace of .NET Framework. Obviously, the people behind HTML5 are aware of the security issues such an object model can create. So, the File API is essentially a cut-down version of a file-handling system in which files can only be read and can't be modified or deleted. Additionally, the File API can't read any random file on the machine. File(s) to be read must be explicitly supplied by the user. Thus, the File API is a safe way to read and optionally upload local files with user consent.

This chapter examines what the File API can do for you and how it can be used in ASP.NET web applications. Specifically, you learn the following:

- Classes available as a part of the File API

- Techniques of selecting files to be used with the File API

- Using HTML5 native drag-and-drop

- Reading files with the File API

- Uploading files to the server

Understanding the File API

The HTML5 File API consists of a set of three objects (see Table 9-1) that allow you to read files residing on the client computer. The files to be read must be explicitly selected by the user using one of the supported techniques discussed in later sections. Once selected, you can read the files using JavaScript code.

Table 9-1. Objects Exposed by the File API

Object	Description
FileList	A list of files selected by the user. A user typically selects files using a file field or by dragging from Windows Explorer and dropping them on a predefined area of a web page.
File	A single file that's used to find information such as file name, size, and MIME type.
FileReader	Allows you to read a file in asynchronous fashion. Once read, you can either upload the contents to the server or use them for custom processing.

The object model of the File API is quite small, but you can use these three objects in creative ways that were impossible (or at least very difficult) prior to HTML5. Some of the creative ways in which you can use the File API are as follows:

- In traditional HTML, when you use a file field to upload files, there is no checking of file size on the client end. Only when the file reaches the server can you perform checks in the server-side code and accept or reject the file. You can now reject files above a certain file size at the client.

- You can read image files on the client side and render a preview or thumbnail before they're uploaded to the server. Such a facility can also be used in social networking applications or photo album applications that deal with images.

- You can validate the content of file before it's uploaded to the server. For example, if your application is supposed to upload XML files, you can validate an XML document before it reaches the server.

- You can develop client-side images or file catalogs that a user can review before finally uploading them to the server.

- You can develop a photo album application that lets the user drag and drop images files rather than individually picking them up.

■ **Note** In the future, HTML5 may add more support for file-system navigation. A draft specification is available at http://dev.w3.org/2009/dap/file-system/pub/FileSystem/. However, as of this writing there is little or no support for these features in the leading browsers.

FileList Object

The FileList object represents a list of File objects. A FileList is returned either from a file field (<input type="file">) placed on a web page or by the user dragging and dropping local files from Windows Explorer on a droppable area of a web page. Normally, you iterate through a FileList to access individual File objects. The FileList object exposes just one property and one method, as described in Table 9-2.

Table 9-2. Properties and Methods of the FileList Object

Property / Method	Description
length	The length property returns a number of File objects from a FileList.
item()	The item() method accepts a zero-based index and returns a File object at that index.

File Object

A File object represents a single file and provides information about it such as its name, size, and MIME type. You also need a File object if you wish to read the contents of a file. Table 9-3 lists the properties of the File object.

Table 9-3. *Properties of the File Object*

Property	Description
name	Name of a File along with its extension
size	Size of a file in bytes
type	MIME type of the file

FileReader Object

A FileReader object allows you to read the contents of a File. The read operation is performed in asynchronous fashion. This way, even very large files can be read without blocking other operations. The FileReader object can read File contents as text, Base64, binary, or ArrayBuffer. Table 9-4 lists the methods of the FileReader object that are responsible for reading a file.

Table 9-4. *Methods of the FileReader Object*

Property / Method	Description
readAsText()	Reads a file as a text file
readAsDataURL()	Reads a file as a data URL (Base64)
readAsBinaryString()	Reads a file as a raw binary string
readAsArrayBuffer()	Reads a file as an ArrayBuffer
abort()	Can be used to abort a file-reading operation

The readAsText() method is intended to be used with text-based files such as plain-text files, CSV files, and XML files. The readAsDataURL() method encodes the file content in Base64 format and returns it as a data URL. As described in more detail in Chapter 4, you know that the data URL format consists of Base64-encoded data prefixed with the MIME type of the file, as shown in the following example:
data:image/png;base64,iVBORw0KGgoAAAANSUh…

The readAsDataURL() method also comes in handy in situations where binary data can't be transferred to the server. One such situation is the jQuery $.ajax() method that sends text data to the server. The readAsBinaryString() method reads files as raw binary data. The readAsArrayBuffer() method reads the file contents as an ArrayBuffer; an ArrayBuffer is a fixed-length binary data buffer.

The file-reading methods discussed here affect certain properties of a FileReader. These properties can then be used to process the file contents or to flag an error to the end user. Table 9-5 lists these properties.

Table 9-5. Properties of the FileReader Object

Property	Description
error	Error that occurred (if any) while reading a file.
readyState	State of a FileReader object. The possible readyState values are 0 (EMPTY), 1 (LOADING), and 2 (DONE).
result	File's contents. This property is valid only after the read operation is complete. The format of the data returned depends on the read method invoked.

The FileReader raises certain events as the file is being read. You can wire up handlers for these events and intercept various stages of the read operation. The events raised by the FileReader object are given in Table 9-6.

Table 9-6. Events of the FileReader Object

Event	Description
load	Raised when a file is successfully read
loadstart	Raised when the reading of file content is about to begin
loadend	Raised when the file-reading operation completes successfully or with an error
loadprogress	Raised periodically when data is being read
error	Raised when there is some error while performing the read operation
abort	Raised when a read operation is aborted

Out of all the events listed in Table 9-6, you must handle the load event because that is where you can access the file content.

Selecting Files to Be Used With the File API

As mentioned previously, files to be accessed using the File API must be explicitly selected by the user in one of the following ways:

- A user can select files using the Open File dialog shown by a file field control.

- As user can drag files from Windows Explorer and drop those files on some predefined area of a web page.

The first way is straightforward and traditional. A variation on this technique is to display the Open File dialog without a visible file field on the page. In such cases, you need to play tricks to achieve the desired behavior. The second way is specific to HTML5, and with the native support for drag-and-drop it's easy to implement in web pages.

The following sections discuss these two ways of selecting files. Note that HTML5 drag-and-drop features aren't restricted to file selection alone and can be used independently in your applications.

Using a File Field to Select Files

Using a file field to select one or more files is the most basic technique of selecting files to be used with the File API. Prior to HTML5, a file field control allowed the selection of only one file at a time. If you wanted to allow users to select five files, you had to place five separate file field controls on the web page. In HTML5, however, users can select multiple files using a single file field control. This is possible with the new `multiple` attribute of the `<input>` element. Listing 9-1 shows how a file field control can be configured for selecting a single and multiple files.

Listing 9-1. *File Field Control Markup*

```
<input id="File1" type="file" />
<input id="File2" type="file" multiple="multiple" />
```

This listing shows two `<input>` elements with the `type` attribute set to file. Notice that the second file field has the `multiple` attribute. When you specify the `multiple` attribute, the resulting Open File dialog allows you to select multiple files using standard Windows techniques (a combination of the Ctrl/Shift key and mouse clicks).

The file fields are displayed differently by different browsers. For example, Figure 9-1 shows how the file fields are displayed in Chrome, Opera, and Firefox.

Figure 9-1. *File fields in different browsers*

Notice how Chrome and Opera show the file field with the `multiple` attribute to indicate that multiple files can be selected. Clicking the Browser, Choose Files, or Add Files button opens a standard Windows Open dialog, as shown in Figure 9-2.

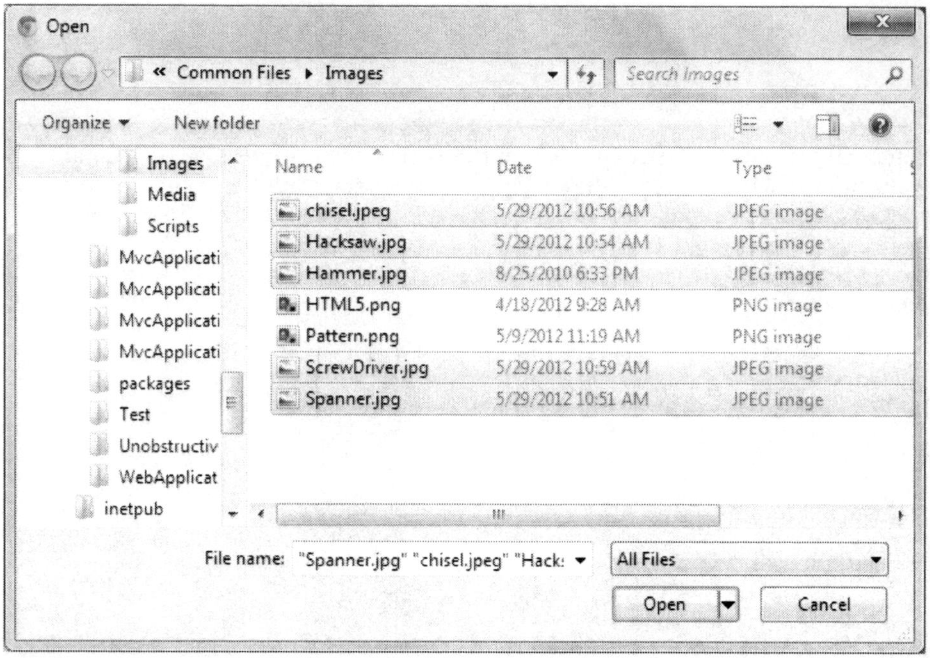

Figure 9-2. *Selecting multiple files using the Open dialog*

Notice that Figure 9-2 shows multiple files selected. When you select multiple files and click the Open button in the Open File dialog, all the selected files are added to the same file field, one after the other. Firefox and Opera display all the selected files in the text box of a file field control, whereas in Chrome you need to hover your mouse over the file field to see a list of selected files (see Figure 9-3).

Figure 9-3. *File field control after selecting files*

If you're developing an ASP.NET Web Forms–based application, you can use the `FileUpload` server control instead of using the raw markup shown in Listing 9-1. The markup in Listing 9-2 shows how you can use `FileUpload` server controls.

Listing 9-2. Using FileUpload Server Controls

```
<asp:FileUpload ID="FileUpload1" runat="server" />
<asp:FileUpload ID="FileUpload2" runat="server" AllowMultiple="True" />
```

The first `FileUpload` server control shown here lets you select a single file. The second `FileUpload` server control has its `AllowMultiple` property set to `True` and allows you to select multiple files.

If you're developing an ASP.NET MVC application, you can either use the plain HTML shown in Listing 9-1 or use an HTML `TextBox` helper to render a file field. Listing 9-3 shows how to use HTML `TextBox` helpers to render file fields.

Listing 9-3. Using TextBox Helpers to Render File Fields

```
<% using (Html.BeginForm("Index","Home","POST")) { %>
<%= Html.TextBox("file1", "",new {type="file"})%>
<br />
<%= Html.TextBox("file2", "",new {type="file",multiple="multiple"})%>
<%}%>
```

As you can see, to render a file field you use `TextBox` helper and supply a `type` property value of `file`. The first call to the `TextBox` helper renders a file field that allows only one file to be selected, whereas the second call sets the `multiple` property to allow multiple files to be selected.

Using a Custom Button to Select Files

Sometimes, using a file field to select files is undesirable for aesthetic reasons. Although you can use CSS to change the look and feel of a file field, its appearance can't be altered drastically. For example, let's say you wish to display an image on a web page, and when a user clicks the image you wish to prompt them to select one or more files. Something like this is impossible using file field because even after applying CSS, the field's basic appearance is governed by the browser.

If you wish to provide such a custom technique for selecting files in your application, you need to use a programmatic trick. You essentially need to add a file field to the web page but keep it hidden from view. When a user clicks a custom graphic or button intended for file selection, you trigger the `click` event on the hidden file field through JavaScript. This way, the Open File dialog is displayed to the user. Once the user selects one or more files, those files are assigned to the hidden file field. You can then access the files for further processing.

Figure 9-4 shows a custom image for selecting files.

Figure 9-4. Selecting files using a custom image button

The web form consists of a Label control, a FileUpload control, and an ImageButton control. Listing 9-4 shows the web form's markup.

Listing 9-4. Prompting for File Selection Using a Custom Image

```
<form id="form1" runat="server">
  <asp:FileUpload ID="FileUpload1" runat="server" AllowMultiple="true"
    CssClass="hidden" />
  <asp:Label ID="Label1" runat="server" CssClass="message"
    Text="Click on the image below to select files" >
  </asp:Label>
  <br />
  <asp:ImageButton ID="ImageButton1" runat="server"
    ImageUrl="~/Images/UploadFile.jpg" />
</form>
```

Notice a couple of things in the markup. First, the AllowMultiple property of the FileUpload control is set to True so as to allow multiple-file selection. Second, its CssClass property is set to a CSS class named hidden. The hidden CSS class looks like this:

```
.hidden {
    display:none;
}
```

The hidden CSS class simply sets the display CSS property to none so that at runtime, the FileUpload control isn't visible. An ImageButton control is used to display a clickable image to the user. In order to trap the client-side click event of the ImageButton and programmatically trigger the click event of the FileUpload control, you need to write some jQuery code. Listing 9-5 shows the jQuery code to add to the web form.

Listing 9-5. Programmatically Triggering the click Event of the File Field

```
$(document).ready(function () {
  $("#FileUpload1").change(function (evt) {
    alert(evt.target.files.length + " file(s) were selected!");
```

```
  });
  $("#ImageButton1").click(function (evt) {
    $("#FileUpload1").click();
    evt.preventDefault();
  });
});
```

This code essentially handles the client-side `click` event of the `ImageButton` control. Inside the `click` event handler, it triggers the `click` event of the `FileUpload` control (the file field). This way, an Open File dialog is shown to the user. Because you don't have any server-side functionality for the `ImageButton` control, you call the `preventDefault()` method to cancel the default action. Upon selecting file(s), the `change` event of the file field is raised. Notice the use of the `files` property that gives you access to all the files selected using the Open File dialog. The `change` event handler displays the number of files selected using the `length` property of the `files` object.

Using Drag-and-Drop to Select Files

Selecting files from an Open File dialog isn't the only option for grabbing files to be read using the File API. A more advanced option lets users drag files from Windows Explorer or the Desktop and drop them onto some area of a web page. This drag-and-drop option requires more coding than the previous options because you need to designate a certain area of a web page where files can be dropped; further, you must handle certain events related to drag-and-drop. In the past, developers used third-party JavaScript libraries or plug-ins to implement drag-and-drop. However, HTML5 provides native support for drag-and-drop. Although implementing drag-and-drop–based file selection requires more code than the other techniques, the overall process is straightforward and can be implemented easily as compared to traditional HTML.

The native drag-and-drop support in HTML5 isn't limited to use with the File API. It's an independent feature of its own and can be used in any situation where drag-and-drop is required. In the section that follows, you learn how to implement drag-and-drop in a web page.

■ **Note** Strictly speaking, selecting files using drag-and-drop requires only the drop operation to be captured. However, the next section covers how to implement dragging as well as dropping operations for the sake of completeness. You can use the native drag-and-drop support in many situations to provide a better user experience.

Working with Drag-and-Drop

Drag-and-drop operations are common in desktop applications. Modern web applications also try to harness the ease and power of drag-and-drop operations to provide an enhanced user experience. Web developers often resorted to third-party JavaScript-based libraries or custom techniques for enabling drag-and-drop behavior in their web applications. Luckily, HTML5 comes with built-in support for drag-and-drop.

Using drag-and-drop features, you can drag an HTML element and drop it onto another. You can also drag files from Windows Explorer or the Desktop and drop them onto a web page for further processing. During the drag-and-drop operation, you can pass data from the source element to the target element.

Implementing drag-and-drop essentially involves the following steps:

1. Enable dragging for one or more HTML elements from a web page.

2. Decide on a drop target, and handle the drop of draggable elements or files.

3. Handle drag-and-drop related events.

4. If required, transfer data between the drag source and the drop target.

Enable Dragging for HTML Elements

The first step in using drag-and-drop in a page is to make one or more elements draggable. You do this by setting the draggable attribute of an HTML element to true. For example, the following piece of markup makes a <div> element draggable:

```
<div class="myclass" draggable="true">Some content</div>
```

Drag-and-Drop Events

Marking one or more DOM elements as draggable is just a part of the story. To actually make your drag-and-drop functional and visually appealing to the end user, you need to handle certain events. These events are listed in Table 9-7.

Table 9-7. Drag-and-Drop Events

Event	Description
dragstart	Raised when the drag operation begins
drag	Raised when an element is dragged
dragenter	Raised when a draggable element is dragged and enters a valid drop target
dragleave	Raised when a draggable element that was dragged on a valid drop target leaves the drop target
dragover	Raised when a draggable element is being dragged over a valid drop target
drop	Raised when a dragged element is dropped onto a valid drop target
dragend	Raised when the drag operation ends

Note that a *drag source* is an element that is being dragged, whereas a *drop target* is an element on which a draggable element is to be dropped. Events from Table 9-7 such as dragstart, drag, and dragend are handled by a drag source, whereas events such as dragenter, dragleave, dragover, and drop are handled by a drop target. You can wire event handlers to these events using JavaScript, as shown in Listing 9-6.

Listing 9-6. Wiring Event Handlers for Drag-and-Drop Events

```
$("div").each(function () {
  this.addEventListener('dragstart', OnDragStart, false);
  this.addEventListener('drop', OnDrop, false);
});
```

In this code, the dragstart and drop events of <div> elements are wired to OnDragStart and OnDrop functions respectively using addEventListener() method.

Transferring Data Between Drag-and-Drop Operations

Most of the time, dragging something and dropping it onto something else also calls for transferring some data between the source and the target elements. To accomplish this data transfer, HTML5 provides the dataTransfer object. The dataTransfer object is accessible in various drag-and-drop events through the event object passed to the event handlers. Table 9-8 lists some of the important properties and methods of dataTransfer object.

Table 9-8. Properties and Methods of the dataTransfer Object

Property / Method	Description
effectAllowed	Indicates the types of operations that are to be allowed. The possible values are none, copy, copyLink, copyMove, link, linkMove, move, all, and uninitialized.
dropEffect	Indicates the type of operation that is currently selected. If the type of operation isn't supported by the effectAllowed attribute, then the operation fails. The possible values are none, copy, link, and move.
setDragImage()	Sets the given element that is shown during drag operation.
setData()	Sets specific data that is to be transferred.
getData()	Retrieves previously set data for further processing.
clearData()	Removes the previously stored data.

You typically use the properties and methods of the dataTransfer object in the dragstart and drop event handlers.

Implementing Drag-and-Drop: A Shopping Cart

Now let's put your knowledge to work in a simple yet functional Shopping Cart web form, shown in Figure 9-5.

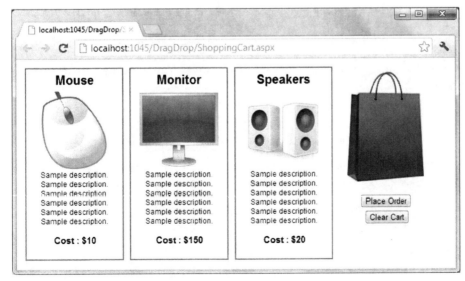

Figure 9-5. Shopping Cart web form

As you can see, the web form represents a simple shopping cart. Various products are represented by
`<div>` elements placed inside a Repeater control. The products can be dragged and dropped onto the
shopping bag. Once all the required products are added, the user can click the Place Order button to send
product data to the server to place an order.

Entity Framework Data Model

The Shopping Cart example stores data in a SQL Server Express database. To get the data in and out of the
database, the application uses the Entity Framework data model, as shown in Figure 9-6.

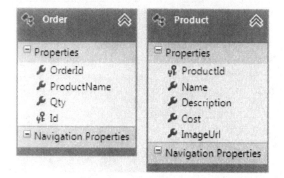

Figure 9-6. Entity Framework data model for the Shopping Cart database

The data model consists of two classes: `Product` and `Order`. The `Product` class captures details such as
`ProductId`, `Name`, `Description`, `Cost`, and `ImageUrl`. The `Order` class captures details such as `OrderId`,
`ProductName`, and `Qty`. Of course, a real-world shopping-cart system captures many more details, but this
data model is sufficient to illustrate this subject.

Product Catalog and Shopping Cart

The product catalog is a `Repeater` control whose `ItemTemplate` contains a draggable `<div>` element. This
`<div>` element wraps all the product details such as `Name`, `Description`, and `Cost` for an individual product.
The `Repeater` control receives its data through an `EntityDataSource` control. The markup of the `Repeater`
control is given in Listing 9-7.

Listing 9-7. Markup of the Product Catalog

```
<asp:Repeater ID="Repeater1" runat="server" DataSourceID="EntityDataSource1">
  <ItemTemplate>
    <div class="product" draggable="true">
      <header><%# Eval("Name") %></header>
      <div>
       <asp:Image runat="server" ID="img1"
          ImageUrl='<%# Eval("ImageUrl") %>' />
      </div>
      <div><%# Eval("Description") %></div>
      <br />
      <div class="cost"><%# Eval("Cost","Cost : ${0}") %></div>
```

```
            <input type="hidden" value="<%# Eval("ProductId") %>" />
        </div>
    </ItemTemplate>
</asp:Repeater>
```

Notice the code in bold. The <div> elements representing products are marked with the draggable attribute set to true. The remaining markup from Listing 9-7 essentially binds various columns of the Products table with HTML elements using the ASP.NET Eval() data-binding expression.

Handling Drag-and-Drop Events

The next step is to wire drag-and-drop event handlers to various elements. The jQuery code that wires various event handlers is shown in Listing 9-8.

Listing 9-8. Wiring Drag and Drop Event Handlers

```
$(document).ready(function () {
    $("div .product").each(function () {
        this.addEventListener('dragstart', OnDragStart, false);
    });

    var cart = $("#divCart").get(0);
    cart.addEventListener('dragenter', OnDragEnter, false);
    cart.addEventListener('dragleave', OnDragLeave, false);
    cart.addEventListener('dragover', OnDragOver, false);
    cart.addEventListener('drop', OnDrop, false);
    cart.addEventListener('dragend', OnDragEnd, false);
})
```

As you can see, first all the <div> elements that have the product CSS class applied to them (that is, the container <div> elements of all the products) are selected using a jQuery selector. Then the each() method is called on the result set to add an event listener for the dragstart event. The addEventListener() method wires an event-handler function to an event. In this case, the dragstart event is handled by the OnDragStart function.

The <div> element that contains the shopping bag and the buttons has the ID divCart. The divCart element should handle other events such as dragenter, dragleave, and drop. A series of addEventListener() method calls attaches event-handler functions to these events. The event-handler functions take the form On*XXXX*, where *XXXX* is the name of the event.

In all, there are six event-handler functions: OnDragStart, OnDragEnter, OnDragLeave, OnDragOver, OnDrop, and OnDragEnd. Let's examine them one by one.

OnDragStart

The dragstart event handler reduces the opacity of the element being dragged so that the end user gets a visual clue about the drag operation. The OnDragStart event-handler function that handles the dragstart event is shown in Listing 9-9.

Listing 9-9. OnDragStart Event Handler Function

```
function OnDragStart(e) {
    this.style.opacity = '0.3';
```

```
        srcElement = this;
        e.dataTransfer.effectAllowed = 'move';
        var product=$(this).find("header")[0].innerHTML;
        e.dataTransfer.setData('text/html', product);
}
```

The OnDragStart event-handler function stores the source of drag operation in a global variable srcElement because you need it later in the drop event handler. The effectAllowed property of the dataTransfer object is set to move. When the user drags a product and drops it on the shopping bag, you need to transfer the corresponding product name to the drop target. In this case, product names are placed inside <header> elements; hence the find() method finds all the header elements and then grabs the innerHTML (the product name) of the header element. The setData() method sets the product name as the data to be transferred via the dataTransfer object. This way, the drop event handler knows which product is to be added to the shopping cart. The first parameter of setData() indicates the MIME type of the data that is being transferred ('text/html' in this case).

OnDragOver

The OnDragOver event-handler function adds a CSS class to the drop target so as to give the user a visual clue about the operation. The OnDragOver function is shown in Listing 9-10.

Listing 9-10. OnDragOver Function

```
function OnDragOver(e) {
    ...
    $(this).addClass('highlight');
    e.dataTransfer.dropEffect = 'move';
}
```

The highlight CSS class essentially adds a highlight to the drop target (shopping bag <div> element) by changing its background color. It's shown here:

```
.highlight
{
    background-color:Yellow;
}
```

The dropEffect property of the dataTransfer object is set to move.

OnDragEnter and OnDragLeave

The OnDragEnter and OnDragLeave event handlers merely add the highlight CSS class to and remove it from the drop target element. These event handlers are shown in Listing 9-11.

Listing 9-11. OnDragEnter and OnDragLeave Functions

```
function OnDragEnter(e) {
    $(this).addClass('highlight');
}

function OnDragLeave(e) {
    $(this).removeClass('highlight');
}
```

OnDrop

The OnDrop event-handler function is the main event handler in which you transfer product names from the DataTransfer objet to the shopping cart. The OnDrop function is shown in Listing 9-12.

Listing 9-12. *OnDrop Function*

```
function OnDrop(e) {
    ...
    srcElement.style.opacity = '1';
    $(this).removeClass('highlight');
    var count = $(this).find("div[data-product-name='" +
                e.dataTransfer.getData('text/html') + "']").length;
    if (count <= 0) {
        $(this).append("<div class='selectedproduct' data-product-name='" +
        e.dataTransfer.getData('text/html') + "'>" +
        e.dataTransfer.getData('text/html') + "</div>");
    }
    else {
        alert("This product is already added to your cart!");
    }
    return false;
}
```

The drop event handler sets the opacity of the source element back to 1 because the drag-and-drop operation is complete. It also removes the highlight CSS class from the target element. It then appends the product being dragged to the target element.

Notice the use of the getData() method to retrieve the data previously set in the OnDragStart event-handler function. There is also a check so the same product can't be added to the cart multiple times. Figure 9-7 shows how an error message is shown to the user if the same product is dragged and dropped multiple times.

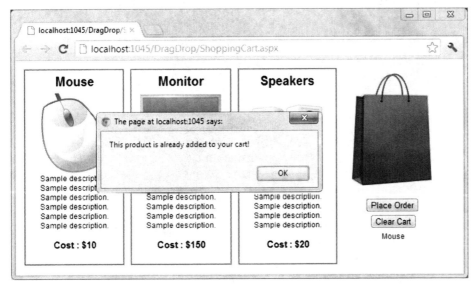

Figure 9-7. *Checking for duplicate products after the drop*

As you can see, Mouse has already been added to the shopping cart. Attempting to drag-and-drop Mouse to the shopping cart again results in an alert box with a message informing the user about the duplication.

OnDragEnd

The OnDragEnd event-handler function simply removes the highlight CSS class from the drop target and is shown in Listing 9-13.

Listing 9-13. OnDragEnd Function

```
function OnDragEnd(e) {
    $("div .bag").removeClass('highlight');
    this.style.opacity = '1';
}
```

Passing Data from Client to Server

To transfer shopping-cart items to the server-side code, you need to use the jQuery $.ajax() method. The click event handler of the Place Order button has the relevant code and is shown in Listing 9-14.

Listing 9-14. Saving Order Data on the Server

```
$("#Button1").click(function () {
    var data = new Array();
    $("div .bag div").each(function (index) {
        data[index] = "'" + this.innerHTML + "'";
    });
    $.ajax({
        type: 'POST',
        url: 'shoppingcart.aspx/PlaceOrder',
        contentType: "application/json; charset=utf-8",
        data: '{ products:[' + data.join() + ']}',
        dataType: 'json',
        success: function (results) { alert(results.d); },
        error: function () { alert('error'); }
    });
});
```

As you can see, first the products in the shopping bag are stored into a JavaScript array. This way, it's easy to pass them to the server by joining the array elements. An Array is created by using the each() method and extracting the innerHTML of individual <div> elements. Then the $.ajax() method invokes a web method, PlaceOrder(), that resides in the ShoppingCart.aspx web form. The PlaceOrder() web method is shown in Listing 9-15.

Listing 9-15. PlaceOrder Web Method

```
[WebMethod]
public static string PlaceOrder(string[] products)
{
    Guid orderId = Guid.NewGuid();
```

```
ShoppingCartEntities db = new ShoppingCartEntities();
foreach (string p in products)
{
    Order order = new Order();
    order.OrderId = orderId;
    order.ProductName = p;
    order.Qty = 1;
    db.Orders.AddObject(order);
}
db.SaveChanges();
return "Order with " + products.Length.ToString() +
        " products has been added!";
}
```

The PlaceOrder() web method puts an order in the Orders table. The method accepts an array of strings that represents product names. Notice how $.ajax() passes the products parameter in JSON format. Upon successful completion of the web method, the success handler function displays an alert to the end user.

To test the drag-and-drop behavior, run the web form and try dragging a product on the shopping bag. Figure 9-8 shows a sample run of the web form.

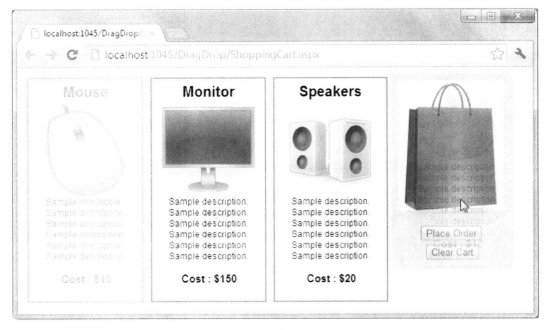

Figure 9-8. Sample run of the Shopping Cart web form

Notice how the product being dragged (Mouse) is shown with less opacity and how the shopping bag is highlighted. If you click the Place Order button, the selected products are saved in the database.

Dragging and Dropping Files

Now that you know how to drag HTML elements and drop them onto a target element, let's see how files can be dragged and dropped onto a web page. In the case of file drag-and-drop, you don't have to worry about marking any HTML elements as draggable because files are external entities and you drag them from outside the browser. You need to take care of dropping of the files.

A page may contain many HTML elements capable of acting as a drop target. However, if you want to access the files dropped from Windows Explorer or the Desktop, you have to "listen" to known elements designated for that purpose. To understand how to do this, let's develop a web form as shown in Figure 9-9.

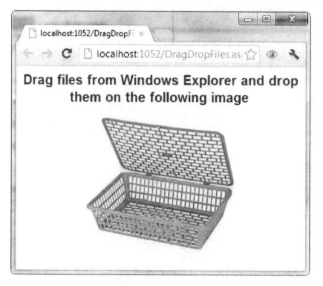

Figure 9-9. Dragging and dropping files on a web form

The web form consists of a `<div>` element whose background image is set to the image of a basket. You can drag files from Windows Explorer or the Desktop and drop them onto this `<div>` element. The `<div>` handles the drop event and displays an alert box that indicates how many files were dropped. The code in Listing 9-16 shows how the required drag-and-drop events are handled.

Listing 9-16. Handling Dropped Files

```
$(document).ready(function () {
  var container;
  container = document.getElementById("container");
  container.addEventListener("dragenter", OnDragEnter, false);
  container.addEventListener("dragover", OnDragOver, false);
  container.addEventListener("dragleave", OnDragLeave, false);
  container.addEventListener("drop", OnDrop, false);
});

function OnDragEnter(e) {
  e.stopPropagation();
  e.preventDefault();
}
```

```
function OnDragLeave(e) {
  e.stopPropagation();
  e.preventDefault();
}

function OnDragOver(e) {
  e.stopPropagation();
  e.preventDefault();
}

function OnDrop(e) {
  e.stopPropagation();
  e.preventDefault();
  var files = e.dataTransfer.files;
  alert(files.length + " file(s) dropped!");
}
```

This code wires event handlers for four events—dragenter, dragover, dragleave, and drop—using the addEventListener() method. Unlike in the Shopping Cart example, the functions OnDragEnter, OnDragLeave, and OnDragOver don't do anything special apart from calling the stopPropagation() and preventDefault() methods. The jQuery stopPropagation() method stops the event from bubbling up the DOM tree, thus preventing any parent handlers from being notified of the event. Similarly, the jQuery preventDefault() method prevents the event's default action.

If you wish, you can set dropEffect or a visual indicator in these event handlers. Also, note that you aren't setting the dataTransfer object anywhere. This is because data (files in this case) comes from an external source. Notice the OnDrop() event-handler function: it uses the files property of the dataTransfer object to access the files that were dropped on the element. It then displays the number of files dropped using the length property.

To test the web form, run it: drag a few files from Windows Explorer and drop them on the basket. As soon as you drop the files, you should see an alert with the number of files dropped.

Reading Files and Displaying File Information

Now that you know the techniques for selecting files—file field, custom button, and drag-and-drop—let's see how to read the selected files using the File API. To understand the process, you develop a web form that resembles Figure 9-10.

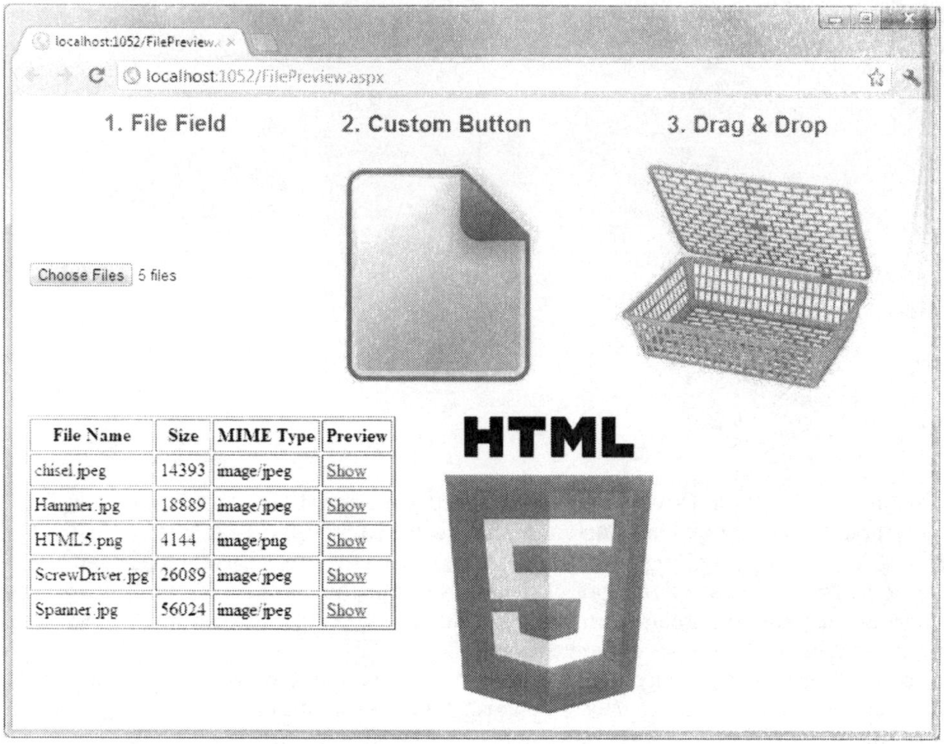

Figure 9-10. Reading files using the File API

The web form is divided into two parts. The top part allows you select image files using all three techniques. Then, the details of the selected files, such as file name, size, and MIME type, are displayed in a table at the bottom. Hovering on the Show link provided in each row of the table shows that image to the right of the table. The markup for the web form is shown in Listing 9-17.

Listing 9-17. Markup for a Web Form That Shows Image Previews

```
<form id="form1" runat="server">
<div>
  <table>
    <tr>
      <th>
        <asp:Label ID="Label1" runat="server" Text="1. File Field"
                          CssClass="message">
        </asp:Label>
      </th>
      <th>
        <asp:Label ID="Label2" runat="server" Text="2. Custom Button"
                          CssClass="message">
        </asp:Label>
      </th>
      <th>
```

```
          <asp:Label ID="Label3" runat="server" Text="3. Drag & Drop"
                            CssClass="message">
          </asp:Label>
        </th>
      </tr>
      <tr>
        <td>
          <asp:FileUpload ID="FileUpload1" runat="server" AllowMultiple="True" />
        </td>
        <td>
          <asp:FileUpload ID="FileUpload2" runat="server" AllowMultiple="true"
                                CssClass="hidden" />
          <asp:ImageButton ID="ImageButton1" runat="server"
            ImageUrl="~/Images/UploadFile.jpg"/>
        </td>
        <td>
          <div id="divBasket" class="dropDiv"></div>
        </td>
      </tr>
    </table>
  </div>
  <div class="divBlock">
    <table id="Table1" border="1" cellPadding="3"></table>
  </div>
  <div class="divBlock">
    <img id="filePreview" />
  </div>
</form>
```

The bold elements in the listing are important to the functioning of the web form. The file field FileUpload1 is used to select files directly, whereas FileUpload2 is kept hidden and shows the Open File dialog when the ImageButton is clicked. The <div> element divBasket is the drop target where files dragged from Windows Explorer can be dropped. The HTML table Table1 is filled dynamically using jQuery depending on the files selected. A preview of the images is shown in filePreview image element.

Various events of the elements are wired in the jQuery ready() function, shown in Listing 9-18.

Listing 9-18. Wiring the Event Handlers of the HTML Elements

```
var files;

$(document).ready(function () {
  $("#FileUpload1").change(OnChange);
  $("#FileUpload2").change(OnChange);

  $("#ImageButton1").click(function (evt) {
    $("#FileUpload2").click();
    evt.preventDefault();
  });

  var basket;
  basket = document.getElementById("divBasket");
```

```
        basket.addEventListener("dragenter", OnDragEnter, false);
        basket.addEventListener("dragover", OnDragOver, false);
        basket.addEventListener("drop", OnDrop, false);
});
```

This code declares a global variable, files, that is used later in the code to store a reference to the selected files. The change event of both file field controls is wired to the OnChange function. Similarly, the dragenter, dragover, and drop events are wired to the OnDragEnter, OnDragOver, and OnDrop functions, respectively. Out of all these event handlers, OnChange and OnDrop are important because they initiate the process of generating the table of files. These two event handlers are shown in Listing 9-19.

Listing 9-19. *OnChange and OnDrop Event Handlers*

```
function OnChange(evt) {
  files = evt.target.files;
  ShowFileDetails(files);
}

function OnDrop(evt) {
  evt.stopPropagation();
  evt.preventDefault();
  files = evt.dataTransfer.files;
  ShowFileDetails(files);
}
```

The OnChange event-handler function grabs the selected files using the files property of the file field control. Note that the change event handler of FileUpload1 as well as FileUpload2 is handled by OnChange. So, the evt.target refers to the respective file field control. OnChange then calls a helper function ShowFileDetails(), which updates the table of files displayed in the page.

The OnDrop event-handler function grabs the files using the files property of the dataTransfer object and cancels the event bubbling. ShowFileDetails() is then called to generate a table of files.

Note that the files property of the file field control and the dataTransfer object is of type FileList (see Table 9-2 earlier for a quick recap of the FileList object). The ShowFileDetails() function used by the OnChange and OnDrop event handlers is shown in Listing 9-20.

Listing 9-20. *Showing File Information Using the File Object*

```
function ShowFileDetails(files) {
  $("#Table1").empty();
  $("#Table1").append("<tr><th>File Name</th><th>Size</th><th>MIME Type</th><th>Preview</th></
tr>");
  for (var i = 0; i < files.length; i++) {
    if (files[i].type == "image/jpeg" ||
        files[i].type == "image/png" ||
        files[i].type == "image/gif") {
            $("#Table1").append("<tr><td>" + files.item(i).name +
                                        "</td><td>" + files[i].size +
                                        "</td><td>" + files[i].type +
                                        "</td><td><a href='#'
                                          data-file-index='" +
                                          i + "'>Show</a></td></tr>");
```

```
    }
    else {
      alert("Only image files are allowed. Other files will be ignored!");
    }
  }
  $("a").hover(ShowPreview, HidePreview);
}
```

ShowFileDetails() first empties the table by removing all its rows using the jQuery empty() method. It then iterates through the FileList and accesses each File object to get the file details. Because the application is intended only for image files, every file's extension is checked. If a file is an image file (.jpg, .jpeg, .png, or .gif) then a new row is added to the table. This checking is done with the help of the File object's type property, which returns the MIME type of a file (image/jpeg, image/png, and so on). The name property returns the name of the file with extension but doesn't include the path information. The size property returns the size of the file in bytes.

You can access individual File objects either using typical collection syntax (files[i]) or using the item() method of the FileList object. The Show hyperlink stores an index of the file using a custom data-* attribute data-file-index. This way, you can determine which image to show.

The actual image preview is shown when you hover the mouse over the Show link. The jQuery hover() method binds two handler functions to the hyperlink elements that are invoked when the mouse pointer enters and leaves the hyperlinks. The ShowPreview() and HidePreview() functions are shown in Listing 9-21.

Listing 9-21. *Showing an Image Preview*

```
function ShowPreview(evt) {
  var reader = new FileReader();
  $(reader).bind("load",function (e) {
    var imgSrc = e.target.result;
    $("#filePreview").attr('src',imgSrc);
  });
  var fileIndex = $(evt.target).attr('data-file-index');
  reader.readAsDataURL(files[fileIndex]);
}

function HidePreview(evt) {
  $("#imgPreview").attr('src', '');
}
```

The ShowPreview() function creates an instance of a FileReader. The FileReader object reads files in asynchronous fashion and raises a load event when a file is successfully read. That is why the event handler for the load event needs to be attached before reading the file. A file is read using the readAsDataURL() method of the FileReader object. readAsDataURL() makes the file content available to the load event handler in the form of a data URL (Base64 encoded). This content can be accessed using the result property of the e.target object. The load event handler retrieves the file content using the result property of the FileReader object and then sets the image's src attribute to the image content.

The HidePreview() method simply removes the image's src attribute.

Uploading Files to the Server

It isn't mandatory that files read by the File API be uploaded to the server. However, in most cases you upload them to the server so that they can be processed or stored. You can, of course, discard some of the selected files based on processing logic and upload a subset of the selected files. As far as the File API is concerned, it doesn't play any role in uploading the files to the server. It's your responsibility to devise a mechanism that takes care of uploading the required files to the server.

Uploading files selected using a file field control or a custom button is easy because all you need to do is POST the web form to the server. In the server-side code, you can then access the selected file as shown in Listing 9-22.

Listing 9-22. Uploading Files by POSTing a Web Form

```
foreach (HttpPostedFile file in FileUpload1.PostedFiles)
{
    string fileName = file.FileName;
    fileName = Server.MapPath("~/uploads/" + fileName);
    file.SaveAs(fileName);
}
```

In the server-side code, you use the PostedFiles collection of the FileUpload control. Each element of PostedFiles is of type HttpPostedFile. The SaveAs() method of the HttpPostedFile class allows you to save an uploaded file to the server.

Uploading files selected using the drag-and-drop technique is slightly tricky. That's because the selected files don't belong to a <form> control, and as such they aren't POSTed to the server. You need to programmatically send them to the server. The jQuery $.ajax() method comes to the rescue here too. Listing 9-23 shows how you can use $.ajax() to upload files.

Listing 9-23. Using $.ajax() to Upload Files

```
function UploadFiles() {
  var data = new FormData();
  for (var i = 0; i < files.length; i++) {
    data.append(files[i].name, files[i]);
  }
  $.ajax({
    type: "POST",
    url: "UploadFiles.ashx",
    contentType: false,
    processData: false,
    data: data,
    success: function (result) {
      alert(result);
    },
    error: function () {
      alert("There was error uploading files!");
    }
  });
}
```

This listing shows the UploadFiles() function that uploads the selected files to the server. You can't send the File objects from the FileList directly to the server; you first need to convert them into FormData objects. As the name suggests, the FormData object represents the form data that should accompany the request. The append() method of the FormData object allows you to append the individual files that you wish to upload. The code makes a POST request to a generic handler UploadFiles.ashx, which is responsible for accepting the posted files and saving them on the server. Upon successful uploading of the files, a success message is shown to the user.

Notice that the $.ajax() call sets contentType and processData options to false. You don't need to provide the content type because the FormData object defaults to a content type of multipart/form-data. If you don't set the processData option to false, $.ajax() automatically converts the data being posted to URL-encoded form, which is undesirable.

Listing 9-24 shows how files POSTed using the $.ajax() method are handled on the server side using the generic handler UploadFiles.ashx.

Listing 9-24. *Saving Files Uploaded Using a Generic Handler*

```
public void ProcessRequest(HttpContext context)
{
    if (context.Request.Files.Count > 0)
    {
        HttpFileCollection files = context.Request.Files;
        foreach (string key in files)
        {
            HttpPostedFile file = files[key];
            string fileName = file.FileName;
            fileName = context.Server.MapPath("~/uploads/" + fileName);
            file.SaveAs(fileName);
        }
    }
    context.Response.ContentType = "text/plain";
    context.Response.Write("File Uploaded Successfully!");
}
```

The generic handler's ProcessRequest() method saves the posted file on the server. ProcessRequest() receives HttpContext as a parameter. This can be used to access intrinsic objects such as Request, Response, and Server.

The uploaded files are accessed using the Request.Files collection. Each element of the Files collection is of type HttpPostedFile. The SaveAs() method of the HttpPostedFile class allows you to save a file on the server. Once all the files are saved, a success message is sent to the client. This message is displayed in the success function of the $.ajax() call.

Using the File API in ASP.NET MVC

In this section, you develop an ASP.NET MVC application that uses the File API. The application is intended to serve two purposes: upload XML files to the server, and validate the uploaded files against an XSD schema.

Consider a hypothetical situation in which a desktop application stores its data as XML files on the local machine. Periodically you're required to upload the XML files thus generated to a central web server for further processing. Such an application can use the File API to do the following:

- Ensure that only XML files are being uploaded to the server.

- Check that the XML files contain specific XML tags. Although such a validation can't replace XSD schema validation, it can act as a first-level validation.

- Show a preview of the XML files being uploaded to the server.

The application that you develop in this section resembles Figure 9-11.

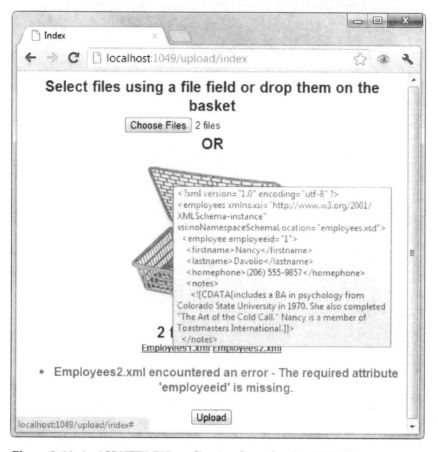

Figure 9-11. An ASP.NET MVC application for uploading XML files

The application lets you select files using a file field control or by dragging them from Windows Explorer. Once the files are selected, the number of files selected is displayed below the basket along with a list of file names as links. If you hover over the file names, a short preview (up to 500 characters) of the file content is displayed in the link's tooltip. When you click the Upload button, all the files are uploaded to the server and are validated against an XSD schema. If the uploaded XML files don't match the schema specifications, an error is returned.

The XML file-uploading application works along the same lines as the image-preview application you developed earlier; hence this section focuses only on the areas that are different. Listing 9-25 shows the markup of the application's index view.

Listing 9-25. Index View of the XML File-Upload Application

```
<% using (Html.BeginForm()) { %>
  <div class="message">
     Select files using a field field or drop them on the basket
  </div>
  <%= Html.TextBox("file1", "",new {type="file",multiple="multiple"})%>
  <div class="message">OR</div>
  <div id="basket" class="dropDiv"></div>
  <div id="filecount" class="message"></div>
  <div id="errors" class="error"></div>
  <input id="upload" type="button" value="Upload" />
<%}%>
```

The `<form>` consists of a file field control and a basket `<div>` element acting as a drop target. The Upload button triggers the file-upload operation. The jQuery code that wires various event handlers is shown in Listing 9-26.

Listing 9-26. Wiring Event Handlers for Drag-and Drop Events

```
var files;
$(document).ready(OnChange);
  var basket;
  basket = document.getElementById("basket");
  basket.addEventListener("dragenter", OnDragEnter, false);
  basket.addEventListener("dragleave", OnDragLeave, false);
  basket.addEventListener("dragover", OnDragOver, false);
  basket.addEventListener("drop", OnDrop, false);


  $("#upload").click(UploadFiles);
});
```

This code declares a global variable, files, that is used later in the code to store a reference to the selected files. The change event handler of the file field is wired to the OnChange function. Similarly, dragenter, dragleave, dragover, and drop are wired to OnDragEnter, OnDragLeave, OnDragOver, and OnDrop, respectively. The OnChange and OnDrop events are important and are shown in Listing 9-27.

Listing 9-27. OnChange and OnDrop Event Handlers

```
function OnChange(evt) {
  files = evt.target.files;
  ShowFileDetails();
}

function OnDrop(e) {
  e.stopPropagation();
  e.preventDefault();
  files = e.dataTransfer.files;
  ShowFileDetails();
}
```

The OnChange event-handler function grabs the selected files using the files property of the file field control. OnChange then calls a helper function ShowFileDetails() that displays a list of files selected as anchor elements.

OnDrop grabs the files using the files property of the dataTransfer object and cancels event bubbling. ShowFileDetails() is then called.

The ShowFileDetails() function is shown in Listing 9-28.

Listing 9-28. ShowFileDetails() Function

```
function ShowFileDetails() {
  var html = "";
  html += files.length + " files selected!";
  html += "<div class='fileName'>"
  for(var i=0;i<files.length;i++)
  {
    if (files[i].type == "text/xml") {
      html += "<a href='#' data-file-index='" + i + "'>" + files[i].name + "</a>   ";
    }
    else {
      html += "<span data-file-index='" + i + "'>" + files[i].name + "</span>   ";
    }
  }
  html += "</div>";
  $("#filecount").html(html);
  $("a").hover(ShowPreview,HidePreview);
}
```

The application is intended to upload XML files only, and hence only XML files can be previewed. ShowFileDetails() iterates through the selected files (files global variable) and checks the type property of every File object. For XML files, the type property returns text/xml; only such file names are displayed as anchors. Other file types are displayed as <span> elements and hence can't be previewed.

The jQuery hover() method binds to the hyperlink elements two handler functions that are invoked when the mouse pointer enters and leaves the hyperlinks. The ShowPreview() function is responsible for displaying a short preview of the XML file in the tooltip. This is done by setting the title attribute of the corresponding anchor elements. Listing 9-29 shows ShowPreview().

Listing 9-29. ShowPreview() Function

```
function ShowPreview(evt) {
  evt.stopPropagation();
  evt.preventDefault();
  var reader = new FileReader();
  $(reader).bind("load", function (e) {
    var xmlData = e.target.result;
    if (xmlData.length > 500) {
      xmlData = xmlData.substr(0, 500);
    }
    $(evt.target).attr('title', xmlData);
  });
  var fileIndex = $(evt.target).attr('data-file-index');
  reader.readAsText(files[fileIndex]);
}
```

ShowPreview() creates a FileReader object. Because XML files are essentially text files, the readAsText() method is used to read the files. The load event handler of the FileReader accesses the XML file content using the result property. The XML file may be very large, and for preview purposes only part of the file (up to 500 characters) is extracted. The title attribute of the underlying anchor element is then set to the extracted XML data.

The HidePreview() function doesn't do anything special in this case because the browser automatically hides the tooltip when mouse pointer leaves a hyperlink under consideration.

The task of uploading the XML files to the server is accomplished by the UploadFiles() function, shown in Listing 9-30.

Listing 9-30. *UploadFiles() Function*

```
function UploadFiles() {
  var data = new FormData();
  for (var i = 0; i < files.length; i++) {
    if (files[i].type == "text/xml") {
      data.append(files[i].name, files[i]);
    }
  }
  $.ajax({
    type: "POST",
    url: "/Upload/UploadFiles",
    contentType: false,
    processData: false,
    data: data,
    success: function (result) {
      $("#errors").empty();
      $("#errors").html(result);
    },
    error: function () {
      alert("There was error uploading files!");
    }
  });
}
```

UploadFile() iterates through the selected files and appends only the XML files to a FormData object. The $.ajax() method then makes a POST request to the UploadFiles() action method of the Upload controller. The contentType and processData options are set to false as before. If there are any schema validation errors, they're displayed in a <div> element.

The UploadFiles() action method that saves and validates the XML files is shown in Listing 9-31.

Listing 9-31. *UploadFiles() Action Method*

```
[HttpPost]
public JsonResult UploadFiles()
{
    if (Request.Files.Count > 0)
    {
        HttpFileCollectionBase files = Request.Files;
        foreach (string key in files)
        {
            HttpPostedFileBase file = files[key];
```

251

```
        string fileName = file.FileName;
        fileName = Server.MapPath("~/Content/Uploads/" + fileName);
        file.SaveAs(fileName);

        XmlReaderSettings settings = new XmlReaderSettings();
        settings.Schemas.Add("", Server.MapPath("~/Content/Employees.xsd"));
        settings.ValidationType = ValidationType.Schema;
        settings.ValidationEventHandler += OnValidationError;
        XmlReader reader = XmlReader.Create(fileName, settings);
        while (reader.Read())
        {
        }
        reader.Close();
    }
}
Response.ContentType = "text/plain";
StringBuilder sb = new StringBuilder();
sb.Append("<ul>");
foreach (string error in errors)
{
    sb.Append("<li>" + error + "</li>");
}
sb.Append("</ul>");
return Json(sb.ToString());
}

void OnValidationError(object sender, ValidationEventArgs e)
{
    string fileName = Path.GetFileName(((XmlReader)sender).BaseURI);
    errors.Add(fileName + " encountered an error - " + e.Exception.Message);
}
```

The code from Listing 9-31 that saves the uploaded XML files is identical to the previous example. The code marked in bold is responsible for validating the XML files against an XSD schema file: Employees.xsd. The Employees.xsd schema file expects the XML markup in the format shown in Listing 9-32.

Listing 9-32. Sample XML File

```
<?xml version="1.0" encoding="utf-8" ?>
<employees>
  <employee employeeid="1">
    <firstname>Nancy</firstname>
    <lastname>Davolio</lastname>
    <homephone>(206) 555-9857</homephone>
    <notes>
      <![CDATA[...]]>
  </notes>
  </employee>
```

Although this example uses a fixed schema file, you can pick a schema file based on a condition. The XmlReader class is used to read XML documents. The XmlReaderSettings class attaches Employees.xsd to the XmlReader. When you call the Read() method of the XmlReader class, the XML document is read and validated against the schema. If there are any validation errors, the `ValidationEventHandler` event is raised. The event-handler function `OnValidationError` stores the XML file name and the error message in a generic list.

Once all the uploaded XML files are validated, the code iterates through the generic list of errors and creates a bulleted list of the error messages. The error list is returned to the jQuery `success` function by converting it to JSON format.

To test the application, run it and try uploading XML files—some matching the schema and some violating the schema (for example, keep some `<employee>` elements without an `employeeid` attribute). You should get error messages for any invalid XML files.

Summary

HTML5's File API allows you to read files residing in the user's local file system. The files, however, must be explicitly selected by the user using a file field control's Open File dialog or by dragging them from Windows Explorer and dropping them onto a predefined area of a web page.

The File API consists of three main objects: `File`, `FileList`, and `FileReader`. The `File` object gives information about a file such as its name, size, and MIME type. The `FileList` object is a collection of `File` objects and is obtained either via the files property of a file field or via the files property of a `dataTransfer` object. The `FileReader` object lets you read selected files in asynchronous fashion.

Although drag-and-drop is an independent feature of HTML5, it can be coupled with the File API to enhance the user experience. Selected files can be uploaded to the server using the `$.ajax()` method.

The next chapter introduces another interesting feature—web workers—that allows you to run code in the background. Web workers are like threads used in a multithreaded desktop application in that they let you run lengthy processes in the background without obstructing the user interface.

■ ■ ■

CHAPTER 10

Multithreading in Web Pages Using Web Workers

The creators of JavaScript invented the language as an aid to developing interactive web pages. HTML markup by itself is purely static in nature and lacks any programming abilities. JavaScript was introduced to compensate for this lack of programmability. Considering the needs that were felt that time, JavaScript was created as a simple, lightweight, easy-to-use language.

In earlier days, JavaScript was primarily used to add interactivity and fancy graphical effects to otherwise static web pages. However, over the years the situation has changed dramatically. Modern web applications rely extensively on JavaScript for a variety of tasks. A web page of a modern web application no longer uses JavaScript merely for fancy hover effects or animations. It relies heavily on JavaScript for business validations, making Ajax calls to the server, and business domain-specific processing.

A web page that uses JavaScript executes the script in foreground. That means as long as the script is running, user interaction with the page is blocked. In other words, user interactions and the script run on a single thread. Such an approach can be troublesome when the script is performing an intensive and time-consuming operation. To overcome this limitation, HTML5 and JavaScript provide *web workers* that allow you to run JavaScript processing in the background. This chapter gives you a detailed understanding of web workers. Specifically, you learn the following:

- What web workers are and how they work

- Flavors of web workers

- Restrictions on web workers

- Using web workers to develop a multithreaded web page

- Communicating with the server from the worker thread

Overview of Multithreading in Web Pages

If you've ever developed desktop applications in C# or Visual Basic, chances are you're aware of the Thread class residing in the System.Threading namespace. The Thread class represents a thread. A *thread* is the smallest unit of processing. When you run any application, the application code runs on a thread. Threads are handled by the operating system, and most modern programming languages provide classes that encapsulate them. A *single-threaded application* runs all the code (including user interface and business processing) in a single thread. A *multithreaded application* runs application code in multiple threads.

A multithreaded application offers the following benefits:

- It can significantly improve the application's user responsiveness. This benefit is useful when you're developing web applications. Rather than your JavaScript code blocking user interactions, by using multithreading you can keep the user interface responsive as the script runs in the background.

- It can improve the overall performance of your application. However, this benefit depends on several other factors such as number of CPUs and whether the code is running locally or remotely. Although a detailed discussion of how multithreading affects application performance is beyond the scope of this book, suffice to say that multithreading can improve the performance of an application that runs on a machine with multiple processors rather than a single processor. This is so because a multiprocessor machine can run different threads on different processors simultaneously, resulting in improved performance.

Now that you have a basic idea of single-threaded and multithreaded applications, let's apply these concepts to a web page. Consider the markup shown in Listing 10-1.

Listing 10-1. Web Page Running the UI and JavaScript in a Single Thread

```
<head>
    ...
    <script type="text/javascript">
      $(document).ready(function () {
        if (!Modernizr.webworkers) {
          alert("This browser doesn't support HTML5 Web Workers!");
          return;
        }
        $("#button1").click(function () {
          alert("Processing started!");
          var date = new Date();
          var currentDate = null;
          do {
            currentDate = new Date();
          }
          while (currentDate - date < 10000);
          alert("Processing done!");
        });
      });
    </script>
</head>
<body>
    ...
        <input id="button1" type="button" value="Click" />
    ...
</body>
```

This markup consists of a button and a block of JavaScript that is executed when the button is clicked. The ready( ) function uses Modernizr to check whether the browser supports web workers. This is done by checking the webworkers property of the Modernizr object. If the browser doesn't support web workers, an error message is displayed to the user.

The button's click event handler first displays an alert box to indicate the start of processing. The do-while condition is written in such a way that it simply loops for 10 seconds. The looping is achieved by calculating the difference between the current date-time and the date-time when the looping operation begins. The do-while loop is intended to mimic lengthy processing. In a real-world application, you have actual business processing instead of the loop. Once the loop is exited, another alert box flags the end of processing.

If you run this web page in the browser and click the button, you obviously get to see the start and end alert boxes; but more important, you observe that while the loop is running, the web page's UI becomes nonresponsive. During this time, your browser stops responding to keyboard inputs and mouse operations such as clicking and scrolling. These operations may be queued and played when the do-while loop is finished, but as long as the loop is running, the UI doesn't respond. The reason for this bottleneck is that the UI and the JavaScript are running on the same thread. So, at any given time, either the script can run or the UI can function.

The UI bottleneck can be avoided if you run the JavaScript code in a thread of its own. Consider Figure 10-1.

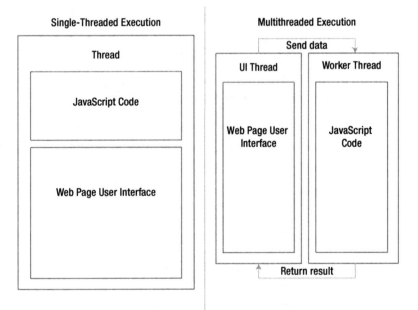

Figure 10-1. Single-threaded and multithreaded execution in web pages

Look at the single-threaded execution model shown in the figure. In this case, the same thread runs the JavaScript code and also handles user interactions. Now look at the multithreaded execution model. Here the UI is handled by a dedicated thread (UI thread), and the JavaScript is executed in a thread of its own. The thread running the JavaScript is often called a *worker thread* because its primary job is processing. Typically, a worker thread doesn't have access to the UI-level elements. It can, however, receive input from the UI thread and may return the result of the processing back to the UI thread. In the multithreaded model, the UI thread is also referred as a *foreground thread* and the worker thread as a *background thread*. In HTML5 terms, a worker thread is called a *web worker* and is represented by the Worker object.

Figure 10-1 shows only one worker thread, but you can spawn as many threads as you want. Remember, though, that each additional thread has overhead and may eventually degrade application performance. In many web applications, just one worker thread is sufficient for background processing needs.

Types of Web Workers

HTML5 web workers come in two flavors: dedicated and shared. *Dedicated* web workers are attached to the web page that creates them. They come into existence and die with the associated web page. Their scope is the web page in which they're created. In other words, dedicated web workers can be used only by a single web page. A dedicated web worker is represented by the Worker object.

Shared web workers are created by a web page, but once created they can be shared by multiple web pages within the same web application (that is, having the same origin). Creating a web worker requires resources. If you find yourself executing the same script in many pages of your web application, you may want to use shared web workers instead of creating a new thread in every web page. However, compared to dedicated web workers, they're more complex to code and are best used only in cases where you need to share a thread across multiple application pages. A shared web worker is represented by the SharedWorker object.

What Web Workers Can Access and What They Can't

Although web workers solve the problem of a blocked UI by running JavaScript processing in a separate thread, they also require careful design of the JavaScript code. As mentioned in the previous sections, web workers are worker threads and can't have any UI-level access. That means you can't access any DOM elements in the JavaScript code that you intend to run using web workers. This implies the following:

- Web workers can't access HTML elements from the web page.

- Web workers don't have access to global variables and JavaScript functions from the web page.

- Web workers can't use functions such as alert() and confirm() that require user attention.

- Objects such as window, document, and parent can't be accessed in the web-worker code.

- You can't use the jQuery library in web-worker code.

You may wonder why web workers can't access the HTML DOM. The main reason behind this restriction is that it isn't thread-safe to do so. Suppose, for example, that two web workers are running in the background. If both are allowed to access the HTML DOM, it's possible that one web worker may accidently overwrite the changes made by the other web worker. In the absence of any synchronization between multiple threads, such an execution is bound to produce unwanted results. That's why HTML5 web workers don't allow individual worker threads to access the DOM elements. When you pass data from the web page to the web worker, a copy of the data is sent to the worker thread. Each worker thread maintains its own data that is local to that worker thread.

A side effect of the "no DOM access" rule is that you can't use the jQuery library in web workers. The jQuery library is tied to the HTML DOM, and allowing it would violate the previous rule. This can be a little painful because even methods such as $.ajax() can't be used in web workers. Luckily, you can use the XMLHttpRequest object to make Ajax requests.

You can access navigator and location objects in the web-worker code. You can also use the setTimeout(), setInterval(), clearTimeout(), and clearInterval() methods in web workers.

■ **Note**   The XMLHttpRequest object is covered in Chapter 11. For the purpose of this chapter, it's sufficient to know that XMLHttpRequest is an object that allows you to make requests (GET/POST) to server-side resources. Instead of using the $.ajax() method you can use XMLHttpRequest object to call web methods, MVC action methods, and generic handlers.

Using Web Workers

Now that you have a basic understanding of what web workers are and what they can do, let's convert the web page from Listing 10-1 so that it doesn't block the UI. This essentially calls for running the processing logic (do-while loop) in a worker thread, to free up the UI thread to handle user interactions. Listing 10-2 shows how this can be done.

Listing 10-2. Creating a Web Worker

```
<script type="text/javascript">
  var worker;
  $(document).ready(function () {
    $("#btnStart").click(function () {
      worker = new Worker("scripts/processing.js");
      worker.addEventListener("message", ReceiveMessageFromWorker, false);
      worker.postMessage("Hello Worker!");
    });
  });
</script>
```

This code creates a global variable—worker—in a web form. This global variable is used to store the web worker object you create in the button's click event handler. The ready() function wires the click event handler of btnStart. In the click event handler the code creates a new Worker object. The JavaScript code that you wish to execute in a worker thread is placed in a separate script file. The path of the script file (scripts/processing.js) that includes the JavaScript code to be executed in the Worker is passed to the constructor.

Although not mandatory, often you're interested in receiving the result of processing from the worker thread so you know the outcome. The message event of the Worker object lets you listen to messages sent by the worker thread. The addEventListener() method wires the message event to the ReceiveMessageFromWorker() function. ReceiveMessageFromWorker()is a developer-defined function and is discussed shortly. The code then calls the postMessage() method of the Worker object. postMessage() acts as a trigger for starting the worker thread. You can pass it input data as a parameter. Although the code passes a string to the worker thread, the data can be in some other form such as a JSON object. If you don't want to pass any data, you can simply pass an empty string.

ReceiveMessageFromWorker() displays the result of processing as returned by the worker thread, like this:

```
function ReceiveMessageFromWorker(evt) {
  alert(evt.data);
}
```

The evt.data property returns the processing result sent by the worker thread. The actual processing (do-while loop) now resides in the Processing.js script file (see Listing 10-3).

Listing 10-3. Code Running in a Worker Thread

```
addEventListener("message", ReceiveMessageFromPage, false);

function ReceiveMessageFromPage(evt) {
    var date = new Date();
    var currentDate = null;
    do {
        currentDate = new Date();
    }
    while (currentDate - date < 10000);
    postMessage("Page said : " + evt.data + "\r\n Worker Replied : Hello Page!" );
}
```

Earlier, you wired the web page's message event handler to receive the message sent by the worker thread. Along the same lines, you need to wire the message event handler for the Worker to receive the message sent by the web form. The addEventHandler() call in Listing 10-3 does that job. The message event for the worker thread is raised when the web form calls the postMessage() method on the Worker object. In this case, the Worker's message event is handled by the ReceiveMessageFromPage() function.

ReceiveMessageFromPage() contains the same do-while loop as before. Notice, however, that there are no alert() calls because the worker thread can't have user interactions. Once the do-while loop completes, the worker thread calls postMessage() to send the processing result back to the web form. Notice how the data sent by the web form ("Hello Worker!") is retrieved in ReceiveMessageFromPage() using the evt.data property.

Figure 10-2 shows a sample run of the web form.

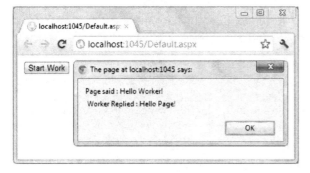

Figure 10-2. Processing.js running in a worker thread

The web form passes the string "Hello Worker!" to the worker thread. The worker thread forms a string by prefixing the evt.data value with "Page said :" and suffixing "Worker Replied : Hello Page!". The string is then returned to the web form. The ReceiveMessageFromWorker() function written in the web form displays the return value in an alert() box. Using the web worker object, the UI isn't blocked when you click the Start Work button. You can interact with the page freely because the processing is taking place in the background. When the processing is finished, you're notified and the result of the processing is displayed.

To make the interaction between the web form and the worker thread clear, Figure 10-3 displays the working of this application in pictorial form.

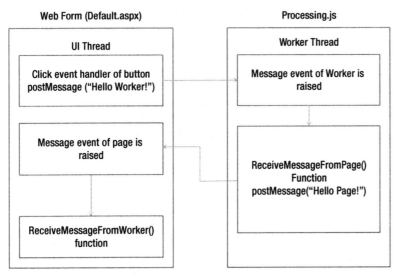

Figure 10-3. *Pictorial representation of web worker execution*

As shown in the figure, the sequence of execution is as follows:

1. The user clicks the Start Work button.

2. postMessage() is called, and "Hello Worker!" is sent to the worker thread.

3. The worker's message event is raised, and the ReceiveMessageFromPage() function handles it.

4. postMessage() is called, and "Hello Page!" is returned to the page.

5. The page's message event is raised, and the ReceiveMessageFromWorker() function handles it.

6. An alert box is shown to the user.

Importing External Script Files

In the preceding example, the entire processing logic was included in a single file. At times, your processing logic may reside in different script files. In a normal web page, one or more <script> tags point to the files and consume their functionality. However, the same trick doesn't work with web workers because web workers don't have access to any DOM elements, including <script>.

There is an alternative with web workers: the importScripts() function. You use importScripts() in the script file intended to run on a worker thread. The importScripts() function takes a comma-separated list of script files that you wish to refer to and imports them into the current file in synchronous fashion. The files are executed in the order you specify when calling importScripts(). The following code shows a sample usage of importScripts():

```
importScripts("Helper1.js");
importScripts("Helper1.js","Helper2.js","Helper3.js");
```

The first call to `importScripts()` imports the `Helper1.js` file. The second call imports three files: `Helper1.js`, `Helper2.js`, and `Helper3.js`. The scripts in the second call are executed in the order specified.

Handling Errors

Typically, web workers involve lengthy processing, and at times they may encounter unexpected errors. Because web workers don't have access to DOM, they can't report the errors by displaying dialog boxes or alerts. Any unhandled errors in the worker thread raise error event. The web page can wire an event handler to the error event of the web worker object and be notified when there is any error. Listing 10-4 shows how this is done.

Listing 10-4. Handling Errors

```
$("#btnStart").click(function () {
  worker = new Worker("scripts/Processing.js");
  worker.addEventListener("message", ReceiveMessageFromWorker, false);
  worker.addEventListener("error", HandleError, false);
  worker.postMessage("Hello Worker!");
});

function HandleError(evt) {
  var msg="There was an error in the worker thread!\r\n";
  msg += "Message : " + evt.message + "\r\n";
  msg += "Source : " + evt.filename + "\r\n";
  msg += "Line No. : " + evt.lineno;
  alert(msg);
}
```

Notice the line of code shown in bold. The `addEventListener()` method attaches an event-handler function `HandleError()` to the error event. The `HandleError()` function receives an `ErrorEvent` object. The three properties of the `ErrorEvent`—message, filename, and lineno—give you the error message, the file name in which error occurred, and the line number at which the error occurred. Figure 10-4 shows a sample run of the `HandleError()` event-handler function.

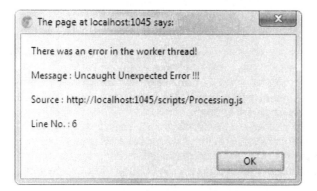

Figure 10-4. Error details being displayed by handling the error event

The alert box shows the error message "Uncaught Unexpected Error !!!". It also tells the user that the source of the error is `Processing.js` and that there is problem at line 6.

Terminating Web Workers

When you trigger a lengthy operation on a web worker, the only way you hear back from the worker thread is when it sends you the result of processing using the `postMessage()` method or when an error takes place during the execution of the worker thread. If the operation being executed on the worker thread is long-running, you may wish to allow the user to cancel the operation before its completion. The `Worker` object's `terminate()` method allows you to do that. The following piece of code shows how you use `terminate()`:

```
$("#btnStop").click(function () {
  worker.terminate();
});
```

This code handles the `click` event of a button (`btnStop`) and cancels the operation running on the worker thread by calling `terminate()`. Once a web worker is terminated, you can't reuse or restart it. The only way to restart the operation is to create a new `Worker` object.

Monitoring Web Workers During Development

As an ASP.NET developer, you interact with web workers using the `Worker` object. You don't need to know the internal details of how the browser creates and manages the threads. However, during the development and testing phase, you may want to see the effect of using web workers on the number of threads created by the browser. If so, you can use the Windows Resource Monitor to peek inside the browser's internal thread handling. You can access the Resource Monitor from the Performance tab of the Task Manager dialog.

Figure 10-5 shows entries for `Chrome.exe` in the Resource Monitor when the web form you developed earlier is loaded in Chrome.

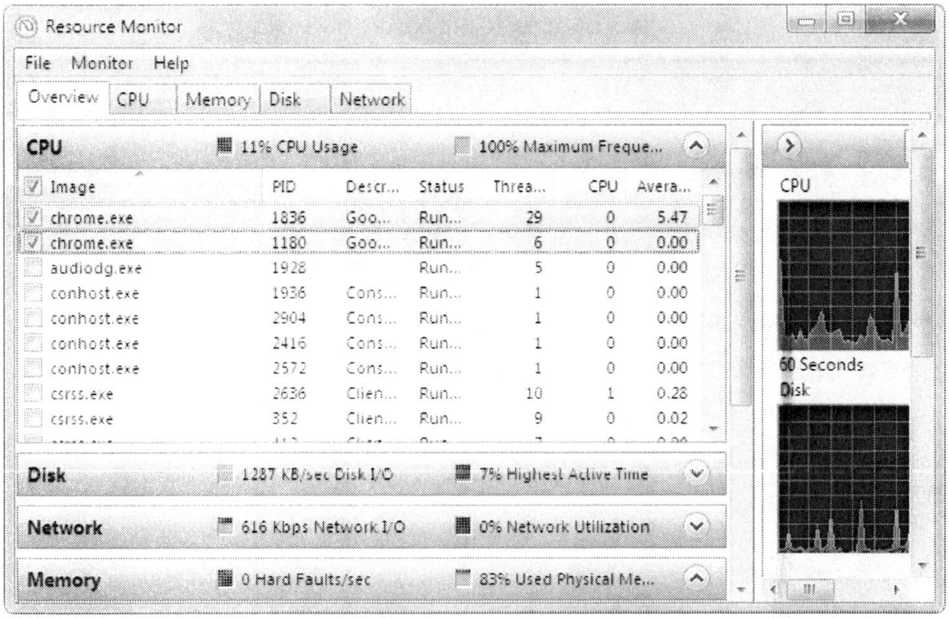

Figure 10-5. *Resource Monitor showing thread utilization*

As you can see, before the Start Work button is clicked, the thread counts for two instances of Chrome.exe are 29 (main process) and 6 (a single tab), respectively. When the Start Work button is clicked, thread utilization changes to 29 and 7, respectively. As you might guess, the thread count increments from 6 to 7 due to the creation of a web worker. When the web worker completes, however, the count doesn't go back to 6: although the operation has completed, the web worker is still active and will be reclaimed when the page is closed. If you click the Stop Work button that calls the terminate() method, the thread count goes back to 6 because you're explicitly terminating the thread. If you click the Start Work button multiple times without first terminating the previous worker thread, the thread count keeps incrementing, indicating that the previous thread isn't immediately reclaimed by the browser.

■ **Note** The previous thread counts (29 and 6) are taken from a sample run of the web form. The values may vary from browser to browser or even across multiple runs on the same browser. The point is to provide insight as to how the browser creates and destroys the worker threads.

Using Shared Web Workers

Creating and managing a worker thread is a resource-intensive operation. As you observed in the preceding section, dedicated web workers are created on per-page basis. If many pages of your web application need to execute the same script, using dedicated web workers may be costly in terms of thread utilization and memory. For example, if you open three web pages in three browser tabs, and each creates a Worker object, then three worker threads are created and naturally resource consumption is high. In such cases, you can use shared web workers, represented by the SharedWorker object.

As the name suggests, shared web workers share a worker thread across multiple pages of the web application. For example, suppose you have three web pages Page1, Page2, and Page3. All of them wish to execute the same script file, SharedProcessing.js. Let's further assume that Page1 is loaded in the browser and an instance of SharedWorker is created for running SharedProcessing.js. Later, Page2 is loaded in the browser and also tries to create an instance of SharedWorker to run SharedProcessing.js. However, because Page1 has already created a SharedWorker for processing SharedProcessing.js, Page2 doesn't create a new worker thread; instead it uses the same SharedWorker created earlier to get the job done. The same procedure is followed if Page3 is loaded in the browser. A shared web worker is reclaimed only when all the connections using it are closed.

Although using shared web workers conserves system resources, the downside is that they're slightly more complex to code than dedicated web workers. To understand how shared web workers are programmed, let's modify the earlier example to use the SharedWorker object.

Listing 10-5 illustrates how a SharedWorker object is created in a web form.

Listing 10-5. Creating a SharedWorker Object

```
<script type="text/javascript">
  var worker;
  $(document).ready(function () {
    $("#btnStart").click(function () {
      worker = new SharedWorker("scripts/SharedProcessing.js");
      worker.port.addEventListener("message", ReceiveMessageFromWorker, false);
      worker.port.start();
      worker.port.postMessage("Hello Shared Worker!");
    });
  });
```

```
...
</script>
```

This code creates a global variable named worker to hold the SharedWorker reference. The ready()
function wires the click event handler of the Start Work button. In the click event handler, an instance of
SharedWorker is created. A JavaScript file path that this shared web worker is supposed to run
(SharedProcessing.js) is passed in the constructor.

In the case of the Worker object, the message event is raised on the object. In the case of SharedWorker,
however, the message event is raised on the port object of the SharedWorker instance. That's why the
addEventListener() method is called on the port object. addEventListener() wires an event handler
function—ReceiveMessageFromWorker()—to the message event. Next, you need to call the port object's
start() method to start that port. Finally, postMessage() is called on the port object, and a string message
is sent to the shared worker thread. The ReceiveMessageFromWorker() function that acts as the message
event handler is as follows:

```
function ReceiveMessageFromWorker(evt) {
  alert(evt.data);
}
```

This function simply displays in an alert box the data sent back by the shared worker thread.

This completes the web form–level code. Now let's see what goes in the SharedProcessing.js file
(Listing 10-6).

Listing 10-6. Code Running in a Shared Web Worker

```
var port;
addEventListener("connect", ReceiveMessageFromPage, false);

function ReceiveMessageFromPage(evt) {
    port = evt.ports[0];
    port.addEventListener("message", SendMessageToPage, false);
    port.start();
}

function SendMessageToPage(evt) {
    var date = new Date();
    var currentDate = null;
    do {
        currentDate = new Date();
    }
    while (currentDate - date < 10000);
    port.postMessage("Page said : " + evt.data +
                            "\r\n Shared Worker Replied : Hello Page!");
}
```

This code begins by creating a global variable named port to hold a reference to a port object.
Whenever a new SharedWorker object obtains a reference to a shared worker thread, the connect event is
raised. To receive any messages from the web form in which the SharedWorker object exists, you need to
handle this event. The addEventListener() method attaches an event-handler function—
ReceiveMessageFromPage()—to the connect event.

The ReceiveMessageFromPage() event-handler function grabs the port object of the incoming
communication using evt.ports[0]. Although it appears that the ports array might have more than one

port object, in the current implementation of shared web workers there is always only one port in the ports array; thus you access the port object at array index 0.

The addEventListener() method wires an event-handler function—SendMessageToPage()—for the port object's message event. The start() method of the port object starts the communication channel.

■ **Note**   Although it isn't used in this example, the port object also has a close() method. This method closes a port and stops any further communication on that port.

The SendMessageToPage() event-handler function contains the same processing logic (do-while loop) as before. To send the result of the processing back to the web form, postMessage() is called on the port object. The string message sent by the web form is retrieved using the evt.data property, and extra string data is appended to it.

If you run the web form and click the Start Work button, you should see an alert box as shown in Figure 10-6.

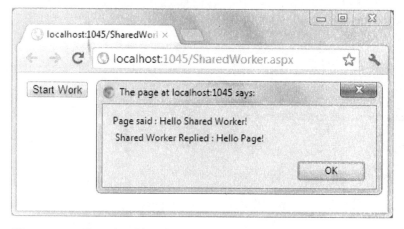

Figure 10-6. *Shared web worker in action*

Figure 10-6 shows that the script is being executed properly by the shared web worker. If you wish to see the effect on thread utilization of using shared web workers, open the Resource Monitor and look at the entries for Chrome.exe as before (Figure 10-7).

Figure 10-7 shows the Resource Monitor when the web form is open in two Chrome tabs. In all, there are four active entries for Chrome.exe. The one with 29 threads is for the main browser window. Every open tab takes 6 threads. So, the 2 entries with 6 threads each are for the 2 tabs in which the web form is loaded. Another set of 6 threads is created when you click the Start Work button for the first time; they're used for running the shared web workers. If you click Start Work multiple times, there is no further increase in the thread count because the previously created shared worker threads are reused by subsequent requests.

■ **Note**   Subsequent executions of the script running in a shared web worker get the previous state of the global variables. Also, if a shared web worker is already being used by a page, other pages interested in gaining access to the same shared web worker need to wait until the current processing is complete.

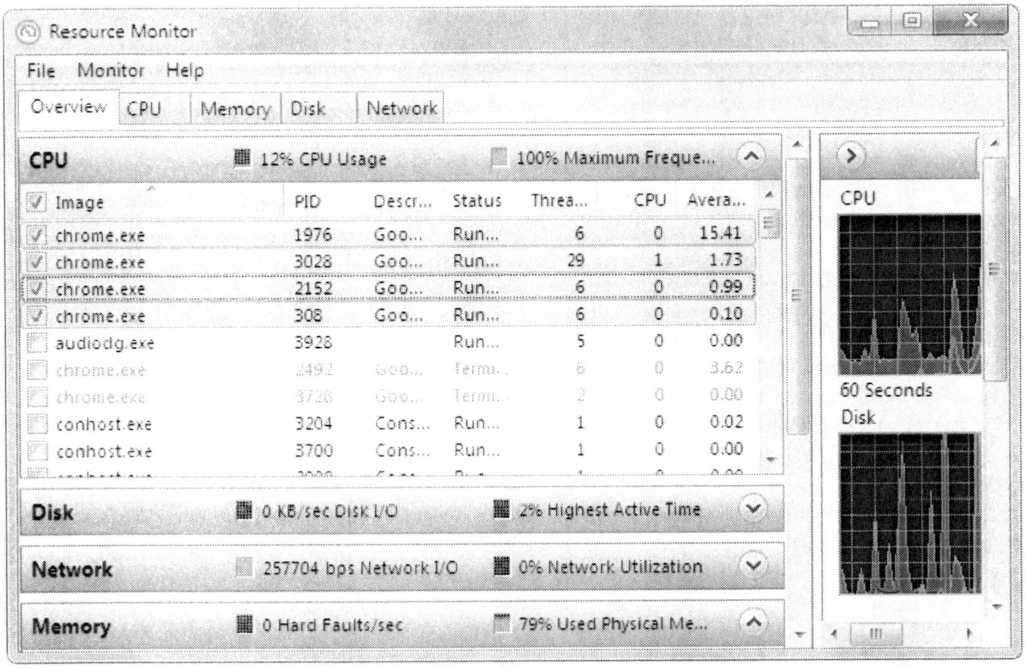

Figure 10-7. Observing shared worker threads using the Resource Monitor

Communicating With the Server

Web workers may need to make requests to server-side resources for their functioning. For example, a script running in a web worker may need to retrieve data residing in a SQL Server database. To fulfill this requirement, you may immediately think of using the jQuery $.ajax() method. After all, throughout this book you've been using jQuery to make Ajax calls to the server. However, you can't use jQuery with web workers because jQuery requires DOM access. As mentioned previously, web workers don't have access to any DOM elements. So, if you wish to make Ajax calls to the server, you need to use the XMLHttpRequest object.

Listing 10-7 uses XMLHttpRequest to access a server-side resource.

Listing 10-7. Using the XMLHttpRequest Object to Make Ajax Calls

```
function GetOrders(customerId) {
    var xhr = new XMLHttpRequest();
    xhr.open("POST", "/Home/GetOrders");
    xhr.setRequestHeader('Content-Type', 'application/json');
    xhr.onreadystatechange = function () {
        if (xhr.readyState == 4) {
            postMessage(xhr.responseText);
        }
    }
    var param = '{ "customerid": "' + customerId + '"}';
    xhr.send(param);
}
```

This code shows a JavaScript function—GetOrders()—intended to retrieve order data for a specific customer from the SQL Server. The GetOrders() function accepts a customer ID whose orders are to be retrieved.

Inside, the function creates a new instance of XMLHttpRequest. The open() method of the XMLHttpRequest object opens a communication channel with a remote request. The first parameter of the open() method is the type of request (GET/POST) being made, and the second parameter is the location of the remote resource. In this example, a POST request is made to an MVC action method named GetOrders. The XMLHttpRequest object's setRequestHeader() method sets the MIME content type of the request to application/json.

The XMLHttpRequest object raises the onreadystatechange event when the state of the request changes. The onreadystatechange event-handler function checks the readyState property of the XMLHttpRequest object. The readyState object indicates the current state of the request and can have values from 0 to 4. A value of 4 indicates that the request is completed. If the request is completed, you can use the postMessage() method to send the data returned by the remote resource back to the web page. The responseText property of the XMLHttpRequest object returns the response from the remote resource. In this case, the MVC action method is assumed to return data in JSON format, and hence responseText is sent directly to the web page.

To initiate the request, you need to call the XMLHttpRequest object's send() method. send() takes request parameters, if any. Because you wish to send request data in JSON format, you convert the customer ID to a JSON object and then pass it as a parameter to send().

Using Web Workers That Require Server-side Data

In this final example, you develop an ASP.NET MVC application that uses web workers to fetch data from the server and display it in a view. The main view of the application is shown in Figure 10-8.

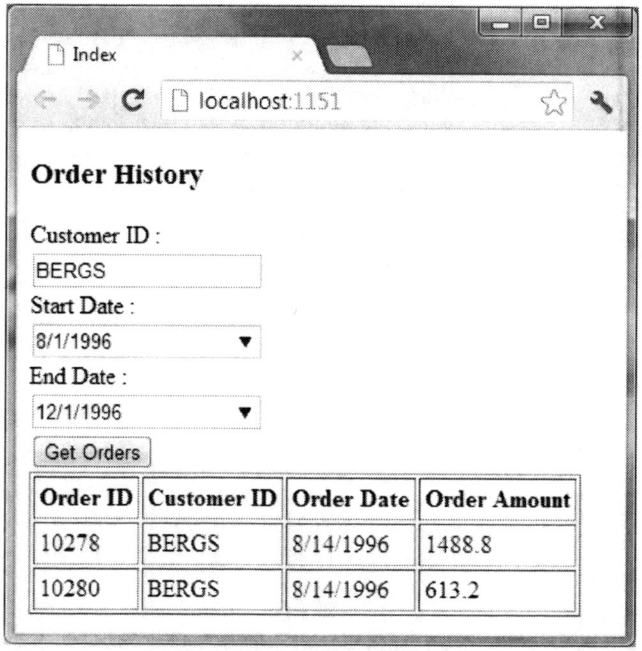

Figure 10-8. Order History application

The Order History application lets the user specify a customer ID along with a date range. It then fetches all the existing order data from the Orders and Order Details tables of the Northwind database and returns them to the view. The Entity Framework data model for the Orders and Order Details tables is shown in Figure 10-9.

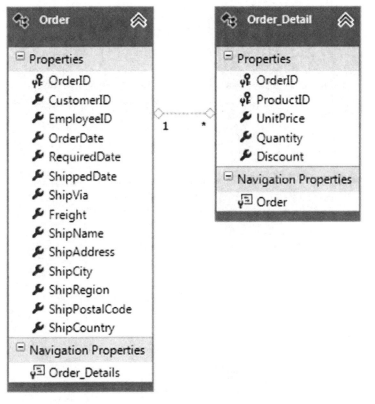

Figure 10-9. *Entity Framework data model for the Orders table*

Although the Order and Order_Detail classes have several properties. For the purpose of this example, you use only some of them: OrderID, CustomerID, OrderDate, Quantity, and UnitPrice. The total amount of an order is calculated in the JavaScript code.

Order History View

The view displays the order information in an HTML table. The task of fetching Order records from the SQL Server database is accomplished using a web worker. The HTML markup from the view is shown in Listing 10-8.

Listing 10-8. HTML Markup of the Order History View

```
<form id="form1" runat="server">
  <h3>Order History</h3>
  <div>Customer ID :</div>
  <input id="customerID" type="text" />
```

```
    <div>Start Date :</div>
    <input id="startDate" type="date" />
    <div>End Date :</div>
    <input id="endDate" type="date" />
    <br />
    <input id="getOrders" type="button" value="Get Orders" />
    <br />
    <table id="orderTable" border="1" cellPadding="3"></table>
</form>
```

The Order History view consists of a text box to specify a customer ID and two date fields. Notice the markup in bold: the <input> fields accepting date range are of type date. This way, browsers capable of showing a pop-up date picker can render the fields accordingly. Clicking the Get Orders button triggers the web-worker operation. The returned order details are displayed in the orderTable HTML table.

Creating a Web Worker

After entering a customer ID and a date range for selecting Order records, the user clicks the Get Orders button. The jQuery code responsible for creating a web worker and executing the required script is contained in this button's click event handler; see Listing 10-9.

Listing 10-9. Creating a Web Worker to Fetch Order Records

```
var worker;
$(document).ready(function () {
  …
  $("#getOrders").click(function () {
    $(this).attr("disabled", "disabled");
    $(this).val("Wait...");
    worker = new Worker("../../scripts/Processing.js");
    worker.addEventListener("message", ReceiveDataFromWorker, false);
    worker.addEventListener("error", HandleError, false);
    var settings = { "CustomerID": $("#customerID").val(),
                     "StartDate": $("#startDate").val(),
                     "EndDate": $("#endDate").val() };
    worker.postMessage(settings);
  });
});
```

The code first declares a global variable (worker) to store a reference to the web worker. The ready() function wires the click event handler of the Get Orders button. The click event-handler function disables the button by adding a disabled attribute to it using the jQuery attr() method. This is done so the user can't click the button multiple times and thus create multiple worker threads. To give a hint to the user that processing is going on, the value of the button is changed to "Wait..." using the val() method.

A new Worker object is then instantiated. The JavaScript code that fetches data from the server resides in Processing.js, and the path of the script file is specified while creating the Worker object. Then the event-handler functions for the message and error events are attached using the addEventListener() method. The respective event-handler functions, ReceiveDataFromWorker() and HandleError(), are discussed shortly.

The view needs to pass three pieces of information to the worker thread: the customer ID whose order details are to be fetched, the start date, and the end date. The postMessage() method can take only one parameter to pass to the worker thread. Hence, these pieces of data are grouped in a JSON object with three properties: CustomerID, StartDate, and EndDate.

To begin processing, the Worker object's postMessage() method is invoked and the JSON settings object is passed to it as a parameter.

Event Handlers for message and error Events

The ReceiveDataFromWorker() event-handler function receives the order data returned by the worker thread. This function is shown in Listing 10-10.

Listing 10-10. Receiving and Displaying Order Details

```
function ReceiveDataFromWorker(evt) {
  var data = evt.data;
  $("#orderTable").empty();
  $("#orderTable").append("<tr><th>Order ID</th><th>Customer ID</th>
  <th>Order Date</th><th>Order Amount</th></tr>");
  for (var i = 0; i < data.length; i++) {
    $("#orderTable").append("<tr>" +
                            "<td>" + data[i].OrderID + "</td>" +
                            "<td>" + data[i].CustomerID + "</td>" +
                            "<td>" + ToJSDate(data[i].OrderDate) + "</td>" +
"<td>" + data[i].OrderAmount + "</td>" +
                            "</tr>");
  }
  $("#getOrders").removeAttr("disabled");
  $("#getOrders").val("Get Orders");
}
```

ReceiveDataFromWorker() receives order data from the worker thread as an array. Each element of the array represents an order and has properties: OrderID, CustomerID, OrderDate, and OrderAmount. The evt. data property gives you access to this array.

The orderTable HTML table is emptied to remove any previously added rows. A for loop iterates through the JSON collection. With every iteration, a row is added to the table and the OrderID, CustomerID, OrderDate, and OrderAmount property values are displayed.

Notice that unlike OrderID and CustomerID, OrderDate isn't directly displayed in the table. The OrderDate value is first passed to a helper function—ToJSDate()—and the return value of ToJSDate() is displayed in the table. The OrderDate column is a date-time column in the database, but the JSON format doesn't have a date data type. So, when dates are serialized from the server to the client, they're sent in a special format. For example, if OrderDate is 8/12/1996 (mm/dd/yyyy) in the database, the JSON equivalent is /Date(839788200000)/. The number in Date() is the number of milliseconds between that date and midnight of 1 January 1970. The ToJSDate() helper function converts this cryptic-looking value into a readable form. ToJSDate() is shown in Listing 10-11.

Listing 10-11. Converting a JSON Date Value into a JavaScript Date

```
function ToJSDate(value) {
  var pattern = /Date\((([^)]+)\)\)/;
  var results = pattern.exec(value);
  var dt = new Date(parseFloat(results[1]));
  return  (dt.getMonth() + 1) + "/" + dt.getDate() + "/" + dt.getFullYear();
}
```

ToJSDate() uses regular expression and the JavaScript exec() method. exec() is called on a regular expression and accepts a parameter. It tests the specified value against the regular expression and returns the matched text. A new JavaScript Date object is then constructed, and a date string in mm/dd/yyyy format is returned to the caller.

■ **Note**   JSON doesn't have a specific format to represent date and time. This poses difficulty when you're serializing and deserializing date-time data between client and server. A recent trend is to use the ISO date and time format on the wire (for example, Json.NET and the Web API use this format). In ISO format, a date and time are represented as follows: YYYY-MM-DDThh:mm:ssTZD (for example, 2010-08-20T19:20:10+01:00).

After the order details are displayed in the HTML table, the button is enabled again by removing the disabled attribute added previously. The button value is again set to Get Orders.

The event handler of the error event simply displays an error message in an alert box, as follows:

```javascript
function HandleError(evt) {
        var msg="There was an error in the worker thread!\r\n\r\n";
        msg += "Message : " + evt.message + "\r\n";
        msg += "Source : " + evt.filename + "\r\n";
        msg += "Line No. : " + evt.lineno;
        alert(msg);
    }
```

The HandleError() function displays the error message, source file name, and line at which the error occurred using the three properties of the ErrorEvent object: message, filename, and lineno.

Code Running in the Web Worker

Now that you've finished coding the view, let's move to the Processing.js file that is executed by the web worker. The JavaScript from Processing.js retrieves order data from the server using the XMLHttpRequest object. Listing 10-12 shows the contents of Processing.js.

Listing 10-12. Retrieving Data from the Server Using XMLHttpRequest

```javascript
addEventListener("message", ReceiveMessageFromPage, false);

function ReceiveMessageFromPage(evt) {
    GetOrders(evt.data);
}

function GetOrders(settings) {
    var xhr = new XMLHttpRequest();
    xhr.open("POST", "/Home/GetOrders");
    xhr.setRequestHeader('Content-Type', 'application/json');
    xhr.onreadystatechange = function () {
        if (xhr.readyState == 4) {
            var data = JSON.parse(xhr.responseText);
            var orderAmount = 0;
            var finalData = new Array();
            var currOrderId = data[0].OrderID;
```

```
        for (var i = 0; i < data.length; i++) {
            if (data[i].OrderID != currOrderId || i == (data.length - 1)) {
                if (i == (data.length - 1)) {
                    orderAmount += (data[i].Quantity * data[i].UnitPrice);
                }
                finalData.push({ CustomerID: data[i].CustomerID,
                                 OrderID: currOrderId,
                                 OrderAmount: orderAmount,
                                 OrderDate: data[i].OrderDate });
                currOrderId = data[i].OrderID;
                orderAmount = 0;
            }
            orderAmount += (data[i].Quantity * data[i].UnitPrice);
        }

        postMessage(finalData);
    }
}
var param = JSON.stringify(settings);
xhr.send(param);
}
```

This code attaches an event handler for the web worker's message event. The event-handler function ReceiveMessageFromPage() calls another function, GetOrders(). Recollect that the view passes a JSON object containing a customer ID and a date range to the worker thread. This JSON object is obtained using the evt.data property and passed to the GetOrders() function.

GetOrders() creates a new instance of XMLHttpRequest and opens a POST request with a controller action method (Home/GetOrders). The Content-Type header is set to application/json because the data being sent as a part of the request is in JSON format.

The onreadystatechange event-handler function checks the readyState property of the XMLHttpRequest object. If readyState is 4 (meaning the request is complete), it processes the returned data. The value of the responseText property is converted into JSON format using the JSON.parse() method. A for loop iterates through the order data and calculates the total amount for each order. It does so by multiplying the Quantity and UnitPrice values.

Based on the processing result, a JSON object is constructed with four properties: CustomerID, OrderID, OrderDate, and OrderAmount. This order data is stored in an array—finalData—using the push() method. Finally, the postMessage() method is invoked on the web worker to send the finalData array to the page. Before the request is initiated, the JSON settings are converted into their string equivalents using the JSON.stringify() method. The send() method makes the request and passes the settings to the GetOrders() action method.

GetOrders() Action Method

The GetOrders() action method resides in the HomeController and returns order data for a specific customer ID and date range. GetOrders() is shown in Listing 10-13.

Listing 10-13. GetOrders() Action Method

```
[HttpPost]
public JsonResult GetOrders(OrderSettings settings)
{
```

```
            NorthwindEntities1 db = new NorthwindEntities1();

var data = from item in db.Orders
                       join item2 in db.Order_Details on item.OrderID
                       equals item2.OrderID
                       where
                       item.CustomerID == settings.CustomerID
                       &&
                       item.OrderDate >= settings.StartDate
                       &&
                       item.OrderDate <= settings.EndDate
                       orderby item.OrderID ascending
                       select new { item.CustomerID, item.OrderID,item.OrderDate,
                                        item2.UnitPrice, item2.Quantity };
            return Json(data.ToArray());
}
```

GetOrders() takes one parameter of type OrderSettings. The OrderSettings class's properties match those of the JSON object being sent from the client. This way, ASP.NET MVC automatically maps incoming JSON object to the OrderSettings class. OrderSettings looks like this:

```
public class OrderSettings
{
    public string CustomerID { get; set; }
    public DateTime StartDate { get; set; }
    public DateTime EndDate { get; set; }
}
```

A LINQ to Entities query then selects all the Order and Order Details records with matching CustomerID and falling within the specified date range. The query returns a custom type that contains the CustomerID, OrderID, and OrderDate properties from the Orders table and the Quantity and UnitPrice properties from the Order Details table. The return type of GetOrders() is JsonResult. The Json() method converts the query results into the equivalent JSON format.

That's it! You can now run the Order History view and test its functionality.

■ **Note**   While testing the Order History application, you may find that the worker thread completes too quickly if the database is running on the local machine. For the sake of testing and confirming that the UI isn't blocked, you can deliberately introduce some delay in the worker thread. As an alternative to adding a dummy do-while loop that introduces delay, you can call the postMessage() method using the setTimeout() function, like this: var t = setTimeout(postMessage, 10000, xhr.responseText);.

Summary

Traditional JavaScript code runs in the same thread as the UI. Due to this single-threaded nature, the UI is blocked when JavaScript code is being executed. HTML5 web workers add multithreaded capabilities to JavaScript. Using web workers, you can execute script files in the background. This way, the UI isn't blocked while the script is running. Web workers can be a great help when a script is lengthy and long-running. Web workers come in two flavors: dedicated and shared, represented by the `Worker` and `SharedWorker` objects, respectively. Web workers don't have access to HTML DOM. Using web workers, you can develop user-responsive web pages and improve the overall user experience.

In this chapter, you saw web applications that benefitted from new multithreading features. The next chapter covers more features that allow client-server communication as well as cross-domain communication.

CHAPTER 11

■ ■ ■

Using the Communication API and Web Sockets

So far in this book, you've learned about HTML5 features that require no server-side communication. Although you used some techniques such as jQuery $.ajax() to send and receive data between the client and the server, doing so wasn't an integral part of the HTML5 feature being discussed. In this chapter, however, you learn about a few HTML5 features that are specifically designed to facilitate communication between the client browser and the server. Using these features, you can pass data to and from web pages from the same web application or from different applications. Additionally, some of these techniques provide one-way (client to server) communication, and others provide two-way (client to server and server to client) communication. Specifically, you learn about the following:

- Cross-document messaging and Cross-Origin Resource Sharing (CORS)
- Using the postMessage API to send data to documents from different web application
- Using the new XMLHttpRequest Level 2 features to make GET and POST requests
- Notifying the client using server-sent events
- Performing two-way communication using Web Sockets

Understanding Cross-Domain Communication

A web application often needs to perform one of the following two kinds of communication:

- A web page may want to communicate with another web page from the same web application.
- A web page may want to communicate with another web page belonging to some another web application.

Performing the first type of communication is relatively simple because there are no restrictions enforced by the browser on such communication. Additionally, JavaScript-based libraries such as jQuery are readily available for performing this type of communication. However, things become tricky when you wish to communicate to web pages from a different web application.

The main problem in achieving the second type of communication is that all browsers prohibit what is known as *cross-domain communication* due to security concerns. If cross-domain communication is allowed, it's possible that a malicious web page may exploit this feature to cause security threats to your web application.

Communication is said to be *cross-domain* if the origin of the two parties taking part in the communication isn't the same. An *origin* consists of a scheme, a host, and a port. For example, consider the origin `http://www.domain1.com`. In this URL, the scheme is `http`, the host is `www.domain1.com`, and no explicit port is specified. If two URLs don't have the same origin, they can't communicate with each other. So, `http://www.domain1.com/Page1.aspx` and `http://www.domain2.com/Page2.aspx` can't communicate because their hosts are different. On the same lines, `https://www.domain1.com` and `http://www.domain1.com` are considered different origins because their schemes are different (`http` and `https`). However, `http://www.domain1.com/Page1.aspx` and `http://www.domain1.com/Page2.aspx` belong to the same origin.

Just because cross-domain communication poses security threats doesn't mean it's unsuitable in every situation. Suppose you're building a network of web sites. Each web site is independent and provides different content to the user. However, a member of the web-site network may want to share some features (member chat, for example) with other web sites in the network. This is a genuine case of cross-domain communication. Luckily, HTML5 understands the problems faced by developers today in achieving cross-domain communication and provides two approaches for doing this:

- Cross-document messaging
- Cross-Origin Resource Sharing (CORS)

Let's look at these in more detail.

Cross-Document Messaging

Cross-domain messaging refers to communication between two or more web pages belonging to different origins, where one web page either embeds or opens another web page. Consider a case where a web page of WebSite1 declares an `<iframe>` and embeds a web page of WebSite2 in that `<iframe>`. A similar situation arises when a web page of WebSite1 opens a web page of WebSite2 using the `window.open()` method. In both of these examples, the two web pages belong to different origins. If they wish to communicate with one another, there was no easy and standard way prior to HTML5.

HTML5 facilitates cross-document messaging with the help of the postMessage API. This is a standard approach that enables secure cross-origin communication across `<iframe>` elements, tabs, and windows. To enable cross-document messaging using the postMessage API, you don't need to do any configuration at the server end. The postMessage API is secure and doesn't pose a security threat because you need to explicitly receive the messages in your web application. The web site receiving the request from a page from another origin must explicitly make available specific pages for accepting the cross-document requests. So, even if someone sends malicious script or data to you, there won't be any damage unless you explicitly permit and receive that data. You'll understand this better when you develop a sample application that uses the postMessage API.

■ **Note** The postMessage API discussed in this chapter bears a striking resemblance to web workers as far as syntax is concerned. That's because they use the same HTML5 messaging system. Web workers, however, serve an entirely different purpose than the postMessage API.

Cross-Origin Resource Sharing (CORS)

During cross-document messaging, one document needs a *handle* to the other document. This handle is typically in the form of an <iframe> or window object. However, in many real-world cases, you just want to make a cross-domain GET or POST request. Cross-document messaging won't allow you to do that. What you need in such cases is Cross-Origin Resource Sharing (CORS).

Unlike the postMessage API, to enable CORS you need to do little configuration at the web server end. All cross-domain requests have an Origin header. This header is added by the browser and provides the request origin to the web server. The application code can't tamper with the header. To accept requests from a different origin, the web server should be configured to have an Access-Control-Allow-Origin HTTP header. You can add this header using either IIS Manager or web.config. Figure 11-1 shows the IIS Manager dialog in which you can add the Access-Control-Allow-Origin header.

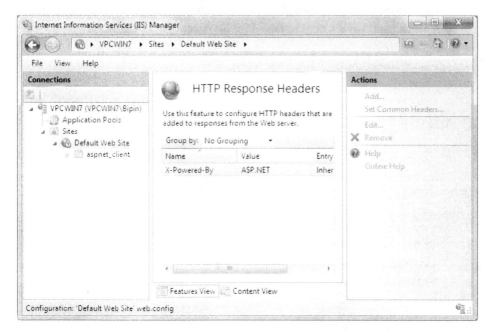

Figure 11-1. Adding the Access-Control-Allow-Origin header using IIS Manager

The value for the Access-Control-Allow-Origin header can be either * (all domains allowed) or a list of specific domains. You can achieve the same effect using the web.config file, as shown in Listing 11-1.

Listing 11-1. Adding the Access-Control-Allow-Origin Header Using web.config

```
<system.webServer>
  <httpProtocol>
    <customHeaders>
      <add name="Access-Control-Allow-Origin" value="*" />
    </customHeaders>
  </httpProtocol>
</system.webServer>
```

The <customHeaders> section of web.config allows you to add custom headers. In this case, the Access-Control-Allow-Origin header is added and its value is set to *, indicating that all domains are allowed.

To implement CORS communication, HTML5 enhances the XMLHttpRequest object (these improvements are collectively referred as *Level 2*) so that cross-domain HTTP requests can be made.

Now that you have a basic understanding of cross-document messaging and CORS, let's peek into the code-level details of these techniques.

■ **Note** A common way to fetch data from another origin without using any specific technology such as cross-document messaging or CORS is JSONP: JSON with Padding. JSONP works on the basis that even though browsers don't allow you to make cross-domain requests, they do allow you to use <script> tags that point to a remote resource. In this technique, the script URL also specifies the name of a callback function in the query string. Instead of returning JSON data, the remote resource returns a function call to this callback function with the JSON data as a parameter. This technique suffers from the drawback that you must trust the remote server, which can pose a security threat.

Using the postMessage API

In order to use the postMessage API, you need a handle to the window of the target document. The target document receives the data sent by the main web page. Optionally, the target document can return a value to the main web page to indicate the result of the operation being performed. To obtain this handle, you can use either of two common techniques:

- Use the <iframe> element in the main web page, and load the target web page in the <iframe>. You can then use the contentWindow property of the <iframe> DOM element to get a reference of the target window.

- Use the window.open() method in the main web page. This method returns the reference to the target window object.

Using postMessage with <iframe>

Using the postMessage API with <iframe> involves embedding the target web page in the main page using the <iframe> element and then sending data to the target page using the postMessage() method. Listing 11-2 shows the main web form with an <iframe> element.

Listing 11-2. Using the <iframe> Element to Embed a Target Web Form

```
<form id="form1" runat="server">
  <div>Send Data :</div>
  <input id="txtData" type="text" /><input id="btnSend" type="button" value="Send" />
  <div>Data Received from Target Web Form :</div>
  <div id="divReceived"></div>
  <h3>Target Page in IFRAME</h3>
  <iframe id="target" src="http://localhost:1052/Target.aspx">
  </iframe>
</form>
```

This listing shows markup of the main web form (Iframe.aspx) that embeds the target web form (Target.aspx) using an <iframe> element. Note that for the sake of testing, Iframe.aspx and Target.aspx are created in two separate web applications. Although this won't make them cross-domain in a real sense, they're still cross-origin because the Visual Studio development web server assigns different port number to different web applications.

The main web form contains a text box to accept the data to be sent to the target web form. The Send button triggers some jQuery code that actually sends the data to the target web form. The src attribute of the <iframe> element points to http://localhost:1052/Target.aspx. The <div> element is used to output the data returned by the target web form.

The target web form markup is simple and consists of a <div> element that outputs the data received from the main web form. The markup of the Target.aspx is shown next:

```
<form id="form1" runat="server">
  <div>Data Received from Main Web Form :</div>
  <div id="divReceived"></div>
</form>
```

Figure 11-2 shows the main web form and the embedded target web form at runtime.

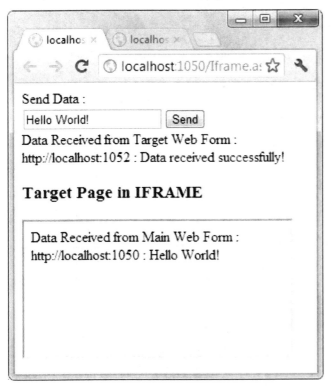

Figure 11-2. Target web form loaded in an <iframe>

Figure 11-2 shows a sample run of the main web form. The main web form sends the string data "Hello World!" to the target web form. The target web form outputs the data and sends back a success message. The origin of the main form as well as that of the target web form are also displayed along with their respective data.

The main web form contains jQuery code that handles the Send button's click event. This code is shown in Listing 11-3.

Listing 11-3. Sending Data to the Target Web Form

```
var targetOrigin = "http://localhost:1052";
$(document).ready(function () {
  if (!Modernizr.postmessage) {
    alert("This browser doesn't support the HTML5 postMessage API!");
    return;
  }
  var targetWindow = $("#target").get(0).contentWindow;
  window.addEventListener("message", ReceiveMessage, false);
  $("#btnSend").click(function () {
    targetWindow.postMessage($("#txtData").val(), targetOrigin);
  });
});
```

This code uses the Modernizr library to detect whether the browser supports the postMessage API. This is done using the postmessage property of the Modernizr object. As mentioned earlier, you need a handle to the target window in order to send data to the target web form. To get the window object attached to the <iframe> element, you use the contentWindow property of the <iframe> DOM element.

If you're interested in receiving the return value sent by the target web form, you need to wire an event handler for the message event. The addEventListener() method can wire an event-handler function—ReceiveMessage, in this example—to the main window's message event.

The Send button's click event handler calls the postMessage() method on the target window object. The first parameter of the postMessage() method is the data you wish to pass to the target web form. The second parameter is the origin of the target web form.

The ReceiveMessage() event-handler function is shown in Listing 11-4.

Listing 11-4. Handling the message Event in the Main Web Form

```
function ReceiveMessage(evt) {
  if (evt.origin != targetOrigin)
    return;
  $("#divReceived").append(evt.origin + " : " + evt.data + "<br/>");
}
```

This code first checks whether the origin of the message being received is a permitted one. It does so using the origin property of the event parameter. This way, the developer of the other web site (the web site whose service is being consumed by your web site) can *white-list* only certain origins. If the origin doesn't belong to the approved set, you can simply ignore it during further processing.

To access the data sent by the target web form, the code uses the data property of the event parameter. The origin and the data are appended to the <div> element using the jQuery append() method.

The target web form contains jQuery code that receives the data sent by the main web form. This code is shown in Listing 11-5.

Listing 11-5. Receiving the Data Sent by the Main Web Form

```
var targetOrigin = "http://localhost:1050";
$(document).ready(function () {
  ...
```

```
window.addEventListener("message", ReceiveMessage, false);
});

function ReceiveMessage(evt) {
  if (evt.origin != targetOrigin)
    return;
  $("#divReceived").append(evt.origin + " : " + evt.data + "<br/>");
  evt.source.postMessage("Data received successfully!", evt.origin);
}
```

Earlier it was mentioned that the postMessage API offers a secure way to do cross-document messaging. Here you can understand why. The author of the main page doesn't get direct access to the target web page: everything is mediated by the code from the target web page.

The code in Listing 11-5 wires an event handler—ReceiveMessage()—to the target window's message event. The ReceiveMessage() event-handler function then performs checking on the origin property and, if the data is being received from an expected origin, appends the data to a <div> element. A success message is sent back to the main web form using the source property of the event parameter. The source property refers to the window object of the main web form.

■ **Note** Unless you're developing a general-purpose service that is exposed for public consumption, it's a good idea to include a white-listing mechanism in applications that use the postMessage API. In the absence of such a white-list, any origin can send data to your web pages, and it will be processed by the message event handler. If your white-list is small, you can store it in an array; otherwise an XML file or a database table is a better choice.

Using postMessage with the window Object

Using the postMessage API with the window object is similar to using it with the <iframe> element. The only difference is that instead of the contentWindow property, you need to use the window reference returned by the window.open() method. Listing 11-6 makes this clear.

Listing 11-6. Using postMessage() with window.open()

```
$(document).ready(function () {
  ...
  var targetWindow = window.open(targetOrigin + "/Target.aspx");

  window.addEventListener("message", ReceiveMessage, false);

  $("#btnSend").click(function () {
    targetWindow.postMessage($("#txtData").val(), targetOrigin);
  });
});
```

This code resides in the main web form. Notice that this time, instead of using an <iframe> to load the target web form, you use the window.open() method. The open() method accepts the URL of the target web form and returns a reference to the window object of the target web form. Once a reference to the target window is obtained, it's used in exactly the same manner as in the <iframe> example discussed earlier.

283

Making Requests Using XMLHttpRequest

A very common and popular way of communicating with the server is the XMLHttpRequest object. The XMLHttpRequest object allows you to programmatically make HTTP requests to the web server, such as GET, POST, PUT, and DELETE. The primary reason for the popularity of XMLHttpRequest is that the leading browsers support it. XMLHttpRequest was first introduced by Internet Explorer, but it was soon absorbed in all the other browsers too. Today, XMLHttpRequest is the basis of most Ajax-based communication. In fact, the jQuery $.ajax() method that you've been using throughout this book internally uses XMLHttpRequest for its functionality. Using XMLHttpRequest, you can make synchronous and asynchronous requests to the web server, although asynchronous mode is used more often.

XMLHttpRequest existed prior to HTML5, but with HTML5 it has been improved. Some of the main improvements include the following:

- You can make cross-origin requests using the XMLHttpRequest object and the CORS specifications.

- You can track the progress of data download and upload operations using progress events.

- XMLHttpRequest now supports sending binary data.

Together, these improvements to the XMLHttpRequest object are referred as *Level 2*. You used XMLHttpRequest briefly while working with web workers. The following sections dissect the XMLHttpRequest object in more details.

Properties of XMLHttpRequest

Before using the XMLHttpRequest object, let's take a quick look at its properties, methods, and events. Table 11-1 lists the properties of XMLHttpRequest. Some of these properties are set before making a request, and others are accessed after the completion of the request.

Table 11-1. Properties of the XMLHttpRequest Object

Property	Description
readyState	Indicates the state of a request at a given point of time. The readyState property can change during the lifetime of a request and can take one of the following values: 0—The request has not yet been sent to the server. 1—The request has been opened by the server using the open() method, but the send() method hasn't yet been called. 2—The send() method has been called, and the response headers and status are available. 3—The response is being downloaded but isn't complete. 4—The operation is complete. The readyState property is commonly used inside the readystatechange event.
responseType	Tells the server the desired response type. Common values include text, json, and document.
responseText	Returns the response to the request as text data.
responseXML	Returns the response to the request as an XML document.
status	Indicates an HTTP status code (such as 200).
statusText	Indicates an HTTP status text (such as "200 OK").

Property	Description
timeout	Specifies the number of milliseconds to wait before terminating a request. A value of 0 indicates no timeout.
upload	Tracks the progress of the data upload.

In a typical usage, you set responseType and timeout before initiating a request. You then track the readyState of the request and, when it becomes 4 (complete), access the responseText, responseXML, status, and statusText properties.

Methods of XMLHttpRequest

The XMLHttpRequest object provides methods that allow you to initiate a request, send data with the request, and terminate a request before its completion. Table 11-2 lists these methods for your quick reference.

Table 11-2. Methods of the XMLHttpRequest Object

Method	Description
open()	Sets the HTTP method and request URL before the request is made. By default, a request is made in asynchronous fashion, but you can make a request synchronously using a parameter.
send()	Actually sends a request to the server. For all request types other than GET, you can also pass data as a parameter. The type of data depends on the content type of the request.
abort()	Cancels a request before its completion.
getResponseHeader()	Returns the value of a specified HTTP response header once a request is complete.
getAllResponseHeaders()	Returns all the HTTP response headers once a request is complete.
setRequestHeader()	Sets a request header (such as Content-Type). This method must be called between open() and send().

In a typical usage, you call the open() method followed by setRequestHeader(), and then call send() to actually make the request. In most cases, you use the GET or POST verb with the open() method. However, open() can be used for other verbs too. For example, while using the ASP.NET Web API, you need to pass PUT and DELETE in addition to GET and POST.

send() can be used to send data depending on the content type. Common data formats are text and JSON. You can also use FormData object to bundle data as key-value pairs and send it to the server.

Events of XMLHttpRequest

Events of the XMLHttpRequest object allow you to track the request being made and determine its status. Table 11-3 lists these events.

Table 11-3. Events of the XMLHttpRequest Object

Event	Description
readystatechange	Raised whenever the readyState value changes for an asynchronous request. You can use this event to track the request from the time it's made to its completion.
loadstart	Indicates that the request operation has begun.
load	Raised when the request has completely downloaded. The load event can be an alternative to using the readystatechange event to track request completion.
loadend	Indicates that the request operation has stopped.
progress	Raised multiple times while the data is being downloaded or uploaded.
timeout	Raised when a request is timed out.
abort	Raised when a request is cancelled.
error	Raised whenever there is an error while making the request.

If you used XMLHttpRequest prior to HTML5, recollect that developers mostly relied on the readystatechange event for any sort of tracking including request completion and error handling. However, XMLHttpRequest Level 2 provides task-specific events that you can use to make your code cleaner and neater.

Note that the progress event is fired for the XMLHttpRequest object itself and also for the upload object of the XMLHttpRequest instance. The former event tracks the progress of data being downloaded, whereas the latter tracks the progress of the data being uploaded. By handling the progress event, you can display the progress of the operation to the user, say in a progress bar.

Making Requests Using XMLHttpRequest

Now that you know the properties, methods, and events of the XMLHttpRequest object, let's develop an application that illustrates how they're used. In this section, you develop an ASP.NET Web Forms–based application as shown in Figure 11-3.

Figure 11-3. Customer List application developed using XMLHttpRequest

This web form displays all the records from the Customers table of the Northwind database in an HTML table. The row at the top allows the user to insert a new customer. Existing customers can be modified or deleted using the Update or Delete button, respectively. The SELECT, INSERT, UPDATE, and DELETE (CRUD) operations are performed through ASP.NET Web API. The methods exposed by the Web API controller class are invoked using the XMLHttpRequest object. The web form markup is simple and is shown in Listing 11-7.

Listing 11-7. *Markup for the Customer List Web Form*

```
<h3>Customer List</h3>
<form id="form1" runat="server">
<table id="tblCustomers">
</table>
</form>
```

The web form consists of a table: tblCustomers. The rows of the table are added programmatically depending on the number of customer records in the database. The Entity Framework data model required by the application is shown in Figure 11-4.

Figure 11-4. *Entity Framework data model class for the Customers table*

The Customer data model class has several properties, but only four are used in the application: CustomerID, CompanyName, ContactName, and Country.

Developing a Web API Controller

To perform CRUD operations on the Customers table, you develop a Web API controller (CustomerController). A Web API controller is a class that inherits from the ApiController base class and contains an implementation for the following methods:

- Get(): Represents an HTTP GET request that SELECTs data items and returns them to the caller.

- Get(id): Represents an HTTP GET request and SELECTs a single data item that is to be returned to the caller based on the ID specified.

- Post(): Represents an HTTP POST request and is used to INSERT a data item into a database.

- Put(id): Represents an HTTP PUT request and is used to UPDATE a data item from the database matching the specified ID.

- Delete(id): Represents an HTTP DELETE request and is used to DELETE a data item from the database.

Note that though this example needs CRUD functionality, it isn't necessary that the Web API and XMLHttpRequest be used exclusively for such scenarios. Listing 11-8 shows the Get() and Post() methods of CustomerController.

Listing 11-8. *Get() and Post() Methods of the CustomerController Class*

```
public class CustomerController : ApiController
{
    public IEnumerable<Customer> Get()
    {
        NorthwindEntities db = new NorthwindEntities();
        var data = from item in db.Customers
                       orderby item.CustomerID
                       select item;
        return data;
    }

    public void Post(Customer obj)
    {
        NorthwindEntities db = new NorthwindEntities();
        db.Customers.AddObject(obj);
        db.SaveChanges();
    }
    ...
}
```

The Get() method returns an IEnumerable of Customer items. Inside, Get() selects all the Customer items and returns them to the caller after sorting them based on the CustomerID column.

The Post() method accepts a Customer object as a parameter. This parameter comes from the jQuery code you writer later. Post() adds the supplied Customer object to the Customers table using the AddObject() method. To persist the data back to the database, you call SaveChanges().

To successfully call a Web API from the client, you also need to add the following routing information in the Global.asax file:

```
protected void Application_Start(object sender, EventArgs e)
{
    RouteTable.Routes.MapHttpRoute(
        name: "DefaultApi",
        routeTemplate: "api/{controller}/{id}",
        defaults: new { id = System.Web.Http.RouteParameter.Optional }
        );
}
```

The `MapHttpRoute()` method maps the incoming requests to the Web API controller classes. For example, a sample URL pointing to the `Customer` Web API controller is `http://localhost:1050/api/Customer`.

Using XMLHttpRequest to Invoke the Web API

Now let's write the client-side jQuery code that invokes the `Customer` Web API controller using the `XMLHttpRequest` object. The jQuery code primarily consists of four functions: `GetCustomers()`, `InsertCustomer()`, `UpdateCustomer()`, and `DeleteCustomer()`. These functions perform the respective operations by calling a Web API method.

When the web form is loaded, it needs to display the `Customer` data; hence the `GetCustomers()` function is called in the jQuery `ready()` function. Listing 11-9 shows how this is done. Some code has been omitted for the sake of readability.

Listing 11-9. Creating an XMLHttpRequest Object and Displaying Data

```
$(document).ready(function () {
  GetCustomers();
});

function GetCustomers() {
  $("#tblCustomers").empty();
  $("#tblCustomers").append("<tr><th>...</tr>");
  var emptyRow = "<tr>";
  emptyRow += "<td><input size='5' type='text'/></td>";
  ...
  emptyRow += "<td><input type='button' value='Insert'/></td>";
  emptyRow += "</tr>";
  $("#tblCustomers").append(emptyRow);

  var xhr = new XMLHttpRequest();
  xhr.open("GET", "api/Customer");
  xhr.setRequestHeader('Accept', 'application/json');
  xhr.setRequestHeader('Content-Type', 'application/json');
  xhr.onreadystatechange = function () {
    if (xhr.readyState == 4) {
      var data = JSON.parse(xhr.responseText);
      for (var i = 0; i < data.length; i++) {
        var row = "<tr>";
        row += "<td><input size='5' type='text' value='" + data[i].CustomerID +
                    "' readonly='readonly'/></td>";
        ...
        row += "<td><input type='button' value='Update'/>";
        row += "<input type='button' value='Delete'/></td>";
        row += "</tr>";
        $("#tblCustomers").append(row);
      }
      $("#tblCustomers input[value='Insert']").click(InsertCustomer);
      $("#tblCustomers input[value='Update']").click(UpdateCustomer);
      $("#tblCustomers input[value='Delete']").click(DeleteCustomer);
```

```
      }
    }
    xhr.send();
}
```

This code declares a global XMLHttpRequest object so that all the other methods can use it. Inside the jQuery ready() function, the GetCustomers() function is called. GetCustomers() first adds table headers and an empty row for accepting new Customer details.

A new XMLHttpRequest object is then created. The open() method of the XMLHttpRequest object specifies the request method as GET and the URL as api/Customer. Note that you need not specify the Web API method name in the URL. Based on the HTTP verb (GET in this case), the appropriate Web API method is automatically invoked.

You set two request headers: Accept and Content-Type. The Accept header is mainly for the Web API and controls the format of the returned data (text, JSON, and so on). Because you want to access the Customer data items in JSON format, the Accept header is set to application/json.

The onreadystatechange event-handler function checks the readyState property of the XMLHttpRequest object. If readyState is 4 (complete), the responseText is parsed into a JSON object using the JSON.parse() method. Recollect that the Get() Web API method returns an IEnumerable of Customer objects. Hence you use a for loop to iterate through the data object. With each iteration, a new table row is added. Each new table row consists of text boxes filled with the existing customer information (for example, data[i].CustomerID).

Next, you add the click event handler for the Insert, Update, and Delete buttons. Note how you use the attribute selector to compare the value of the <input> elements against Insert, Update, and Delete. The corresponding InsertCustomer, UpdateCustomer, and DeleteCustomer functions are wired as the event handlers.

Once the readystatechange event-handler function is wired, the request is sent to the server using the XMLHttpRequest object's send() method.

The InsertCustomer(), UpdateCustomer(), and DeleteCustomer() functions are similar as far as their usage of XMLHttpRequest is concerned. InsertCustomer() is shown in Listing 11-10. The other functions follow a similar pattern.

Listing 11-10. Inserting a New Customer

```
function InsertCustomer(evt) {
  var customerID = $(this).closest('tr').children().eq(0).children().eq(0).val();
  var companyName = $(this).closest('tr').children().eq(1).children().eq(0).val();
  var contactName = $(this).closest('tr').children().eq(2).children().eq(0).val();
  var country = $(this).closest('tr').children().eq(3).children().eq(0).val();
  var obj = { "CustomerID": customerID, "CompanyName": companyName,
              "ContactName": contactName, "Country": country };

  var xhr = new XMLHttpRequest();
  xhr.open("POST", "api/Customer");
  xhr.setRequestHeader('Content-Type', 'application/json');
  xhr.onreadystatechange = function () {
    if (xhr.readyState == 4) {
      alert("Customer Inserted!");
      GetCustomers();
    }
  }
```

```
    var param = JSON.stringify(obj);
    xhr.send(param);
}
```

InsertCustomer() acts as the event handler for the Insert button. The first thing the function does is grab the newly entered Customer details, such as CustomerID, CompanyName, ContactName, and Country. Observe how the jQuery selector retrieves the values from the <input> elements. Inside the InsertCustomer() function, the keyword this refers to the Insert button. The jQuery closest() method returns the nearest surrounding <tr> element. This way, you reach the table row that contains the text boxes. The children() method called on the table row returns all the <td> elements it contains. The eq() method returns a specified child element based on the index, allowing you to reach the individual <td> element. Another set of children() and eq() methods gives you access to the <input> elements in the table cells.

The values entered in the text boxes are stored in local variables: customerID, companyName, contactName, and country. A JSON object is formed using these values. Note that the JSON object must have the same key names as the Customer data-model property names so that ASP.NET can map the JSON object to the data-model class.

A new XMLHttpRequest object is then created, and a POST request is opened using its open() method. Because you're sending JSON data to the server, the Content-Type header is set to application/json using the setRequestHeader() method. The readystatechange event handler displays a success message to the user if readyState is 4 (complete). GetCustomers() is called again to refresh the customer list with the newly added record.

After you wire the readystatechange event handler, the request is sent to the server using send(). The send() method takes the string representation of the JSON Customer object as its parameter. This JSON object is received by the Post() method of the Customer Web API controller.

You can now run the Customer List application and test the CRUD operations on it. You might wonder how you can make cross-origin requests using the XMLHttpRequest object. Luckily, you need not make any code-level changes to XMLHttpRequest to make cross-origin requests. All you need to do is ensure that the IIS running the other domain allows CORS requests. You can configure the CORS header using either IIS Manager or web.config, as described earlier.

Uploading Files Using XMLHttpRequest

In Chapter 9, you learned about the File API. In that chapter you also learned how to select and upload files from the client machine onto the web server using the jQuery $.ajax() method. You can accomplish the same task using the XMLHttpRequest object. One advantage of using XMLHttpRequest is that it allows you to track the upload operation via progress events. By handling the progress event, you can display some sort of progress indicator (say, a progress bar) to the user. Figure 11-5 shows a web form that uses the upload progress event.

Figure 11-5. The progress of a file upload is shown using a progress bar.

This web form should look familiar: you developed something similar in Chapter 9. The web form allows you to drag and drop files from Windows Explorer or the Desktop onto the basket image. You can then upload the files to the server using the Upload button. An upload operation can be cancelled with the Cancel button. The progress of the file-upload operation is shown in a progress bar.

The web form's markup is straightforward. The only unfamiliar element is the HTML5 <progress> element, which render a progress bar at the bottom of the web form. The <progress> element looks like this:

```
<progress id="uploadProgress" value="1" max="100"></progress>
```

This <progress> element uses two attributes: value and max. The value attribute indicates progress made by an operation. The max attribute controls the scale of the value attribute. For example, if you wish to display upload progress as a percentage (%), you need to set the max attribute to 100 so the value attribute can take a maximum value of 100. Note that the <progress> element by itself doesn't automatically increment. You need to set the value attribute programmatically in order for the progress bar to show the correct progress.

When you click the Upload button, a JavaScript function—UploadFiles()—is called that initiates the upload operation. UploadFiles() is shown in Listing 11-11.

Listing 11-11. Uploading Files Using the XMLHttpRequest Object

```
var xhr = new XMLHttpRequest();

function UploadFiles() {
  var data = new FormData();
  for (var i = 0; i < files.length; i++) {
      data.append(files[i].name, files[i]);
  }
  xhr.upload.addEventListener("progress", OnProgress, false);
  xhr.addEventListener("load", OnComplete, false);
  xhr.addEventListener("error", OnError, false);
  xhr.addEventListener("abort", OnAbort, false);
  xhr.open("POST", "UploadHandler.ashx");
  xhr.send(data);
}
```

This code declares a global XMLHttpRequest object (xhr). The UploadFiles() function first creates a new FormData object. It then iterates through all the files selected by the user. The files collection contains the File objects as selected using the drag-and-drop operation. All the selected files are appended to the FormData object using the FormData object's append() method.

Next, the addEventListener() method wires event handlers for the four events: progress, load, error, and abort. Note that because you're interested in tracking the progress of the data-upload operation, the progress event of the upload object is handled rather than the progress event of the XMLHttpRequest object. The event-handler functions OnProgress(), OnComplete(), OnError(), and OnAbort() are discussed shortly.

The XMLHttpRequest object's open() method is then called by specifying POST as the request type and UploadHandler.ashx as the URL. UploadHandler.ashx is an ASP.NET generic handler that saves the uploaded files on the server. Finally, you call the XMLHttpRequest object's send() method and pass the FormData object to it as a parameter.

The Cancel button calls the XMLHttpRequest object's abort() method, as shown here:

```
function CancelUpload() {
  xhr.abort();
}
```

The event-handler functions that handle the progress, load, error, and abort events are shown in Listing 11-12.

Listing 11-12. Handling Events of the XMLHttpRequest Object

```
function OnProgress(evt) {
  if (evt.lengthComputable) {
    var progress = Math.round(evt.loaded * 100 / evt.total);
    $("#uploadProgress").attr("value", progress);
  }
}

function OnComplete(evt) {
  alert(evt.target.responseText);
}

function OnError(evt) {
  alert("Error Uploading File(s)!");
```

```
}

function OnAbort(evt) {
  alert("File Upload Aborted!");
}
```

The OnProgress() event-handler function receives an event parameter of type ProgressEvent that provides progress information about the upload operation. The lengthComputable property returns a Boolean value indicating whether the progress of the operation can be determined. The loaded and total properties indicate the number of bytes uploaded and the total number of bytes to be uploaded. Based on these two values, a progress percentage is calculated. The value attribute of the <progress> element is set to this calculated value using the jQuery attr() method.

The other event-handler functions are straightforward and simply display a message (success, error, or cancellation) to the user.

Notifying the Browser Using Server-Sent Events

So far in this book you've been using techniques that initiate communication from the client to the server ($.ajax() or XMLHttpRequest, for example). In such client-to-server techniques, once a request is sent and a response is received from the server, the underlying communication channel is closed. Consider a case where a server is continuously performing a business operation. A web page displays the status of the processing for the user. Because the operation is continuing on the server, you want that status to be periodically updated. How do you accomplish this task? A common approach is to poll the server periodically and retrieve the status of the operation. You can use functions such as setTimeout() and setInterval() and make a request to the server in an attempt to retrieve the operation's status.

The disadvantage of this polling technique is that there are too many request-response cycles. The client keeps sending requests, and the server keeps responding to every request. Each request-response cycle needs its own communication channel, which is closed once the cycle is complete. Wouldn't it be nice if the server notified you when something interesting happened, without any need for polling? This is what *server-sent events* allow you to do.

As the name suggests, server-sent events are dispatched by the server. Instead of the client periodically checking the server for updates, the server notifies the client if anything interesting happens on the server. Server-sent events use a common communication channel to send multiple notifications, thus avoiding continuous request-response cycles. The server-side resource that sends the notifications to the client is wrapped in an EventSource object. The open, message, and error events of the EventSource object are then used to open a communication channel, receive messages from the server, and deal with the errors, respectively.

Let's develop an application that illustrates how to use server-sent events. Figure 11-6 shows the application's main web form.

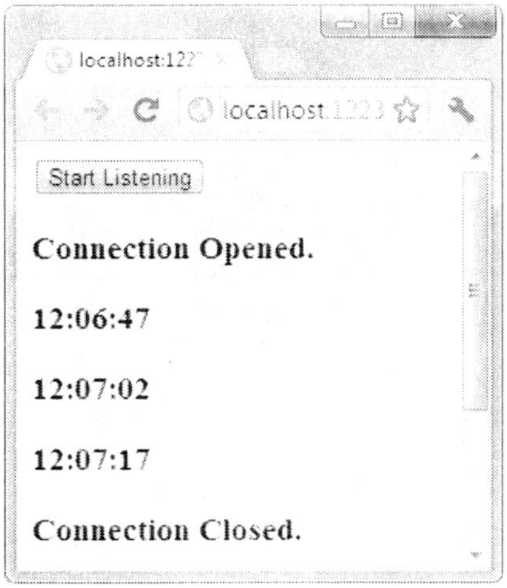

Figure 11-6. Server-sent events in action

The web form consists of a Start Listening button. Clicking the button opens a connection with a generic handler (ClientNotifier.ashx) residing on the server. The generic handler is designed in such a way that it sends a notification in the form of the server time to the client every 15 seconds for 1 minute. You see the outputted time at those intervals. The messages, including the notification data, are displayed in a <div> element.

The JavaScript code behind the working of the web form is shown in Listing 11-13.

Listing 11-13. Initiating the Server-Sent Events

```
$(document).ready(function () {
  if (window.EventSource == undefined) {
    alert("This browser doesn't support HTML5 Server Sent Events.");
    return;
  }

  $("#btnListen").click(function () {
    var source = new EventSource('ClientNotifier.ashx');
    source.addEventListener("open", function (event) {
      $('#targetDiv').append('<h3>Connection Opened.</h3>');
    },false);

  source.addEventListener("error", function (event) {
    if (event.eventPhase == EventSource.CLOSED) {
      $('#targetDiv').append('<h3>Connection Closed.</h3>');
    }
  },false);

  source.addEventListener("message",function (event) {
    $('#targetDiv').append('<h3>' + event.data + '</h3>');
  },false);
});
});
```

This code first checks whether the browser supports server-sent events. It does so by checking for the existence of the window.EventSource object.

The code then proceeds to wire the click event handler of the Start Listening button. This event handler creates a new EventSource object. The path of the ASP.NET generic handler that sends the events is passed as the parameter while creating the EventSource.

Event handlers are then wired for the EventSource object's three events: open, message, and error. The open event is raised when the browser makes a request to the server resource for the first time. When the data sent by the server arrives at the client, the message event is raised. In case of an error, such as closed connection, the error event is raised. The open and error event handlers add a message to the targetDiv <div> element. The error handler uses the eventPhase property to decide whether the underlying connection is closed. The possible values for eventPhase are CONNECTING (0), OPEN (1), and CLOSED (2). The message event handler receives an event parameter, and its data property returns the data sent by the server.

The server-side code that sends the events to the client resides in the ASP.NET generic handler, ClientNotifier.ashx. This code is shown in Listing 11-14.

Listing 11-14. Sending Events to the Client

```
public void ProcessRequest(HttpContext context)
{
    HttpResponse Response = context.Response;
    DateTime startDate = DateTime.Now;
    Response.ContentType = "text/event-stream";
    while (startDate.AddMinutes(1) > DateTime.Now)
    {
        Response.Write(string.Format("data: {0}\n\n", DateTime.Now.ToString("hh:mm:ss")));
        Response.Flush();
        System.Threading.Thread.Sleep(15000);
    }
    Response.Close();
}
```

This code sets the ContentType of the Response to text/event-stream. This way, the client browser knows that this response belongs to server-sent events. A while loop then iterates for 1 minute. Within the loop, the event data is dispatched to the client in batches. The Response.Write() method writes the event data on the response stream, and Response.Flush() ensures that it's sent directly to the client without any buffering. The event data sent to the client must be in a predefined format. A sample format is as follows:

```
data: Hello World!\n\n
```

Every piece of event data should begin with data: and end with two newline characters (\n\n). The event data can also be sent in multiple-line format:

```
data: {\n
data: "CustomerID": "ALFKI",\n
data: "Country": "USA"\n
data: }\n\n
```

This markup sends data to the client in JSON format. The client can parse the data to construct a JSON object.

The operation is halted for 15 seconds using the Thread.Sleep() method, to introduce a delay between notifications. In addition to the developer-defined data, the server also sends the client a unique event ID and a retry interval. These pieces of information can be accessed as the id and retry properties of the event parameter.

Although you don't need to do so in this example, you can stop receiving server-sent events by calling the EventSource object's close() method.

■ **Note** In the example discussed in this section, server-side processing takes place for 1 minute, after which the server terminates the underlying connection. The browser, however, thinks there was a connection problem and after a brief interval tries to reconnect with the server, causing the same logic to run again. If you don't wish to receive further events, you need to call the EventSource object's close() method.

Two-Way Communication Using Web Sockets

Typically, communication over the Web consists of two distinct parties participating: the client and the web server. So far in this chapter you've learned about two client-server communication techniques: one-way communication and request-response communication.

Server-sent events use the one-way communication model. In one-way communication, one party communicates with the other party. In the case of server-sent events, the server keeps "talking" with the client by sending notifications. This is also referred to as *simplex* communication. A real-life example of simplex communication is radio broadcasting, where radio signals are sent from the radio station but the station doesn't receive anything back.

The postMessage API and XMLHttpRequest object use the request-response model to communicate with the server. In this model, a client initiates a request with the server to trigger some processing or fetch some data. The server then sends the response back to the client once the processing is finished. The underlying communication channel is held open during only one request-response cycle. If you send multiple requests to the server, you're essentially opening and closing the communication channel that many times. Such a communication pattern is sometimes called *half-duplex* communication because at any one time, either the client or the server is talking to the other party. Of course, in a web application, the browser has to initiate communication with the server; only then is the server allowed to respond. A real-life example of half-duplex communication is a walkie-talkie: only one person can talk at a time.

There is a third type of communication—two-way or *duplex* communication. In this case, both parties can communicate at the same time. A real-life example is a telephone call: both the parties can talk simultaneously. A common application of duplex communication in software applications is chat systems such as MSN, Yahoo! Messenger, and Google Talk. In any chat system, two or more members can chat with each other at the same time. Another example is multiplayer online games, where multiple players can participate at once. As far as HTML5 is concerned, the technique to achieve two-way communication is Web Sockets.

Understanding Web Sockets

Unlike the request-response model, Web Sockets keep the underlying communication channel open throughout the course of communication. Web Socket–based communication typically involves three steps:

1. Establish a connection between the client and the server or handshake.

2. Ask the Web Socket server to listen to the incoming communication.

3. Send and receive data.

Web applications use the HTTP protocol for their functioning, and HTTP essentially uses the request-response model. Plain HTTP isn't well suited for performing two-way communication. Web Sockets, therefore, need to upgrade plain HTTP to the WebSocket protocol. This upgrade takes place while establishing the connection between the client and the server. WebSocket is a TCP-based protocol and uses HTTP only during the handshake and upgrade process. Once a connection is established between the client and the server, WebSocket communication takes place over a single TCP connection. The WebSocket protocol can deal with text as well as binary data. Due to these features, the WebSocket protocol offers performance benefits over the HTTP request-response model.

The request and response headers in Figure 11-7 show how this upgrade takes place.

Figure 11-7. Request and response during a handshake, shown in Chrome Developer Tools

Notice how the request and response headers set the Connection and Upgrade headers. In order to upgrade the communication from plain HTTP to WebSocket, you need a web server that is capable of doing this upgrade. IIS 8.0, which ships with Windows 8, can accept Web Socket communications. If you're developing a web application that uses HTML5 Web Sockets, you may need to install WebSocket support in IIS 8.0. Figure 11-8 shows how you can use the "Turn Windows features on or off" option from the Control Panel to install the WebSocket protocol.

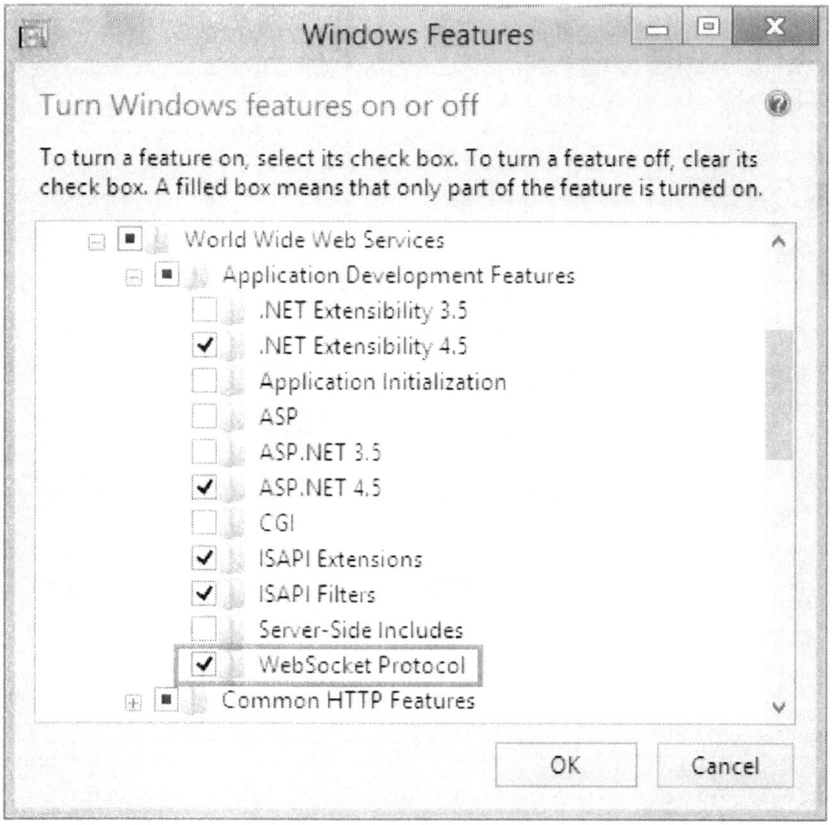

Figure 11-8. Enabling WebSocket protocol support in IIS 8.0

If the WebSocket protocol isn't enabled, your ASP.NET applications won't be able to receive and respond to Web Socket requests on the server.

Once a handshake takes place between the client and the server, and a communication channel is established between them, you can communicate using the upgraded connection. A Web Socket–based application consists of code divided into two parts: Web Socket server-side code and Web Socket client-side code. The Web Socket server-side code resides on the web server and listens to incoming communication from clients. When a communication is received from the client, the Web Socket server-side code processes the communication and typically sends a communication back to the client. If there is no communication from the client, the Web Socket server can either keep waiting or can terminate the communication channel.

Although you can develop Web Socket server-side code from scratch, many times you can use a third-party server. For example, if you wish to implement online chat in your web application, you can use a third-party or open source chat server and develop the client web pages as needed.

Note that HTML5 restricts itself to developing the Web Socket clients. Different web servers and server side technologies may have their own way of developing the Web Socket server. The Web Socket client and the Web Socket server can now communicate with each other and transmit data. Web Socket clients use the HTML5 WebSocket object to send data to and receive data from the Web Socket server.

The WebSocket Object

The HTML5 WebSocket object provides properties, methods, and events that you can use to develop a Web Socket client application. Table 11-4 shows them for your quick reference.

Table 11-4. Properties, Methods, and Events of the WebSocket Class

Member	Property / Method / Event	Description
readyState	Property	Read-only property that returns the current state of the connection. Possible values are 0 (CONNECTING), 1 (OPEN), 2 (CLOSING), and 3 (CLOSED).
bufferedAmount	Property	Read-only property that returns the number of bytes of data that have been queued for transmission over the network.
send()	Method	Sends data to the Web Socket server over an established connection.
close()	Method	Closes the previously established connection with the Web Socket server.
open	Event	Raised when the readyState property changes to 1 (OPEN) and indicates that the connection is ready to send and receive data.
close	Event	Raised when the readyState property changes to 3 (CLOSED).
message	Event	Raised when a message is received from the Web Socket server.
error	Event	Raised when an error occurs during communication with the Web Socket server.

When you create an instance of WebSocket, you need to supply the endpoint URL that connects the client to the Web Socket server. As you can see from Table 11-4, the data-sending and -receiving pattern used by WebSocket is similar to earlier techniques. Once a connection is established, you send data using send() as and when required. At the same time, the message event-handler function keeps receiving messages sent by the server.

Using WebSocket in ASP.NET

As mentioned earlier, while developing a Web Socket application you have two distinct pieces of code: the Web Socket client and the Web Socket server. The Web Socket client is developed using JavaScript and the HTML5 WebSocket object. So, this piece of code follows the same coding pattern regardless of your web server software. However, when you're developing the Web Socket server, you need to use the framework provided by the web server software and the server-side framework you're using. As far as ASP.NET is concerned, IIS 8 and certain .NET framework classes together allow you to develop a Web Socket server.

To understand how the client-side and server-side code go hand in hand, let's develop a simple Echo server that echoes whatever the client sends to it. Although the Echo server doesn't perform simultaneous two-way communication like a chat application, it does illustrate how the Web Socket client and server interact. The web form that acts as a Web Socket client is shown in Figure 11-9.

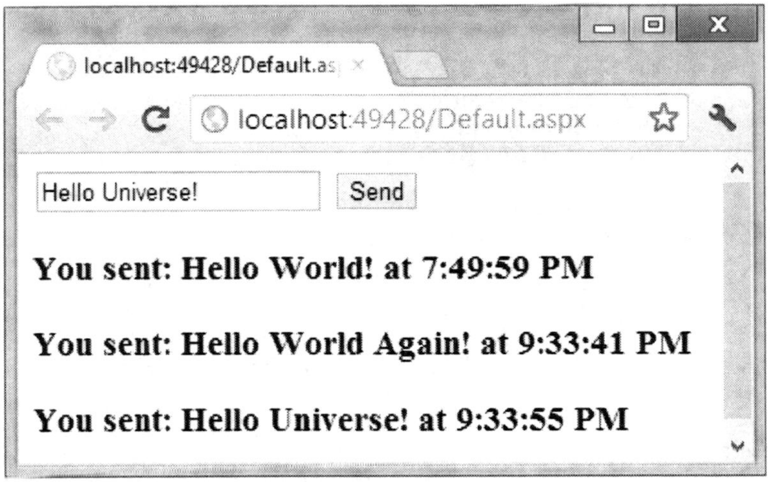

Figure 11-9. Web Form acting as a Web Socket client

As you can see, the Web Socket client web form consists of a text box and a button. The user enters some data in the text box and clicks the Send button. The Web Socket server sitting on IIS 8.0 listens to the incoming communication, receives the data sent by the client, and echoes it back to the client. The echoed data is displayed on the web form by appending it to a <div> element.

■ **Note**   Although you can develop this application using Visual Studio 2012 installed on Windows 7, you won't be able to run and test it. To run the example, you need Windows 8 with IIS 8.0 installed. You must also enable the WebSocket protocol in IIS 8.0 if it's not already enabled.

Developing the Echo Server

Before developing the Web Socket client, let's develop the server part. You develop the Echo server as an ASP.NET generic handler (.ashx). The job of the generic handler is to trigger the listening code. Listing 11-15 shows how this is done.

Listing 11-15. Using a Generic Handler to Start the Echo Server

```
public class WebSocketGenericHandler : IHttpHandler
{
    public void ProcessRequest(HttpContext context)
    {
        if (context.IsWebSocketRequest)
        {
            context.AcceptWebSocketRequest(EchoServer);
        }
    }
    ...
}
```

This code shows a generic handler—WebSocketGenericHandler—that triggers the Web Socket server. The generic handler's ProcessRequest() method first checks whether the incoming request is a Web Socket request. It does so by checking the IsWebSocketRequest property of the HttpContext object. This property works hand in hand with the IIS 8.0 WebSocket module and returns true if an incoming request is a WebSocket request. A WebSocket request is different than an ordinary HTTP request in that instead of using the http:// protocol it uses the ws:// (WebSocket) protocol. For example, a WebSocket request to this generic handler looks like this:

```
ws://localhost:49428/WebSocketGenericHandler.ashx
```

If IsWebSocketRequest returns true, the AcceptWebSocketRequest() method of the HttpContext is called. This method takes one parameter—a user function—that supplies a function that listens and responds to the client requests. In this case, the EchoServer function contains the logic to listen to the incoming data and echo it to the client. The user function supplied to the AcceptWebSocketRequest() method should be an asynchronous function, as shown in Listing 11-16.

Listing 11-16. EchoServer Asynchronous Function

```
public async Task EchoServer(AspNetWebSocketContext context)
{
    WebSocket socket = context.WebSocket;
    while (true)
    {
        ArraySegment<byte> buffer = new ArraySegment<byte>(new byte[1024]);
        WebSocketReceiveResult result = await
        socket.ReceiveAsync(buffer, CancellationToken.None);
        if (socket.State == WebSocketState.Open)
        {
            string userMessage = Encoding.UTF8.GetString(buffer.Array, 0, result.Count);
            userMessage = "You sent: " + userMessage + " at " +
            DateTime.Now.ToLongTimeString();
            buffer = new ArraySegment<byte>(Encoding.UTF8.GetBytes(userMessage));
            await socket.SendAsync(buffer, WebSocketMessageType.Text,
                                            true, CancellationToken.None);
        }
        else
        {
            break;
        }
    }
}
```

The EchoServer() method is marked as async, indicating that the code inside it runs in asynchronous fashion. An async method is a convenient way to execute a long-running operation without blocking the main thread. In this example, the Echo server is supposed to continuously listen for incoming requests—that is, a long-running operation. EchoServer() returns a Task object. The Task class acts as a wrapper to the asynchronous code. EchoServer() receives a parameter of type AspNetWebSocketContext. The AspNetWebSocketContext class gives you access to the WebSocket through its WebSocket property. The WebSocket class is the server-side counterpart of the HTML5 WebSocket object. An endless while loop is then started so the Echo server can continuously listen to incoming requests.

To receive incoming data, you use the WebSocket class's ReceiveAsync() method. This method is invoked along with the await operator. The await operator indicates that the execution of the calling method will be suspended until the awaited task completes. In this case, the awaited task is to receive incoming data and store it in an ArraySegment, a byte array. The results of the receive operation are stored in a WebSocketReceiveResult object.

If the WebSocket is open, as indicated by the State property, the received data is echoed to the client using the SendAsync() method. Before sending the message back to the client, you append a date-time stamp to the message. If the State property has any value other than Open, the while loop is exited, thus terminating the server.

■ **Note**   The System.Net.WebSockets and System.Web.WebSockets namespaces contain classes that deal with server-side Web Socket programming. Detailed discussion of asynchronous programming in .NET and using Web Socket classes is beyond the scope of this book. Refer to the MSDN documentation to learn more about these topics.

Developing the Web Socket Client

Now that you've completed the Echo server, let's develop the client web form that sends data to the Echo server and receives echoed messages. Listing 11-17 shows the jQuery code that uses the HTML5 WebSocket object.

Listing 11-17. Using the HTML5 WebSocket Object

```
var socket;
$(document).ready(function () {
    if (!Modernizr.websockets) {
      alert("This browser doesn't support HTML5 Web Sockets!");
      return;
    }
    socket = new WebSocket("ws://localhost:49428/WebSocketGenericHandler.ashx");
    socket.addEventListener("open", function (evt) {
        $("#divHistory").append('<h3>Connection Opened with the Echo server.</h3>');
    }, false);
    socket.addEventListener("message", function (evt) {
        $("#divHistory").append('<h3>' + evt.data + '</h3>');
    }, false);
    socket.addEventListener("error", function (evt) {
        $("#divHistory").append('<h3>Unexpected Error.</h3>');
    }, false);
    ...
});
```

This code declares a global variable named socket to hold a reference to a WebSocket object. The jQuery ready() method first checks whether HTML5 Web Sockets are supported in the client browser. It does so using the Modernizr's websockets property.

You then create a WebSocket instance by passing the URL of WebSocketGenericHandler.ashx. Notice how the URL uses ws:// instead of http://. Next, event handlers for the three events—open, message, and error—are wired using the addEventListener() method. In the message event handler, the data sent by the Echo server is retrieved using the evt.data property. The echoed data is then appended to a <div> element. The other event handlers output the specified messages in the <div> element.

The data from the client is sent to the server when you click the Send button. The Send button's click event handler looks like this:

```
$("#btnSend").clickhow(function () {
    if (socket.readyState == WebSocket.OPEN) {
        socket.send($("#txtMsg").val());
    }
    else {
        $("#divHistory").append('<h3>The underlying connection is closed.</h3>');
    }
});
```

The click event handler checks the readyState property of the WebSocket object. If it's OPEN, the click event handler calls the WebSocket instance's send() method. The text entered in the text box is passed as a parameter to send(). Although not used in this application, you can close the underlying connection by calling the WebSocket object's close() method:
```
socket.close();
```
That's it! You can now run the web form and test the Echo server by sending messages to the server.

▪ **Note** The Windows Communication Foundation (WCF) in .NET Framework 4.5 also supports Web Sockets. Two new bindings have been added to WCF for this purpose: NetHttpBinding and NetHttpsBinding. Detailed discussion of how WCF supports Web Sockets is beyond the scope of this book. Refer to the MSDN documentation for more details.

Summary

Web applications often need to communicate with the server. Especially in Ajax-driven applications, you need to communicate with the server without a full page post-back. HTML5 offers several ways to achieve client-server communication. The postMessage API allows you to perform cross-document messaging, by means of which you can send data to a web page having a different origin. XMLHttpRequest is the basis of Ajax-based communication between the client and the server. XMLHttpRequest Level 2 lets you monitor the progress of the data-upload and -download operations. It also allows cross-origin communication through CORS.

Typical web communication uses the request-response model. You can use server-sent events if you need one-way communication from server to client. This way, the server can notify the client about happenings on the server. Web Sockets offer full-duplex communication between client and server. IIS 8.0, which ships with Windows 8, provides server-side support for the WebSocket protocol. The .NET framework also offers a set of classes to work with Web Sockets.

The next chapter peeks into yet another feature that can be useful in certain types of web applications: geolocation. Using geolocation, you can determine the geographical location of a user and change how your web application responds accordingly.

CHAPTER 12

■ ■ ■

Finding Location with the Geolocation API

Most of today's web applications don't care where you're accessing them from. Regardless of your geographical location, they present the same content in the browser. However, if you make such information available to web applications, they can make innovative use of it. For example, a social networking web application can suggest friends who are in the same locality as you. User-location information can also be used in job portals to suggest jobs near the user's geographical location.

The idea of tracking user location isn't new, but at first there was no standard way to find this information. Luckily, over the years a standardized approach—geolocation—has evolved to address this need. The Geolocation API allows you to find a user's location by using various location sources such as IP address, Global Positioning System (GPS), Global System for Mobile Communications (GSM), and general packet radio service (GPRS). Strictly speaking, the Geolocation API isn't part of HTML5. However, most often it's used and grouped with HTML5 features and technologies. This chapter gives you a detailed introduction to the Geolocation API. Specifically, you learn the following:

- What is geolocation?
- Finding and tracking user location using the Geolocation API
- Integrating the Geolocation API with Google Maps and Bing Maps
- Using the Geolocation API to present location-specific data to the user

Overview of the Latitude and Longitude Coordinate System

To convey a user's geographical location, you need a standard system that can be understood by all the parties involved in the process. In day-to-day life, location information is expressed in terms of city, state, country, and so on. However, such information is of little use for calculation purposes. For example, looking at two city names, you can't tell the distance between them. That is why location is specified using a geographic coordinate system. The system used by the Geolocation API consists of latitude and longitude coordinates.

A latitude coordinate specifies the north-south position of a point on the Earth's surface. Points with the same latitude run east-west as circles parallel to the equator. Latitude is an angle ranging from 0° at the equator to 90° (north or south) at the poles.

A longitude coordinate specifies the east-west position of a point on the Earth's surface. Points with the same longitude lie on lines running from the North Pole to the South Pole. Longitude is an angle that varies between 0° at the Prime Meridian to 180° toward the east or west.

Latitude and longitude coordinates are specified in decimal/minute/second (DMS) format or decimal degrees. For example, in DMS format, the latitude of Mumbai is 18° 55' N and the longitude is 72° 54' E. In decimal format, the same coordinates are represented as 18.91667 and 72.9, respectively. Positive decimal numbers indicate north-east positions, whereas negative decimal numbers indicate south-west positions. The Geolocation API uses latitude and longitude values in decimal format.

Sources of Location Information

The Geolocation API doesn't dictate where the location information is to be fetched from. The source of location information can vary greatly depending on the type of device you're using. For example, a desktop computer may use an IP address as the source of information, whereas a mobile phone may use GPS-based location information. The common sources of location information include the following:

- IP address
- GPS
- Wi-Fi
- Mobile phones (GSM or Code-Division Multiple Access [CDMA])

These location sources are discussed briefly in the following sections.

IP Address

Using the IP address through which a user is accessing a web application is possibly the oldest way of determining the user's location. With this technique, the IP address allotted to a user by the Internet service provider (ISP) is used to detect the origin of requests. This technique is only a guess, rather than a precise result, because the ISP might be located far from the user's actual location—so, you can't rely on the location information provided by this technique.

In addition to being widely used, this technique offers the advantage that the IP-detection and location-finding logic happen in the server-side code. The client browser doesn't come into picture at all. However, due to its lack of precision, you can't use this technique in situations where a higher degree of accuracy is expected.

GPS

You can use signals from GPS satellite stations located around the globe to determine a user's exact location. Although GPS gives much more accurate location information than other techniques, it's not well suited for closed or indoor locations. Another pitfall of using GPS is the associated higher battery consumption, which may require the user to charge the device frequently.

Wi-Fi

Using the Wi-Fi technique, the user's location is determined by calculating the distance between Wi-Fi access points and the user. This technique works well in closed and indoor locations and gives accurate results. However, it suffers from the disadvantage that Wi-Fi access isn't available everywhere. Especially in rural areas, the availability of Wi-Fi connectivity is often poor, and location information may become unavailable.

Mobile Phones (GSM or CDMA)

This technique uses the distance between mobile-phone towers and the user to determine the user's location. The technique works only with mobile phones and only in the areas where mobile stations are available. The results are reasonably accurate and can be used for applications specifically developed for mobile phones.

■ **Note** The specific technique used by the Geolocation API is determined by the device and the software that is using the Geolocation API, and not by the Geolocation API itself.

The Geolocation API

The Geolocation API allow you to perform three operations: find a user's location at a given point in time, track a user's location as the user moves from one place to another, and stop tracking the user's location. The API is encapsulated in a geolocation object that's available as a property on the browser window's navigator object. These three tasks are accomplished with the help of three methods: getCurrentPosition(), watchPosition(), and clearWatch(). These three methods are described in Table 12-1.

Table 12-1. *Methods of the geolocation Object*

Method	Description
getCurrentPosition()	Determines the user's current location. It accepts a success function, an error function, and an options object as parameters. The success function is then used to find the latitude and longitude coordinates of the user's location. You can use the error function to flag the user about an error while determining the location. The latitude and longitude values are in decimal format.
watchPosition()	Similar to getCurrentPosition() but keeps monitoring the user's location periodically unless the clearWatch() method is called. This method is suited for tracking user movements as the user moves from one place to another.
clearWatch()	Stops monitoring the user's location. This method is triggered using the watchPosition() method.

Looking at Table 12-1, you might wonder how these results can benefit the end user. The Geolocation API merely gives you the user's location. How you use this data in innovative ways is up to you. Consider the following situations in which the Geolocation API can be of great use:

- Travel companies can use the location to provide a list of nearby pick-up points.

- A mapping application can suggest driving directions to the user based on the location information.

- A job portal can present only those jobs located within a specified distance of the user.

- E-commerce web sites can use the location information to suggest shipping costs to the user.

- Real-estate applications can customize search results based on the user's location.

- Museums, theaters, gathering halls, and such establishments can calculate the approximate travel time from a user's location to the venue.

Geolocation and User Privacy

The user's geographical location is considered a private piece of information, and the user needs to provide explicit approval before the browser can send the data to the server for further processing. Whenever you access a web page that uses the Geolocation API, the browser notifies you that you're about to share your location information with the page and prompts you to confirm this action. For example, Figure 12-1 shows how Firefox, Chrome, and IE9 prompt the user to confirm the use of Geolocation API.

Figure 12-1. Browsers asking permission to send location information to the server

As you can see, unless the user explicitly grants permission to transmit their location on the Web, the web application can't use the Geolocation API. The user can revoke this permission at any time using their browser options.

In certain cases, you may also want to send the user's location information to a third-party system. As a good practice, it's better to keep the user informed about such sharing.

Using the Geolocation API to obtain User's Location

Now that you have a basic understanding of what the Geolocation API does, let's develop a simple Web Forms–based application that illustrates how you can use the getCurrentPosition() method to find the user's location. The application's main web form is shown in Figure 12-2.

Figure 12-2. Finding the user's location using the getCurrentPosition() method

The web form consists of a button and a table. Clicking the Show Current Location button fills the table with the location information. Note that some of the table cells contain undefined values, indicating that those pieces of information are unavailable.

The jQuery code responsible for retrieving the location information is given in Listing 12-1.

Listing 12-1. Retrieving the User's Location Information

```
$(document).ready(function () {

  if (!Modernizr.geolocation) {
    alert("This browser doesn't support the Geolocation API.");
    return;
  }

  $("#btnShowCurrent").click(function () {
    var options = {
      enableHighAccuracy: false,
      timeout: 5000,
      maximumAge: 3000
    };
    window.navigator.geolocation.getCurrentPosition(OnSuccess, OnError, options);
  });

});
```

This code shows the ready() function that checks whether the Geolocation API is supported in the browser. This is done using the geolocation property of the Modernizr object. The code then wires an event-handler function to the click event of the Show Current Location button.

The click event-handler function defines an options object with three settings: enableHighAccuracy, timeout, and maximumAge. This object specifies the options to be used by the getCurrentPosition() method. The significance of these three options is described in Table 12-2.

Table 12-2. Options for the getCurrentPosition() Method

Option	Description
enableHighAccuracy	Boolean option that indicates whether to use the high-accuracy GPS technique to find the user's location. A value of true indicates that GPS is to be used if available. Of course, the device must have GPS support as well as the user's permission to use this mode. Otherwise, this setting is ignored.
timeout	Indicates the number of milliseconds the web page should wait before giving up location detection.
maximumAge	Indicates how much old cached location data can be used. The value is in milliseconds. The default is 0, indicating that cached data is never used. You may set this option if you wish to reduce the number of geolocation calls or save power. However, the downside of setting maximumAge is that the location information can be outdated, in which case the specified value may cause calculation errors.

The code in Listing 12-1 then calls the geolocation object's getCurrentPosition() method. This method accepts three parameters: a success function that is called when the geolocation data is successfully retrieved, an error function that is called if an error occurs while retrieving the geolocation information, and the options object. Specifying the error function and options object is optional.

The OnSuccess() function that acts as a success callback is shown in Listing 12-2.

Listing 12-2. OnSuccess() Callback Function

```
function OnSuccess(position) {
  var html = "";
  html += "<tr><td>Latitude : </td>";
  html += "<td>" + position.coords.latitude + "</td></tr>";
  html += "<tr><td>Longitude : </td>";
  html += "<td>" + position.coords.longitude + "</td></tr>";
  html += "<tr><td>Accuracy : </td>";
  html += "<td>" + position.coords.accuracy + "</td></tr>";
  html += "<tr><td>Altitude : </td>";
  html += "<td>" + position.coords.altitude + "</td></tr>";
  html += "<tr><td>Altitude Accuracy : </td>";
  html += "<td>" + position.coords.altitudeAccuracy + "</td></tr>";
  html += "<tr><td>Heading : </td>";
  html += "<td>" + position.coords.heading + "</td></tr>";
  html += "<tr><td>Speed : </td>";
  html += "<td>" + position.coords.speed + "</td></tr>";
  html += "<tr><td>Timestamp : </td>";
  html += "<td>" + new Date(position.timestamp).toString() + "</td></tr>";
  $("#tblInfo").append(html);
}
```

OnSuccess() receives a position object that provides information about the user's location including latitude and longitude. Most of these properties (except the timestamp) are available in the position object's coords property. The pieces of information given by the position object are listed in Table 12-3.

Table 12-3. Properties of the position Object

Property	Description
latitude	Returns the latitude value in decimal format.
longitude	Returns the longitude value in decimal format.
accuracy	Contains a distance in meters that specifies how close the latitude and longitude values are to the actual location. The value of the accuracy property increases as the accuracy of the location data decreases.
altitude	Returns the height of the user's location in meters above the ellipsoid.
altitudeAccuracy	Provides the accuracy of the altitude value in meters.
heading	Indicates the direction of travel in degrees relative to north.
speed	Gives the ground speed in meters per second.
timestamp	Gives the timestamp at which the location data was returned. It's returned as number of milliseconds since 1 January 1970. You can convert this value into a JavaScript Date object for further use.

Not all the properties discussed in Table 12-3 are available on all the devices. For example, a desktop computer doesn't supply properties such as speed and heading. The four properties latitude, longitude, accuracy, and timestamp are available on all devices; the other properties aren't guaranteed to be supported. If no data is available for a property, null is returned.

The code in Listing 12-2 reads various properties and appends the values in a HTML table (tblInfo). If an error occurs while finding the user location, the OnError() function is called. OnError() is shown in Listing 12-3.

Listing 12-3. OnError() Function to Display Error Information

```
function OnError(err) {
  alert(err.code + " : " + err.message);
}
```

The OnError() function is quite straightforward. The err object passed to the function has two properties that give more information about the error: code and message. The possible error codes are 1 (PERMISSION_DENIED), 2 (POSITION_UNAVAILABLE), and 3 (TIMEOUT). The message property gives a descriptive error message. Figure 12-3 shows an error message when permission to use the Geolocation API is denied.

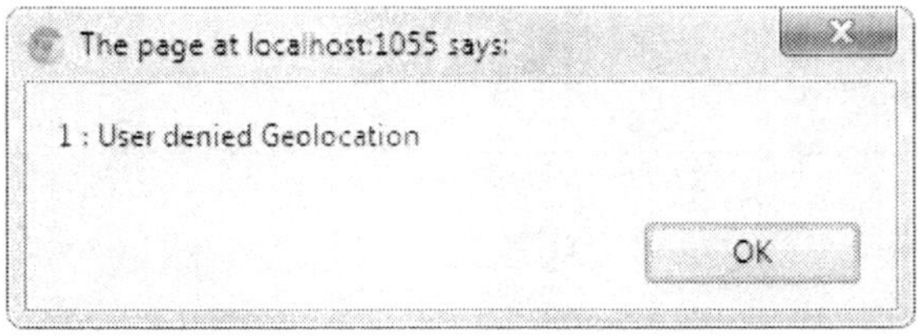

Figure 12-3. Error message after permission to use the Geolocation API is denied

Figure 12-3 shows the code and message properties in an alert box. You can, of course, check the code property and display a friendlier message for each error code.

Using the Geolocation API with Mapping Applications

One of the common uses of the Geolocation API is integrating mapping services with web applications. Such integration can be useful for showing the user's location with respect to a set of other locations, suggesting driving routes, and calculating the distance between two places. The Google Maps and Bing Maps mapping services are popular and commonly used by developers in web applications. Using these services involves the following steps:

1. Obtain an API key from the service provider (Google or Bing).

2. Refer to the map API library that allows you to program the mapping service in your web page.

3. Embed a map into your ASP.NET web application.

4. Integrate the mapping service with the Geolocation API to customize the map as per your need.

Google Maps and Bing Maps require that you have an API key to consume their mapping services in your web application. An API key is allotted for an account, and you can obtain the API key from the corresponding web site. The examples discussed later in this section assume that you've obtained a valid API key from the mapping service provider.

Google Maps and Bing Maps allow you to program a map using a JavaScript-based API developed by the provider. You need to add a reference to this JavaScript library in your web pages to consume its features. The features exposed by these libraries include showing a particular location on a map, setting a map's zooming level, showing a callout for a location, and many others. The examples in this section use some of the libraries' basic features.

Using the JavaScript libraries, you can easily embed a map into your own web page. For example, you can show a map in a `<div>` element.

The Geolocation API and the mapping services are independent of each other. However, you can integrate them to provide a better user experience. For example, instead of showing a map of a fixed location and expecting users to zoom in or out to their location, it's better if by default the map shows the user's location prominently.

■ **Note**   The Google Maps API and Bing Maps API expose many programmable features that you can use in a web application. Detailed discussion of these features is beyond the scope of this book. This chapter uses Google Maps and Bing Maps only to the extent of illustrating the integration of the Geolocation API with mapping services. You can visit the mapping service providers' web sites (`https://developers.google.com/maps` and `www.microsoft.com/maps/developers/web.aspx`) for complete documentation.

Integrating the Geolocation API with Google Maps

In this section, you learn to integrate the Geolocation API with Google Maps. Figure 12-4 shows the web form you develop.

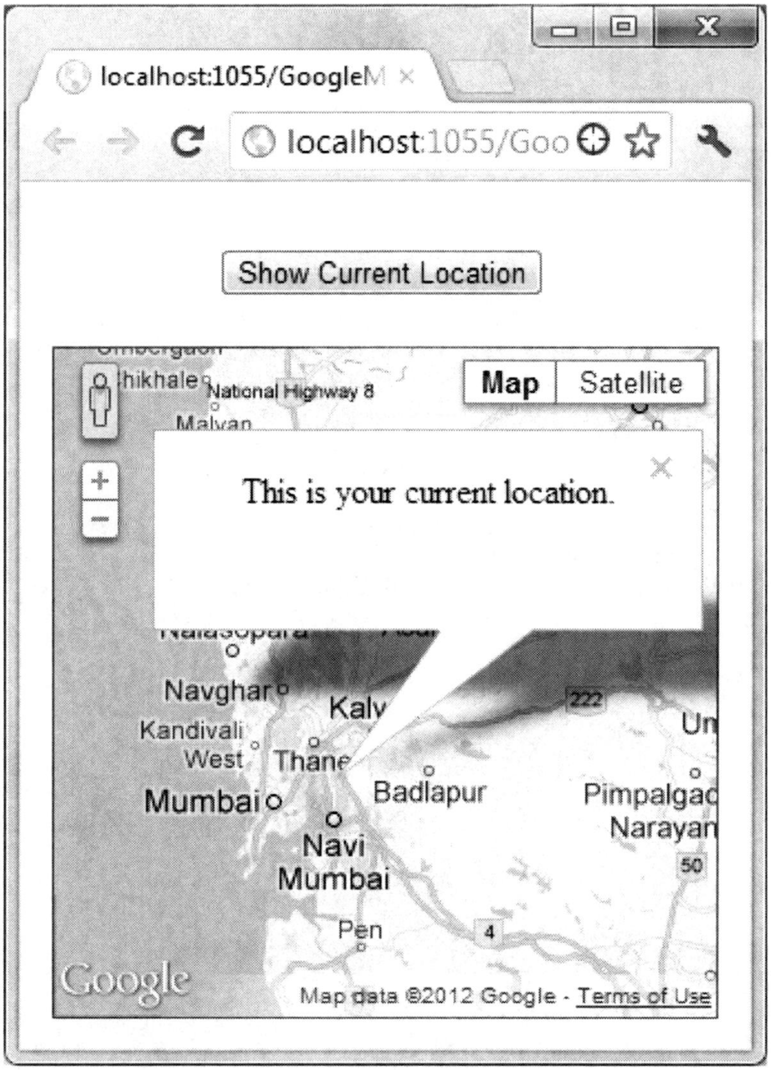

Figure 12-4. Integrating the Geolocation API with Google Maps

As you can see, the web form consists of a button and a `<div>` element that holds a map. When the page is loaded in the browser, by default the map is centered on Mumbai. If you click Show Current Location, a callout is displayed that points to the user's current location.

To develop this application, you need to reference the Google Maps JavaScript library in the markup. Listing 12-4 shows how this is done.

Listing 12-4. Referencing the Google Maps API Library

```
<html>
  <head>
    ...
```

```
    <script type="text/javascript" src="http://maps.googleapis.com/maps/api/
      js?key=<%= ConfigurationManager.AppSettings["GoogleMapsAPIKey"] %>&
      sensor=true">
</script>
    ...
    <input type="button" id="btnShowCurrent" value="Show Current Location" />
    ...
    <div id="divMap" style="..."></div>
    ...
</html>
```

The line of markup shown in bold refers to the Google Maps API library. The URL includes two mandatory query string parameters: key and sensor. The key query string parameter specifies an API key. Because the key may change depending on the Google account being used, it isn't embedded in the markup. Instead, the key is stored in the <appSettings> section of the web.config file and retrieved in the <%= and %> block. GoogleMapsAPIKey is the name of the key in the <appSettings> section. The sensor query string parameter indicates whether the device running this web application uses a sensor such as a GPS locator to determine the user's location.

The other markup in Listing 12-4 is simple and includes an <input> tag that renders the Show Current Location button and a <div> that acts as a container for the map.

The jQuery code that uses the Google Maps API to display Mumbai when the page loads in the browser is shown in Listing 12-5.

Listing 12-5. Displaying a Map Using the Google Maps API

```
var map;
var defaultPos;

$(document).ready(function () {
  ...
  defaultPos = new google.maps.LatLng(18.916667, 72.9);
  var mapOptions = {
    center: defaultPos,
    zoom: 8,
    mapTypeId: google.maps.MapTypeId.ROADMAP
  };
  map = new google.maps.Map($("#divMap").get(0), mapOptions);

  $("#btnShowCurrent").click(function () {
    window.navigator.geolocation.getCurrentPosition(OnSuccess, OnError);
  });
});
```

This code begins by declaring two global variables named map and defaultPos. The map variable holds a reference to a Google Map object, whereas the defaultPos variable holds a default position on the map. The ready() method handler creates a LatLng object provided by the Google Maps API by passing the latitude and longitude of Mumbai. This LatLng object acts as the default center of the map. The code then creates a mapOptions object containing configuration settings for the map. The center option defines the map's center coordinate. The zoom setting affects the map's zoom level. The larger the zoom value, the more magnified the map is. The mapTypeId setting governs the type of map displayed. The value for mapTypeId can be assigned from constants such as ROADMAP, SATELLITE, HYBRID, and TERRAIN. The value of ROADMAP means that a two-dimensional map is displayed. A Map object is then constructed by passing the DOM reference to the <div> element that is acting as the map container, and the map options. This displays a map in the <div> element with Mumbai as its center.

The code also shows the click event-handler function of the Show Current Position button. The click event handler calls the getCurrentPosition() method on the geolocation object and passes two callback functions—OnSuccess() and OnError()—in the parameter. OnSuccess() and OnError() are shown in Listing 12-6.

Listing 12-6. OnSuccess() and OnError() Callback Functions

```
function OnSuccess(position) {
  var curPos = new google.maps.LatLng(position.coords.latitude,
                        position.coords.longitude);
  map.setCenter(curPos);
  var callout = new google.maps.InfoWindow();
  callout.setContent("This is your current location.");
  callout.setPosition(curPos);
  callout.open(map);
}

function OnError(err) {
  alert(err.message);
  map.setCenter(defaultPos);
  var callout = new google.maps.InfoWindow();
  callout.setContent("This is the default location.");
  callout.setPosition(defaultPos);
  callout.open(map);
}
```

OnSuccess() creates a new LatLng object using the latitude and longitude properties provided by the coords object. This LatLng object represents the user's location. The setCenter() method of the map object is then used to set the center to the new LatLng object. To display a callout to the user pointing to the user's location, you use an InfoWindow object provided by the Google Maps API. The setContent() method of the InfoWindow object indicates the callout's content. The setPosition() method of the InfoWindow object governs the location where the callout is to be placed. Finally, the open() method of the InfoWindow object shows the callout on the specified map object.

OnError() is similar to OnSuccess() but is called in the event of an error while retrieving the user's location. OnError() displays an error message to the user and displays a callout at the default position (Mumbai, in this case).

Integrating the Geolocation API with Bing Maps

The process of integrating the Geolocation API with Bing Maps is similar to that used for Google Maps. This time, however, you need to use the Bing Maps API and the corresponding API key. The following line of markup shows how to reference the Bing Maps API in a web page:

```
<script src="http://dev.virtualearth.net/mapcontrol/
mapcontrol.ashx?v=7.0" type="text/javascript">
</script>
```

Note that the Bing Maps documentation refers this library as an Ajax control but it's actually a JavaScript library and can be referenced using the normal <script> tag as shown. This time, the API key isn't added in the library's URL. Instead, the API key is specified in the map options, as illustrated in Listing 12-7.

Listing 12-7. Displaying a Map Using the Bing Maps API

```
$(document).ready(function () {
  ...
  defaultPos = new Microsoft.Maps.Location(18.916667, 72.9);
  var mapOptions = {
    credentials: '<%= ConfigurationManager.AppSettings["BingMapsAPIKey"] %>',
    center: defaultPos,
    mapTypeId: Microsoft.Maps.MapTypeId.road,
    zoom: 8
  };
  map = new Microsoft.Maps.Map($("#divMap").get(0), mapOptions);
  ...
});
```

This listing is similar to the previous example. Here, instead of a LatLng object, a Location object is used to represent a map location. The map options include credentials, center, zoom, and mapTypeId. The credentials setting holds the Bing Map API key stored in the <appSettings> section of the web.config file. The other settings are obvious and need no explanation.

The OnSuccess() and OnError() functions this time use an Infobox object to display the location callout. These functions are shown in Listing 12-8.

Listing 12-8. Using the Infobox Object of the Bing Maps API

```
function OnSuccess(position) {
  var curPos = new Microsoft.Maps.Location(position.coords.latitude,
                        position.coords.longitude);
  var calloutOptions = {title: "Location Information",
                                description: "This is your current location."};
  var callout = new Microsoft.Maps.Infobox(curPos, calloutOptions);
  map.entities.push(callout);
}

function OnError(err) {
  alert(err.message);
  var calloutOptions = {title: "Location Information",
                                description: "This is the default location."};
  var callout = new Microsoft.Maps.Infobox(defaultPos, calloutOptions);
  map.entities.push(callout);
}
```

A new Location object is created based on the user's location. The calloutOptions object holds the title and description shown in the callout. An Infobox object is created by passing the desired location (the user's location, in this case) and the calloutOptions object. Finally, the callout is displayed by calling the push() method of the entities object and passing the Infobox as the parameter. Figure 12-5 shows a map in Bing Maps.

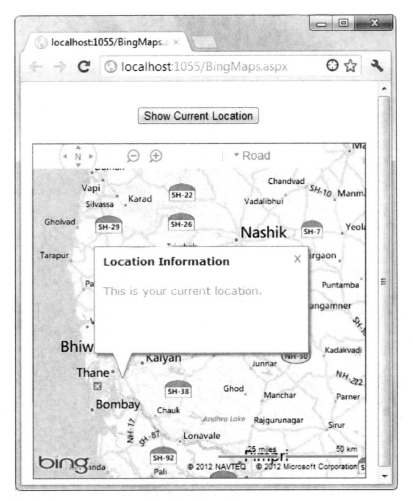

Figure 12-5. Bing Maps showing an Infobox

As you can see, clicking the Show Current Location button opens the Infobox. The title setting controls the title of the Infobox, and the description setting controls its content.

Using the Geolocation API to Present Location-Specific Data

The Geolocation API isn't restricted to mapping applications. You can use it in innovative ways to add location awareness to your web applications. In this section, you develop an ASP.NET MVC application that displays job openings based on the user's location. The application consists of a single view that looks like Figure 12-6.

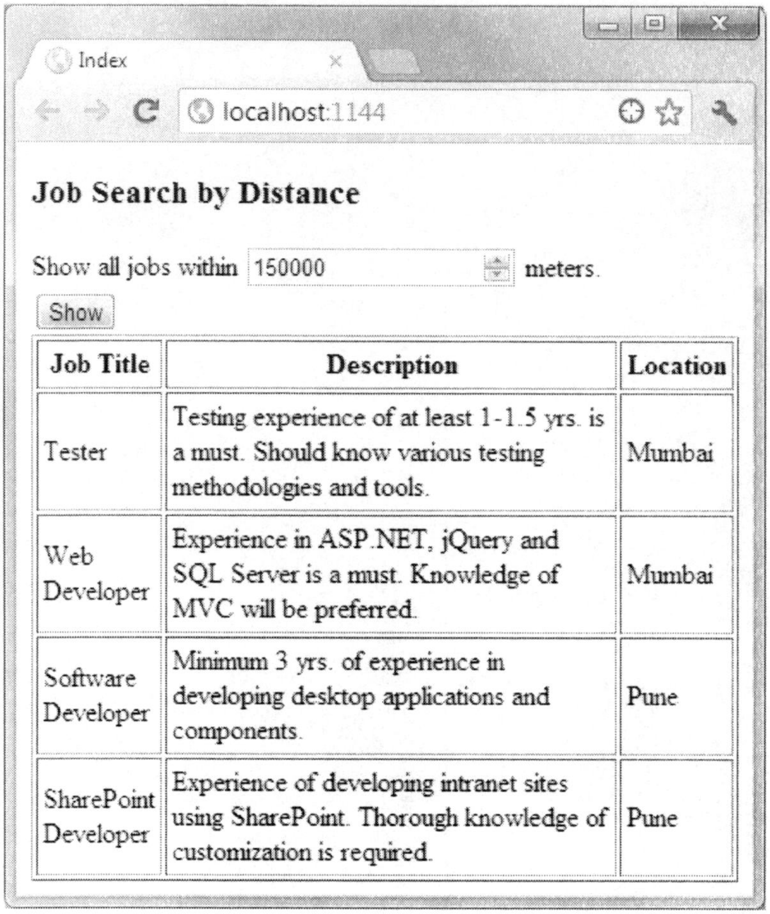

Figure 12-6. Searching for jobs based on the user's location

The view has a numeric `<input>` field at the top. The user can specify a distance in meters to indicate that only jobs within the specified distance are to be listed. When the user clicks the Show button, their location is captured using the Geolocation API; based on the user's location and the distance specified, only job postings that fall within the specified distance range are displayed. For example, if the user's location is Mumbai and the distance specified is 150000 meters (150km), then job postings from Mumbai and Pune will be displayed because these two locations fall within the specified range of 150km. Job postings from Bangalore and Chennai won't be displayed because those locations are outside the specified range.

The application uses two tables—`Jobs` and `Locations`—that store job postings and location, coordinates respectively. The Entity Framework data model for these tables is shown in Figure 12-7.

Figure 12-7. Entity Framework data model forJobs and Location tables

The Jobs table stores JobTitle, Description, and LocationName, whereas the Locations table stores LocationName, Latitude, and Longitude. The code that performs the job of finding the user's location and fetching the relevant job postings is shown in Listing 12-9.

Listing 12-9. Finding Job Postings Based on User Location and Ddistance

```
$(document).ready(function () {
...
  $("#btnShow").click(function () {
    window.navigator.geolocation.getCurrentPosition(function (position) {
      var lat1 = position.coords.latitude;
      var long1 = position.coords.longitude;
      var distance = $("#txtDistance").val();
      var data = '{ "lat1" : "' + lat1 + '","long1":"' + long1 +
                        '","distance":"' + distance + '"}';
      $.ajax({
        type: "POST",
        url: '/home/GetJobs',
        data: data,
        contentType: "application/json; charset=utf-8",
        dataType: "json",
        success: function (jobs) {
          $("#tblJobs").empty();
          $("#tblJobs").append("<tr><th>Job Title</th><th>Description</th><th>Location</th></
tr>");
          for (var i = 0;i<jobs.length;i++)
          {
            $("#tblJobs").append("<tr><td>" + jobs[i].JobTitle + "</td><td>" +
            jobs[i].Description + "</td><td>" + jobs[i].LocationName +
                                        "</td></tr>");
          }
        },
        error: function (err) {
          alert(err.status + " - " + err.statusText);
        }
      });
```

319

```
        });
    });
});
```

This code shows the Show button's `click` event-handler function. It first retrieves the user's location using the `getCurrentPosition()` method of the geolocation object. This time, a `success` function is provided inline with the `getCurrentPosition()` call instead of as a separate function. The user's location's latitude and longitude values are stored in the local variables `lat1` and `long1`. A JSON object with three keys—`lat1`, `long1`, and `distance`—is formed using the values from the variables and the `<input>` field.

Next, an Ajax request is made to the `GetJobs()` action method using the jQuery `$.ajax()` method. `GetJobs()` returns zero or more `Job` objects and is discussed shortly. The `success` function of the `$.ajax()` method receives the `Job` objects returned by `GetJobs()`. It then iterates through the jobs array and adds the jobs to an HTML table. The table contains the `Title`, `Description`, and `LocationName` properties of the `Job` objects.

The error-handler function of the `$.ajax()` method displays the error message in an alert box. The `GetJobs()` action method that returns the relevant jobs based on the user's location and the specified distance is shown in Listing 12-10.

Listing 12-10. *GetJobs() Action Method*

```
[HttpPost]
public JsonResult GetJobs(double lat1, double long1, double distance)
{
    JobsDbEntities db = new JobsDbEntities();
    var data = from item in db.Jobs
                    select item;
    List<Job> selectedJobs = new List<Job>();

    foreach(Job job in data)
    {
        var temp = from item in db.Locations
                        where item.LocationName==job.LocationName
                        select item;

        double lat2 = (double)((Location)temp.SingleOrDefault()).Latitude;
        double long2 = (double)((Location)temp.SingleOrDefault()).Longitude;

        if (GetDistance(lat1, long1, lat2, long2) <= distance)
        {
            selectedJobs.Add(job);
        }
    }
    var finalData = from obj in selectedJobs
                        orderby obj.LocationName
                        select obj;
    return Json(finalData);
}
```

The `GetJobs()` action method from the Home controller takes three parameters of type double. The `lat1` and `long1` parameters represent the latitude and longitude of the user's location. The `distance` parameter represents the distance specified by the user. The method then iterates through all the available job postings. With each iteration, the latitude and longitude of the job location are determined. The

GetDistance() helper method determines the distance between the user's location (lat1, long2) and the job location (lat2, long2). If the distance returned by GetDistance() is less than or equal to the distance specified by the user, the job posting is added to a generic List of Job objects. Before the filtered job postings are sent to the user, the selectedJobs generic List is sorted on LocationName. Finally, the sorted list of Job objects is sent to the caller in JSON format using the Json() method. The GetDistance() method that determines the distance between the user's location and the job location is shown in Listing 12-11.

Listing 12-11. Finding the Distance Between the User's Location and the Job Location

```
private double GetDistance(double lat1,double long1,double lat2,double long2)
{
    GeoCoordinate point1 = new GeoCoordinate(lat1, long1);
    GeoCoordinate point2 = new GeoCoordinate(lat2, long2);
    double distance = point1.GetDistanceTo(point2);
    return distance;
}
```

This code uses the GeoCoordinate class from the System.Device.Location namespace (located in the System.Device.dll assembly). GeoCoordinates represents the geographical coordinates of a location. The GeoCoordinate constructor accepts a location's latitude and longitude. The GetDistance() method of the GeoCoordinate class returns the distance between that point and another point as specified in the parameter. The distance, in meters, is then returned to the caller.

Note that for the sake of simplicity, this code retrieves all the rows from the table and then iterates through them one by one. A more sophisticated solution would calculate the maximum latitude and longitude values and then retrieve only rows that fall in that range.

■ **Note** The .NET Framework's GeoCoordinate class is similar to the Geolocation API's coords object in terms of its properties. GeoCoordinate uses the haversine formula to calculate the distance. This formula treats Earth as spherical rather than an ellipsoid and doesn't use altitude for distance calculation. The haversine formula introduces an error of less than 0.1 percent while calculating long distances.

Tracking Movement Using the Geolocation API

In the preceding examples, you used the geolocation object's getCurrentPosition() method to get the user's current location. This works well when you want to know the user's location at the time you call the method and you aren't interested in continuously tracking the user. In some cases, however, you need to keep watching the user's location as the user moves from one place to the other. For example, you may want to monitor the distance travelled by a user who is moving from a location toward some other location, and you may want to inform the user regularly about the distance remaining to the target location. You can use the watchPosition() method of the geolocation object in such cases. This method is similar to getCurrentPosition() in terms of syntax; but unlike getCurrentPosition(), it keeps invoking the success function at regular intervals. The exact interval between successive calls to the success function is governed by the device. The success callback function is invoked only if the user's location has changed. So, on a desktop computer, getCurrentPosition() and watchPosition() behave in the same fashion because the location of the computer doesn't change.

What if, based on a condition, you wish to stop watching the user's location? The watchPosition() method returns a number that acts like a handle to that invocation of watchPosition(). You can pass this number to the clearWatch() method to stop watching the user's location. The code in Listing 12-12 shows how you can use watchPosition() and clearWatch().

Listing 12-12. Using the watchPosition() and clearWatch() Methods

```
var watchId;
function StartWatch() {
  watchId = window.navigator.geolocation.watchPosition(OnSuccess, OnError);
}

function StopWatch() {
  window.navigator.geolocation.clearWatch(watchId);
};
```

This code defines a global variable named watchId to store the watch handle returned by watchPosition(). The StartWatch() function calls geolocation object's watchPosition() method and passes OnSuccess and OnError callback functions as before. The returned numeric handle is stored in the watchId variable. StopWatch() calls the geolocation object's clearWatch() method and passes watchId as a parameter to clear that watch.

Summary

The Geolocation API allows you to find the user's geographic location in terms of latitude and longitude. The geolocation object property of the navigator object exposes the methods responsible for retrieving the user's location. The getCurrentPosition() method returns the user's current location. The watchPosition() method keeps monitoring that location until the clearWatch() method is called.

Using the Geolocation API, you can build location-aware web applications that present data based on the user's location. You can also integrate the Geolocation API with mapping services such as Google Maps and Bing Maps.

You've learned about all of HTML5's prominent programmable features. Although, as a web developer, your core focus is on programmable features, at times you also need to style your web applications using Cascading Style Sheets (CSS). CSS3 offers the latest in this area. The next chapter covers some new and improved features.

CHAPTER 13

Styling Web Forms and Views with CSS3

As an ASP.NET developer wishing to harness the power of HTML5, your primary area of interest is the programmable features of HTML5. However, as a part of developing real-world professional web applications, you also need to look into the styling aspects of those web applications. When it comes to styling web forms and views, Cascading Style Sheets (CSS) is the de facto standard, and CSS3 adds many enhancements that make styling even better. CSS3 isn't part of HTML5, but they're evolving together and complement each other well.

CSS3 specifications group improvements over CSS 2.1 into what are known as *modules*. There are around 50 modules in CSS3. The idea behind grouping the improvements and additions into modules is that browser vendors can decide which modules to implement in their products. When a module is implemented, developers also know which features they can use. Because CSS3 is still an evolving specification, this modular approach makes it easy for browser vendors to support and refine CSS3 features in an incremental fashion.

There are many new additions to CSS3, including things such as rounded borders, web fonts, shadows, transparency, and transforms. This chapter gives you a detailed overview of some important CSS3 features that are frequently needed by developers because they're commonly used while styling web pages. Using these features, you can beautify web forms and views in a better way. Specifically, you learn the following:

- Working with CSS3 selectors
- Using custom fonts that are downloaded automatically at the client side
- Enhancing boxes using rounded corners, shadows, gradients, and transparency
- Using transitions and transforms
- Targeting different devices with media queries

The chapter concludes with information about using Modernizr to apply CSS3-specific features.

CSS3 Selectors

In Chapter 2, you learned about jQuery selectors that allow you to select elements for further manipulation in your jQuery code. CSS selectors do exactly the same job, with the difference that they select elements for the sake of applying styling. In fact, jQuery selectors are based on the idea of CSS selectors. CSS3 adds many new selectors to those that already existed in CSS. This section introduces some of the important ones.

If you've used CSS in the past, chances are you're already familiar with the concept of selectors. Consider the following CSS class:

```
#mydiv{ border: 2px #f00 solid; }
```

This class uses the *ID selector* and is applied to a DOM element whose ID attribute is mydiv. The other two commonly used CSS selectors are the element selector and the class selector. An *element selector* selects all the elements of specific tag name, whereas a *class selector* selects all the elements whose class attribute is set to a specific CSS class name. The following examples show these two selectors:

```
div{ border: 2px #f00 solid; }
.myclass{ border: 2px #f00 solid; }
```

The first CSS class uses an element selector that selects all the <div> elements and applies to them a border with a specified color and width. The second class selects all the DOM elements whose class attribute is set to myclass and applies to them a border with a specified color and width.

■ **Note** In addition to the selectors just discussed, CSS 2.1 offers a few others, but this chapter doesn't discuss them. Here we focus only on the newly added selectors in CSS3.

The newly added selectors of CSS3 that are discussed in the following sections can be grouped in four categories:

- *Attribute-substring selectors:* Allow you to select elements whose attribute value starts with, ends with, or contains a specified string

- *Structural pseudo-classes:* Let you select elements based on their structural position, such as a specific child element

- *Element-state pseudo-classes:* Allow you to select elements that are in a specific state, such as enabled, disabled, or checked

- *Miscellaneous pseudo-classes:* Provide miscellaneous functionality that doesn't fit in any other category

The following sections discuss each of these groups of selectors in detail.

Attribute-Substring Selectors

The attribute-substring selectors allow you to select DOM elements whose attribute values start with, ends with, or contain a specified string. These three selectors are listed in Table 13-1.

Table 13-1. Attribute Substring Selectors

Selector	Operator	Description
Attribute starts with	^=	Matches the start of an attribute value with a specified string
Attribute ends with	$=	Matches the end of an attribute value with a specified string
Attribute contains	*=	Checks whether an attribute value contains a specified string

Let's illustrate these three attribute-substring selectors with an example. Suppose you have a web page with multiple hyperlinks. Some of them point to URLs and some point to e-mail addresses, as shown here:

```
<a href="http://www.microsoft.com">Go to Microsoft's website.</a>
<a href="mailto:contact@somedomain.com">Contact us here.</a>
```

Now assume that you wish to display all hyperlinks starting with http:// in red and all hyperlinks starting with mailto: in blue. You can do so using an attribute-substring selector:

```
a[href^="http://"] {
  color:red;
  font-size:30px;
}
a[href^="mailto:"] {
  color:blue;
  font-size:30px;
}
```

The CSS selectors used in these classes use ^= operator to match the start of the href attribute of anchor elements with a specific string. The first selector selects all hyperlinks that begin with http:// and sets their color to red; the other selector selects all hyperlinks that begin with mailto: and sets their color to blue. Figure 13-1 shows how these links look in the browser.

Figure 13-1. *"Attribute starts with" selector in action*

Now, further assume that the same page contains the URLs of certain PDF files, and you wish to render these hyperlinks in green. In this case, you can use the "attribute ends with" selector as shown next:

```
a[href$=".pdf"] {
  color:green;
  font-size:30px;
}
```

The "attribute ends with" selector uses the $= operator to match the end of an attribute value with a specified string. In this example, the end of the href attribute value is matched against ".pdf", and all hyperlinks that match the criteria are shown in green. An example of a matching hyperlink is as follows:

```
<a href="downloads/ebook.pdf">Download eBook here.</a>
```

Extending the idea further, you can also display hyperlinks that contain (rather than start or end with) specific text. For example, to display in orange all hyperlinks that contain the word *google*, you use

```
a[href*="google"] {
  color:orange;
  font-size:30px;
}
```

As you can see, the *= operator checks the href attribute of each hyperlink element to see if it contains the word *google*. If so, the hyperlink color is set to orange. Here's an example of a matching hyperlink:

```
<a href="http://www.somedomain.com/google/api">…</a>
```

The specified string can exist at the start of the attribute value, at the end of the attribute value, or anywhere in between.

Structural Pseudo-Classes

Sometimes you want to apply styling to elements based on their structural position in the DOM tree. For example, you may want to apply certain styling to the first and last rows of a table. In such cases, structural pseudo-classes come in handy. Table 13-2 lists the structural pseudo-classes.

Table 13-2. Structural Pseudo-Classes

Pseudo-Class	Description
:root	Matches an element that is the root of the document (typically the <html> element)
:first-child	Matches any element that is the first child of its parent
:last-child	Matches any element that is the last child of its parent
:nth-child	Matches any element that is the nth child of its parent
:nth-last-child	Matches any element that is the nth child of its parent, counting from the last child
:only-child	Matches any elements that is the only child of its parent
:first-of-type	Matches any element that is the first sibling of its type
:last-of-type	Matches any element that is the last sibling of its type
:nth-of-type	Matches any element that is the nth sibling element of its type
:nth-last-of-type	Matches any element that is the nth sibling element of its type, counting from the last child
:only-of-type	Matches any element that is the only sibling of its type
:empty	Matches any element that has no children

Let's see some examples of using structural pseudo-classes. Suppose you wish to display the last row of an HTML table in a certain color. You can do so using the :last-child pseudo-class, as shown here:

```
tr:last-child {
  background-color:#808080;
  font-size:20px;
}
```

This CSS selector selects all <tr> elements that are the last child of their parent (that is, the <table> element) and applies to them the specified background color and font size. Figure 13-2 shows how a table looks with the styling applied.

Figure 13-2. Last row of a table styled using the :last-child pseudo-class

A common requirement while working with tables is to show the alternate rows in different colors. This can be achieved using the :nth-child selector. The following CSS selectors apply different styling to the odd and even rows of a table:

```
tr:nth-child(odd) {
  background-color:#fff;
}
tr:nth-child(even) {
  background-color:#808080;
}
```

Here, all the odd rows have the background color #fff and all the even rows have the background color #808080. The resulting table is shown in Figure 13-3.

Figure 13-3. Odd and even rows of a table with different styles applied using an :nth-child pseudo-class

The odd and even keywords denote odd and even rows, respectively. You can also specify a row number: for example, tr:nth-child(2) {...}. The numbering starts from 1.

The type selectors are similar to child selectors, but they're applicable to siblings of a specified type rather than children. Consider a case where you have many <p> elements and you want the first letter of

327

the first paragraph to be displayed in a specific way. Because all the <p> elements are siblings of each other, you use a type pseudo-class. For this particular case, you can use :first-of-type as follows:

```
p:first-of-type::first-letter {
  font-size:50px;
  float:left;
  line-height:1;
  margin-right:5px;
}
```

This :first-of-type selector selects the first <p> element. The double colon (::) syntax then selects the first letter of that paragraph using the ::first-letter pseudo-element and applies the styling as specified. Figure 13-4 shows how the paragraph looks.

Figure 13-4. Using a :first-of-type selector to select the first paragraph of content

Note that the specific styling is applied only to the first letter of the first paragraph because the :first-of-type pseudo-class is used. The other <p> elements remain unaffected by the styling.

■ **Note** Prior to CSS3, pseudo-classes and pseudo-elements were prefixed by a colon (:). To distinguish between them, CSS3 prefixes pseudo-classes with a single colon (:) and pseudo-elements with a double colon (::). This enables you to quickly identify that :first-of-type is a pseudo-class whereas ::first-letter is a pseudo-element.

Element-State Pseudo-Classes

The element-state pseudo-classes are useful when you're working with form fields because they select elements based on their state. For example, suppose you want to apply specific styling to all check boxes that are checked, or display disabled elements in a specific way. These pseudo-classes are listed in Table 13-3.

Table 13-3. Element-State Pseudo-Classes

Pseudo-Class	Description
:enabled	Matches any form field that is enabled
:disabled	Matches any form field that is disabled
:checked	Matches any form field that is checked

To understand how element-state pseudo-classes are used, consider the following selectors:

```
input[type="text"]:enabled { background:#fff; }
input[type="text"]:disabled { background:#808080; }
input:checked { border:2px #f00 solid; }
```

The :enabled pseudo-class, when applied to input elements of type text, returns all text boxes that are enabled and applies the specified styling to them. Similarly, the :disabled pseudo-class selects all text boxes that are disabled and applies the specified styling. The :checked pseudo-class selects all check boxes and adds a border to them as specified. Figure 13-5 shows these pseudo-classes in action.

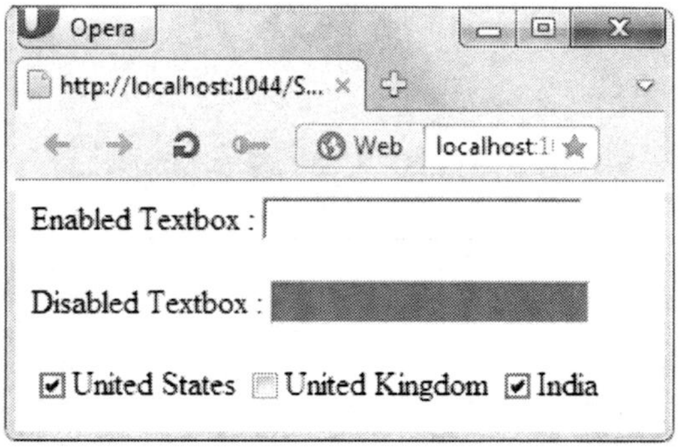

Figure 13-5. :enabled, :disabled, and :checked pseudo-classes in action

Miscellaneous Pseudo-Classes

The CSS pseudo-classes discussed in this section don't fit in any of the categories discussed earlier. These pseudo-classes include the negation pseudo-class (:not()) and the general sibling combinator pseudo-class.

The negation pseudo-class is used when you wish to select elements that don't match a specific condition. For example, suppose a form contains several <input> elements. Of all those <input> elements, only one is of type submit; all the rest are of type text, checkbox, and radio. If you wish to apply styling to all of the <input> elements except the Submit button, you can do so using the :not() pseudo-class as shown next:

```
input:not([type="submit"]) {
  background-color:#808080;
}
```

This selector selects elements whose type attribute isn't submit. The background color of these elements is then set to #808080.

The general sibling combinator consists of two simple selectors separated by a tilde (~) character. It selects elements of the second type that are preceded by an element of the first type. Both elements must have the same parent, but the second element doesn't have to be immediately preceded by the first element. For example, let's say you have a <div> element containing other elements such as <ul>, <input>, and <span>, as shown here:

```
<div>
  <ul>
    <li>One</li>
    <li>Two</li>
  </ul>
</div>
<ul>
  <li>Three</li>
  <li>Four</li>
</ul>
```

You wish to apply styling to <ul> sibling elements that appear after the <div> element and occurring anywhere within the <div>. You can do so using the following CSS rule:

```
div ~ ul {
  background-color:#ff6a00;
}
```

Figure 13-6 shows the final outcome.

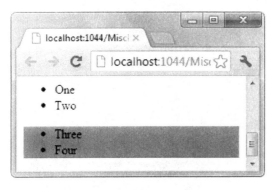

Figure 13-6. General sibling combinator

As you can see, the first <ul> is a child of the <div> and not a sibling, and hence the specified styling isn't applied it to it. The second <ul> is a sibling of the <div> element, so the general sibling combinator selects it and applies the specified background color.

Browser-Specific Property Prefixes

As mentioned earlier, the CSS3 specifications are still evolving, and different browser vendors support them in varying degrees. Currently, the CSS3-specific features implemented by browsers fall into two broad categories: features that meet the specification completely, and features that are implemented but don't yet meet the specifications completely. To distinguish between these two types, the browser vendors use their own prefixes for the features belonging to the second category. These prefixes are listed in Table 13-4.

Table 13-4. *Browser-Specific Prefixes for CSS3 Properties*

Prefix	Description
-ms-	Used by Microsoft Internet Explorer
-moz-	Used by Mozilla Firefox
-webkit-	Used by Google Chrome and Apple Safari
-o-	Used by Opera

Consider a CSS class named rotate, as shown next:

```
.rotate
{
  border-radius: 25px;
  -ms-transform: rotate(10deg);
}
```

The rotate CSS class uses two CSS3 properties: border-radius and -ms-transform. The border-radius property doesn't have a prefix attached to it, which indicates that it's feature-complete. The transform property, on the other hand, uses the -ms- prefix, indicating that the feature-incomplete implementation specific to Internet Explorer should be used. You use the browser-specific prefixes listed in Table 13-4 in some of the examples discussed later.

■ **Note**　You can use Modernizr to detect browser support of CSS3 features in JavaScript code just like other HTML5 features. However, Modernizr doesn't provide detection properties for all CSS3 features.

Using Web Fonts

You can make your web pages catchy and easy to read by making the proper use of fonts. Unfortunately, web developers and designers have had to be satisfied with a small set of fonts to ensure that their web applications look the same on all browsers running on a variety of operating systems. If you use a font in your web pages that doesn't come bundled with the operating system, there is no guarantee that the client machine has the same font installed. As a result, your web page may look different to the end user than it does on your machine. That is why web developers and designers have often restricted themselves to using well-known web-safe fonts, which are likely to be available on a wide range of computer systems; these fonts include Arial, Verdana, and Times New Roman.

CSS3 provides a new way to use fonts called *web fonts*. Using this feature, you can host nonstandard fonts used by web pages on your web site. You then declare a custom font definition using the @font-face CSS3 rule. At runtime, the client browser reads the custom font definition from the style sheet and downloads the font to the client machine. The font is then used for your web pages. Each web site that wants to use a nonstandard font must define it in the web site's style sheet.

331

Web Font Formats

Although CSS3 makes it easy for you to use nonstandard fonts in your web pages, one more area needs to be addressed: font file formats. Just like media files, font files come in a variety of formats, and there is no one web standard for these formats. Table 13-5 shows a list of font file formats that are in use today.

Table 13-5. Font Formats Used on the Web

Format	Description	Browser Support
True Type Font (.ttf) Open Type Font (.otf)	The TTF and OTF formats are most commonly used on desktop computers.	Firefox, Chrome, Opera, and Safari
Embedded Open Type (.eot)	EOT is a proprietary Microsoft format and is used mainly in older versions of IE	IE
Scalable Vector Graphics (SVG)	SVG is a general graphical format.	Mobile devices using the Android operating system and Safari Mobile
Web Open Font Format (.woff)	All newer versions of browsers support WOFF. It may become a standard at some point.	All newer versions of IE, Firefox, Chrome, Opera, and Safari

Because there is no single standard file format for web fonts, and developers may need to host multiple file formats on their web sites, some web sites offer fonts in these file formats for downloading. One popular web site is Font Squirrel (www.fontsquirrel.com), which provides what is known as @font-face kits—sets of fonts in these file formats. Figure 13-7 shows the Font Squirrel download page for a font named Magenta.

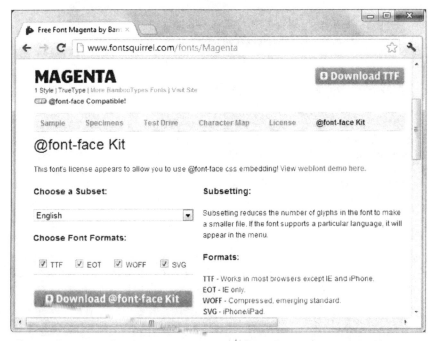

Figure 13-7. Downloading a @font-face kit from the Font Squirrel web site

You can select font formats to download. By default, the TIF, EOT, WOFF, and SVG formats are selected. The downloaded @font-face kit (a Zip file) contains all the font formats, licensing information, and a demo HTML page.

There is an alternative to downloading a @font-face kit from a web site and then uploading it to your own web site: Google Web Fonts. Google Web Fonts offer web fonts to use in your web pages without any need to download them. All you need to do is to add a Style Sheet reference in your web pages, as instructed on the Google Web Font web site (www.google.com/webfonts). At runtime, the Google Web Font web site automatically detects the browser and sends it a font in a supported format. Figure 13-8 shows the Google Web Fonts web site.

Figure 13-8. Google Web Fonts web site

In the following section, you learn how to use @font-face kit files as well as the Google Web Fonts web site.

Using @font-face Rules

Now that you know what web fonts are and how to get them, let's see how you can put them to use in a web page. Suppose you've downloaded the Magenta font mentioned in the preceding example. To use that web font, you need to create a custom font definition in your style-sheet file. A sample font definition is shown here:

```
@font-face
{
font-family: MyWebFont;
src: url('Fonts/Magenta_BBT-webfont.ttf'),
    url('Fonts/Magenta_BBT-webfont.eot'),
```

```
        url('Fonts/Magenta_BBT-webfont.svg'),
        url('Fonts/Magenta_BBT-webfont.woff');
}
```

The @font-face rule begins by defining a font family named MyWebFont. The font-family name can be any developer-defined name. If you have multiple @font-face rules, each should have a unique font-family name to avoid ambiguity. The src property then points to one or more URLs where the font files are located, using the url() function. In this example, all the font files are located in a folder named Fonts. For each font format that you wish to support, you must specify a URL.

Once you define a custom font definition using @font-face, you can use that font in other CSS rules. For example, the following CSS rule uses MyWebFont for <h1> tags:

```
h1 {
    font-family: 'MyWebFont';
    font-size:40px;
    text-align:center;
}
```

As you can see, in a CSS rule you can use the custom font like any other standard font. In this case, the font-family property is set to MyWebFont, and the font-size and text-align properties are also set. Figure 13-9 shows a top-level heading in the browser.

Figure 13-9. @font-face applied to a page heading

Even if the local machine doesn't have a specific font, the web page can display text in that font because @font-face provides the location of the font files.

If you're using a font from Google Web Fonts, then you don't need to define a font with @font-face because that is already done for you. All you have to do is refer to a style sheet provided by Google Web Fonts and then use the font-family name in your CSS rules. For example, if you click the Quick Use button for the font Peralta, you see a style-sheet reference link and a font-family name (Peralta). With this information, you can define a CSS rule as follows:

```
h2 {
    font-family:'Peralta';
    font-size:20px;
    text-align:center;
}
```

Here, you create a CSS rule for <h2> elements and specify the font-family as Peralta. You can then refer to the style sheets in a web page as follows:

```
<link href='http://fonts.googleapis.com/
 css?family=Peralta' rel='stylesheet' type='text/css'>
<link rel="stylesheet" type="text/css" href="StyleSheet.css" />
```

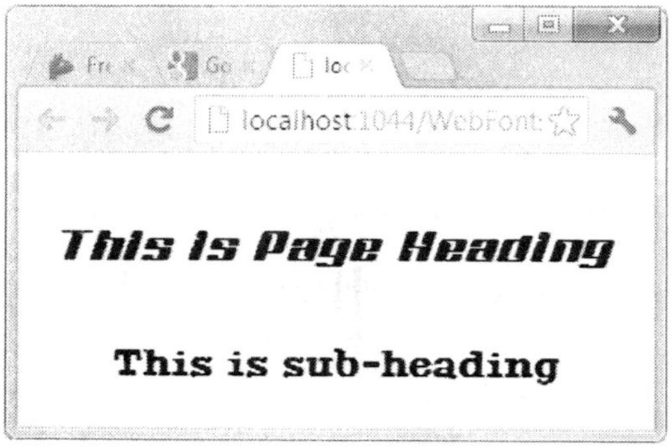

Figure 13-10. *Using web fonts from Google Web Fonts*

Note that you should refer to the style sheet provided by Google Web Fonts prior to using the Peralta font definition in your own style sheet (StyleSheet.css). Figure 13-10 shows how <h2> headings look in the browser.

As you can see, the subheading is displayed using the Peralta font face provided by Google Web Fonts.

In the preceding examples, you used fonts provided by a third party (Font Squirrel or Google), but if required you can also use your own fonts by generating a @font-face kit for them. The Font Squirrel web site allows you to generate your own @font-face kits by uploading your own fonts. Once the @font-face kit is generated for such fonts, you can use them in your web pages as discussed in this section.

Rounded Corners, Shadows, Gradients, and Transparency

One of the most common effects applied to DOM elements in a web page is to put them in a box. Box attributes such as borders, border width and style, color, and so on are configured using various CSS properties. CSS3 offers features that help you enhance the box layout even further. These cool additions may very well become the CSS3 features you use most frequently. Using them, you can do the following:

- Add boxes with rounded corners to DOM elements.

- Add shadows to boxes.

- Set more than one image as the background.

- Add a gradient fill to the background.

Let's see how you can apply each of these features to DOM elements.

Rounded Corners

Whenever you put a box around an element using border properties, by default the box gets sharp corners. You can turn a box with sharp corners into a box with rounded corners using the border-radius property. With border-radius, you can specify the radius of a circle whose circumference governs the rounding of the corners. The following CSS rule shows how to use the border-radius property:

```
.boxRoundedCorners {
    padding:15px;
    background-color:#d0bdbd;
    border: 2px solid #071394;
    border-radius: 25px 25px 25px 25px;
}
```

border-radius sets the radius of the circles for the rectangle's four corners in the order top-left, top-right, bottom-right, and bottom-left. Although this example sets the radius of every circle to 25px, that's not necessary. You can specify that a radius value be different, and the corresponding corner (top-left, top-right, bottom-right, or bottom-left) will change its curve accordingly.

You can also use an ellipse to control the curve rather than a circle. This way, the horizontal curve and vertical curve can be different. To do this, you need to set the border radius of the individual corners as follows:

```
.boxRoundedCorners2 {
    padding:15px;
    background-color:#d0bdbd;
    border: 2px solid #071394;
    border-top-left-radius: 25px 15px;
    border-top-right-radius: 25px 15px;
    border-bottom-left-radius: 50px 40px;
    border-bottom-right-radius: 50px 40px;
}
```

This time, individual properties—border-top-left-radius, border-top-right-radius, border-bottom-left-radius, and border-bottom-right-radius—specify the horizontal and vertical radius of the ellipse, respectively. Figure 13-11 shows two ASP.NET FormView server controls placed inside <div> elements that have the boxRoundedCorners and boxRoundedCorners2 CSS classes applied.

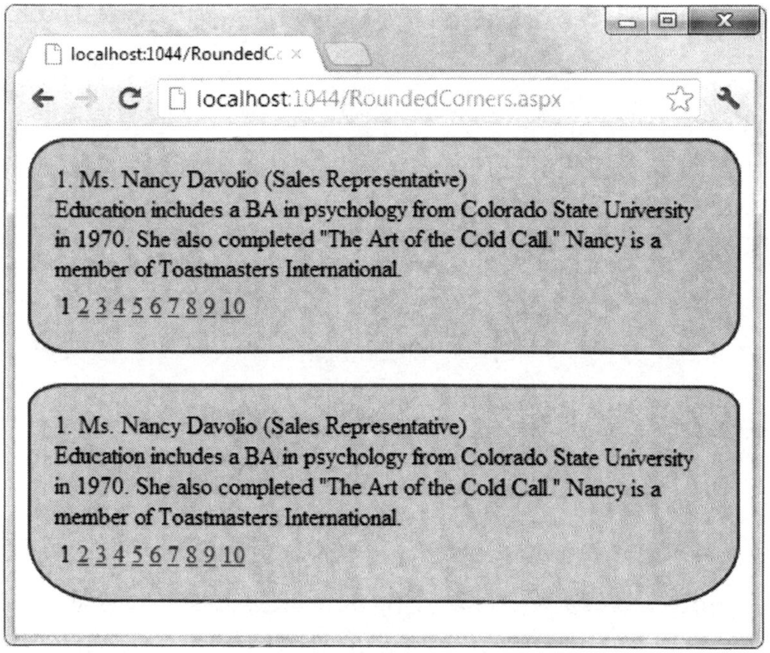

Figure 13-11. `FormView` *controls with rounded corners*

The first `FormView`'s borders all have an equal radius of 25px, as specified in the `border-radius` property. The second `FormView` has top corners with radii of 25px, 15px and bottom corners with radii of 50px, 40px respectively.

Shadows

CSS3 lets you add shadows to boxes as well as text. The `box-shadow` and `text-shadow` properties control the box shadow and text shadow, respectively. You can specify a horizontal offset, a vertical offset, a blur amount, and a color for both types of shadows.

The following CSS rule uses the `box-shadow` and `text-shadow` properties just discussed:

```
.shadow {
    padding:15px;
    background-color:#d0bdbd;
    border: 2px solid #071394;
    border-radius: 25px 25px 25px 25px;
    box-shadow: 5px 5px 5px #808080;
    text-shadow: 2px 2px 2px #808080;
}
```

As you can see, `box-shadow` specifies horizontal and vertical offsets of 5px. A positive offset means the shadow is dropped down and to the right with respect to the box, whereas a negative value means the shadow is dropped up and to the left. The `box-shadow` property specifies the blur amount as 5px. The larger the value, the more blurred the shadow is. Finally, the shadow color is specified as #808080 (grey).

The text-shadow property is similar and specifies the horizontal and vertical offset as 2px. The blur value is also set to 2px. Figure 13-12 shows the resulting box.

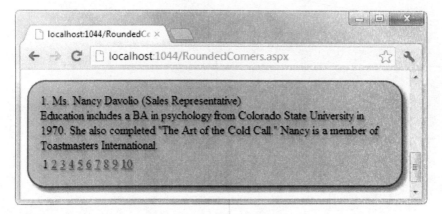

Figure 13-12. Adding shadows to the box and the text

Note that text-shadow isn't supported in all browsers (IE9 for example), but box-shadow has good support in all the leading browsers.

By default, a box shadow is placed outside the box. You can change this behavior using the inset keyword like this:

```
box-shadow: 5px 5px 5px #808080 inset;
```

When you add the inset keyword at the end, the shadow appears inside the box rather than outside (Figure 13-13).

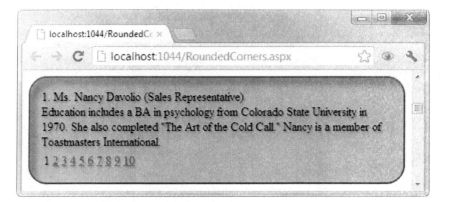

Figure 13-13. Shadow after adding the inset keyword

Image Backgrounds

In the preceding examples, the CSS rules used a color for the box's background. Instead of specifying a background color, you can use a background image. New in CSS3 is the ability to use multiple images in a single background. For example, you can use four different images and place them in the top-left, top-right, bottom-left, and bottom-left areas of the box. Of course, the actual area occupied by the image is governed by the image's size. Consider the following CSS rule:

```
.imageBackground {
    padding:15px;
    font-size:20px;
    border: 2px solid #071394;
    border-radius: 25px 25px 25px 25px;
    background-image: url('images/RedFlower.png'), url('images/BlueFlower.png');
    background-position: left top, right bottom;
    background-repeat: no-repeat, no-repeat;
    height:300px;
}
```

This CSS rule uses the background-image property to specify two image URLs: RedFlower.png and BlueFlower.png. The placement of these two images is controlled by the background-position property. For every image URL in the background-image property, there must be an entry in the background-position property. In this example, RedFlower.png is placed in the top-left corner of the box and BlueFlower.png is placed in the bottom-right corner.

You also need to specify the background-repeat property. In this example, because you don't repeat the images horizontally or vertically, you set background-repeat to no-repeat. Figure 13-14 shows the resulting box background.

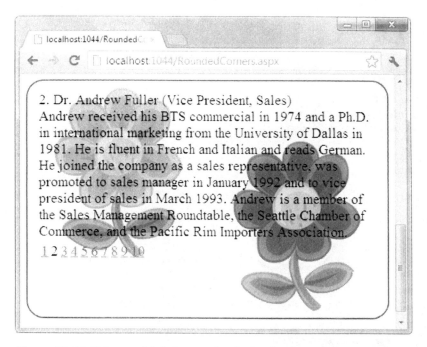

Figure 13-14. *Using multiple images for the box background*

RedFlower.png appears at upper left and BlueFlower.png appears at lower right.

Gradients

In Chapter 4, you learned to draw gradients—linear and radial—on the canvas. CSS3 provides ways to draw a gradient background. You can do this using two CSS functions: linear-gradient() and radial-gradient(). They draw box backgrounds with linear and radial gradients, respectively. As of this writing, linear-gradient() and radial-gradient() aren't fully implemented by some browsers, so you need to use them with the browser prefixes (-ms-, -moz-, -webkit-, and so on) discussed earlier. The following CSS rule shows how to use linear-gradient():

```
.linearGradient {
    padding:15px;
    background-color:#d0bdbd;
    border: 2px solid #071394;
    background: -moz-linear-gradient(left, yellow, white);
    background: -webkit-linear-gradient(left, yellow, white);
    background: -o-linear-gradient(left, yellow, white);
}
```

The function prefixed with -moz- targets Firefox, the one prefixed with -webkit- targets Chrome and Safari, and the one prefixed with -o- targets Opera. The function's first parameter specifies the starting edge for drawing a gradient. Left means a gradient is drawn starting from the left until it reaches the right side of the box. If you specify top, the direction of gradient is from top to bottom. The second and the third parameters specify the start and end colors for the gradient. Figure 13-15 shows how this gradient looks.

Figure 13-15. *Drawing a linear gradient*

The example gradient starts with a yellow color and gradually fades to white. You can also specify the starting point (first parameter) as an angle. For example, 0deg, 90deg, 180deg, and 270deg mean left, bottom, right, and top, respectively. Any angle between these values shifts the starting point in the corner accordingly. Additionally, you can specify a series of colors for the gradient rather than just the start and end colors:

```
-webkit-linear-gradient(left, orange, yellow, white);
```

In this example, three colors are specified: orange, yellow, and white. So, the gradient is orange to begin with, then turns yellow, and finally fades to white.

Drawing a radial gradient is similar to drawing a linear gradient. The only difference is that instead of starting from one edge and ending at another edge, the gradient begins in the center and ends at the box's boundary. The following CSS rule shows how to use radial-gradient():

```
.radialGradient {
    padding:15px;
    background-color:#d0bdbd;
    border: 2px solid #071394;
    background: -moz-radial-gradient(circle, yellow, white);
    background: -webkit-radial-gradient(circle, yellow, white);
    background: -o-radial-gradient(circle, yellow, white);

}
```

The first parameter of the radial-gradient() function indicates the start position of the gradient's center. The most common value is center, which means the center of the box is the starting point. The other two parameters represent the start and end color of the gradient, as with linear-gradient(). Figure 13-16 shows the radial gradient.

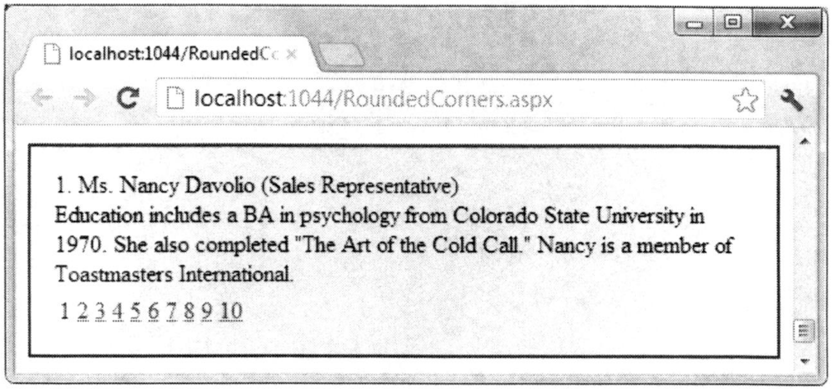

Figure 13-16. Using the radial-gradient() *function to draw a radial gradient*

Note that this section discusses only basic use of the gradient functions. These functions provide more complex ways of drawing and fine-tuning gradients. You can read more on the Internet (https://developer.mozilla.org/en-US/docs/CSS/CSS_Reference, for example).

Transparency

In addition to displaying a background, you can control the box's opacity. CSS3 provides two ways to handle the opacity of an element: the rgba() function and the opacity property. The rgba() function specifies red, green, and blue color values as numbers as well as an alpha value that controls an element's opacity. The r, g, and b numbers take a value between 0 and 255; the alpha parameter can be any value between 0 to 1, where 0 means fully transparent and 1 means fully opaque. The following CSS rule shows how to use rgba():

```
.transparency {
    padding:15px;
    background-color:rgba(10,200,0,0.3);
    border: 2px solid #071394;
}
```

This function specifies the red, green, and blue components as 10, 200, and 0, respectively. The alpha parameter is specified as 0.3. Figure 13-17 shows how a box looks when you apply transparency of 0.3.

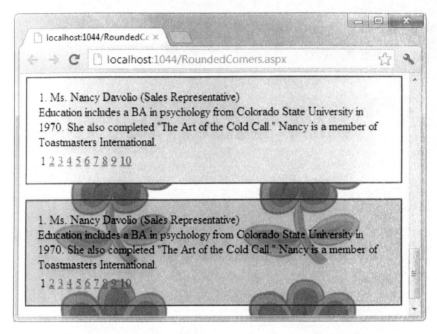

Figure 13-17. Setting a box's transparency using the rgba() function

In the figure, the second box is styled using rgba(). Notice how the background doesn't show through the first box but does show through the second box, due to the transparency alpha value of 0.3.

You can obtain a similar effect using the opacity property instead of rgba():

```
.transparency2 {
    padding:15px;
    background-color:#ffd800;
    opacity:0.75;
    border: 2px solid #071394;
}
```

The opacity property takes any value between 0 and 1, just like the alpha parameter discussed earlier. Figure 13-18 shows the resulting box .

Figure 13-18. Setting transparency using the opacity *property*

There are some differences between using rgba() and the opacity property. rgba() only makes the background color transparent, whereas opacity makes the background, the border, and text inside the element transparent. The opacity property also comes in handy if you wish to control the opacity (but not the background color) programmatically (say, by using the jQuery css() method). This way, without knowing or touching the background color, you can set the opacity property and achieve the desired level of transparency. The following line of code shows how to do this:

```
$("<jQuery_selector>").css("opacity", "0.75");
```

This code uses the jQuery css() method to set to 0.75 the opacity of all the elements matched by a jQuery selector.

Adding Effects Using Transitions and Transforms

Professional web sites often spice up their pages by adding jazzy and attractive effects. CSS3 provides two techniques that allow you to add cool effects to your web pages: transitions and transforms. CSS3 transitions let you add effects to an element as the element is transitioning from one CSS rule to another. On the other hand, CSS3 transforms change an element's appearance by adding effects such as rotating or skewing the element.

Transitions

CSS pseudo-classes such as :hover allow you to change the styling rules applied to an element when the user interacts with the element in a specific way. For example, using the :hover pseudo-class, you can change an element's appearance when the user hovers the mouse pointer over the element. The limitation with pseudo-classes is that they toggle the element's appearance from one state to another. You can't control the element's appearance between the "about to change" and "changed" stages. That means you can't add animation effects during this change of CSS rules.

CSS3 transitions are means to fill this gap. Consider the following CSS rules that define the styling for a <div> element in the normal and hover states:

```
.employeeData {
    padding:15px;
    background-color:#f3f3f3;
    border: 2px solid #071394;
}
```

```
.employeeData:hover {
    color:#682020;
    background-color:#ff6a00;
    font-weight:bold;
}
```

The CSS properties specified in employeeData are applied when the <div> is in the normal state (the user isn't hovering the mouse over it), whereas the CSS properties specified in employeeData:hover are applied when the user hovers the mouse pointer over the <div>. Currently, using these CSS rules doesn't add any transition effect to the <div>. To add a transition effect, you need to modify the employeeData rule as follows:

```
.employeeData {
    ...
    -moz-transition: color 3s,background-color 3s;
    -webkit-transition: color 3s,background-color 3s;
    -o-transition: color 3s,background-color 3s;
}
```

The modified employeeData rule uses the transition property prefixed with browser-specific prefixes. The transition property consists of a comma-separated list of properties to be included in the transition effect and the time duration in seconds for which the transition effect is played. In this example, the color and background-color properties change from their old values to new values in three seconds. Figure 13-19 shows how the <div> looks before and after the transition.

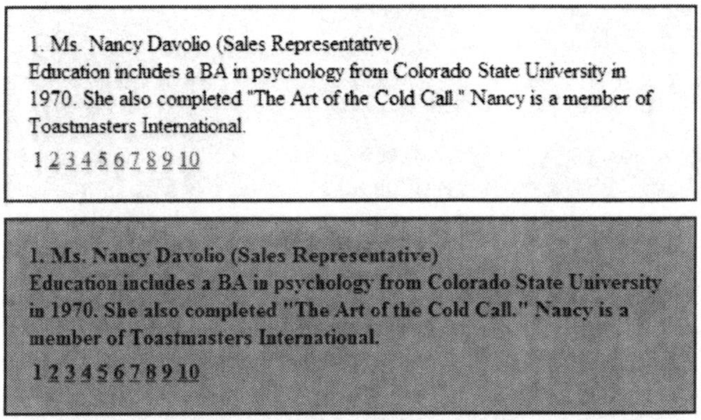

Figure 13-19. Applying transitions during mouse hover

In the absence of the transition property, the <div> instantaneously changes its background color from #f3f3f3 to #ff6a00 when hovering begins and from #ff6a00 to #f3f3f3 when the mouse leaves the <div>. However, with transition in place, the same change of background color takes place in three seconds rather than instantly, resulting in an animation effect.

■ **Note**　You can also add other details to the transition effect, such as timing functions. You can read more at www.w3.org/TR/css3-transitions and https://developer.mozilla.org/en-US/docs/CSS/CSS_transitions.

Transforms

Transitions add effects during the transition from one style to another. Transforms, on the other hand, change the appearance of an element using effects such as rotating, skewing, and scaling. Consider the following CSS rule:

```
.rotate {
    padding:15px;
    margin:20px;
    background-color:#f3f3f3;
    border: 2px solid #071394;
    -ms-transform:rotate(5deg);
    -moz-transform:rotate(10deg);
    -webkit-transform:rotate(10deg);
    -o-transform:rotate(10deg);
}
```

This rule uses the transform property prefixed with vendor prefixes to rotate the element by 10 degrees. The rotate function accepts an angle by which the element is to be rotated. A positive number indicates rotation in the clockwise direction, and a negative number indicates rotation in the counterclockwise direction. Figure 13-20 shows the resulting <div>.

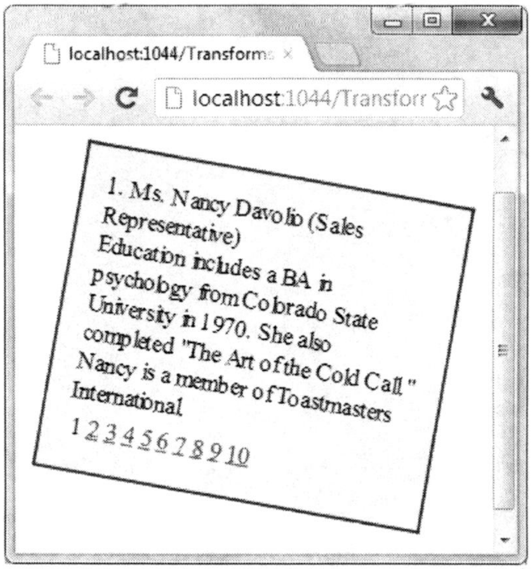

Figure 13-20. Rotating an element using the transform property

As you can see, the <div> element and the FormView inside it are rotated 10 degrees clockwise.

You can also add a skewing effect and change the scaling using the skew() and scale() functions, respectively. You can also use multiple functions together, as the following CSS rule shows:

```
.skew {
    padding:15px;
    margin:20px;
    background-color:#f3f3f3;
```

345

```
    border: 2px solid #071394;
    -ms-transform:skew(10deg) scale(0.9);
    -moz-transform:skew(10deg) scale(0.9);
    -webkit-transform:skew(-10deg) scale(0.9);
    -o-transform:skew(10deg) scale(0.9);
}
```

This rule uses the skew() function as well as the scale() function. skew() takes an angle in degrees that specifies how much the element is skewed. scale() takes a number indicating how much the element should be shrunk or stretched. For example, a scale value of 2 means the element is stretched to twice its original size. You can also use the scaleX() and scaleY() functions to control x and y scaling values, respectively. Figure 13-21 shows the resulting element.

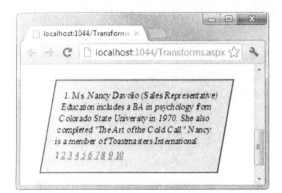

Figure 13-21. Skewing and scaling effects applied to an element

You can also use transforms and transitions together, as shown in the following CSS rules:

```
.myclass {
    -moz-transition: all 3s;
    -webkit-transition: all 3s;
    -o-transition: all 3s;
}

.myclass:hover {
    -ms-transform:rotate(10deg);
    -moz-transform:rotate(10deg);
    -webkit-transform:rotate(10deg);
    -o-transform:rotate(10deg);
}
```

The .myclass:hover rule uses the rotate() function to transform the element. The .myclass rule uses the transition property to specify that all properties from the :hover pseudo-class should be animated for three seconds. This way, when you hover mouse pointer on the <div>, the <div> is rotated 10 degrees clockwise.

■ **Note**   You can read about more transform techniques at https://developer.mozilla.org/en-US/docs/CSS/transform.

Using Media Queries to Target Different Devices

As the use of mobile devices such as smart phones and tablets increases, more people are accessing web sites over mobile devices. A problem in such cases is that a web page designed for a desktop browser doesn't look as expected when viewed on a mobile browser. For example, a hover menu with a sleek animation effect that looks stunning in a desktop browser may not display correctly in a mobile browser and may appear overlapped and disproportionate. A traditional approach to deal with users accessing a web application via both desktop computers and mobile devices is to develop two versions of the web application—a normal version and a mobile version. Although this approach works, the downside is that you need to maintain two different versions of the web application.

CSS3 offers some help when you're targeting your web application to mobile devices. Support for *media queries* allows you to detect certain features of the requesting device and apply a styling rule accordingly. This way, you don't need to create different versions of the web site targeting different devices. You can dynamically change the styles being applied to page elements in two ways:

- You can attach a different style sheet (.css) to a page if the requesting device meets certain criteria.

- You can change the CSS rules, depending on the requesting device.

▓ **Note** This book isn't about developing web sites for mobile devices and hence discusses media queries only to make you familiar with this new CSS3 feature. See `www.w3.org/TR/css3-mediaqueries` for more details.

Typically, media queries use the following parameters to change the style rules being applied to a page or element:

- Minimum and maximum width of the browser window (`min-width` and `max-width`)

- Width of the device screen (`max-device-width`)

- Orientation of the device screen (horizontal or vertical: `orientation`)

- Height of the device screen (`device-height`)

Changing a Style Sheet Using Media Queries

Using media queries and device properties as discussed in the preceding section, you can attach a different style sheet to a web page at runtime. Suppose you have two style sheets `Desktop.css` and `Mobile.css` that contain CSS style rules to be used when the target is a desktop or a mobile device, respectively. You want to attach `Desktop.css` to a web page if it's being viewed by a device with a minimum width of 800 pixels (if a device's screen is at least this wide, chances are it's a desktop computer). Along the same lines, if the screen width is a maximum of 480 pixels (a typical value for mobile phones), then you wish to attach `Mobile.css`. You can accomplish this task by referring to the style sheets as follows:

```
<link rel="stylesheet" type="text/css"
 media="(min-device-width:800px)" href="Desktop.css" />
<link rel="stylesheet" type="text/css"
 media="(max-width:480px) and (orientation:portrait)" href="Mobile.css" />
```

The first <link> element tells the browser that if the device's minimum width is 800 pixels, it should attach Desktop.css to the page. The second <link> element says that if this device has a maximum width of 480 pixels and is using portrait mode, the browser should attach Mobile.css to the page.

Note the use of the and operator in the second <link> element, to check multiple conditions. You can also use the all, not, and only keywords: all indicates that the style sheet applies to all media types, not negates the result of the query, and only hides style sheets from older browsers. Although older browsers ignore such a style sheet, browsers that support CSS3 media queries process media queries starting with only as if the only keyword wasn't present.

If you don't have a mobile device on which to test this page, you can change the min-device-width property to something higher than your desktop screen resolution and then view the page in your desktop browser. Because none of the <link> elements match the criteria, the browser won't apply a style sheet, resulting in a plain default rendering of the HTML elements. Then change min-device-width to a value smaller than the screen resolution and view the page again. The browser should display the HTML elements as per the style rules defined in Desktop.css.

Changing a Style Rule Using Media Queries

In the preceding example, you changed the entire style sheet at runtime based on device properties. This approach works well if the two style sheets are different. However, if only a few CSS rules need to be tweaked to target different devices, you can put them in a single style sheet. In this case, you need to use a @media block in your style sheet. The following example illustrates how to use a @media block:

```
@media (min-device-width: 800px) {
    body {
        background-color:blue;
        color:white;
    }
}

@media (max-width: 480px) and (orientation:portrait) {
    body {
        background-color:red;
        color:white;
    }
}
```

The first @media block groups CSS rules for a device whose minimum screen width is 800 pixels. The second @media block groups CSS rules for devices with a maximum width of 480 pixels and portrait orientation. This style sheet is attached to a web page as usual:

```
<link rel="stylesheet" type="text/css" href="StyleSheet.css" />
```

If you run a web page with this style sheet attached on a desktop computer, you should see the web page background painted blue color. On mobile phones, the background is red.

Using Modernizr to Apply CSS3-Specific Features

As mentioned earlier, CSS3 is an evolving specification. Not all browsers support all CSS3 features. If you know that your web application will be used by the modern browsers, you can use the CSS3 features that they all support. The advantage of this approach is that you have a good number of CSS3 features at your disposal that you can use in your web applications. However, the downside is that very old browsers may not display your web pages as expected. A solution to tackle this problem is to create different CSS classes encapsulating traditional versus CSS3-specific properties. At runtime, based on whether a browser supports a specific CSS3 feature, either a CSS3-specific class or a class with traditional properties is applied to an element. But doing so calls for more work because it involves creating multiple CSS classes and applying them at runtime based on the level of support offered by the target browser.

To assist you in this job, you can use the Modernizr library. Throughout this book, you've been using Modernizr to detect HTML5 features. The same Modernizr library also allows you to detect support for CSS3 features. Let's see how.

A web page that uses Modernizr refers to it using a `<script>` tag as shown next:

```
<script type="text/javascript" src="scripts/modernizr.js"></script>
```

At runtime, the Modernizr library modifies the `<html>` tag of the HTML5 document to include all supported HTML5 and CSS3 features as well as those not supported on a given browser. The following `<html>` tag from a sample HTML5 document shows how this happens:

```
<html class=" js flexbox canvas canvastext webgl no-touch geolocation
postmessage websqldatabase indexeddb hashchange history draganddrop websockets
rgba hsla multiplebgs backgroundsize borderimage borderradius boxshadow
textshadow opacity cssanimations csscolumns cssgradients cssreflections
csstransforms csstransforms3d csstransitions fontface generatedcontent video
audio localstorage sessionstorage webworkers applicationcache svg inlinesvg
smil svgclippaths">
```

In this markup, Modernizr has added a `class` attribute to the `<html>` tag. The value of the `class` attribute is a string containing CSS classes separated by white space. Each class represents an HTML5 or CSS3 feature. The features that aren't supported on a given browser are prefixed with `no-`. For example, this markup includes a `no-touch` class, indicating that touch events aren't supported. The plain feature names (such as `video`, `audio`, and `webworkers`) indicate that they're supported by the browser.

■ **Note** The `<html>` tag with the `class` attribute added isn't visible in the HTML source of the web page because it's added programmatically by Modernizr. You need to inspect the page in a tool such as Chrome Developer Tools.

Now, suppose you have a `<div>` element on the page and you wish to set its `background-color`, `text-align`, `padding`, `border`, and `border-radius` CSS properties. Of these, `border-radius` is CSS3-specific, whereas the others are traditional CSS properties. The `border-radius` property allows you to create borders with rounded corners, as discussed earlier in this chapter. You can create three CSS classes as shown here:

```
.div {
  background-color: #d3a584;
  padding: 10px;
  text-align: center;
}
.borderradius .div {
  border: 2px #f00 solid;
  border-radius: 25px;
}
.no-borderradius .div {
  border: 2px #f00 solid;
}
```

One CSS class contains CSS properties that are to be applied regardless of whether border-radius is supported, another contains CSS properties that are to be applied when border-radius is supported, and the third contains CSS properties that are to be applied when border-radius isn't supported. Note that the second (borderradius) and third (no-borderradius) CSS class names are the same as the corresponding class names from the <html> tag. The borderradius class sets the border and border-radius properties, whereas the no-borderradius class sets only the border property. Once the CSS classes are created, you can use them on a <div> element as follows:

```
<div class="div">Hello World!</div>
```

At runtime, the div CSS class is applied to the <div> element. Additionally, one of the two classes (borderradius or no-borderradius) is applied depending on whether the border-radius property is supported. Figure 13-22 shows a sample run of the web page in Chrome.

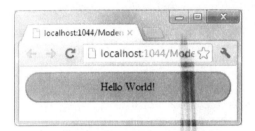

Figure 13-22. Modernizr applies the borderradius CSS class in Chrome.

As you can see, because Chrome supports the border-radius property, the CSS properties from the div and borderradius CSS classes are applied to the <div> element.

Summary

CSS is a de facto standard for applying styling rules to web pages. CSS3 adds many new features to CSS 2.1 to make it more appealing and useful to web developers. This chapter covered some of the important features of CSS3.

With CSS3, you can use nonstandard fonts in web pages by creating custom font definitions using @ font-face. At runtime, the font file is downloaded at the client and is used to display the web page's text. Another nice improvement of CSS3 is the ability to add fancy frills to box layouts, such as shadows, gradients, and transparency. You can also add effects using transitions and transforms.

As mobile and handheld devices become more common, web sites are increasingly being accessed over mobile devices. Using media queries, you can detect device properties such as width and orientation. You can then apply different styling rules to web pages or elements to ensure that they look great in the target device.

HTML5, JavaScript, and CSS3 together will, no doubt, change the way people develop and use web applications. The momentum has begun, and in the future you'll see these technologies gain increasing acceptance and widespread use. This book has attempted to give you all the necessary skills to ride the HTML5 wave and harness the power of this futuristic technology.

HTML5 Learning Resources

W3C and WHATWG Specifications

W3C HTML5 specifications
http://www.w3.org/TR/2011/WD-html5-20110525/

WHATWG HTML5 specifications for developers
http://developers.whatwg.org

Documentation from Browser Companies

Microsoft Internet Explorer documentation on MSDN
http://msdn.microsoft.com/en-us/library/ie/

HTML5 page on Mozilla Developer Network
https://developer.mozilla.org/en-US/docs/HTML/HTML5

HTML5 articles on Dev.Opera
http://dev.opera.com/articles/tags/html5

HTML5 page on Apple Developer
https://developer.apple.com/technologies/safari/html5.html

Other Web Sites of Interest

W3Schools.com HTML5 tutorials
http://www.w3schools.com/html5/default.asp

HTML5 Rocks
www.html5rocks.com/en/

HTML Goodies, HTML5 Development Center
www.htmlgoodies.com/html5/index.php

Author's web site presenting HTML5- and ASP.NET-related articles
www.bipinjoshi.net

HTML5 section of *Visual Studio Magazine*
http://visualstudiomagazine.com/articles/list/html5.aspx

Index

CPSIA information can be obtained at www.ICGtesting.com
Printed in the USA
LVOW111604131112

307155LV00003B/3/P